HAPPINESS ON YOUR TERMS

(Re) Design your life
& live with courage

SANJU AHMED

Inspired by Positive Psychology & the Science of Happiness

Copyright © 2025 by d brilliance, a brand of Mx Lane Australia Pty Ltd. All rights reserved.

ISBN (Paperback): 978-1-7640494-0-5
ISBN (eBook): 978-1-7640494-1-2

No portion of this book may be reproduced in any form without written permission from the publisher or author, except as permitted by U.S. copyright law.

This publication is designed to provide accurate and authoritative information in regard to the subject matter covered. It is sold with the understanding that neither the author nor the publisher is engaged in rendering legal, investment, accounting or other professional services. While the publisher and author have used their best efforts in preparing this book, they make no representations or warranties with respect to the accuracy or completeness of the contents of this book and specifically disclaim any implied warranties of merchantability or fitness for a particular purpose. No warranty may be created or extended by sales representatives or written sales materials. The advice and strategies contained herein may not be suitable for your situation. You should consult with a professional when appropriate. Neither the publisher nor the author shall be liable for any loss of profit or any other commercial damages, including but not limited to special, incidental, consequential, personal, or other damages.

The strategies and tools in this book are inspired by the science of happiness research under positive psychology. Feel free to use them responsibly. Seek professional help if you feel the need to do so. The author is not liable for any actions you take. The results outlined are subjective and can vary widely depending on many factors. Living or happiness on your terms does not mean being harmful to yourself, anyone, or anything in any way. Many of the stories used in this book are inspired by true events, but names, locations, and a few details have been changed to protect the privacy of the people involved. They are not intended to breach anyone's privacy or confidentiality in anyway. The responsibility of the outcome or results of any actions taken by the reader upon reading this book lies with the reader.

Interior book design and layout by, Ellie Bockert Augsburger of CreativeDigitalStudios.com

Cover design features stock images from:
by Aditya / Stock.Adobe.com
by Tartila / Stock.Adobe.com
by Teerapat / Stock.Adobe.com

First edition 2025

I am a reflection of my mother,
and my wife completes me.

TABLE OF CONTENTS

Preface 1

I'm Thankful 8

PART 1:
YOUR HAPPINESS AND SATISFACTION 11

The Power of Your Happiness 13

The Default Life 23

My Quest for Life by Design 36

The Science of Happiness 45

The Satisfying Life and the Happy Life 55

Three Things to Remember 65

PART 2:
YOUR RESULTS, RESILIENCE, PERMISSION, AND MONEY 79

Measure Your Happiness 81

What Results Can You Expect 85

How to Recover from a Setback 93

How to Permit Yourself to Be Happy 106

How Much Money Do You Need 115

PART 3:
THE SIX ELEMENTS OF YOUR SATISFYING LIFE BY DESIGN 123

Meaning 126

Engagement (Flow) 138

Love and Connections 146

Pleasure 157

    Health 163

    Achievements 173

    Your Life By Design 184

PART 4:
YOUR SKILLS TO LIVE A HAPPY LIFE 191

    Your Happiness is Your Responsibility 193

    Three Lanes of Happiness 199

    How to Be Happy 214

    How to Stay Happy 225

    The Eleven Happiness Habits - Create Happy Moments 236

    The Seven Emotional Habits - Protect Your Happy Moments 265

PART 5:
BUILDING YOUR HAPPINESS HABITS ON YOUR TERMS 275

    John or Mike - Who Will Be Happier at Ninety 277

    All on One Page 283

    Discover Your Natural Happiness Habits 284

    Your Six-Week Intervention Program 290

    Build Your Own Happiness Habits 308

PART 6:
STAY HAPPY BY YOURSELF 313

    Stay Happy When Alone 315

PART 7:
STAY HAPPY AT HOME. 329

    Stay Happy with Your Loved Ones at Home 331

PART 8:
STAY HAPPY AT WORK..339

Why Does Happiness at Work Matter?............................341
What Does It Mean to Be Happy at Work?........................342
How Can You Stay Happy at Work................................343
How to Stay Happy with Others at Work.........................355
Creating a Happy Workplace....................................367

MY EMBARRASSING STORY AND CONCLUSION..................385

NOTES..387

PREFACE

I thought I would write this preface after finishing my book and it would be easy. But when I started, I had been staring at the blank page for a long time. I didn't know where to start or how to start it. I couldn't come up with anything I liked, so I procrastinated for a few weeks and hoped I would come up with something amazing.

But I couldn't.

So I decided to speak my mind. When I was about thirty-five, I remember one evening when I got stuck in freeway traffic on my way home from work. I'd had a long day and couldn't wait to get home. Back then, I was at a job I didn't like, and I had to travel more than three hours every day. Even though I was in a high-paying corporate role, the job had become meaningless. After that long day at work, I didn't feel a sense of achievement. Instead, I was going home drained and unfulfilled.

That day, I asked myself, "What am I doing? Why am I spending so much time travelling to work, where the work doesn't even fulfil me?" I could have spent that time doing something I love or being with my loved ones. It didn't make any sense. I realized that, at the time, I was not doing anything that made a meaningful difference to anyone or anything.

A few months later, I realized I had more than ten years of experience in corporate work and I could coach people who wanted to climb the corporate ladders. So, in the next few years, I got trained in neurolinguistic programming, hypnosis, and matrix therapies and became a professional coach. I started to help people out. My new role as a coach became very meaningful for me.

Since then, over the years, I have specialized in human behavioral strength development and small business consulting, but in my early months of coaching, I realized that the clients I worked with wanted to do something, be someone, or have something to improve the quality of their lives, whether it was getting that promotion, applying for that dream role, or even making a career change. When I asked them what their future achievements would give them, they all said things like "Joy," "peace," "fulfilment," "excitement," or "happiness." But I noticed a pattern that, one way or the other, they all wanted some kind of positive emotion. The word was not always "happiness," but often it was.

I wondered, "Isn't happiness at the core of almost everything we do?" I became very curious and started to explore happiness. The more I learned, the more surprised

I became. In fact, as part of my exploration, many stats I learned were shocking. According to the WHO, 280 million people suffer from depression worldwide. A recent world happiness report says that in the US, the general happiness has been declining over the last decade and hit a record low in 2019. I also found that many people have regrets at their deathbeds and say things like "I wish I'd had the courage to live a life true to myself, not what others expected of me." According to a recent Gallup study, over 80 per cent of the global workforce is not engaged at work. I was like, "Seriously!" I never thought or knew about these statistics before.

I can go on and on with more statistics, but the thing is, these numbers are worrying. With so many advancements everywhere in science, technology, and lifestyle, you may think the quality of our lives must have improved. It has done so externally in many ways, but internally it hasn't. According to many statistics, we have not been happier.

Then what's the point?

Even if I didn't worry about the world (most people don't), I could still relate to my own life. Remember I was already unfulfilled with the job I didn't like. Well, I was one of that 80 per cent of people who were not engaged at work. Also, I was not healthy and fit, had relationships with a number of toxic people, and wasn't doing the things I loved. I was following the crowd and doing what everybody around me was doing.

In short, I realized I was living a life of others that I didn't like.

I started searching for alternatives, and after a few months, I came across the science of happiness. The research on happiness falls under the umbrella of positive psychology. In 2000, the top scientists and psychologists worldwide started a new area of study, and they called it positive psychology. It is a relatively new area of study where scientists focus on things like what makes a good life, what the elements necessary for a fulfilled life are, how we can not only survive but also thrive as human beings, and how can we live to our highest potentials.

Personally, I believe everybody should live to his or her true brilliance. We should live the way that makes sense to us and not based on what others impose on us or expect us to do.

In other words, we should live on our own terms.

That's why I started to study happiness and positive psychology at Harvard University Extension School in 2017. The more I learned, the more intrigued I became. Professor Tal Ben-Shahar of Harvard created the most popular course in Harvard's history, which I studied. Even though the academic journals published by the researchers are based on real-life data and we can use their remarkable findings, the irony is that they are not easily accessible and not read by many people. When I was studying, I was like, "Wow! Why do we not know them?"

Almost everything around us is governed by science. When I was growing up, I learned physics, chemistry, mathematics, and many other things in school,

but I didn't learn how to be happy.

Nobody goes to school to learn happiness. That would be a crazy idea, especially when there was no such thing as the science of happiness. But now that science exists. As happiness is at the core of almost everything we do,

shouldn't we all learn and master the skills of happiness?

I am not a researcher, but as a coach, I use those research findings in my practice. Also, as an advocate of positive psychology, my job is to apply the wisdom I learned in my own life and relay it to the people I work with to help them improve the quality of their lives. It is very meaningful for me. But I felt an obligation to share the wisdom I learned with more people. I thought, "What else can I do?"

All my life, I have always enjoyed writing, but I wrote only small pieces, mainly for myself. I never thought I would write a book, especially on a topic like happiness. When I was considering this idea of a book, I asked myself, "Why should I write a book?" But then I asked, "Why not?" I didn't have an answer.

So I decided to go ahead.

In my journey, I realized that I loved studying happiness, and every time I talked about it, I got excited. There was so much to explore and share. I can talk about this topic for hours without getting tired. But it was often very hard to express the learnings and feelings in words in my book.

But why would you care to read it?

Over the last five years of writing this book, I have gone through many struggles, especially during the COVID-19 times (like many others). I lost one aunt and another uncle in my close family and others in my wider circles who died of COVID. The COVID lockdowns were not easy either. In fact, Melbourne, where I live, was one of the world's most "locked down" cities. I felt stuck and helpless. I often questioned my ability to finish my book. Does it really matter? Is it worth the effort? Is it going to really help someone? I felt small, doubted myself, and felt very low at times.

Two of the most important people on earth are my wife and my mother. They were also going through very hard times coping with the recent uncertain times. Whether in health and fitness, business, relationships, or anything else, they also felt very low emotionally.

During these times, my personal challenge was to stay strong and happy. I helped my intimate family members do the same. I believe that if I cannot stay happy myself and cannot make my better half and mother happy, all my studies of happiness and life experiences don't matter.

Honestly, over the last seven years, I have walked the talk. I implemented in my personal life and the lives of others around me many of the tools and strategies from the science of happiness I talk about in this book. And I can tell you, not surprisingly, the science strategies helped me and my close family members survive the hard times. In fact, we bounced back stronger, happier, and more satisfied than before.

Even though my book is inspired by the research on the science of happiness and positive psychology, I don't just write about graphs, stats, and studies. You can just google them. Rather, I also write about how I and others implemented the science tools in our own lives and transformed to live happier and more satisfying lives.

The stories I share in my book are from my personal life, the lives of those I know very closely, and the lives of people who lived very fulfilling and successful lives that we all can learn from. I have changed the names, locations, dates, and some other details to protect the privacy of others. Almost 100 per cent of the stories are inspired by true events.

In my journey of transforming my life, I have been blessed to learn directly from amazing people like Marc Randolph, one of the co-founders and former CEO of Netflix; Randi Zuckerberg, the former director of market development at Facebook (Meta); Brian Nieves, a former US senator of Missouri; and a few others like them. They not only built very successful businesses that changed the world but also live very fulfilling lives. I have shared a few key insights I learned from them.

As this is my first book and I don't have many years of writing experience, it may not be polished, eloquently written, formal, or a New York Times best-selling book, but it is authentic, true to my heart, and inspired by the science from world's best happiness researchers, and it conveys my genuine desire to help you live a happy and satisfying life on your terms. I didn't try to be someone else. This is how I talk, write, and make a point. When you meet me, you will have the same experience.

My book is an extension of me.

So what's in my book for you?

People link money, success, close relationships, health, and many other things with happiness and satisfaction. One way or the other, we all chase them in our own ways. But most people don't live the lives they desire. They don't have the health and body, money, relationships, freedom, peace, happiness, or fulfilment they truly want, because when it comes to living a fulfilling life, we assume and follow the crowd, and often when we are old, we regret our past decisions and actions.

But what if we could live by a solid design?

PREFACE

What if there was a framework for a satisfying life? What if we live less on assumptions and more on the science framework and strategies so we have more happiness, more fulfilment, and fewer regrets?

The science of happiness gives us that ability.

In my journey, I found that even though we use the terms "happiness" and "satisfaction" interchangeably, they are not quite the same. That's why I discuss how you can actually design and live a satisfying life. What skills will you need to live a happy life? And how can you protect your happiness? Almost all of what I have written is inspired by the research of positive psychology. At the end of the day, if you are not happy and fulfilled, nothing really matters.

By the way, did you know you can measure your happiness?

Scientists have been using many tools for years to measure people's happiness. You can also use a few tools by yourself, which are almost as good. I have talked about how you can do that.

You might be wondering what results you can expect from my book. Reading a book takes time and effort. If you read my book and do not become and stay happy, then it isn't worth it. That's why in the second part, I first discuss results. A few years ago, in that endeavor, I ran a six-week intervention program with a group of everyday people to see whether the science strategies actually worked. I also reached out to one of the top researchers in the world, Professor Sonja Lyubomirsky, from the University of California–Riverside. She helped me clarify the results of my participants. She was very kind, and I'm very thankful to her. But I'm delighted to tell you that over 80 per cent of my participants became happier in the six-week program. We measured their happiness every week and shared their results and feedback with you so you get an idea of what is possible.

But life is not always about colors and rainbows. We face hard times and go through trauma and many other things that make us unhappy. So, I write about resilience, how you can bounce back from a setback, and how it impacts your happiness over time. Next I discuss what prevents us from being happy, why it is so hard for us to allow ourselves to be happy even when we all want to be happy, and how we can handle that. Finally, I discuss money—how it relates to your happiness and how much money you will need to be lastingly happy.

I have told a story of John and Mike, who are very different people from the same age group. I demonstrated how scientific tools and strategies could potentially make a measurable difference in happiness over their lifetimes. I developed and shared a discovery test for you to find out your natural habits. You can implement them in a sample six-week intervention program I designed to make you happier (similar to what I used with my participants mentioned earlier).

Finally, in the last three parts, I have discussed how you can use the tools and strategies of science to be and stay happy when you are by yourself, at home, and at work.

I want to quickly point out three things you can do to get the most out of my book. Firstly, when you read, please read with an open mind and a genuine desire to live a happy and satisfying life on your terms. Secondly, there are some questions (mostly in the reflection sections) in each chapter that are designed to help you internalize the concepts presented. I humbly request you to read and write the answers to those questions for yourself as honestly as possible (as you will be designing your life of happiness and satisfaction on your terms). And finally, with the tools and interventions, please take actions consistently to get the results.

Remember nothing will change unless you take intentional, meaningful, and consistent actions.

Many people think living a happier and more satisfying life is just a dream far away, or that it comes about by chance, luck, or destiny and may not happen in their lifetimes. Over many years, I have realized that living a happy live does not occur based on chance, luck, destiny, or your ability.

Rather, it happens only if you genuinely want it.

It's always the decisions you make and the actions you take every day that shape your life. That includes living a happy and satisfying life.

You may remember, many years ago, I was driving home and got stuck in traffic. I was tired and unfulfilled, and I started to question my life choices. At the time, I was thirty-five and living the default life of others. I was not happy or fulfilled even though I was in a high-paying role and had achieved many goals.

All my life, I have been an optimist. This is one of my greatest powers. So I thought, "What if it was the opposite?" What if that day when I was stuck on the freeway, I was not tired and unfulfilled by my work? What if instead I were excited, had a sense of achievement, and felt satisfied after an engaging day at work? What if I were healthy and fit? What if I had deep, loving, and meaningful connections with people around me who inspired me to live to my highest potential? What if I could live on my terms instead of living a default and unhappy life of others?

My life didn't change overnight, and I'm not living "happily ever after." But in my journey of transforming my life, I made the decisions over the years to redesign my life, and I took actions to make changes to it using the framework of the science of happiness.

Honestly, I have never been happier and more fulfilled in my life.

What if you could do the same or even better?

I believe you should be able to do what you love and care about at work and be fulfilled. Have enough money so it's not a problem in your life. Be healthy and fit. Surround yourself with people you love. Do what makes you happy and satisfied not just once in a while, but every day.

No matter how hard it seems, you still deserve to live on your terms.

If I can transform my life, you can do it too.

My book may not change the world, but for those who read my book, it will change their worlds within. You can change your world when you want to, the way you want to, and as much as you want to.

And that's why I wrote this book.

Learning and mastering the skills of happiness is a lifelong process. As long as I live, I will continue to do that. But I also feel that after spending more than forty years on this planet (fifteen years in the corporate workforce), I have learned some valuable lessons that I would be honored to share with you.

If you are at a stage of life where you believe that you deserve and genuinely want to live a happier and more satisfying life on your terms, I humbly invite you inside my book and encourage you to read it with an open mind and genuine desire. Whether a concept, an aha moment, or a perception, I truly believe something will move you in an empowering way, and that will be my two cents to your extraordinary life on your terms.

No matter what you do, if you are blessed to live up to ninety or when your time approaches to leave this planet, you might look back on your life and ask two simple questions,

Did you live a happy life?

And did you live a satisfying life?

My aim in this book is to inspire you to live such a life that you would say yes to both.

- Sanju Ahmed

I'M THANKFUL

In my journey of writing this book, I have interviewed many people. They have believed in me, inspired me, and, often guided me.

Firstly, I specially thank Glenn Simmons, Bec Truong, Jessica Baker, Rakesh Kadian, Manohar Singh, Alex Tomic, Kim La Ferla, and others for being part of my happiness intervention group and sharing some of their stories with me, as well as for permitting me to put them in my book.

Secondly, I want to sincerely thank Phil Nguyen, Ashraf Alam, Tiff Any, Tanvi Rahman, Oliver Tham, and Richard Tan for their valuable insights and inspirations, which I have shared in different sections. I want to thank Catherine Bell and Jo Wise, my teachers during my neurolinguistic programming course, which has given me a new perspective on life, for which I am very grateful. Also, I want to express my gratitude to Professor Sonja Lyubomirsky for guiding me and helping me understand some of the concepts of her research a few years ago. It was very kind of her to help me out in my journey. I want to thank my direct and indirect mentors and teachers, Randi Zuckerberg, Gerry Robert, Brian Nieves, Ashley Lazaro, Marc Randolph, Joseph McLendon III and Raza Aziz for their wisdom, which is truly world-changing. I have learned so much from them and put the knowledge into practice in my own life.

Someone I must mention is Mr. Anthony Robbins. I have attended many of his seminars. While I haven't gotten a chance to have him as my direct mentor yet, his teachings have changed my life for the better, and if I do not say he is special, it will be very unfair and not right. In fact, you probably wouldn't be reading this book if it were not for his inspiration. Like millions of others, I'm indebted to Mr. Robbins for the better life I'm living.

I want to sincerely thank my sister Sonia, my father and mother. I shared a few of their stories that I have learned from in my book.

And my highest gratitude is for my better half, Mahin Eshita, who relentlessly supported me in my journey in many ways and spent numerous sleepless nights with me. I could list many things that I'm thankful to her for, but I just want to say that without her, I wouldn't be the person I am today, and she is the reason why I do (or at least try to do) better every day.

Finally, I want to thank God for creating me and giving me this opportunity to humbly share some of what I have learned in my positive psychology studies and throughout my life in this book.

PART 1:
Your Happiness and Satisfaction

In this part, we will discuss the following:

- why being happy is at the center of everything we do
- why the default life of assumptions makes us unhappy
- what is life by design
- your happiness and satisfaction are not the same
- what science tells us about a satisfying life
- what science tells us about a happy life
- why you should protect your precious moments
- the four types of lives, which one are you living
- what is a life of harmony
- how it all comes down to three things

THE POWER OF YOUR HAPPINESS

"Believe that life is worth living, and your belief will help create the fact."
—William James

THE GIRL AT THE COFFEE SHOP

It was about 7:00 a.m. I was travelling from a New York train station to Boston. My wife, Mahin, wanted to have green tea and needed hot water. I looked around and found a coffee shop nearby. I walked up to the ordering counter, and a girl approached to take my order. She didn't ask me what I wanted. Instead she just looked at me for a few seconds with no expression and said nothing. She didn't seem to be present or willing to take my order. I asked whether I could get a cup of hot water. She looked very annoyed and suddenly turned around. I took my wallet out and asked her, "How much is it?" She turned back and looked at me and then looked down; then, with a very annoyed tone, she said, "It's free." I was like, "Ah, okay, thank you." After a minute, she gave me a cup of hot water.

She looked very unhappy. I didn't know her. I had no idea whether she'd had a fight with someone earlier or was just having an unpleasant morning. But the five-second (Hi, Water, Free, Thanks) type conversation I had with her didn't make me feel good, and I never expected to be served that way. Generally, we judge people based on our experiences with them. Most people (sometimes including me) do not look at why others behave the way they do, especially when those others are strangers. Who wants to interact with an unpleasant person every day? Probably no one. I may have judged too early, but honestly, my experience at the coffee shop was not great.

On the same morning, at the same station, I went to another shop specializing in bagels. The girl at the shop didn't know me but greeted me with a smile. She asked, "Good morning. What can I get you?" I smiled back, shrugged, and said, "I never tried bagels in New York before, and you have so many different types. So I'm not sure." She smiled again and replied, "Yeah, we have a huge range. But I will help you. We have cinnamon, we have chocolate …" As she spoke, she kept a big smile on her face. I was amazed and asked, "What's your best seller? Maybe I can try that." She said, "That's a good idea. It's cinnamon. How do you like it?" She was very friendly, I was comfortable talking to her, and she made me feel important. She was present as she served me and looked genuinely happy and engaged.

As a result, I had a great customer experience.

Next time I'm at that New York station, which shop will I prefer? The coffee shop or the bagel shop?

The happy girl at the bagel shop had the power to convince me.

Being unhappy not only impacts your mood and well-being but also impacts the people around you. If you always feel blue (even for genuine reasons) or in a low emotional state, it may stop people from coming close to you. They may feel uncomfortable talking to you or approaching you.

We all feel unhappiness one way or the other, but staying that way takes a toll on every area of our lives. For example, as human beings, we are hard-wired for love and connections. We cannot deny that. Remember what COVID-19 lockdowns did to our mental health? Most people want to be loved and connected to others.

The longest scientific study on happiness, which started in 1938 in Boston, followed 724 men over their lifetimes and continues today. More than seventy-seven years of research concludes that for us it is the quality of close relationships that matters the most for happiness (more on this later).

But we do not necessarily focus on building those warm and loving connections with others. A study by the American Psychological Association finds that recent generations have been focusing on money and fame.

But, why do so many people want to be rich and famous?

John Dewey was an American philosopher and psychologist, as well as one of the greatest thinkers of the twentieth century. His ideas have been influential in education and social reform. He was one of the most prominent scholars during that time. He said, "The deepest urge in human nature is the desire to be important." This principle has been used (and is still being used) for many years in education, building social connections, business, and everywhere else where human beings are involved.

Being rich and famous serves that urge. If you are rich or famous, generally, you will have more money, fame, status, power, fewer rejections, privilege, and many benefits beyond those of an average person. Honestly, these are essential. However, they may not automatically help you build deep, meaningful, and loving connections with people.

Imagine you have two friends, Peter and Steve. Peter is rich and famous but often grumpy, and his behavior changes frequently. He often becomes depressed or angry without any warning. He drives an expensive Mercedes. But Steve is an average person and is generally nicer, kinder, and happier than Peter. Steve drives an average-priced Toyota. Both of them live about twenty minutes away from you.

Now think about a situation in which you need to drop your kid at school but your car has broken down in the middle of the road. Whom would you call for help? Peter or Steve?

Generally, happy people are nice, kind, and more willing to help than others who are not so happy. But yes, there are certainly people who are rich, famous, and happy; who wouldn't want them as friends?

But if someone is generally annoyed, grumpy, and complaining most of the time, would you invite this person for dinner? Or to go on a date? Or to do business or work with? Your happiness or unhappiness has a very high impact on the people around you. Your health, relationships, work, performance, business, social interactions, and many other aspects of your life will have a ripple effect. (You may or may not believe this now, but as you continue reading, you might feel differently.)

Being happy is a likeable trait. If you are happy, you will not only live a happy life but will also notice that people will love you, trust you, rely on you, and care for you more. As a result, you will make deeper, more meaningful, and loving connections with the people around you.

And the feeling of importance? You will automatically feel it.

HER HAPPINESS HELPED HER SURVIVE

I want to talk about a person I admire so much that I couldn't resist but share a little about him here. As of this writing, he is sixty-eight, but he is one of the fittest people of his age and his body has the shape of a twenty-four-year-old. He probably has a six-pack too.

How unbelievably cool is that?

This man, John, is one of the best peak-performance coaches on earth, has authored several books, is an instructor at a major University in California–Los Angeles, holds a doctorate in neuropsychology, and has taught success and peak performance principles to more than three million people worldwide in the last thirty-five years. (I'm really struggling to shorten his bio.) He lives what he teaches and has helped transform the lives of many, including mine.

In other words, he is one of my favorite people.

I first met John at a conference in Sydney in 2016. In his talk, he shared his personal story about his mother.

He lives in California. More than thirty years ago, he attended a three-week-long workshop away from LA. At the time, there were no mobile phones, and people used to rely on wired telephones at home. When he finished the workshop and flew back home, he found that his sister had left a voice message on his answering machine. It said that his mother was severely ill and had been taken to a hospital. He had no idea at that time because he had been away for the last three weeks. So he rushed to the hospital. The physician said his mother had undergone surgery because she was diagnosed with terminal cancer and had only two months to live.

It was like a sudden punch in the face to John. He was devastated. The doctor was a very compassionate man, and he said, "I'm very sorry, but you know it is time to get her affairs in order." Even though medical science was not as developed then as it is these days, John couldn't believe that his mother had only two months to live.

Earlier, through a lot of personal development, John became a big believer in how our bodies are miraculous in healing themselves from diseases through more natural ways than traditional medicines. He believed there must be something that could be done. He told the doctor, "I appreciate your diagnosis, but I do not accept your verdict."

When people become desperate and there is no other way out of a situation, they try anything and everything. John was worried and anxious but was eager to find something to help his mother. He remembered that he had read a book by Dr. Norman Cousins, who had helped himself and several other people heal themselves from terminal diseases through laughter.

He decided to give it a try.

At the time, people used cassette tapes in VCRs (some of you may remember them) to watch movies. John found a bunch of books and tapes on comedy in a video store. Later, he organized everything and went back to the hospital. They let him set up the VCR with the giant television in his mother's room. He sourced everything while his mother was still unconscious from the surgery. He was waiting for her to wake up.

When she woke up, he said to his mother, "All right, Mum, the doctor said you have cancer, but there are only two kinds of cancer. Can-surrender, or can-survive. We decided that we can survive. So here is what we want to do." And then he told her what to do with the comedy tapes and books. He spent many weeks in that hospital room helping his mother have a good time, with laughter, jokes, and great conversations. He tried his best to help her be and stay happy as much as possible. He was relentless and never gave up on his mother. He was all in.

To everybody's surprise, his mother's condition improved over the next few months, and she lived another 11.5 years cancer-free.

John's story is one of many examples of how being and staying happy, in addition to modern medical treatments, can help your body heal itself. You are born with this miraculous machine that is your body. It knows how to fix itself if you give it what it needs and often it is happiness.

That's why feeding your mind is also super essential in addition to healthy eating and exercise. Feeling more peace, calmness, excitement, satisfaction, happiness, or anything that makes you feel good in some way is absolutely necessary. Yes, we will always have opposites; that's life. But the idea is to live in more happy states than unhappy ones.

As John's mother was going through the recovery process, it was hard, but being and staying happy during those tough times turned her life around.

If you can be and stay happy, you can turn things around not only in your health but in almost every area of your life.

YOUR HAPPINESS FUELS YOUR SUCCESS

A few years ago, I talked about the relationship between success and happiness at a small conference of 150 people. After I finished my talk, one of my friends came and introduced me to Jane. She said, "This is Jane, and your talk made her cry," and she was smiling. I wasn't sure how to react. I turned to Jane and said, "Hi, Jane. How so?" She greeted me and looked a little embarrassed. She said, "I didn't really cry, but some of the things you said made me a little emotional." I said, "Okay, tell me more" Then she took a pause and said, "After working eight years full-time for an agency, I had to be a part-timer with three days a week for some personal reasons. But they took my dedicated desk, laptop, and mobile phone away. My manager said they were only for full-timers. The part-timers must bring their own devices. I was very upset with their decision and couldn't take it easy, and I felt that I was not part of the team anymore."

She went on, "I have a good track record over the years, but because of this change, my monthly sales dropped from twenty-five to six. It was because I was upset and could not concentrate on my work. My manager also noticed the drop in my performance. Even though she was initially not very supportive, she later talked to HR, and I got my desk and laptop back—but not the mobile phone. I realized that I didn't need a mobile phone for my work. I used my desk phone instead. A couple of weeks later, my sales went up again. It was because I felt happy again. I became emotional because what you said in your talk resonated with my work situation. As you said, happiness comes first, and then success follows."

We constantly hear about working hard so we can be successful and then be happy. But over the years, I learned from the science of happiness that reality is actually the opposite. If we are happy, we are more likely to be successful, not the other way around.

You might wonder, "How?"

For most people, happiness relates to something in the future (i.e., getting that promotion, going on that holiday). If that resonates with you, you may not be ready to be happy yet. If you know that your target is months away, your brain does not allow you to be happy today. And finally, when you hit your target, you will get a spike of happiness that may not last. So next time, you may set a bigger goal, and the same pattern continues.

Author Shawn Achor is one of the leading experts in happiness. In his TEDx talk, He said, "If your happiness is on the other side of success, your brain never gets there." They also found that when your brain is in a positive state in a work or business situation, you are likely to be 31 per cent more productive. Your intelligence, creativity, and energy level rise. Shawn also said, "Your brain at positive performs significantly better than it does in negative, neutral, or stressed."

Jane's performance dropped when she was upset at work. But later, when she got her desk and laptop back, she became happier, and her sales numbers went up again.

Your happiness fuels your success in every area of your life.

Many studies suggest that happy people are more successful, have stronger relationships, make more money, and are more attractive. They are also better leaders and negotiators, have more robust immune systems and resilience, and live longer than unhappy people. And honestly, the list of the good things that come from living a happier life goes on.

In the end, no matter who you are, what you do, or what you have, you might want to ask yourself, "Am I happy?"

HAPPINESS HAS MANY NAMES

Happiness is not only about laughter or being excited all the time. It is much deeper than that. I will talk about this throughout the book. It is also very individualistic, and everybody has his or her own definition of it.

In 2016, when I first started studying the science of happiness at the University of California–Berkeley, I found it significantly transforming. After I finished, I was privileged to serve as a community teaching assistant for a few months. During that time, I had to read comments and remarks on happiness made by students from all over the world. These remarks related to what made them happy and what happiness meant to them. They shared their own experiences, what they learned in the course, and how they were using the science of happiness in their lives. Sometimes as a community TA, I would have to explain things to them from a scientific point of view based on the findings of the leading happiness researchers. I enjoyed doing that.

In that journey, I came across thousands of people talking about happiness. When they were asked about happiness, they mentioned numerous things, sleeping, walking the dogs, listening to music, exercising, painting, spending quality time with loved ones—and the list goes on. These things made them feel good in some way. But those good feelings were not always labelled by them as "happiness." They expressed them in many different ways, "I feel energized," "I feel strong," "I love doing that," "I feel satisfied," "I feel at peace," and so on.

Everybody is wired differently. The other day my wife and I watched a film. I liked it; it was awesome for me. But for my wife, it was just okay. This was the same film, but with very different feelings and labels. What happiness is to you may not be the same for your loved ones. Even if we are in the same family, we all see, love, and experience things differently. That's why happiness is subjective. I love how Harvard professor Dan Gilbert explained it. He said, "Happiness is, of course, just something your brain is doing. It is an experience you have because your brain - your neurons are in a certain dance."

Even though the "dance" of our neurons we feel every day may seem similar, each one of us feels and names those good feelings of happiness in our own unique ways.

WE ALL CRAVE IT

In my journey of writing this book in the last five years, I spoke to many people from various backgrounds and age groups. When I asked them what happiness means to them, many knew straight away, but I also came across some who were surprised by this question. It felt as if I had asked them for directions to a place and they were unsure how to get there. Some smiled and said, "I have never thought about it" or "I have no idea." And some got stuck in thinking and just shrugged. Sometimes, for many, the face of happiness is not very clear.

Many of us believe happiness is out there and must be found in the future. We say things like "When this happens, then I will be happy" or "My happiness does not last long, so what's the point?" We also say, "I'm not a happy person. I'm not that lucky to be happy. I don't worry about happiness; it happens when it happens." These are very common beliefs.

Although sometimes the idea of happiness may look fuzzy, I have an interesting observation. I was talking to a friend, and she said, "I want to improve how I manage my time." I asked her, "Why is that important to you?" She replied, "I would like to finish the tasks during the day on time, so I can ensure my time with my children at night." I asked her, "What would that give you?" She said straight away, "That would give me joy." I continued, "What would joy give you?" She took a moment and said, "Pleasure! Maybe enjoyment." Like a recorded voice, I asked her again, "What would enjoyment give you?" Now she paused, and with a smile, she said, "Happiness?"

That day, I realized something and asked myself, "Isn't that the case in pretty much everything we do?"

Anything we willingly do every day has a purpose. For example, you brush your teeth in the morning to keep your teeth healthy and free of germs. That helps your health. But what does health give you? Or you may drive your kids to school because you want them to be educated. And what does their education give you? Or, if you are working on a project at work, you want to be successful. But what would that success give you?

Your answers could be "joy," "satisfaction," "peace," "achievements," "fulfilment," or the like. But if you ask the same question a few times, you will likely have similar answers, which is some kind of good feeling.

We are hard-wired to seek pleasure and avoid pain. No one wants to do something she doesn't like or anything against her will. But we think that almost everything we willingly do will eventually lead to feeling good in some way.

And often that is happiness.

Whether we realize it or not, we seek happiness anyway.

OFTEN THE PRICE WE PAY

Many years ago, I used to own an old car. At the time, I was studying, and a car was an expensive thing for me. Instead of doing regular servicing, I used to do "reactive" servicing to save money. That means I wouldn't worry about any servicing as long as the car was running. And most of the time, it took me to places without much problem.

One day, the car stopped in the middle of the road, and I noticed the engine light was on. I didn't know (and still don't know) much about cars, so I had no idea what that meant. After going through the car handbook, I found the instructions to not drive the car and take it to a service center as soon as possible. Later the mechanics told me that the radiator had been leaking for a long time and the coolant had run out (which I had no idea about). That's why the car engine got overheated and was not responding.

I asked them, "So what's next?" They said they would need to replace the engine.

I had to live without my car for a week, and it cost me $3,800.

For all those months, I thought the car was running just fine (at least to me, it looked fine). The radiator leak went unnoticed for a long time because I did not do regular checks and servicing of the car, but it survived as long as possible.

Just as our cars need regular servicing, our bodies and minds also need regular nurturing. We know we need food at least a few times a day to have the physical energy to survive. We do everything we can to avoid the physical breakdown of our bodies.

But historically, we do not have a concept of feeding our minds.

If we fast for a day, our bodies will complain and may even break down. If we do not feed our minds regularly, that essentially means we have been fasting for our minds forever. Like our cars or bodies, our minds also break down. They are not like our stomachs and do not complain as fast. Our minds are much more intelligent and complicated. Our minds do not complain in the short term, as they are very resilient, but they absolutely need nurturing and fueling regularly. Our minds need to feel energized, relaxed, at peace, and happy. Otherwise, we will experience sadness, boredom, and many other negative feelings in the longer term. If we do not notice those engine lights in our minds and take necessary actions with awareness, or if we ignore them, the price we will pay is too high, and we run into depression, anxiety, and other mental issues.

Not only that, but if you feel low, sad, depressed, or generally unhappy, your negative mental state will adversely impact everyone else around you and everything you do.

You might ask, "Okay, I get it, so what do we do?" As you do for your body, you must start "feeding" your mind. Being and staying happy is not a luxury. Rather, it is a necessity.

HAPPINESS IS LIKE PLANTS

Leslie Williamson was one of my teachers when I was studying positive psychology at Harvard. She is also the president of the Academy for Brain Health and Performance. I remember I submitted a reflection for her review. She emailed me her response, and the first line said, "There you go, you have an analogy for everything." This was followed by a smiley face.

What can I do? I love analogies.

Over many years, I have realized that happiness is like plants. Feeling good, energized, excited, fulfilled, or happy is a beautiful thing, like flowers. And feeling low, sad, depressed, or angry is like the weeds.

But beautiful flowers do not just grow automatically. Weeds do.

Your mind is like a garden. If you nurture more beautiful flowers and take the weeds out regularly, your garden will look nice and feel great. But if you don't, you will have more weeds than flowers.

What comes into our minds automatically and quickly? A positive thought or a worry? For most people, it is the worry.

If you have five plants and you water only two of them and leave the other three untouched and uncared for, then what happens to those three plants? Yes, they all die.

Anything worth having, doing, or experiencing takes nurturing. If you want to have a successful business, you need to build it. If you want a great body, you must put in the effort. If you want a great relationship with your partner, you must focus on and nurture it. Your happiness also grows over time through your focus and careful nurturing, like the plants.

Nurturing good thoughts and feelings and reducing the negative ones is a continuous and never-ending process. A nice-looking garden is a result of the gardening skill of the gardener. Your happiness on your terms is also a result of your skill. I sincerely believe my book will help you build that.

REFLECTION

Have you ever thought, how would you measure the quality of your life?

Take a moment and ponder.

Is it your career, health, money, loving connections or anything else?

As you grow older and look back on your life, you will see many things you once wished wouldn't matter anymore.

But, whoever you are, whatever you do or have, the bottom line is to ask yourself, "Am I happy today? Do I feel satisfied with my life?"

If the answer is yes to both, nothing really matters.

If I were given a chance to pick just one ability I desire, I would like to be and stay happy on my terms for the rest of my life.

What would yours be?

THE DEFAULT LIFE

"We forget the chains we wear in life."
—Charles Dickens

WE ASSUME

Jason is eighty-eight years old. When he was young, he studied law at a reputed university. He then joined a big corporate in his twenties. After six years, he quit his job and founded his own consulting firm, which became very successful over the years. He also invested in real estate. He made his first million before he was thirty-five. Then he married a beautiful girl and had three children. He worked so hard that almost all of his goals came true.

But his working habits took a toll on his family life. He and his wife separated when he was in his mid-fifties. He never remarried, but all his children were grown up and moved out. He hardly was in touch with them. By the age of seventy, he was one of the wealthiest people in his town, but he didn't stop. He kept growing and increased his investment portfolio even more. But in his eighties, he got diagnosed with Parkinson's disease and has been suffering from that since. He lives in his exquisite big house pretty much by himself. He has a caretaker who comes in daily and helps him with his daily activities, and she leaves at night.

One day when they were talking, Jason said to her, "I know you are in your twenties. Can I give you a piece of advice?" She said, "Sure, what is it?" Jason smiled and said, "All my life, I have achieved a lot. I had a good marriage which I couldn't keep. I have three children, but I failed to spend quality time with them. They don't even call me anymore. I realized that I worked too hard for so many years. I never paid attention to my family, and now I'm old and alone. I wish I could have my family and friends around me." Then he paused and looked through the window and said, "If you have a family and good friends, never let them go."

Why would an eighty-eight-year-old say that?

Most people would dream of what Jason achieved in his life. From the outside, it looks like he had a very busy and successful life. But still, at the age of eighty-eight, he is alone and has no one to share his life with. He regrets not having his family by his side in his old age.

But what went wrong?

When he was young, he assumed and imagined what he needed to achieve for a successful and happy life. He reached most of his goals, but he dropped the ball somewhere without even knowing. In his old age, he realized that his assumptions regarding a successful and happy life didn't serve him as well as he thought they would.

And now he is eighty-eight years old, alone, and not very satisfied.

YOUR DEFAULT LIFE

Most people are not as successful as Jason. Honestly, he is one of the very few. While old age is not promised to anyone, I wondered what my life will look like when I am eighty-eight. I looked at many people of different ages. Most of their lives look like this:

- You are born.
- You have to go to school.
- You must get good grades.
- You should graduate with flying colors.
- You must land a high-paying prestigious job.
- You must get married to someone who is socially accepted.
- You should buy a fantastic house and a car so people will notice you.
- You should take luxurious holidays.
- You must become a parent and raise your kids to the best standards.
- You should have social status.
- You must have a solid bank balance and retirement plan.
- You should plan for reliable aged care.
- You die.

Guess what? Unlike Jason, many people do not even get to the age of aged care. I don't know about you, but this was the life for most people in my close family, friends, and acquaintances. Why would mine be any different? I don't know what the future holds, but I was like, "Are these the primary goals of my life?" I thought, "I have ticked some of the things in this list already," and I asked myself, "Did those things make me lastingly happy? Did they make me fully satisfied with my life?"

The answers were no and no.

One way or the other, most people chase these milestones to live happy and satisfying lives. And yes, of course, some things (e.g., illness, losing a loved one, or injury) are not in our control. But even if we become successful in ticking all these milestones in this default life, we still might end up regretting, as Jason did.

I thought, "The default life looked pretty good and accomplished, but why is it not fulfilling me in my forties, or people like Jason in their eighties? Am I missing something?" I wanted to find out why.

What most people want at every stage of life is very similar. For example, when you are in your teens, you might want to go to the best school, look beautiful and smart, and do the cool things that your friends admire. When you are in your twenties, you want to land your dream job at a big corporation, get credit cards, have social status, buy your house and dream car, possibly fall in love, and get married.

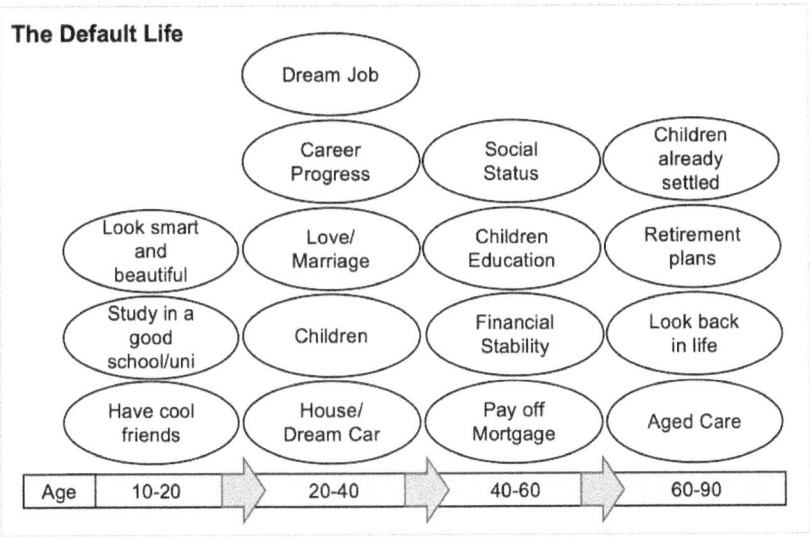

Then you want to have children, raise them with your blood and sweat, pay off your mortgage, and have some level of financial stability. Before you realize it, you may already be sixty-five and planning retirement and eventually going to aged care.

Take a piece of paper and spend five minutes pondering and briefly writing your life story. What have you ticked already on or outside of this list above? How has doing so made you happy and satisfied?

There is no right or wrong way to write, but express yourself as honestly as possible. I don't know if I missed something on the list, and your life goals may differ. But most people assume this default life is the formula for a happy and satisfying life. Generally, if you can reach the age of seventy-five and successfully tick these boxes, you might be considered and automatically assumed to be successful and happy.

Yes, you might have dreamed of climbing that mountain, running that marathon, writing that book, working on the passion project you truly believe in and care for, travelling the world, and so on. But you may have postponed those dreams for "other responsibilities" when you had the time, money, or chance to do them. These things could have made you happier and helped you create good memories. But these are not generally treated as life goals, as are the milestones in the default life. No one will ask you whether you have worked on your passion project or followed your calling, or whether you are happy and satisfied. But if you don't have a proper job, marriage, or children, you may seem like a "failure" in life.

Strangely enough, living a happy life is at the top of what most people want and is not even on the list of life goals in the default life. If I ask someone, "What do you want from life in the next five years?" She might just say, "Finishing graduation, having a job, being a parent, buying a house, paying off my mortgage," or something similar.

But if she says, "Living a happier life," people might call this person "crazy." Because the default life is the only socially accepted pattern of a successful and happy life. Any deviation is not appreciated.

I realized that I was living someone else's default life.

REFLECTING ON THE DEFAULT LIFE

Your own experience can be different, and you might just say, "Meh ... I'm just too busy to think about my life, happiness, or satisfaction right now. Everybody is living the default life. Nothing is wrong with it, and I'm pretty happy and satisfied with my current life."

You might be right.

If somebody had asked me to reflect on my life ten years ago, I would have probably thought the same way. The truth is that many people are not even ready for these questions. They are not prepared to even deeply think about happiness or satisfaction yet. I'm not saying you should stop everything and ponder upon your life choices right now. People reflect in different stages of their lives. You will likely stop and reflect when it is time for you, but being a little more aware is probably a good starting point.

For me, it started with my dad. He is about eighty-two years old. Even though he had a remarkable and successful career, my dad has always talked about his dreams and his passion projects outside of his work. But he never got the time or money to pursue them, mainly because he wanted to ensure we were okay. Dad followed this default life. Many do the same and later in life regret it.

I was terrified when I pondered upon my own life. I always thought that my life would be interesting in the future and I would do incredible things when the time was right. These included things like building a school, learning to fly a helicopter, writing more, travelling more, and having experiences like hot air balloon rides. But after spending about thirty-five years in this existence, I realized I never got the time right to do the things I truly wanted to do. Like my dad, I was stuck in a rut and lived the default life that everybody around me was living.

I didn't see myself continuing to live that life. It scared me.

I was talking to an old friend over dinner. He is in his mid-forties and lives in Sydney. He said, "I love mountain climbing, and last year I wanted to go. I booked everything with a group. One of my friends wanted to join me, but he got too scared and cancelled on the day. And I couldn't go." I said, "Why not? You could have joined the rest of the group." He said, "I thought about it. But I didn't want to disappoint my friend by going alone. It wouldn't look good."

I asked him, "So your friend is joining you to try again?" He said, "I don't think he will ever go mountain climbing. But what can you do?" Then he sadly shrugged. See, my friend couldn't go mountain climbing because his friend cancelled, and he is already regretting it.

That also got me thinking, What are the things I truly wanted to do but couldn't? And how would that make me feel now and later?

I wanted to dig deep and came across author Bronnie Ware.

WE REGRET ON OUR DEATHBEDS

Bronnie spent about eight years as a palliative nurse. She helped people get through the final stages of their lives. As she was nursing them in their final weeks, many patients shared their regrets with her. Bronnie wrote a book titled The 5 Regrets of the Dying. She talked about the most common regrets of all in her book.

The top one is "I wish I'd had the courage to live a life true to myself, not the life others expected of me." Bronnie states, "This was the most common regret of all. When people realize that their life is almost over and look back clearly on it. It is easy to see how many dreams have gone unfulfilled. Most people had not honored even half of their dreams and had to die knowing that they were because of the choices they had made or not made. Health brings a freedom very few realize until they no longer have it."

"I wish I hadn't worked so hard," "I wish I had the courage to express my feelings," "I wish I had stayed in touch with my friends," and "I wish that I had let myself be happier" were the other top four regrets. We do not realize some of our regrets until we realize that our time is up. There are some we know that we have, but we cannot necessarily do anything about them.

Why would the dying regret? And why are such regrets so common?

Bronnie also states, "Common themes surfaced again and again." Most of us may be chasing the wrong things in our lives, which we may regret later in old age.

One answer to the question of why the dying regret could be that they are living the default life of others.

BUT WHERE DID THE DEFAULT LIFE COME FROM?

Think about the time when we didn't have Google Maps, or even any maps at all. How did our ancestors go from place A to place B? They used the information on hand. Sometimes they followed the sun, asked people for directions, and relied on their assumptions.

If you want to go from place A to place B today, you never look at the sun for directions or ask other people. You use Google Maps and completely trust that it will accurately direct you from place A to place B. But if you don't have Google Maps, what are your chances of getting lost? They are likely high. Why? Because you don't have an authentic and accurate map. You have to rely on a bit of information, assumptions, and directions from other people (who may or may not know where you are going) and could spend a lot of your valuable time "figuring out" the path.

When it comes to happiness, we say things like, "I just want to be happy" or "I just want my kids to be happy." We send our kids to schools to learn physics, chemistry, literature, and many other things, but we do not learn happiness at school. Historically, there was no science or evidence-based teaching around living a happy life.

Most of us want to be happy and satisfied in life, but we never had a reliable source of guidance (or map).

Isn't it strange?

There was no "Google Maps for a Happy Life", no science of happiness to guide us based on more accurate data and facts. So we relied on our imaginations, assumptions, and advice from others. Living a happy and satisfying life is not as straightforward as going from place A to place B, but living based on assumptions may lead to unhappiness and regrets.

Remember Jason? He followed the default life and achieved many of his goals but still wasn't satisfied with his life at age eighty-eight.

Our default life has evolved over many years from the time of our ancestors. The one I referred to earlier is a more current and modern version of it. But no matter how updated or modern the default life is, it is still not based on facts or empirical evidence, but rather on our collective and historical assumptions.

WHY MAY OUR ASSUMPTIONS FAIL US?

When we do not have enough information about something, we assume. We basically make things up using our imaginations. The part of our brain that allows us to imagine is called the prefrontal cortex and is the newest part of our brain, from an evolutionary point of view. As human beings, we can imagine something without actually experiencing it. No other animals can do this as well as humans. When it comes to happiness, we imagine things like how good it would be to have a promotion or a new car. We can imagine the feeling of the promotion and the new car without actually having them.

But there is a slight problem with this experience simulator in our brains. It turns out our imaginations often fail us and we overestimate or underestimate the happiness or unhappiness that might come from a future event. This is because the brain's prefrontal cortex is still very new, in evolutionary terms, and not quite perfect. Professor Daniel Gilbert from Harvard University states, "Study after study in the last two decades have shown that people make a systematic series of errors when they try to predict not what will happen but how they will feel about it." Professor Gilbert also says that our imaginations for the future are based on our present conditions. When we imagine something in the future, we underestimate the change that will occur to our current situations. That means that if you are dreaming about a car you want today, the idea might make you very happy today. But when you actually buy that car in the future, you might not feel as happy as you are feeling today, or your happiness may not last as long as you thought it would because of other changes in your life.

And that's when our imaginations and assumptions fail us.

The other risk is that we get bad advice from the people around us. And obviously, they also advise us based on their imaginations, which could be wrong because their prefrontal cortexes will likely make errors too. However, their advice may not always be from their imaginations but may be from their own real experiences. For example, to have a happy life, one of the most common pieces of advice you may get is to get married, have children, and make your marriage work. Another common statement is that getting divorced is a terrible thing for happiness. The people who give you this advice may have actually experienced joy derived from their marriage and kids. They genuinely believe it, and that's why they think you should get married and have children to be happy.

Studies suggest that before getting married, people become very happy. And that boost of happiness remains for a few years before it starts to wear off. Surprisingly, studies also suggest that getting divorced also makes people happy. Professor Gilbert states, "When you look at divorced statistics, people get much happier after a divorce." He also concludes, "It isn't marriage that makes us happy. It's a good marriage that makes us happy." Many people love parenting, and children make them happy, but for many, parenting is hard work that makes them unhappy.

> "The fewer the facts, the stronger the opinion."
> —Arnold H. Glasow

Your individual experience may differ, but these conclusions are drawn from studies done on thousands of people from many different data sets. The bottom line is that when we imagine our futures regarding both good and bad events, we may often be mistaken because of our reliance on our imaginations and advice from others.

THE "WHEN THIS HAPPENS, THEN I WILL BE HAPPY" FORMULA

Most people assume that we must achieve every milestone in this default life formula to be happy. That means landing your dream job, buying a house, having kids, and paying off your mortgage are all milestones. The milestones in the default life are important life goals, and every time we tick one of them, we become happy. But as a society, we have also learned to postpone being happy until we become successful. We do not allow ourselves to be happy today as we wait for our success, special days, or hitting the milestones of the default life.

"When this happens, then I will be happy" is the most widely used but mistaken formula. We subconsciously start to believe that until we have some kind of success, it's not the time to be happy yet. So we do not even think about being happy until we have success.

For example, we call our wedding days the happiest days of our lives, or you become "very special" only on your birthdays. For many people, this belief may automatically imply that the other ordinary days are not "happy days." That's why celebrating new jobs, promotions, births of children, and things like these are the only things we treat as happy days. We focus so much on those default happy days that we postpone being happy and forget to live on our ordinary days.

We make success the primary condition of being happy. We believe our happiness is on the other side of success in our default lives. Days, months, and sometimes years pass, but we do not allow ourselves to be happy. The treadmill of life continues, and in chasing so many milestones, we lose so much time and become old and tired without even realizing it.

The funny thing is that many of those milestones were set by others and are probably not your own. You spend your whole life chasing other people's goals of the default life, and they don't even make you lastingly happy.

Is it worth the effort?

When did you actually live on your terms?

I CAN'T BE HAPPY BECAUSE OF THIS

Many of us also believe that we can't be happy now because of some undesired condition that we are going through. "I can't be happy because my marriage is falling apart," "I have an illness," "I lost my job," "I am not pregnant yet," "My son has an exam next week." These are some of the common beliefs that hold us back from being happy.

You might say, "How can you be happy when these things happen?"

Yes, of course, going through tough times is not fun for anyone. But do you know someone whose life is perfect? You might be screening through the people you know who look to have everything and seem very happy. You may well know someone perfect. But deep down, you and I both know that no matter how good someone's life looks from the outside, that person also has struggles. Whether they relate to material wealth, relationships, health, children, career, or other areas, everyone has his or her own struggle stories of hardship that we don't necessarily know. And you will always find someone who is worse off.

But the moment you start to believe and say to yourself, "I can't be happy because ..." your brain stops trying to be happy. It just does not allow you to be happy until your reason is resolved. If you notice, this belief is slightly different looking. Still, it essentially relates to the same phenomenon of "When this happens, then I will be happy," which tricks you into postponing your happiness today.

Also, if you believe things like, "Happiness is out there, and I must find it," "Happiness is not for me," "I'm not usually that happy," "I'm not that lucky to be happy," "Only rich people are happy," or "I don't have the perfect guy, so I can't be happy" then you might find it very difficult to be happy.

Whatever you choose to believe about being happy has a powerful influence on how you feel every day.

Often our beliefs come from our incorrect assumptions.

THE RESULTS OF THE DEFAULT LIFE

Many people might disagree with me for challenging the status quo or the default life because they believe that the default life is the only way to have a happy life. They might also say, "This blueprint has been there for hundreds of years, and all my ancestors lived a very happy and fulfilled life following this blueprint. Who are you to question this?"

Well, they may have a valid point.

Some people do live happy lives using this formula. But if we knew what it takes to live happy lives and lived using these "success-driven" default life strategies, most people would be happy and have great lives. So I wanted to find out how well this default life and our assumptions have performed in the past.

In terms of success, business, innovation, financial wealth, being a superpower, and in many other dimensions, the United States is considered one of the best countries in the world having the largest nominal GDP of about $30 trillion. Many other countries aspire to be like the US. But if you look at the recent World Happiness Report published in 2019, you will see that the US is not "The happiest country" globally. Instead, the general happiness of adult population in 2019 was at a record low in recent years since 1973.

Surprise!

With more recent data, the US is the 24th country by life evaluations, and Finland ranks 1st in the world as of World Happiness Report 2025.

The 2019 report also says, "By most accounts, Americans should be happier now than ever. The violent crime rate is low, as is the unemployment rate. The income per capita has steadily grown over the last few decades. This is the Easterlin paradox, As the standard of living improves, so should happiness – but it has not."

Also, the 2025 report says, "In general, the western industrial countries are now less happy than they were between 2005 and 2010."

In addition, the 2019 report also revealed that there are many indicators of low psychological well-being. For instance, depression, suicidal ideation, and self-harm increased among adolescents since 2010. According to the World Health Organization, about 264 million people of all ages suffer from depression worldwide. One study found that 23 per cent of people reported midlife crisis. According to ADAA, about 40 million US adults suffer from anxiety each year. That is almost one in five people. Another study found that 90 per cent of people say they have a major regret. The American Psychological Association also finds that 76 per cent of people mentioned an "action" they did not take that would have helped them realize their "ideal self." These are reported numbers, and the actual numbers might be higher.

Why would so many people become depressed, suffer anxiety, or have regrets?

I also found that the typical happiness curve in almost every culture is U-shaped. This reflects that people are happier when young (less than twenty) or older (over sixty), but your happiness drops and remains low between ages twenty and sixty. That's about forty years of happiness lost.

There must be something wrong.

I believe no one deserves to be depressed or thinking of committing suicide or anxiously living an obligated default life.

Also, my intention is not to highlight how bad people's mental well-being is in the United States and worldwide, but to indicate that most of us want to live happy and satisfying lives that make sense to us individually. But our traditional approach to happiness and the ways of the default life based on our assumptions are not leading to long-term happiness and satisfaction. It would be nice if they were effective, but the truth is that they are not.

THE BOTTOM LINE

My book is not the solution to all these global issues, and I'm not saying you should drop everything and reset your life. Honestly, you may already have a good education, a high-paying job, marriage, children, material wealth, and so on, and these are important. With your current life, you may actually be very happy and fulfilled. Many people are.

"Tailor-made" is a concept many of us use when buying dresses, cars, houses, and many other things. Whether it is the perfect fitting for your dress, the exact leather interior for your car, or that perfect living room for your house, having something tailor made allows you to individualize your experience. You cannot get that in a standard dress, car, or house.

The default life is like a standard car. Some people are okay with it, but some are not. The default life stands very strongly because it works and makes some people happy and fulfilled.

The problem is that it does not work for everybody.

As humans, we like to follow what other people do in our circles. But just because everyone is following this default life does not make it right, especially when the global happiness reports are not encouraging. You don't necessarily have to follow the crowd and risk regret or losing forty years of happiness. Everybody is different, and their happiness and satisfaction are also individually defined. What makes your partner happy may not necessarily make you happy and satisfied. That's why, by definition, you have the best chance to live on your terms, which are tailor made only for you. And that is living a life by your own design.

> "There is no passion to be found playing small-in settling for
> a life that is less than the one you are capable of living."
> —Nelson Mandela

Personally, I believe my happiness and satisfaction in my life should not be determined by the default life of others. I want to live a life by my design that makes sense to me. But, yes, I may risk imagining the wrong things (because of my assumptions like everyone else's) and making life choices that I might regret. But my decisions would still be mine, and the responsibility would be on me than on someone else.

It is impossible to eliminate all regrets from our lives. Still, it is possible to minimize them through awareness and taking action. Whether it is working on your dream project, building a loving relationship, creating a business, or doing anything you genuinely love and care about, it can still scare you into taking action, and it is very easy to delay for the "right time."

I love the way author Brené Brown said, "Yeah, it's so scary to show up, and it feels dangerous to be seen, it's terrifying. But it is not as scary, dangerous, or terrifying as getting to the end of our lives and thinking, what if I would have shown up, what would have been different?"

Yes, there will still be regrets, but they will be fewer.

I looked at the default life blueprint (mentioned earlier) again, and I thought, "This can't be it. There must be a better way."

I decided to live my life by design.

REFLECTION

We don't go to a restaurant and order what other people want. We order what we want. Similarly, be, do and have what you want in life.

Do you love your work?

Do you genuinely respect your boss or coworkers?

Are you in a passionate romantic relationship?

Are you a part of a strong circle of good friends where you belong?

Do you generally feel high physical energy?

Do you emotionally feel good most of the time?

Do you earn enough so money is not a problem for you?

Your answers to these questions will trigger some thoughts in you and if you ponder upon them, you will have an indication if you are living according to your own life choices or by the opinions of others.

At the time, I knew I wasn't living by mine.

MY QUEST FOR LIFE BY DESIGN

"Dream as if you'll live forever. live as if you'll die today."
—James Dean

WHAT IS LIFE BY DESIGN?

You might be wondering what "life by design" means? How do you design such a thing as life and then live it?

Honestly, when I first heard about this, I had no idea. And it means different things to different people. Everybody has a version of this, and no one design would fit everybody. You don't want another version of the default life. And there shouldn't be one, because everyone is unique, and the design should also be unique.

As I was saying, I initially had no idea what that meant. But one thing I had already decided was that I wasn't going to live the default life; instead, I would live it the way it makes sense to me. But unfortunately, I did not know anything about it. And I kept searching for it in many different places. I spent my time, effort, and money on various courses, seminars, and conferences for a few years. But the more information I received, the more confused I had become. Some said I should design my life based on money; some said relationships, higher purpose, and similar things.

I felt stuck, and I became frustrated and helpless.

One day, I asked one of my mentors, and he said, "The design of life is not like a design of a building; it can change, and it will. But in this ever-changing life, you must ensure your health, wealth, relationships, and anything important to you match your expectations."

That statement didn't change my life, but it changed my perception.

My first-hand experience of going through this realization has enabled me to look at my life differently. I started reviewing my previous life choices to know where I was. I had to, because I had already decided to live by design.

HAVE TO VS. LOVE TO

So what did I review? And what did I find?

I had to look at my life as a whole, as if from a bird's-eye view, spanning across multiple areas, such as my health, relationships, money, career, and wealth. For each area, I asked, "Do I love this area the way it is today? If not, what would I want it to be?" Then I did a "gap analysis" on each area of my life.

But my answers surprised me. I realized I was doing many things during my typical day because I had to do them and not because I loved to do them.

Every morning till midnight, I found that I did things I didn't like and spent time with people I didn't respect or love. I was doing them only out of my obligations in my default life. They made me feel controlled and forced. I listed them on paper and called this the "Have To" list.

But I also found other things and people that I liked and loved. So I listed those items and people on another sheet of paper and called it the "Love To" list. The challenge is to be completely honest in your answers.

Have To (Default Life)	Love To (Life By Design)
• Waking up at 5 am for work	• Having green smoothies in the morning
• Staying in a job I don't like	
• Facing my unfair boss every day	• Spending time with my partner
	• Writing
• Being in a relationship that does not serve me anymore	• Being helpful to others
• Fitting in a group where I don't feel appreciated	• Talking to my best friend

The items you see on the list are a few examples from all areas of my life. These lists didn't give me a complete audit of my life, but they were simple starting points. If you have more items in the "Have To" list, you are likely living the default life out of obligation. I will discuss more about life by design in part 3.

As I stopped and pondered upon the various areas of my life, I found that I hated my fitness level and a few of my relationships with some people. I'm not a person who likes to spend a lot of time in the past. So instead of blaming myself and asking, "How did that happen?" I started to ask more empowering questions, such as "What can I do about it?"

I realized I needed to do something about my "Have To" list, as it contained too many items and people. I picked two major things that made me disgusted every day and decided to work on them. I intended to adjust and improve them from my "Have To" list to the "Love To" list or completely eliminate them.

Some things are easier to fix (e.g., lawn mowing). And some are more complicated (e.g., a job you hate, a relationship that does not serve you anymore). The latter will naturally take more time to fix. However, if you actively work on them without quitting, it is absolutely possible to see improvements or fix them entirely (e.g., you land a better job that you like or you begin a new relationship)

Create a "Love To" and "Have To" list and see where you are at.

I also understood that the "Have To" list will always have something. But when we are talking about a happy and fulfilling life, we must have more items in the "Love To" list than the "Have To" list. That is essential for living on your terms. But my initial audit had the opposite, and I realized it was time to make some immediate changes.

THE FOUR TYPES OF LIVES: THE LIFE QUADRANT

My dad likes to analyze everything. He spends a lot of time thinking before he makes a move. My mum is very different. She is quick to make a decision and act. My dad's beliefs and values are different from my mum's. Has it ever occurred to you that you just "connect" with someone more easily than with others? It's most likely because your beliefs and values match with that person's. You may feel a disconnect when those beliefs and values do not match. For example, some people are naturally courageous and live very different lives than others. Our behavior comes from our beliefs and values, which shape our lives, including our happiness and satisfaction.

There are no right or wrong ways to live, and there is no one correct way to measure the quality of our lives. But when it comes to living a happy and satisfying life, you will see that some people have everything but are still miserable emotionally. You will also see people who live very happy and satisfying lives with what they have. In my review of my life, I wanted to find out where I stood. What type of life was I living?

Based on years of observation and learning, I summarized lives into four general types. I presented them in the life quadrant.

The determinants of the quality of these lives are not based on power, money, social status, or anything like that, but they are more about living on your terms to stay happy and satisfied—things like what you generally believe about life; whether you love, enjoy, and care about your work; whether you have a deep and loving connection with yourself and others; whether you physically and emotionally feel good; and how you deal with life challenges.

A "survivor life" is a life in which a person believes life is hard and there is not much he or she can do. People living survivor lives do not have specific goals. They are not open to new ideas and hold on to their traditional beliefs. They may not like their jobs. Their relationships are not great either. They may or may not have some money, but it does not fulfil them. They often play the victim and blame others. Health is not a priority for them. Their average emotional state is worried or anxious, and they may rarely feel happy or satisfied.

An "average life" is one in which people believe, "It is what it is," and only react to things and follow the crowd. Their main goal is to make a smooth living. They somewhat hold on to their traditional beliefs. They may just feel "okay" with their jobs, and their relationships are average. They may or may not have a lot of money, but they don't know how to use it to be happy. They often are the victims of circumstances. Health is somewhat important for them. Their average emotional state is better than that of survivors; however, they can easily get worried or anxious. They may occasionally feel happy or satisfied on special occasions (e.g., birthdays).

A "good life" is a life in which a person believes life can be beautiful. Those who live good lives have a few goals, but they work on them only when they feel comfortable and feel like it. They are open to new ideas and approaches. They may generally feel better than okay regarding their work. Also, they pay close attention to their relationships. They may have a sufficient amount of money, and they use it wisely. They don't complain or blame much and can pivot when challenged. They take care of their health. They feel worried or anxious like everyone else, but their average emotional state is better than that of survivors or average people. They can feel happy or satisfied on their ordinary days.

The Life Quadrant

Survivor	Good
You believe, life is hard and there is not much you can do.	*You believe, life can be beautiful and you work for it.*
You have no goals and just surviving.	*You have a few life goals and work on them when you feel like.*
Average	**Extraordinary**
You believe, it is what it is, you react to things and go with the crowd.	*You believe, your life must be on your terms. You make regular progress towards your vision of life.*
Your only goal is to make a smooth living.	*You have clear goals and you actively work on them everyday.*

An "extraordinary life" is a life which a person believes is a blessing. Those who live extraordinary lives have a vision and actively work on their goals every day. They live on their terms as much as they can. They are not afraid to say no when it is needed. They are open to new ideas and approaches. However, they rarely change their goals. They aim for excellence in what they do. They never give up on their dreams and constantly make progress towards them. They feel alive in their work. They develop deep and meaningful relationships with others. They surround themselves with people they love and are inspired by. They may or may not have a lot of money, but they know how to use it for their souls. They rarely complain or blame others. They are masters at pivoting when they are challenged. Health is vital for them, and they work on it regularly. They feel worried or anxious like everyone else, but they are emotionally clever and deal with adversities very differently. They can bounce back after setbacks much more quickly than others.

Most people don't live the lives they truly want, and many fall between average lives and good lives. These labels do not mean one has average money, wealth, or fame. One may have attained a lot of success and material wealth. However, if one is constantly worried, anxious, or unfulfilled, he or she may still be living an average life or survivor life.

The extraordinary life may look hard to achieve. But think about it, many people aren't famous or rich. They don't have expensive material wealth and still live extraordinary lives on their terms. They are some of the happiest and most satisfied people on earth. I know some people who live such lives. Honestly, an extraordinary life can be much simpler and cheaper than other lives.

I want to tell you about one person I admire so much that I cannot even express it in words. I would love to include some of his wisdom here. He is Anthony Robbins. He is considered the world's number-one life and business strategist. He explained it very well after serving millions of people in over one hundred countries over the last forty-four years. One of the most important life lessons I learned from him was that people feel happy when their blueprints of life match their current life conditions.

Your blueprint is what you believe your life should be. If there is one area of your life that you are proud of (e.g., you love your job or body), you may be proud not because you have the best body or have the highest-paying job in the world but because your current job or body matches your expectations. So you may feel good, proud, or satisfied with them. Notice that it is about your expectations and not someone else's. The more areas about which you feel good or which you love about your life, the more you live on your terms.

> "I intend to live life, not just exist."
> —George Takei

When I first did a review on my life, I was in the average quadrant. However, over the years, I did make small changes to my life to get to good, but I still don't think I'm in extraordinary yet. I might be somewhere between good and extraordinary. But that does not mean I settle there. The best thing about extraordinary people is that they never stop growing. They continue to progress and prosper regardless of their age.

Tao Porchon-Lynch was the "Oldest Yoga Teacher." She recently died at 101. She had a remarkable life, and what amazed me about her was that at the age of eighty, she started to dance and became a competitive dancer. She still taught yoga classes when she was nearing one hundred. You might think this is crazy. Yes, it is. But the point is, you can live more on your terms if you strongly believe in, decide on, and act on them.

For me, the mantra is to make regular progress.

Which life quadrant do you feel you are in today? And which quadrant would you rather live the rest of your life in?

Think about it.

Wherever you feel you are ("survivor," "average," "good," or "extraordinary"), you can always make the changes and progress to the next level. If you are already living an extraordinary life, don't settle there. Make progress anyway.

One of the simplest ways to live an extraordinary life is to have much more on your "Love To" list than your "Have To" list. People who live extraordinary lives surround themselves with people they love and are inspired by than the people who annoy them. They don't waste time worrying about the things they don't control (e.g., government rules, weather). They minimize the tasks they don't like doing (e.g., doing taxes, being stuck in traffic). Also, they maximize the tasks they love doing (e.g., painting, presenting). Your transition from your current life to the next level may look like the one below.

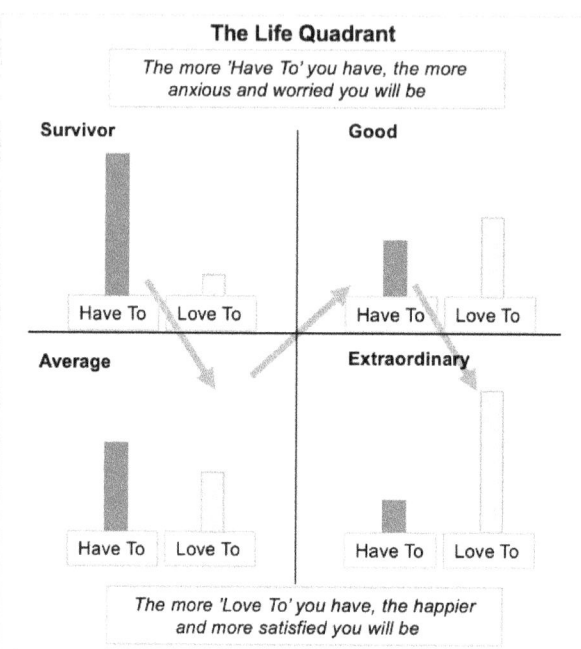

As you move to the next level, the items in your love to list will increase, and items in the "Have To" list will shrink.

Extraordinary people are careful about their thoughts and actions. They understand that emotions are like clouds and change every moment. Feeling hopeful and excited is good, but experiencing worries and anxiety is also part of life, so they intentionally build their emotional muscles (just as we build physical muscles) to deal with low mental states. They don't wait to be happy on special occasions (e.g., birthdays, promotions). Instead, they create small happy moments and celebrate satisfaction on their ordinary days.

The more "Have To" you have, the more anxious and worried you become, but the more "Love To" you have, the happier and more satisfied you will be.

Remember, living an extraordinary life is not about being famous, being rich, or having high social status or expensive material wealth; it is about creating such a life that you live every day not because you have to but because you love to.

MY JOURNEY TOOK A TURN

At this point of my review and exploration, I learned about the default life, regrets, global happiness results, the concept of life by design, and the four types of lives. I understood the power of having more "Love To" items than "Have To" items. I decided to live an extraordinary life on my terms.

But how, exactly, do you design and live such a life? Where to start?

After moving away from the default life, I came across some life strategies from various sources and got a little overwhelmed. I wanted something more solid and reliable.

I kept searching but wasn't getting anywhere.

A few weeks later, I saw Catherine's post on my LinkedIn account. She was one of my NLP instructors. I read what she wrote, then I clicked on her profile and found that one of her qualifications was having completed the Science of Happiness course through UC Berkeley.

I had no idea about any science for something like happiness. I was like, "Wow, that is interesting," and I was hooked. I researched and realized that I had been looking for answers everywhere, but I never thought of looking into science. I felt that almost everything we do in our everyday modern lives is governed by science.

So why not our happiness?

It made sense, and I decided to learn and take guidance from the best source with the highest visibility and authority on the subject. Who can better guide us than the scientists and researchers of happiness? That's when my quest for living a life by design took a timely and authentic turn towards the science of happiness.

I signed up for the course. That was the first time I started to study the science of happiness in an actual university with many other students, in 2016. The more I learned, the more I got intrigued. I loved the whole experience. Then in 2017, I studied positive psychology at Harvard extension school, and my learning continued. I realized that learning about the science of happiness was an amazing experience for me. I thought, "One way or the other, we all seek happiness and satisfaction."

I started to believe that mastering happiness is the most important skill we can build in our lives.

I also felt very strongly that what I learned about happiness and life satisfaction must be shared. And that's one of the reasons you are reading this book.

I haven't talked about it yet, but have you been curious?

In the previous section, how did I compose the determinants of the life quadrant—especially those of the extraordinary life? These factors are not set in stone. However, I derived them from a solid framework of science that I learned during my studies. Instead of living the default life of assumptions, science gave me much more confidence to rely on a solid framework backed by research and empirical evidence. I shall talk about it in the next chapter and throughout the book.

One of my favorite quotes from Confucius states, "I hear and I forget. I see and I remember. I do and I understand." I knew studying the science of happiness would only give me knowledge, but I wanted to be happier and more satisfied. For that to happen, I needed to implement the science framework and strategies in my life. I knew I wanted to "walk the talk." I started to act on my learnings. And slowly the life by design on my terms started to emerge. I can't wait to share it with you.

REFLECTION

Remember, living an extraordinary life is about taking charge of your life and living on your terms. That means you say, "I've had enough," and you don't continue to do things you don't like and don't spend your precious time with people you don't respect or love.

Identify Things

Write three things you do out of obligation (things you have to do) every day. Then, next to these items, write what you can replace them with (things you love to do).

Identify People

Now list three people you don't like but have to deal with regularly. For these people, write what you can do (potentially) to avoid them, get along with them better (so they have less power over you), or replace them.

If you say you can, you will. But if you say you can't, you will not.

THE SCIENCE OF HAPPINESS

*"Scientists have become the bearers of the torch
of discovery in our quest for knowledge."*
—Stephen Hawking

TRUSTING IN SCIENCE

At the time of this writing, the whole world is going through a pandemic caused by COVID-19. Almost every country is looking to collect as many vaccines as possible. Now the world is eagerly waiting for vaccine manufacturers to catch up with the demand for billions of doses.

To produce a solid traditional vaccine takes about five to seven years of data with extensive research. But scientists worldwide came together to fight COVID-19. They have produced vaccines for emergency use within just eighteen months to save millions of lives. Countries had no choice but to rely on science and scientists to fight COVID-19.

If you want to be a doctor, you must attend medical school. But medical schools don't just teach whatever they like. They must follow a well-analyzed curriculum, researched and structured by medical scientists and approved by a governing body of experts with many years of medical knowledge and experience. As medical science advances, the curricula in medical schools also get updated.

Not only for medicine but in every possible area of life, including mathematics, engineering, chemistry, and physics, scientists do the research and share their findings with the world to apply their wisdom in our lives. You cannot learn medicine or any other subjects from your family and friends. You must rely on science.

But historically, when it comes to happiness, we turn to our friends, families, and people around us. This does not make a lot of sense, but it is true. No one goes to school to learn happiness; it seems crazy. If you talk to people and say you went to school to learn happiness, they will give you a blank look; I got it many times. In 2016, when I was studying the science of happiness at UC Berkeley, I had to explain what it was to some people, and they were quite surprised.

You may well be feeling the same as they did. Most people do. You might ask, "Is there such a thing?" Yes, there is. Happiness is slowly becoming one of those subjects we can learn from science and research in top universities around the world.

My mother didn't go to school to study happiness. She and my other families and friends are not experts in this area. Yet I still get advice from them. Our families and friends do not intend to mislead us. Most of them genuinely believe that their advice will make us happy. And sometimes they are correct. I love my family and friends, but as I'm aware of the science of happiness, I would rather turn to the research and findings of the scientists who are the experts and learn from them.

Over the next decade or so, the science of happiness will get much more attention, and we will learn more and more about it and use it in our daily lives. But our perception of happiness, which we have built over hundreds of years, will prevail for some time until most people truly realize the power of the science of happiness.

Today, almost everything we do, see, or experience results from someone's imagination, innovation, and research.

It all comes down to just one word - "science."

When we go to space, go inside a submarine, take medication, undergo surgery, drive a car, or do other various things in our modern-day lives, we do not worry; we feel safe, and we trust.

For our happiness, trusting in science is also the safest option.

OUR AWARENESS OF THE SCIENCE OF HAPPINESS

I walked into Jerry's office for a business meeting and saw a man talking to him. He was probably in his seventies, wearing a nice suit. They looked at me and paused. We greeted one another and Jerry introduced me to this man; he also mentioned that I was writing a book on happiness. The man turned and looked at me for a few seconds, then said, "That's nice. Let me guess, is your book based on the life of Gandhi or Muhammad?" I was not expecting that question. I stopped for a bit, looking for an answer that would make sense in that situation. I then smiled and asked him, "Do you think the book of happiness will be about someone?" He shrugged and said, "Well, I think happiness is something that can be learned by studying someone's life." In my head I was thinking, that's certainly one way of looking at it, but in that case, we would only know one person's view of happiness. And that would not necessarily work for other people. He stood up and was about to leave, but he seemed curious. I thought, I had just met this person and didn't want to strike up a long conversation on this topic, especially as he was about to leave. So I didn't say anything I smiled and just nodded. But he asked again, "Is it based on anyone's life?" I smiled again and said, "No, it is inspired by science." He looked at me in disbelief and asked, "Is there a science behind happiness?" I said, "Fifty years ago, there wasn't, but now there is."

Another day, I went to a friend's place on a Friday night. I took a chair and sat down. Next to me, there was a girl wearing a red jacket. She smiled and asked me, "Are you the guy who runs the happiness sessions?" I thought, "Am I being talked about? Or am I missing something?" But in the previous year, I ran some happiness sessions, and some attendees were at that party. I assumed they must have talked about it. So, I said, "Yes, I ran some sessions last year, but how did you know it was me?" She said, "Bec talked about you and the science of happiness. Is there such a thing?"

I wasn't surprised that the man at Jerry's office or the girl at the party had no idea about the science of happiness.

Most of us are not aware of it yet.

THE POSITIVE PSYCHOLOGY MOVEMENT

There was a time when there were not enough scientists and there was a lack of research on happiness. Between 1967 and 2000, most of the studies done under traditional psychology focused on repairing mental issues associated with negative emotions, such as anxiety, depression, anger, and grief. But there was not much work being done on positive emotions, such as joy, happiness, and gratitude.

It wasn't until around the year 2000 that psychologists started to focus on the big picture. They asked questions like, "Why are we only fixing human mental issues?" They found that previous research on negative emotions was much more robust than research on positive emotions. For example, the number of studies on negative emotion (i.e., depression) was 54,040, whereas only 2,582 studies on positive emotion (i.e., happiness) had been published. The lopsided ratio was about 21 to 1.

Professor Martin Seligman from the University of Pennsylvania was the president of the American Psychological Association. He, with Professor Mihaly Csikszentmihalyi, published a paper proposing a new dimension of psychology in 2000 as positive psychology. Positive psychology is essentially about studies that focus on human potential by nurturing our positive emotions. The science of happiness came up under the umbrella of this new dimension called positive psychology.

In short, traditional psychology concentrates on resolving mental issues. It is essential, but positive psychology focuses on how a person can flourish. It tackles the questions like "What makes a good life?" "What elements must be present in life for complete satisfaction?" "What is happiness?" and "What makes people happy, and how can they stay happy and satisfied over their lifetimes?"

Over the last twenty years, positive psychology has revealed many previously unknown facts about happiness and satisfaction, and has also become a global movement. I'm excited to share some of the facts relating to happiness with you throughout my book.

YOUR HAPPINESS CAN BE MEASURED

I know it may surprise you, but happiness can be measured.

But, how can you measure a feeling?

I was in Kuala Lumpur and caught up with Tahir, one of Malaysia's top peak-performance coaches. Obviously, we talked about happiness, and he said, "It would be awesome if we could measure happiness." I smiled and said, "It surely can be measured. Scientists have measured happiness for years for their research." He was pleasantly surprised. Not many people know that there is an actual science of happiness, and there is no science without measurement.

Your and my happiness can be measured today and observed over time, just like when you go to a doctor and have your blood pressure checked. The blood pressure in our bodies goes up and down all the time, but it generally falls into a certain range. Happiness is kind of the same. When you measure yours over time, you may fall into a range.

But how exactly do scientists measure happiness?

Happiness happens in your brain, so, obviously, looking at brain scans makes sense in the study of happiness. Technologies like fMRI can help. I learned that when there is more blood flow on one side of the brain than the other, that indicates that you're feeling good. When we feel happy, it doesn't just happen inside our brains but affects our facial muscles; it can increase our heart rates, give us goosebumps, and cause other such reactions. Scientists use all kinds of methods and technologies to measure how we feel before, during, or after an event.

But all those methods require a lab environment, which is not always a feasible option. That's why scientists have also developed a specific questionnaire for people to measure happiness. Using this, they can accurately determine your current happiness level.

But how accurate is this questionnaire method?

Scientists have compared the brain scanning methods in the lab environment with the questionnaire method and found that the accuracy is almost the same. Professor Daniel Gilbert from Harvard University says, "I can do all sorts of things, but you know what, it turns out saying to people on a scale of 1-10 about how do you feel right now is just as good as those other methods."

This questionnaire to measure happiness is very similar to tests that measure your IQ, depression level, strength, and many other things. The Oxford Happiness Questionnaire was developed by Michael Argyle and Peter Hills from Oxford Brookes University. It was initially published in 2002 in the Journal of Personality and Individual Differences. It is one of the most widely used methods to measure happiness. Happiness is very individualistic, and it is also called "subjective well-being."

When implementing new interventions and methods to be and stay happy, we want to know whether they are actually working. We can track our progress and adjust the methods being used if needed. Clarity and visibility give us the perspective of what we need to do and what we need to avoid. Whether the focus is our blood pressure, driving a car, or happiness, measuring allows us to get insights and adjust our actions.

And the science of happiness gives us the ability to do that.

YOUR GENETIC HAPPINESS

Scientists have been studying happiness for a long time (technically since the 1930s—can you believe it!). It is the work of many of them from top universities worldwide. Some of the most prominent happiness research in recent times was done by Professor Sonja Lyubomirsky from the University of California–Riverside and her team. They wanted to find out what influences our happiness and why some people are happier than others. They found that about 50 per cent of the answers lie in genetics. That means about 50 per cent of our happiness is determined before birth. Even though it may seem as if 50 per cent of our happiness is already gone, but that genetic part is not all zero. It has both genetic happiness and unhappiness components in it. Some people are generally very happy, and some not so much. Whether you are white, black, or brown, your physical build, look, voice, hair color, and almost every other characteristic you have has a genetic component. We have some level of predisposition in nearly everything. Some things, such as your birth nationality, parents, and siblings, were preset before you were born.

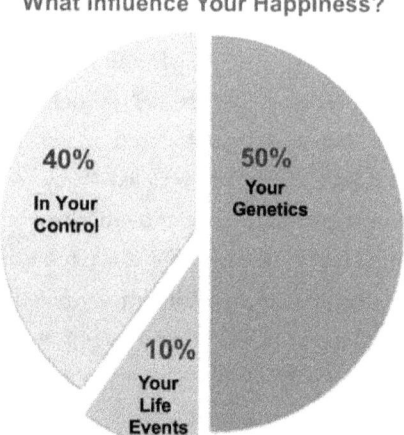

YOUR HAPPINESS FROM LIFE EVENTS

So what about the rest? Well, things like having a high-paying job or earning average, having tremendous success or failure, and living in a mansion or a typical house are important to most of us. And they are our general life situations. And the positive and negative life events we face (such as getting promoted or fired) impact only about 10 percent of our happiness.

I know, seriously! I couldn't believe it either. Most people would think this number would be much higher. After studying Sonja's research and putting thought into it, I realized that the 10 per cent influence of life situations and events on our happiness is not too bad. Honestly, when it comes to happiness, someone rich, good-looking, married, or with high social status should not have an advantage over others without those characteristics. In the next section, you will find out why this 10 per cent influence of life events may be a good thing.

YOUR RETURN TO GENETIC SET POINT

According to Professor Lyubomirsky's research, every one of us has a genetic set point. That accounts for 50 per cent of our happiness, which is the "Default range" we always come back to after a positive or negative event. For example, suppose your happiness genetic set point is 2 out of 6. Today you get promoted at work, and you feel very happy. If you measure your happiness today, you may score 5 out of 6. You may enjoy that for a bit, but you will adapt to your new lifestyle over time, and your happiness will return to your genetic set point of 2. The return to the set point happens because of a phenomenon called "hedonic adaptation." We adapt to our new ways of living much quicker than we usually think.

For staying happy, this phenomenon is not very helpful. In fact, this enemy does not allow us to stay happy for a long time from one event.

The reason why this hedonic adaptation can be a good thing relates to negative events. For instance, if you lost your job today and your happiness is measured, you may score 1 out of 6. You will be unhappy, and the shock will remain with you for some time. But over time, your happiness will also bounce back to 2 (or very close) because you will adapt to your new lifestyle. As human beings, we are very resilient to negative events, and we have a remarkable ability to bounce back. Scientists call this our "psychological immune system," and our hedonic adaptation fuels it. Whether an event that we experience in our lives is a positive or negative event, we will fall back to our genetic set points.

In her book The How of Happiness, Professor Sonja Lyubomirsky states, "Each of us is born with a particular happiness setpoint that originates from our biological mother or father or both. A baseline or potential for happiness to which we are bound to return, even after major setbacks or triumphs."

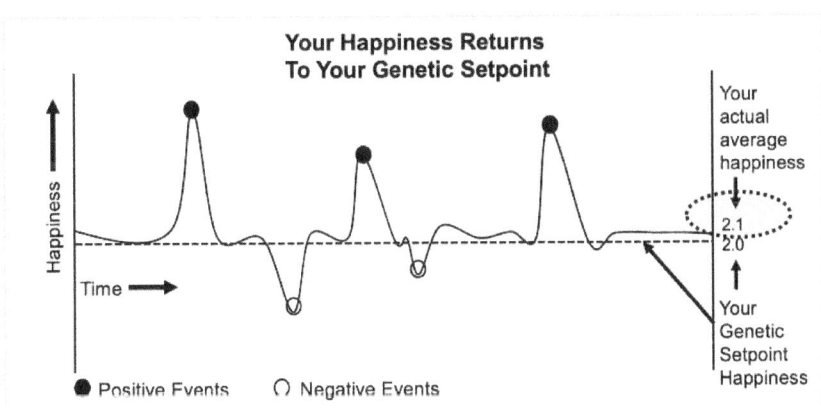

You might think, "What's the point of trying for the good things in life when your happiness is not likely to last for a long time?"

Well, getting a promotion, buying a new house or car, having your dream wedding, being a parent, and other similar events are significant milestones for most of us. We expect to become happy and stay that way from that single event for a long time. But no matter how excited we are or how hard we work for these events, deep down, you and I both know that the spike of happiness we get from these events doesn't last forever. We eventually adapt and get on to our new normal lives.

Professor Lyubomirsky's research is just a testament to this fact. These milestone events make us happy, but not for a long time.

So the question is, How can we achieve long-term happiness?

In her research, Professor Lyubomirsky and her team concluded that the remaining 40 per cent of our happiness is what we can totally control by our own "behavior and acts." We will be capitalizing on this 40 per cent to achieve long-term happiness.

You may wonder, "What does that really mean?"

USING THE 40 PER CENT HAPPINESS IN YOUR CONTROL

Genetic factors play a vital role in our physical build, how we look, our skin color, our hair, our voices, and many other things. Some people are naturally skinnier than others. There is not much we can do about it.

For example, I am naturally skinny, which means I maintain a healthy weight of seventy kilos; I don't necessarily need to watch my diet or exercise every day. My genetics already play a big role in that. But my friend Jack is genetically chubby. To maintain a healthy weight of seventy kilos, he needs to be careful what he eats and burns.

But we can indeed maintain our healthy weight with our lifestyles and habits, which are in our control. If we choose to eat healthy foods rather than eating junk, and do exercise rather than sitting on the couch, then we certainly can maintain a healthy weight. For Jack, the effort is higher than mine because of our different genetic differences.

For happiness, hypothetically, if Jack has a genetic happiness set point of 3 (out of 6) and I have a genetic set point of 2 (out of 6), Jack has a genetic advantage over me for happiness, and he is genetically happier than I am. Now, if we both target and want to stay happy at the range of 3.6 (out of 6), Jack has to come up only 0.6 to hit the goal of 3.6 (genetic 3.0 + 0.6 his behavior). But I have to put in more effort and come up by 1.6 (genetic 2.0 + my behavior 1.6) in addition to my genetic set point. So my effort to stay happy at 3.6 (out of 6) has to be more than Jack's to hit the same happiness target range of 3.6.

How can we do that? By using our 40 per cent happiness in our control. That means using our own behavior and acts in our lifestyles. To maintain our healthy weight, we can eat healthy foods and exercise more. But to maintain our good happiness levels (e.g., 3.6), we can do the things that make us happy in our lifestyles—for example, regularly working on our passion projects, spending time with family, playing piano, or going for a run. Notice these are not big things (e.g., getting a promotion, getting married). They are small things as part of our everyday lifestyles. They give us small happy moments but are much easier to attain and more reliable. If you do these regularly, your happiness over a period of time may look like this and can stay at 3.6 (or whatever you prefer).

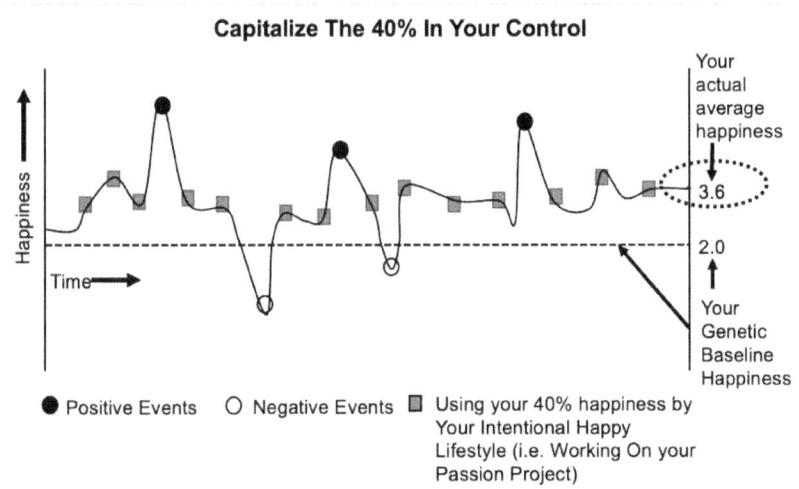

Remember, this happy lifestyle (e.g., creating small happy moments by doing what you love and being with people you love) is "intentional." You will need to make sure that you do them regularly (precisely like you eat healthy foods and exercise to maintain your healthy weight). You may also notice in the above graph that because of your intentional happy lifestyle, your actual average happiness over a period of time is higher (3.6) than your genetic baseline (2.0).

And that's how you will stay happy every day.

The positive events (e.g., birthdays, promotions, buying of new houses) and negative events (loss of someone, getting fired, illness) will happen in their due course. They will give you a spike of happiness or unhappiness for the short term, and they account for only 10 per cent of your happiness. But your daily lifestyle (behavior and acts) will contribute to your 40 per cent happiness.

Yes, you might already be doing such regular activities without knowing it. For example, being kind to others or being grateful can make you happy. Some people are naturally kind and appreciative and may already be cultivating some of that 40 per cent. The good news is, with awareness, they can absolutely become happier. I will talk about them in the next chapter.

Your short-term spikes of happiness and unhappiness come from the positive and negative events you experience (10 per cent). But your long-term happiness essentially has two parts: your genetic disposition (50 per cent) and your lifestyle (40 per cent).

The genetic happiness or unhappiness part is fixed. But for most people, the 40 per cent happy lifestyle part is a chance for grab.

REFLECTION

What three things surprised you about the science of happiness?
Which one have you found most interesting, and why?

THE SATISFYING LIFE AND THE HAPPY LIFE

"In the end, it's not the years in your life that count. It's the life in your years."
—Abraham Lincoln

ONE DAY IN SAN FRANCISCO

At 8:00 a.m., we landed at San Francisco International Airport for a quick day trip. We had another flight to catch at 4:30 p.m., to Las Vegas. As you can imagine, there were so many things to see, and we had only seven hours, so we had to narrow it down to three major attractions. I am a very loyal supporter of Apple computers and wanted to see the Apple Garage in Los Altos, where Steve Jobs started Apple in his parents' garage.

My wife wanted to see the Golden Gate Bridge. We have seen this bridge in movies many times, so we definitely wanted to visit that. We also found a very nice seafood place near Fisherman's Wharf through Trip Advisor reviews, and we wanted to have lunch there on our way back to the airport.

After we landed, we picked up the car from the airport and started driving to the Apple Garage in Los Altos. They drive on the right-hand side of the road in the US, opposite what we do in Australia. For me, that was the first time driving in that condition, and the first ten minutes felt very strange, but I adapted later. But as it was a weekday, there was a lot of traffic on the way. I started to worry about the time, as the Golden Gate Bridge was an hour's drive in the opposite direction. But at the same time, I was excited to see the Apple Garage first.

When we arrived at the Apple Garage, we found it was literally a normal house in a suburb, and people live there now. In fact, while we were there, someone came out of the house and put the rubbish bin out. We parked the car and took selfies, which felt really good. We saw some other people come up and take photos too. We felt that the neighbors were familiar with this paradigm. I tried to imagine the early days of Apple in this house.

We also went to nearby areas, including Apple Park and the Google Garage (where Google started). We bought some souvenirs and then started driving to the Golden Gate Bridge.

Half an hour later, we got stuck in traffic and realized we were falling behind our schedule. But the drive was lovely, and many people were on the streets. We could see the blue water lines through the buildings. Our only worry was getting back to the airport on time. After going through really slow traffic, we finally reached and drove across the Golden Gate Bridge and stopped at an excellent vantage point. The area and the view were fantastic. We took some more photos. We were running about an hour late and realized we might not make it to the seafood place for lunch, so we decided to head back to the airport directly.

On our way back, we stopped at a gas station. I wanted to fill up the car tank before returning the car, but there was no such option on the machine. There were only fixed amounts ($10, $20, and so forth). So I spoke to the guy at the counter, and he said that I had to deposit $100 from my card and fill up the tank, and then they would refund the remaining amount to my card within seven days. That was a very strange and inconvenient way to fill up. As we were already behind time, I was literally counting every minute, and I decided not to argue with him. Even though I took only $30 worth of gas, I paid a $100 deposit. But it didn't make any sense, and it made me very annoyed with their system. The guy at the counter was not helpful either. Anyway, we drove back to the airport, returned the car, and were able to catch our next flight at 4:30 p.m.

WAS I SATISFIED WITH MY DAY IN SAN FRANCISCO?

I had three main expectations in San Francisco: to visit the Apple Garage, to see the Golden Gate Bridge, and to dine at the seafood place. The first two items we did, and we enjoyed the experiences, but we couldn't go to the seafood place, as we ran out of time. But later we thought that we at least enjoyed the two primary expectations thoroughly. The seafood experience was something that we'd had many times before, just not in the Bay Area, and that's fine. So overall, yes, I was satisfied.

WAS IT A HAPPY DAY FOR ME?

I suppose there were some moments during the day when I felt really good and excited, and I enjoyed them. When we entered Los Altos and went to the Apple Garage, I felt excited. When I took the selfies, I felt thrilled. Later, we went to Google Garage and Apple Park, bought souvenirs, and drove across the Golden Gate Bridge. Those moments felt amazing, and I loved every bit of them.

But there were other moments when I felt worried, frustrated, and annoyed. When we realized that we would not be able to go to the seafood place because of time, I thought I didn't plan it well. I felt frustrated at being stuck in traffic and worried about making it to the airport on time. Also, the guy at the gas station made me very annoyed. In those moments, I wasn't very happy.

But when I look back on that day and ponder, I think there were more happy moments than unhappy moments, and I wouldn't mind calling it a "happy day."

A SATISFYING DAY VS. A HAPPY DAY

We use the words "happy" and "satisfied" interchangeably all the time. If I were to ask you the difference between the two, you would have a subjective answer different from others. We all have our own interpretations of events and meanings, and we name the feelings we feel differently.

Over the years, I have realized that even though the words "satisfied" and "happy" both represent positive feelings, they are not the same.

We think we want to be happy in life, but often we want to be satisfied; these are two different things. Let me unfold this a bit more.

You may feel satisfied when your expectations are met. When we landed in San Francisco, we had three major attractions to visit; that we would visit all of them was our expectation for the day. At the end of the day, at 4:00 p.m., we had two of the significant attractions ticked off but couldn't do the other one. But a few years later, when I look at that day today, I only see the things that really mattered to us. Those two ticked off expectations stand out. And I feel satisfied.

Satisfaction is more like an outcome or a destination that you reach (e.g., my visiting the Apple Garage, which is now on my "done" list; becoming a doctor, climbing a mountain, seeing your children graduate from school, or winning an Olympic medal—things that you have successfully achieved or completed). These things are outcomes from your initial expectations. Generally, as you look back in the past for the things that went well for you, you may not feel very excited about them today. However, the feelings you have from them are good feelings that are permanent. You may still feel a sense of satisfaction from them today.

But happiness or unhappiness is more like the feelings we feel in the moment. When I took the photo at the Golden Gate Bridge, visited Google Garage, or drove to Los Altos, I felt really good and was very excited. But those moments of good feelings or joy were short-lived and didn't last long. Also, when I was stuck in traffic, I felt frustrated, worried about the time, and annoyed with the guy at the gas station. Those bad feelings were also gone after those moments. Yes, some good or bad memories (such as our defining moments) remain much longer than a few minutes, but generally those happy or unhappy feelings come and go with the moments. They are like clouds. One moment, you feel happy, but in the next, not so much. Unlike satisfaction, happy or unhappy moments can be impacted easily. For example, I felt very happy at the Golden Gate Bridge, but ten minutes later, I felt very annoyed with the guy at the gas station.

My expectations, happy and unhappy moments, and satisfaction throughout that day in San Francisco may look like this.

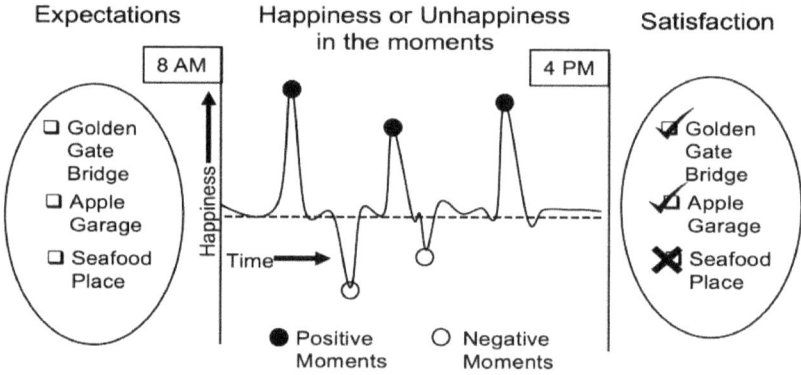

You may have an important presentation at work in the afternoon. You may have worked so hard for it that you didn't eat lunch or take a break. You were anxious and worried all day, but your presentation went well. The moments during the day didn't make you feel very happy. Instead, the moments made you feel anxious and worried all day. However, you may still feel satisfied before going to bed if your presentation went well, according to your expectations.

On the other hand, you may have had a very happy and exciting day. Perhaps you went to lunch and then had coffee with your colleagues and had a great time working on your presentation, and your moments during the day made you feel good. But maybe when you gave your presentation, someone important didn't like it much, which made you feel upset. Even though you had some happy moments during the day, you still may not feel very satisfied because your presentation didn't meet your expectations.

The Nobel Prize–winning psychologist Daniel Kahneman nicely summarized this: "Altogether, I don't think that people maximize happiness in that sense. This doesn't seem to be what people want to do. They actually want to maximize their satisfaction with themselves and with their lives. And that leads in completely different directions than the maximization of happiness."

A few years later, as I'm writing this section, I feel that my happy and unhappy moments that day in San Francisco are gone. But after visiting the Apple Garage and the Golden Gate Bridge, I felt a sense of satisfaction that still makes me feel good.

When you achieve or complete something, your excitement will not last long. However, your sense of satisfaction with something you deeply care about is more permanent and may remain for a lifetime. For example, you may feel good about winning an Olympic medal as long as you live. But your feelings of happiness or unhappiness occur in the moment and will likely perish when the moment disappears.

A SATISFYING LIFE

That day in San Francisco was a satisfying day for me, as my primary expectations were met.

But what about a satisfying life?

I have been talking about living the default life of others. Honestly, in living that life, other people's expectations become our own. Most people believe that good education, a high-paying job, a dream house and car, marriage, children, social status, and the like make for a happy and satisfied life. But that is based on our assumptions and not on science. I previously mentioned people having regrets in old age about having only chased these things. I wanted to find out what science tells us about living a satisfying life. The findings of the science may surprise you.

After studying thousands of people over many years, scientists have narrowed the elements needed to live a fully satisfying life down to six. I have presented those six elements of satisfaction using a star that I have termed the Star of Life. It was inspired by the concept of the PERMA Model introduced by Professor Martin Seligman in 2012. He is often considered the father of positive psychology. PERMA stands for pleasure, engagement, relationships, meaning, and achievements. All of these elements are internally motivating, and they contribute to subjective well-being. The scientists examined many interventions that helped them understand a life worth living. They understood how to define, quantify, and create a sense of well-being. Later, when I studied positive psychology at Harvard, I came across a slightly modified version of PERMA. That was PERMA+H, and the H stands for "health."

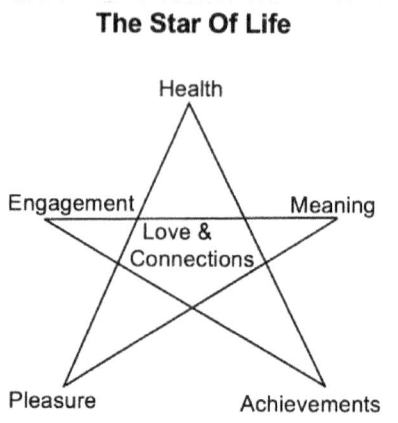

The Six Elements Of A Satisfying Life

So what do these elements mean?

You can look at your life today or when you are ninety years old. Engagement refers to doing the things that engage you and that you love so much that you lose track of time (e.g., talking, painting, running). Next is love and connections, which refers to building deep and loving connections with the people around you, and trusting and counting on them (e.g., having three very close friends). Meaning is super important. It relates to doing something every day that is meaningful for you or having something you believe in your core (e.g., that your work makes other people's lives better). Achievement pertains to achieving the things that matter to you (e.g., building a school, running a marathon). Pleasure relates to enjoyment in living your life (e.g., watching a film, going on a holiday). And finally, health (e.g., eating healthy foods and exercising) allows you to do everything else. I dig deep into each one of these elements in part 3.

Having these elements in your life will not necessarily make you high and happy all the time. But if you have met your expectations on each of, or most of, the elements, you will feel a sense of satisfaction when you look at your life today or when you are ninety.

One of the authors of the World Happiness Report, John F. Helliwell, stated, "Happy people wouldn't have the highest smile factor, they do trust each other and care about each other, and that's what fundamentally makes for a better life."

Remember Jason? At the age of eighty-eight, he realized that even though he became one of the wealthiest in his town, he regretted ignoring his family and children. He was living by himself alone in his big, elegant house. He achieved a lot in his life, but at least one important element was missing, and that was his love and connections. For others, it could be meaning, achievements, health, or anything else.

Metaphorically, if you are cooking a dish and don't know the proper recipe, your dish might taste strange. It can feel as if something is missing. Who can give you a better recipe for life satisfaction than science? The Star of Life is like a recipe for life. If all the six recipe elements are not present and balanced, you may feel that you are missing something in your life. Many feel unfulfillment, midlife crisis, boredom, regrets, and such. You might say that one cannot expect a perfect life—that such a thing never happens. I agree.

But after knowing about these six elements in the Star of Life, I believe that many things are not in our control, but many are. Old age is not promised to anyone. While that is true, we have a good chance to craft our lives based on this framework from science, so we can have the best shot at living our lives to our satisfaction.

Regrets happen when our expectations are not met—especially when we didn't do the things we truly wanted to do. Science gives us the recipe for life satisfaction through the lenses of many who have already lived till old age. And this recipe has been reverse engineered to these six elements. The people who genuinely want to can reset their expectations and priorities in life. Doing so requires you to redesign your life and live on your terms.

Personally, I have aligned and continue to align my life expectations to the six elements of satisfaction using the Star of Life framework.

Remember, it's not about how high or low your expectations are; what matters is whether they are your own.

A HAPPY LIFE

That day I spent in San Francisco was a happy day for me. This means that I had more happy moments than unhappy moments during the day.

So what about a happy life?

A happy life is nothing but a collection of your happy days. Feeling happiness happens in your everyday moments. Many studies show that we adapt to good feelings very quickly because of the phenomenon of hedonic adaptation which you already know. Most of our happy feelings are very short-lived and don't last. The same applies to our unhappy feelings, and we adapt to both.

As human beings, most of us look forward to special events, such as wedding days, the birth of a child, and promotions. And many of us experience frustration, trauma, or unhappiness from the same marriages, children, or jobs later. But, yes, those special days do make us happy, and we may strongly remember them, but you and I also know that those spikes of happiness don't last long.

Remember, we control 40 per cent of our happiness through our lifestyles and behavior. That means we can intentionally create small but happy moments in our ordinary days. That's how we make our happiness last. Creating happy moments every day is a skill. You can absolutely build and live a happy life.

BUT, PROTECT YOUR HAPPY MOMENTS

My run-in with the unhelpful guy at the gas station in San Francisco occurred ten minutes after I had a few happy moments on the Golden Gate Bridge. And the time when I was stuck in traffic and was feeling very frustrated came thirty minutes after I had a great time in Apple Park.

See, our happy moments are very susceptible. Our thoughts can easily impact them (as in my case of being worried about getting back to the airport on time). We interact with people, and they usually have a high influence on our moments (such as the guy at the gas station). Finally, the things we have no control over (my frustration at being stuck in traffic) also impact our moods. We constantly get bombarded with things, whether inside our brains or from outside. And our happy moments are not always guarded. Our ability to protect our emotional states is often referred to as emotional intelligence. Defending our own happy moments is just as important. Personally, I believe this is one of the best skills to build.

THE LIFE OF HARMONY

If you focus only on creating happy moments every day, you might risk missing one or more of those six elements for satisfaction. Also, if you focus only on achievements, you might lose your health, love and connections, or meaning. You must have harmony in all six elements.

Yes, it is possible, as long as the expectations are your own.

When we put life expectations, happiness, unhappiness, and satisfaction all together for the rest of our lives, they might look like this:

THE SATISFYING LIFE AND THE HAPPY LIFE

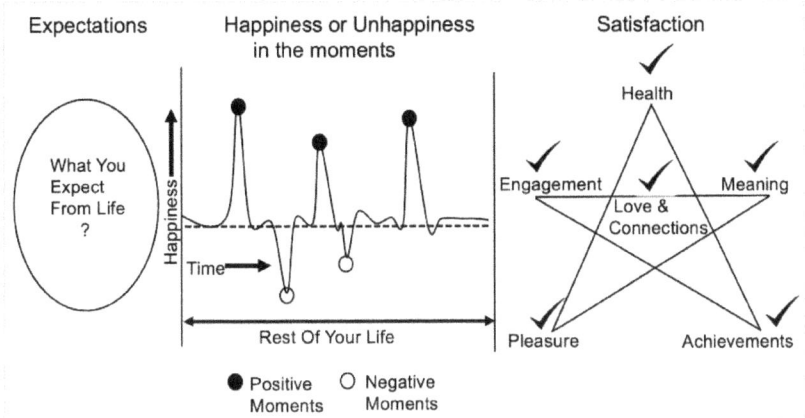

Whatever you expect from life, make sure it aligns with the six elements of the Star of Life. At the end of the day, those six elements are the ones that matter so that, either today or when you are ninety, you can look back at your life and say, "I have a great life."

A happy and satisfying life is about creating more happy moments every day and guarding them, as well as ensuring your life expectations are met in harmony with the six elements of the Star of Life.

MY SINCERE HOPE

What if you could live a life with far fewer assumptions? What if you could live a life more on your terms? The six elements in the Star of Life give us the framework based on science to live a satisfying life.

And what if you could create more happy moments in your ordinary days to live a happy life? Also, what if you could guard your happy moments?

Over the last seven years, I have redesigned my life using the framework of the Star of Life. With the tools and methods of science, I have built the skills (and continue to build) to create more happy moments every day, and I have become more aware of guarding them.

And I can honestly say I have never been more satisfied or happy.

I sincerely hope you do the same or better and live an extraordinary life on your terms—not by chance, but by science.

And throughout my book, you will enjoy and discover how.

REFLECTION

It is your life.

The harmony you want must be on your terms.

And that means you must keep the "key to the kingdom" to yourself at all times (or at least most of the time).

To live a life of harmony, whatever you do, ask yourself the following questions:

- Do you live a satisfying life?
- Do you live a happy life?
- Do you guard your happy moments?
- And make sure you say yes, yes, and yes.

THREE THINGS TO REMEMBER

"Happiness is when what you think, what you say, and what you do are in harmony."
—Mahatma Gandhi

In my journey of discovering, understanding, and mastering the skills of happiness and satisfaction, I have arrived at a profound realization. I believe everything I discussed throughout the book (including the science tools and strategies) comes mainly from three things: your heart, your time, and your decisions.

YOUR HEART

Years ago, I went to a theme park with some friends. They said, "Let's go to the next roller coaster ride." I said nothing and didn't move. Someone said, "Hurry up." I said, "Nope, I shall pass," but they insisted. So I said yes, but I really wanted to say no. I was scared of the ride. When I got off, I felt that was one of the worst five minutes of my life. The whole time I was on the ride, I had my eyes closed and tried to hold my breath.

Yes, I was, and still am, scared of roller coaster rides. But my friends loved them. People love bungee jumping, underwater adventures, sky diving, and all sorts of things. I recently watched a documentary on Netflix about a French high-wire artist, Philippe Petit, who loved walking on high wires. He had very high ambitions. And after eight months of preparation, on the seventh of August in 1974, he walked on a wire between the former Twin Towers in New York (417m above the ground). With a balancing pole, he performed on the wire for forty-five minutes to the New Yorkers below. Was this crazy and dangerous? Absolutely. But he loved it.

These things might be weird and dangerous to you and me, but for others it is total bliss.

Recently, my wife, Mahin, and I went to the Apple Store to upgrade her iMac. Apple had just launched the new iMac series. The saleslady explained all the latest and cool features of the new iMac, but Mahin didn't seem very convinced. I asked, "What do you think?" She said, "Good features, but I don't like the shape of the new ones. I like the older ones better."

You see, our emotional minds play a very powerful role in everyday decision-making. I'm sure you have seen people trying to lose weight eat junk food instead of salads or seen someone who really cannot afford an expensive car buy one anyway. There are countless examples of decisions that are not so logical.

Our logic is dictated by our feelings, such as "I like," "I love," "I enjoy," "I hate," "I am afraid," and so on. They come from our limbic brain and often refer to our hearts, but our logic comes from our analytical brain.

The brain says, "Eat salad"; the heart says, "Nah, I don't like it." Or the brain says, "Don't buy that expensive car," but the heart says, "I love this so much. I will handle it." It happens all the time. According to a Harvard study, 95 per cent of purchasing decisions are emotional. When our hearts and brains are in a battle to win, we feel confused.

But often, our hearts trump our brains.

You may not love someone because she is highly educated or has an excellent track record. Instead, you may love this person because of how she makes you feel. Being happy and satisfied is also about what you love, care about, or enjoy. And those feelings come from your heart and not from your brain.

THE CLOSEST THING ON EARTH

Your heart pumps more than one hundred thousand times a day without you even asking for it. It makes sure that all your organs get the necessary blood supply, it regulates thousands of other things inside your body, but most importantly, it keeps you alive.

You didn't have to earn it. You have been blessed with it. We all have. But your heart longs for something. Your heart sings a unique song. No one can hear it singing. It is only you who can feel what it feels, and it is only you who can hear its longing.

A physical heart has about forty thousand neurons, and some experts believe that the heart's power over our emotions is not just poetic but also biological.

In the journeys that our hearts take throughout our lifetimes, our hearts always sing. Whether or not we listen to the songs is up to us. The unique song of your heart is what you like, love, care about, and enjoy that often relates to living your purpose, passion, or dreams. The adventures that my friends loved came from the songs of their hearts.

What your heart longs for is not necessarily the same as the longings of your loved ones. Their hearts sing their unique songs.

Whether you feel it or not, the closest thing you have on earth is your heart.

BUT WE IGNORE THAT SONG

Even though our hearts have so much power over our emotions, it's not easy to just listen to our hearts. We are bound to be influenced by the people we spend time with. We often feel stuck in our responsibilities. Honestly, often we live our whole lives ignoring our hearts.

When I was six years old, I built a helicopter with Lego bricks. I loved it so much that I put all my other toys away and started creating different things. I used to spend hours building. I forgot to eat. I did not talk to anyone. I also forgot to do my school homework. My imagination was at a peak. Everybody was annoyed with me, I didn't care what other people thought, and I had a great time. I followed the song of my heart.

Then, over time, I started to get told that I was supposed to do homework first and then play with my Lego bricks. I could not play with them all day. I started to grow up, and I learned to ignore my heart.

I was talking to the twelve-year-old daughter of a friend, and I asked her, "What do you love doing?" I noticed she felt a little shy, and she started to look down as if she were hiding something. She said, "I don't know," and started scratching her nails. I insisted, "Come on, what is it?" She hesitantly said, "I love to paint, and I want to be a painter," and then she showed me some of her works. They were amazing. Then her face turned sad, and she said, "But I cannot do a lot of them. I have to study more than I can paint."

I asked the same question to a twenty-four-year-old, and she said, "I love dancing." I noticed that her eyes were sparkling with joy. Her face was glowing when she said that. I asked, "Do you dance regularly?" She sadly said, "Not really. Last time I danced was a few years ago, and these days, I do not have the environment or space at my home to do that."

I realized that, like me, those two have learned to ignore their hearts.

Most of us have similar stories about countless things we love, care about, and enjoy, but our hands are tied. We are guilty of not trying. We live in fear of embarrassment, anxiety about what other people will think if we fail, and many other valid reasons. Many of us have built worlds around us in which our circumstances basically imprison our hearts.

As I mentioned previously, the number-one regret of the dying is "I wish I'd had the courage to live the life true to myself, not what others expected of me." Most of our dreams, passions, and purposes can easily go untouched, unrealized, and unfulfilled because of the choices we make every day.

We may or may not feel regret until our time is up. I have already discussed regret, but I felt it is important to mention it again here, as almost all of them relate to ignoring your heart.

It's not just regrets in old age that matter but also our ability to feel good, have a sense of belonging and purpose, and enjoy and live our lives on our terms. All of these make us feel happy and satisfied every day.

Also, much research suggests that our emotional well-being impacts our physical hearts. For example, if you have severe physical or emotional stress, such as that resulting from an illness, the loss of a loved one, an accident, or a natural disaster, some of your heart cells can get shocked, and the shape of your heart can change over time. This is called broken heart syndrome, or Takotsubo cardiomyopathy. The bottom line is that the more you feel emotionally well, the better your physical heart will be, and then your whole body will function optimally.

In 2005 in a Stanford commencement speech, Steve Jobs said, "Almost everything, all external expectations, or pride, or fear of embarrassment or failure, these things just fall away in the face of death, leaving only what is truly important, remembering that you're going to die is the best way I know, to avoid the trap of thinking that you have something to lose. You are already naked. There is no reason not to follow your heart."

But, listening to your heart demands that you act on the things you love with courage and without guilt every day.

Living your life with courage does not mean having to climb mountains, but rather taking more small but courageous steps every day. This includes things like going for a ten-minute walk when you don't feel like it, giving a random hug to your partner without any reason, saying yes to a date after heartbreak, saying no to friends who don't appreciate you, or following up with a potential client who hasn't called you back.

Remember, courage comes by taking action.

Sometimes it can all feel overwhelming to listen to your heart, take some rest, start fresh, and never stop progressing. Every time you go against your heart and stay that way, you will likely feel unhappy and unsatisfied.

Your heart can absolutely trump your brain, but only if you allow it to do so.

My dad had a super busy and rewarding career, but he always wanted to work on his passion projects on electronics. He never had the courage to leave his job and follow his dream. All his life, he was busy making sure that we were okay. That's what dads and moms do. It wasn't until he was seventy-one that he started to play with his electronic circuit boards again. He spends hours on them, never gets tired of them, and is always excited about them. Age has not been able to stop him from what he truly loves doing. His small projects in his seventies might not change the world, but they make him happy every day.

My sister loves photography. At thirty-five, she quit her job and started to act on her passion. Phil is one of my close friends. He loves wealth building, and he started a wealth education program at age forty. Another friend of mine, Ashraf, loves arm wrestling, and he reignited his passion after twenty years of ignoring it. Since then, he has been ranked seventh in the whole of Australia. These are just a few of many I know and admire.

These people also have responsibilities, but they choose to listen to their hearts anyway and take small, courageous actions every day. Their ages and lack of money, time, or anything else haven't been able to stop them. They allow themselves to live on their terms with courage and without (or with minimal) guilt. They listen to their hearts more than their brains. They do more things that they "love to" than those they "have to."

When it is time for us to leave the planet, we look back and regret not standing up for ourselves when we could have or should have. We may regret breaking up with our true love or letting our marriage fall apart. We may regret worrying and following other people's opinions. We may regret not going on a dream holiday. We may regret not applying for a dream job. We may regret not spending enough time with our loved ones and telling them how much we love them. We may have wanted to do these things, but we couldn't.

We need to free our hearts and truly listen to them.

Even if you have ignored your heart in the past, you can always restart, reset, or reignite what you are passionate about. Yes, people around you might tell you to be realistic, but remember, they will not miss out and regret what you love in your old age.

You will.

So ask yourself what makes you come alive? Whether it is something you enjoy doing or love and care about, or something that you always wanted to do but have never done, do it today, tomorrow, and every day.

I personally believe I have a great life. When I look back in time, I recall that years ago I loved computer coding, photography, and writing. Over time, things have changed. Some things I don't like anymore, and some new things I started to love. But I realized I had ignored my heart for many years, and I hadn't been true to myself.

Today, I had a long day. I have a busy day tomorrow. It is 1:17 a.m. as I'm writing this section of my book. I'm not tired. I'm not stressed. I'm not worried about anything else, I have intense concentration, I'm excited, and I have no plans to slow down anytime soon. This is making me happy.

Why?

Because I have started to listen to my heart, again.

YOUR TIME

I grew up in Dhaka. I remember that when I was about twenty years old at work, I was talking to one of my colleagues in the morning, and I received a call on my mobile.

"Hello? Sanju [that's what my family and friends call me]? Where are you?" The voice on the other side was one of my cousins. I said, "I'm at work. What's up?"

There was silence on the other end. I said, "Are you there? Hello."

He said, "Are you able to come directly to Uncle Rose's house?"

Uncle Rose was my mother's younger brother. He was one of those people who loved to be in the service of others and not brag about it. He had two beautiful children and a lovely wife and lived in a small town called Savar, about an hour's drive from Dhaka. As a medical doctor, he loved his work and the people in his community. He used to respond to medical calls in the middle of the night. He spent hours serving the poor for free. He had a mission. The people in Savar loved him.

On the phone, I asked, "Now? Why? What happened?"

My cousin said, "Uncle Rose has been involved in a road accident."

I was like, "Really? Is he okay?"

Silence again.

I didn't ask anything else. I said, "I'm on my way."

I got on the bus and sat at a window seat, looking outside throughout the journey. I was looking but not really looking. I kept playing the memories of my uncle in my head. That was one of those moments when you know something is terribly wrong but are still hoping for the best. We all loved Uncle Rose, and I didn't have the guts to ask my cousin the hard questions. I was just praying that he would be alive.

When I reached his home, I saw everybody looking quiet and sad. No one was talking. Most of them were my wider family members. After a little while, somebody spoke to me. "In the morning, Uncle Rose left for work as usual with his bike. On the way, he was going to drop his son at school. When he was on the main road, he saw an old lady crossing the road, but she was unaware of her surroundings. Uncle Rose stopped his bike to save that old lady, but his bike got hit by a truck from the other side. His son was sitting behind him. He pushed his son off the bike and saved him, but he couldn't save himself."

In a fraction of a second, our beloved Uncle Rose was no more. The lives of his two beautiful children and wife had changed forever.

A few years ago, a friend shared a philosophy of life. He said, "Imagine you are living in a room lit by a candle behind you. You can see the light, but you cannot see the candle itself. You enjoy the light, and you know that one day the candle will be fully burnt out and stop. But you do not know how much of the burning is left. You keep thinking the candle has enough for many more days." And one day, the candle suddenly stops. But you had no idea.

Our lives are like the candle, and we keep thinking that we have more time, but generally, no one knows how much time he or she has left. Uncle Rose was not ill, and he was living a great life with a definite purpose. He had a beautiful family, and he was making good money. Most people in his position would not think about dying, but Uncle Rose's candle was burnt out, which he probably had no idea about.

Remember, the closest thing on earth is your heart, but the most precious thing is your time.

When considering a job offer, one of the most important things for many of us is how much the pay is. When we go shopping, most people look at the price tag. Whether looking at the restaurant menu, a house, a car, or even booking a holiday, we want to know how much money we can save. We try our best to save money. But when it comes to our time, many of us act as if we have an unlimited amount of it.

Think about it. If you have $4,000 in your bank and decide not to spend any money, after ten days, your balance remains the same—$4000. But if you have 4,000 days left in your life, after ten days, the balance is 3990 days.

Spending money is your decision; spending time is not.

Most people want to save money on numerous things because we all want to maximize the use of our hard-earned money. But when it comes to spending our time, we do not necessarily want to maximize our time, primarily for two reasons. Firstly, we think we have unlimited time. Secondly, our time on this planet is not hard-earned.

In 2018, when my family and I visited Kuala Lumpur for the first time, we had only three days to explore the city. Except for the traffic, we enjoyed every bit of it. The people, the attractions, the food were amazing. I realized that I was very curious about the little things: the colors of the taxis, the shapes of the buildings, the smiles of the people, and the textures of their foods. When we returned to Melbourne, I realized I had been focusing on those little things because I knew that our time in KL was limited to three days. I never notice the same things in Melbourne. We valued our time and wanted to experience the good things and create good memories during our short time in KL.

Our time is also limited on this planet. Shouldn't we do the same?

Living a happy and satisfying life is really about your time. Is it well spent on your terms?

WHAT IS A WASTE OF TIME?

If you were in a crowd and someone pointed to the sky and said, "Hey, look; there is something in the sky," and you looked up, and someone took your wallet, how would that make you feel? Regretting about the past or worrying about the future is like this. They transport you to another time, and your present moments are stolen. Wasting your time can also be about spending time with people who don't appreciate or love you, or doing something you do not enjoy. Basically, anything that makes you feel bad in some way is a waste of your limited precious time on earth.

WHAT IS A GOOD USE OF TIME?

Whether it is talking to your best friend, running, living your passion, spending time with your loved ones, refreshing your good memories from the past, being excited about the future, or just enjoying the present, whatever it is that makes you "come alive" is a good use of your time.

Nothing and no one should ruin your time. Unlike money, you never get your time back. When it is gone, it's gone. Letting other people ruin your time is like letting other people steal your most precious gift. With money, it is your decision whether to spend it, but with time you don't get that decision, because the clock keeps ticking.

Any time spent on what make you feel bad is just too expensive, and any time spent on what you love is just too valuable to miss.

As long as your candle keeps burning, do more of what you love and less of what you don't.

YOUR DECISIONS

For many years, I listened to other people's opinions and made many of my life choices based on them. Except for my intimate relationship, their influence impacted almost every area of my life. I didn't even realize that I was living the default life of others.

I always thought there was only one way to live my life, and that was doing what my close family and friends did. Their opinions matter, and honestly, I wouldn't be the person I am today if it weren't for them. But I also realized that I did what most people around me did. And years later, I found a quote from one of my favorite authors, Jim Rohn. He said, "You are the average of the five people you spend the most time with."

I couldn't agree more.

When I stopped and reviewed my life, I noticed I was hanging out with people who were not healthy and fit. They didn't enjoy their jobs, had average relationships, and were obsessed with success and social status. They used to talk more about other people than good ideas.

Slowly, I became one of them.

I found that I was not true to myself, and I was not very satisfied. Even if there was influence from other people in my life, no one forced me into it (although many of us get forced). When I looked back on my life and pondered, I had a profound realization that in the past, every step of the way, I had a choice to make. And I realized that I often said yes when I wanted to say no. The life I had been living before was the result of my own decisions.

I didn't like the level of fitness I had, didn't like the way people were treating me, and was at a meaningless job that I didn't like. I was making good money, but I was not fulfilled.

Over the last seven years, I have redesigned my life using the science of happiness framework. I'm living more on my terms than before. Since I started transforming my life, I have met many amazing people and created deep and meaningful relationships. I have become more fit and healthy. I have successfully built one online and one offline business that I love, and they are meaningful to me. Honestly, I make more money than before. I have been to places I had never been to and done things I had never done.

I had the opportunity to learn directly from some amazing people, such as the former CEO and co-founder of Netflix, Marc Randolph, and the former director of market development of Facebook, Randi Zuckerberg and others. She is also the creator of Facebook Live.

I realized that we can be the architects of our lives if we commit.

Years ago, I never thought I would ever meet these amazing people or study something like happiness. If I hadn't decided to live my life on my terms, you wouldn't even be reading this book.

I'm telling you these things not to brag (okay, maybe a little) but to give you some evidence from my own life that it is not just talking. It is definitely possible to transform your life and live your life on your terms. The newer way of life has given my family and me more freedom to do what we love than before.

But have I been happier and more satisfied than before? Yes. Honestly, I can assure you that none of this would be possible if I hadn't taken the new strong decisions and acted on them.

IF YOU DON'T KNOW WHAT YOU WANT

You might think, "Okay, I want to live on my terms, but I don't know what I want, or I don't know where to start."

You can spend a lot of time thinking and being confused, as I did. In my book, you will take a systematic approach using the framework of science to make the changes you want. Making many changes to your life at once will be overwhelming, and you may end up taking no action at all.

Oprah Winfrey once said, "What is your next right move? Not think about; oh, I got all of these to figure out. What is the next right move? And from that space, make the next right move, and the next right move, then you won't be overwhelmed by it." I used these principles when I was going through challenges when I started to make changes to my life.

Remember to focus on the next right move, not all the moves.

You may not necessarily want a full reset of your life. I personally did change several things, but your current life may well be very good already. One idea could be asking yourself is "What is that one thing I always wanted to do but have never done?"

You don't have to, but you can start with that. The trick is to take one small step at a time.

THE TRAP OF "YEAH, BUT ..."

You can think to yourself, "Yeah, but I don't have..."

Do you know why most people don't live the way they want? They don't apply for their dream job. They don't say how much they love others, and they don't do what they always wanted to do.

What stops them is just one word: "fear." Their fear can be a fear of what other people will say, a fear of rejection, a fear of not being good enough, a fear of poverty, or a fear of losing something. Fear often comes disguised as excuses: "I do not have time," "I am too busy," "I do not have money," and so on. If you fall into that trap and procrastinate, you might risk regrets later in life.

I also had (and have) those fears.

When you start to make little changes to your life—for example, starting a yoga class, beginning to speak up in meetings at work, investing somewhere, or doing something that you have never done before—people around you (including your loved ones) may not understand why or what you are doing, and they may not be very supportive, but that's to be expected. I experienced this myself, but I learned over the years and from my mentors that you must take action and not let other people's opinions dictate what you do.

Otherwise, how can you live on your own terms?

So do what makes sense to you anyway.

I have seen people get out of abusive relationships and quit their jobs to get out from a micromanaging boss. They have landed their dream jobs, started their own businesses, and become more healthy and fit. They have done so many other things regardless of age, sex, finances, and other circumstances. They have successfully transformed their lives on their terms. None of this would be possible without their courageous decisions and actions.

As Henry Ford once said, "If you think you can do a thing or you can't do a thing, you are right."

THE ROLE OF LUCK

I got a call from one of my friends, and he asked me, "How was your day?" I said, "I just came home from a workshop." He said, "Whose workshop was it?" I replied, "It was Brian's. He is a former US senator," he said, "Wow, really? You are so lucky." I smiled and said nothing.

I had the opportunity to be at Brian's workshop when he visited Melbourne. I had two of his mentoring sessions. I made a decision to be there. In fact, after I paid for the workshop, which I could barely afford at that time, I ended up with only $200 in my bank.

But it was all worth it. I learned a lot from him.

I wasn't lucky to meet and learn directly from people like Brian, Randi, or Marc. I wasn't lucky to build two successful businesses or the things I have done during the transformation of my life. I made thousands of small decisions over the years. Some of them worked, and some didn't. So I made alternate decisions and acted on them to make them work.

There will always be something that is not in your control, but making solid decisions and acting on them is the only way to live on your terms. When we get things in life without much effort, we often attribute it to good luck, but when things don't go our way, we blame bad luck.

Every time you point your own failure toward God or sometimes luck and say, "God hasn't written this for me," "My luck is bad," etc. These names, like God or things like Luck, are so powerful that your brain feels it's not worth trying anymore. And you may completely stop trying.

When you do that, your life does not change.

Things that don't go your way just take more effort or a different approach. But, yes, sometimes you did everything right to the best of your abilities but still didn't get what you wanted. At the time, you may feel frustrated and unhappy, but later, you may get something better than expected. This happens all the time. I have many examples of this that have occurred in my life.

Steve Jobs once said, "You can't connect the dots looking forward; you can only connect them looking backward. So you have to trust that the dots will somehow connect in your future." The dots he is referring to are both positive and negative events that happen in our lives.

In the face of challenges, the people who live extraordinary lives never stop trying. They trust themselves, make 'alternate decisions,' and act accordingly to live on their terms.

The only things that come from luck or chance are the ones you are born with: being born into a rich or poor family, being white or black, being tall or short, and so forth. Those things can potentially give you an edge over other people. But having that edge does not automatically mean you will live a happier or more satisfying life than others.

Think about Prince Harry. He moved out of the palace. He literally is a prince. He was born into a royal family that ruled the world for hundreds of years. He is white; he is good-looking and skinny; he has money.

But he was not living on his terms.

After he and Megan left the royal family, He said, "It was so many months of talks after so many years of challenges. And I know I haven't always gotten it right, but as far as this goes, there really was no other option." Even being royalty, he and his wife didn't like where they were. So Harry and Megan made a strong decision to move out of the palace, which made sense to them. Then they took action and moved out. Was it easy for Harry and Megan? No way. Were they worried about what the royal family and other people (including media) thought? Sure they were. But they took the decision and action to live on their terms anyway.

Think about the areas of your life you built and are proud of—your body, relationships, business, or anything else. Were they just given to you? What decisions have you made in the past, and what actions did you take that made them so great?

The bottom line is that even though there could be some influence of luck or chance (if you believe in them), our lives are primarily shaped by our decisions and acts.

BIG DECISIONS, SMALL DECISIONS

We make decisions all day every day. Some are big, and some are small. For example, running a marathon next year is a big decision, but going for a 10k run today is a small decision. Planning a $10k holiday next year is a big decision, but saving $100 for that today is a small decision.

Living an extraordinary life is a big decision, but choosing more things that you love to do rather than those you have to do involves small decisions you take today.

No matter what big decisions you make for the longer term, your small decisions and acts you do today must align with your big decisions.

Your small decisions and acts every day shape your days, and your days shape your life

ACT ON THREE DECISIONS EVERY DAY

Seven years ago, I made three big and strong decisions:

- The decision to live an extraordinary life on my terms.
- The decision to listen to my heart.
- The decision to value my precious time and live every moment.

In any situation when I make small decisions, I remind myself of those three big decisions I already made. If I hit a roadblock today, I remember my decision to live an extraordinary life, which means I pivot and never give up. If I have a chance to do something I love, I take it, and if I have a chance to avoid something I hate, I avoid it as my decision to listen to my heart. And when I feel low, I remember my decision to value my time, which is too precious to waste on regret or worry.

In your journey to living a happier and more satisfying life on your terms, you will surely hit obstacles and fail; this is expected. We all did and still do. But your firm decision to bounce back and your consistent actions will make all the difference.

I can give you hundreds of science-based facts, but they wouldn't matter unless you make a firm decision and act every day to live a happy and satisfying life on your terms.

Remember, your daily decisions and actions shape your life.

My book is my two cents to your extraordinary life.

REFLECTION

In different phases of life, you will see that nothing is permanent and change is inevitable. Your money, health, and loving relationships will likely change. But as long as you live, your heart will keep pumping and be there for you. It is the closest thing that you have in the whole world, and it keeps you alive.

Thank your heart.

The most precious blessing you have is your time.

No matter what decisions and actions you take every day, make sure they align with your heart for the rest of your precious time on earth.

PART 2:
Your Results, Resilience, Permission, and Money

In this part, we will discuss the following:

- how to measure your happiness
- what results you can expect from reading this book
- how to bounce back from a negative life event
- how to allow yourself to be happy
- whether you can buy happiness with money

MEASURE YOUR HAPPINESS

"The heart of science is measurement."
—Erik Brynjolfsson

Happiness researchers have been using many methods to measure happiness. The Oxford Happiness Scale is one of the easiest yet most authentic methods which is widely used. As I mentioned earlier, this questionnaire method is almost as good as other methods in a lab environment (e.g., fMRI).

The Oxford Happiness Scale has twenty-nine questions. Each of the questions has six possible answers, as below:

- Strongly disagree (1)
- Moderately disagree (2)
- Slightly disagree (3)
- Slightly agree (4)
- Moderately agree (5)
- Strongly agree (6)

Answer as honestly and as accurately as possible when you take it. For each question, select one answer and move on to the next. Do not overthink the answers. Your first instinct is most likely the most accurate. There is no right or wrong answer. It just asks about your emotional level at that point in time, which is likely to change later. Once you finish all twenty-nine questions, this will give you a result on a scale of 1 to 6. Depending on when you take this test, the result is your happiness level at that time. You want to record the result with the date.

One reading does not mean that you are unhappy or super happy. You should take a number of measurements over a long time (e.g., every week for four to six weeks) and then average the results. With the permission from Elsevier the publisher of the original journal published in 2002, I have included this test in the next page for you.

THE OXFORD HAPPINESS SCALE

ANSWER EACH QUESTION AND SCORE (1 TO 6) IN "S"	S	R
1. I don't feel particularly pleased with the way I am. (R)		
2. I am intensely interested in other people.		
3. I feel that life is very rewarding.		
4. I have very warm feelings towards almost everyone.		
5. I rarely wake up feeling rested. (R)		
6. I am not particularly optimistic about the future. (R)		
7. I find most things amusing.		
8. I am always committed and involved.		
9. Life is good.		
10. I do not think that the world is a good place. (R)		
11. I laugh a lot.		
12. I am well satisfied about everything in my life.		
13. I don't think I look attractive. (R)		
14. There is a gap between what I would like to do and what I have done. (R)		
15. I am very happy.		
16. I find beauty in some things.		
17. I always have a cheerful effect on others.		
18. I can fit in everything I want to.		
19. I feel that I am not especially in control of my life. (R)		
20. I feel able to take anything on.		
21. I feel fully mentally alert.		
22. I often experience joy and elation.		

ANSWER EACH QUESTION AND SCORE (1 TO 6) IN "S"	S	R
23. I do not find it easy to make decisions. (R)		
24. I do not have a particular sense of meaning and purpose in my life. (R)		
25. I feel I have a great deal of energy.		
26. I usually have a good influence on events.		
27. I do not have fun with other people. (R)		
28. I don't feel particularly healthy. (R)		
29. I do not have particularly happy memories of the past. (R)		
TOTAL		

CALCULATE YOUR HAPPINESS SCORE

Step 1

Once you have scored all twenty-nine questions, you may have noticed a number of questions ended with (R). The answers for these questions should be reversed. So for each one of those twelve questions, change your scores as below:

- If you scored 1, cross it out and change it to 6.
- If you scored 2, cross it out and change it to 5.
- If you scored 3, cross it out and change it to 4.
- If you scored 4, cross it out and change it to 3.
- If you scored 5, cross it out and change it to 2.
- If you scored 6, cross it out and change it to 1.

You can use the R column in the table for the changed scores if you like.

Step 2

Once you have updated those twelve answers, add all twenty-nine of your scores (seventeen unchanged plus twelve changed) to get a total number.

Step 3

Once you have that total number (from step 2), divide that by 29. The result is your happiness level.

Alternatively, you can Google "The Oxford happiness scale" and take this test on various authentic sites, this option can save you some time by calculating your scores automatically every time you take this test.

Remember, wherever you take this test, the questions and how the answers are measured are the same, and your results should be on a scale between 1 and 6. The average for people is about 4.3 out of 6.

WHAT RESULTS CAN YOU EXPECT

"Change is the end result of all true learning."
—Leo Buscaglia

RESULTS NEVER LIE

I do not expect you to read my book and not be happier. There are many books on happiness. Many of us (including me) get confused and skeptical if the books bring about results. Some surely do. Reading a book requires time, which is the most precious resource that you have. I have invited you to read my book, and I genuinely want you to get the results that matter to you and your loved ones.

Otherwise, what's the point?

That's why, at this point, I wish to discuss the results.

I believe that the happiness principles I preach must work for me. I need to live by them and experience the results myself. Then I use them with my close family members and with people I work with. In this endeavor, I tried the interventions on myself and my close family. And I had a profound realization that the interventions were simple but very powerful. They certainly made me and my family members happier.

Then I wanted to test these principles for a wider audience.

A few years ago, I designed and ran a six-week-long workshop for a small group of participants based on the principles I learned from studying the science of happiness. Each week for six weeks, participants did the interventions and recorded their happiness levels (as results). It turns out about 80 per cent of the participants became happier.

It was a fantastic experience for me and my participants. It gave me immense honor and pleasure to help the small group of participants become happier using the interventions.

I believe that whoever you are, you can expect to be happier. We all have our unique stories, but most people want a happy life.

By sharing the results from my workshop, I want to give you a glimpse of what is possible.

I sincerely hope that reading my book and doing the interventions will give you tools and strategies from science so you can live a happier life. But reading alone will not give you results; actually doing will. I truly want you to feel and say, "Yes, that was worth it."

HOW TO MEASURE YOUR HAPPINESS

As discussed earlier, scientists developed several ways to measure happiness. But one of the simplest and most accurate ways is to use the Oxford Happiness Scale, developed by Michael Argyle and Peter Hills of Oxford Brookes University. It asks specially designed questions to generate a person's emotional responses. As the answers are subjective to the person, this measure is also called "Subjective Well-Being." Researchers have been using these types of measures for years. This scale has twenty-nine multiple-choice questions that can accurately determine your happiness on a scale of 1 to 6.

According to top happiness researchers, these measures are almost as good as having an fMRI of your brain and looking at which part of your brain lights up when you feel positive emotions. Your happiness is very accurately measurable using these measures. You can measure your happiness using the Oxford Happiness Scale on the previous chapter.

THE PARTICIPANTS

My workshop participants were not psychologists, therapists, coaches, or positive psychology students. They were just everyday people from different walks of life, of varying sexes, age groups, and backgrounds. They live in either Melbourne or Sydney. I also have obtained their permission to share these results in this book.

Life is not always about colors and rainbows. It is also not about being happy and high all the time. We all face challenges in our lives. During the six-week interventions, the participants were going through hard times. Someone lost his dear friend. Others either lost their businesses or had tough times at work. One was going through her brother's battle with cancer. One had to be away from her three children for a long time. Yet they could get through life and managed to take time from their busy schedules to do the interventions every week. I'm glad to say that 80 per cent of them became happier. I cannot thank them enough for participating in my program.

THE FORMAT OF THE INTERVENTIONS

The participants joined an hour-long group session with me every week. We talked about the theory and how to do the interventions. The participants spent about an hour every week completing the weekly interventions. They also measured and recorded their happiness levels every week for six weeks using the Oxford Happiness Scale.

I received many positive reflections from the participants, including a few about their struggles. But in general, the results were very inspiring. As I'm not a researcher, I needed some help interpreting the results. So I reached out to one of the most prominent happiness scientists in the world, Sonja Lyubomirsky, from the University of California–Riverside, for some clarification. She was very kind to help me understand some of the concepts from her research.

THE RESULTS

Firstly, I want to show you the results for Kate. She can be considered someone from a control group. That means she didn't do any interventions over the six weeks. As you can see, in week 1, her happiness level was 4.79, and her week-six happiness level was 4.62.

In the weeks in the middle, she had a few ups and downs, but her average happiness stayed in the same range (between 4.7 and 4.6). The purpose of the control group was to compare Kate's results with the results of other participants who did the interventions. She did not become happier. And that was expected.

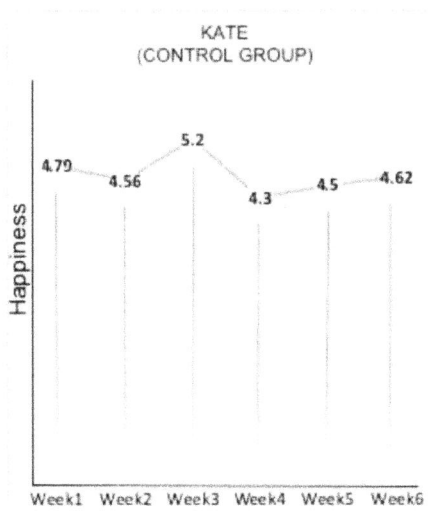

Now, let's look at the results of Amy, who did the interventions over the six weeks. However, she did not do the interventions every week. She was not very consistent in doing them, as you can see below.

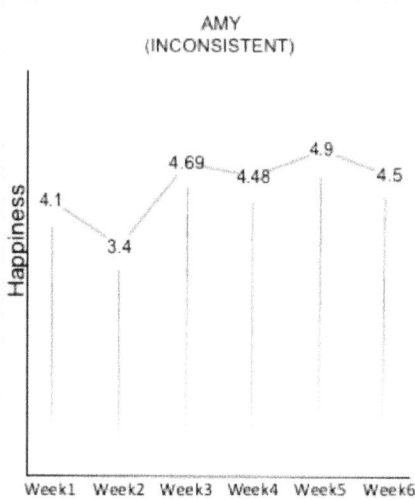

Amy started at 4.1 in week one but didn't do the interventions in weeks 2, 4, and 6. You can see that her happiness levels dropped in those weeks. Her happiness increased over the six weeks (to 4.69 and 4.9 in weeks 3 and 5). But as you can see, because of her inconsistency in doing the interventions, she couldn't maintain that higher range.

That means that if she had done those interventions every week, it would have been possible for her to maintain that higher range (4.69 or above) over six weeks. Maintaining higher happiness levels relates to our lifestyles and behavior. You may remember that is the 40 per cent of our happiness which is in our control, from Professor Sonja Lyubomirsky's research.

Finally, I want to show you Glenn's results. He started with a score of 4.31 in week 1, and he had an increase in the following week to 4.6. In the third week, he reached 5.20, and then, in the remaining three weeks, he maintained that higher level of happiness (above 5).

WHAT RESULTS CAN YOU EXPECT

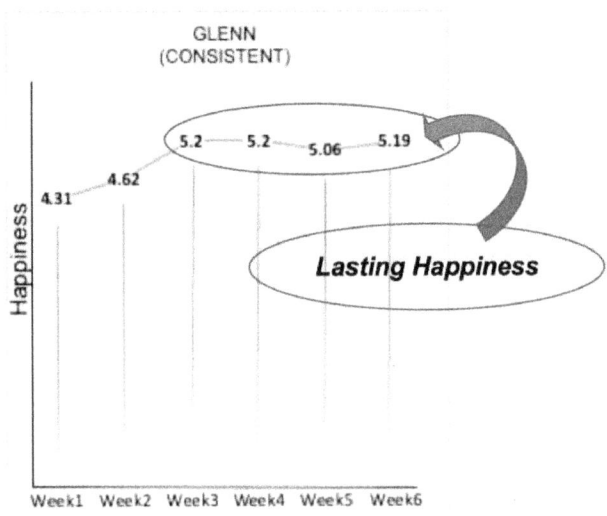

So what was Glenn's secret? It was the consistency in doing the interventions. That means he repeatedly took action every week. Eventually, doing those interventions became his habits. Anything you do every day becomes part of your habits. I call the interventions "happiness habits." I will explain more about them in part 4. Glenn's consistent actions in doing the interventions as happiness habits helped him stay happy.

Almost all the participants had a very positive experience with the workshop. They sent me many messages and reflections. They talked about their experiences, struggles, and challenges during those six weeks.

One of my participants, Albert, said,

> I had a realization that I've been very inconsistent and haven't kept myself accountable for my own happiness. My happiness was reliant on my interactions with other people. I also realized how effective writing or journaling is in soothing the soul. By journaling more consistently, I was able to find solutions to the challenges I had. Every single time, without fail, I felt better once I finished the actual journaling session.
>
> I never really thought about happiness as something we can 'feed' ourselves. I used to practice gratitude more consistently when I utilized the miracle morning strategies, like exercising, reading, journaling, meditating. But I basically stopped doing that after taking a holiday. I liked that this program has made me more accountable and consistent with my strategies and just becoming happy in general.

Another participant, Kate, was going through some challenges. She said,

> I am happy inside and out. I consistently practice gratitude in activities that occur throughout the day. I am blessed to be living such a beautiful life, even when life throws you a curveball! Practicing the happiness interventions helped me through these challenges knowing that there is always someone with more serious problems, just like my brother fighting his way through cancer.

> Yes, the interventions came at a perfect time in my life as I was helping my brother fight his way through Colon Cancer. Never before had I the need to visit Peter Mac hospital. And in a very short period, I was there more often than not. In such an unfamiliar environment with so many unhappy people, I practiced by greeting people and asking them 'how their day had been and how they were feeling.' It surprised me how lonely these people actually were and how they were truly touched by someone noticing them. Particularly when they had bandages and bags hanging off different parts of their bodies. As a result, I felt happy that I was able to bring happiness to them, even if it was for a short time.

At the end of the day, everybody's life is uniquely different, and we face many situations and challenges. The happiness interventions helped my participants build a "happiness habit and muscle," which they used to tackle life challenges better.

I already shared Glenn's results, and here is what he said:

> The experience for me was incredible. The sessions were enjoyable, and the education. They gave me insight and further knowledge, which definitely improved my happiness. With Sanju's assistance, these sessions made me aware that I already did many things required to be happy. But they also showed me how to improve what I was already doing. He also gave me additional tools, simple things that made sense, worked, and made life more enjoyable.

> One of the things that I believed most helped me was to write things down. For example, for a long time before going to sleep, I thought of all the things that I was grateful for, my family, friends, food, shelter, etc. The intervention made me aware that writing these down gave me greater awareness and allowed me to review these, which gave me a better understanding of how

> fortunate I really was. Sanju triggered many things, but another was telling family, friends, and others how much we love and value them.
>
> I have always done whatever I could to show people that I cared. But actually, seeing someone or calling them to tell them how valued and loved they are is amazing for them and yourself.
>
> We all go through challenging times. During the course, we lost a dear friend. I believe the tools which I learned helped me deal with this. I still struggled, but it also helped me refocus and plan a different and better future. I recommend the Happiness Intervention to everyone as I thought I was happy. But this has proven to me that there are simple science tools that we could use to improve and learn. Sanju and the rest of the participants thank you for your support and time.
>
> Glenn

It was an absolute honor and privilege for me to serve them in my workshop. Personally, it gives me a lot of fulfilment.

LASTING HAPPINESS

Over the years I have learned that happiness is not something that you get; it is something that you do. For most people, the challenge is not to be happy but to stay happy. Many people talk about finding lasting happiness and spend their lives looking for the one "secret" that will allow them to achieve it. What that really means is their maintenance of their happiness levels in a higher bracket most of the time. (It is much like your blood pressure, which your habits and lifestyle can maintain).

Lasting happiness is absolutely possible, but not from just one big positive event (e.g., graduation, wedding day, becoming mortgage-free,). It is not about getting that one thing (e.g., a house, dream car) that would make you happy forever.

Rather it is about doing the things you love every day as your happiness habits.

Glenn kept doing the happiness interventions during the last three weeks of the workshop, and he did have lasting happiness. You don't find lasting happiness. Rather, you do it every day, as Glenn, Kate, and Albert did. You can do the same or better.

REFLECTION

I believe in outcomes. Out of all my workshop participants, 80 per cent became happier, that was an amazing result.

The purpose of my book is not just to give you facts and graphs from science, but also to give you perspectives, inspirations, tools, and strategies from the science of happiness and over thirty-eight years of my life experience, which will help you be and stay happy on your terms.

After you finish reading my book, I genuinely want you to get your desired results for you and your loved ones. Also, I want to make sure that your precious time is well spent.

Have you measured your happiness yet?

If not, take five minutes and do it now ("Measure Your Happiness" Chapter).

HOW TO RECOVER FROM A SETBACK

"When one door of happiness closes, another opens, but often we look so long at the closed door that we do not see the one that has been opened for us."
—Helen Keller

HOW SHE LOST EVERYONE IN JUST TWO YEARS

Janvi and Pavan were two lovebirds in college. Everybody thought that they were made for each other. As expected, after college, they got married. They wanted to start a family, but Janvi hadn't been able to get pregnant after trying for a few years. The doctors said that it would be very hard for her to get pregnant naturally because of some complications.

This came as a big surprise. So they got a second opinion, and the doctor suggested the same but said IVF could be an alternative. Pavan was not quite sure about IVF, but Janvi was open to the idea.

After some time, Pavan reluctantly agreed, even though he wanted a natural baby. They started the IVF process. But halfway through the process, Janvi noticed that Pavan was delaying and was not going to the doctor. Janvi gave him some more time, but it wasn't getting anywhere. Having been with Pavan for so long, Janvi realized that something was not right. One day, Janvi came home early from work and was pondering the whole pregnancy thing. Pavan came home looking very tired, but she couldn't just wait another day, so she said, "You know that I can't be pregnant naturally. Are you thinking of a second marriage?"

When I was interviewing Janvi for my book, I stopped her and asked, "Seriously? You asked him that?" I know that she asks straightforward questions, but that was a jaw-dropper for me. I asked her how he responded. She paused for a bit as she was trying to hold back her tears. Pavan had said to her, "I have thought about it, but I can't imagine that I shall have no connection with you." She heard that, turned around and said nothing, and went to bed. Pavan didn't follow her to the bedroom but stayed in the living room.

A few days after this conversation, she went to her parents' place and stayed there a few nights. After hearing what Pavan had said, her dad was so shocked that he suffered a stroke and later started slurring his words. Her mother was already a patient with schizophrenia and bipolar disorder, and her condition worsened. Janvi felt so guilty and thought that all of that happened because her parents were worried about her.

She started to have issues with her sleep. She cried every night and went to work in the morning. She couldn't eat, and basically, her life slowly became miserable. Pavan checked on her a few times during this period, but he never took his words back or talked about pregnancy. Given her history with Pavan, Janvi was not just upset; she couldn't believe it, and she became angry with herself for loving him. She was hurt so much that she didn't bring up the pregnancy conversation anymore. Pavan didn't even apologize or try to make this work. He went on trips for work to other cities and stayed there for weeks and didn't call her. Slowly, their distance widened. They agreed to remain separated and finally got divorced.

As Janvi was going through this trauma, her mother got diagnosed with stage IV cancer. Even though both of her parents were ill, they cared for her. Janvi's brother and his wife were relentlessly preventing the whole family from falling apart. But during this challenging time, her father had a heart attack and suddenly died.

Janvi's whole world had gone black.

Nine months later, her mother became sick and was taken to the hospital. Taking care of her mother every day became a routine for Janvi and her brother. Relatives would come and visit them, and they would tell the same story over and over again. Doctors said one more surgery could give her some time. But twenty-six days later, her mother passed away.

You might think that must have been very hard for her. She was going through this excruciating pain for several different reasons: her failing marriage, knowing that she was never going to be a mother naturally, her father passing away, and the loss of her mother. It feels like a movie sequence. You can imagine how hard it would be to go through such life events.

During all these events, Janvi's brother was very supportive. He was the only person who stood by her following her marriage and through everything else she was experiencing. But one day she got a call from her brother's wife that her brother had been taken to hospital because of a stroke. She rushed to the hospital, but he was no more.

In less than two years, she had lost every member of her family.

I had no words as she was telling me this. I didn't know what to say. I didn't know what to ask. I was just silent. I felt as though if I said a word, it would be a crime.

But she smiled. I dared to ask, "Then?"

She said that the whole story felt like an illusion to her. She was just responding to the events and didn't really have enough time to think or become sad. She was sinking and swimming.

But she kept going to her work—not because she had to, but because she needed to escape. She was the head of her department and had a good team of people supporting her. Everybody told her to take some time off. But what would she do with that time? She spoke to her boss, and he said, "You do not have to do any work; just come and spend some time with your team." Even though it seemed impossible at first, she started to spend more time at work with her colleagues. The hardest part was when she came home, as there was no one there. She didn't have a lot of friends because her family was her whole world, and all of a sudden, they were no more.

A few weeks later, one day at work, she found herself laughing with a few of her colleagues. She was so surprised and felt so guilty that she asked her boss, "Why am I laughing? Am I a sick person and have no emotions?" Her boss said, "You may have been tired of feeling pain."

That little laugh at work was a silver lining.

Her colleagues at work and a few friends continued to make her laugh. But some people thought otherwise, wondering how she could allow herself to laugh after such life events. Some people started judging her.

She had nothing and no one left to lose. She had only two options: she could live the rest of her life in pain and grief, or she could accept the events and live for herself.

With time, she slowly realized that even though she had lost her whole family, she needed to do something meaningful for them. She was not a religious person, but she believed in God. She believes that her father, mother, and brother are with God, having passed away. She believes that all her good deeds will help them rest in peace.

A few months later, with her saved money, she opened a school for underprivileged kids. The kids are either orphans or poor. She supports them with food, shelter, education, clothing, and almost everything a little kid needs for basic life. She has been running her school with over seventy kids enrolled for more than three years now. During the day, she spends time with her team at work. In the evenings and weekends, she spends time with the kids. She talks to them and teaches them good values. She cares for them in every possible way, as if they were her own.

Janvi has evolved into a different person. She has become more confident, smarter, more mature, and more courageous, and she has a strong sense of freedom. No words can describe this, but you can feel it when you talk to her.

I dared to ask her, "So are you happy with your life now?"

She didn't give me a diplomatic answer. As she is straightforward, she took a moment and said, "Yes, I am."

Then I asked, "Do you think you would have been better off with a life that most people want? Like having a husband, kids, and family?" Now I got her to think for a moment. She said, "I have seen many of my friends living that life. And I understood and saw so much of it. I believe my purpose is not to live that life, but to live the life I'm living right now. I have created this life for myself. So no, I do not think that way."

I asked her, "Where did you find the idea of the school?"

She said, "I asked, 'Why? Why me? What does God want from me? What should I do when I have no one left in my family?' I realized that I wanted to serve. I am someone who needs to be serving the people in need. That's why I founded my school. Every day, I serve over seventy kids. They need me. That gives me fulfilment. Those little kids make my day. I listen to their thoughts. In my free time, I cook for them. I laugh when they laugh, and I cry when they are sad. They are my family. I belong there.

"Then I understood; to be able to serve them, I need to be strong. I need to make more money. I need to be there for them. I started to pay attention to my sleep. I try to stay active. I eat good food. Those give me physical strength so I can serve them better. About my parents and brother, I believe that if you are blessed to have yours, you will have them for a limited time, and I had used up that time."

Why did she start all these? Because she believes that her father, mother, and brother will rest in peace with God as a result. And every good deed she does today pleases God. She also believes that God made her recovery easier and prepared her for this more meaningful life she is living today.

Everyone has a story. Often the truth is stranger than fiction. I heard that phrase when I was little but didn't really understand what it meant. Janvi's story, for many people, is unimaginable. But her strong decisions made all the difference for her recovery. God didn't talk to her and say, "Build your school; this is your purpose to serve." She gave her own meaning to what happened in her life. She allowed herself to feel the sadness, the grief, the guilt, and the pain. She could have settled with thinking, "As I lost my family, I must live in pain and guilt for the rest of my life." But she chose to give a very different meaning to those events and realized, "Through these events, I have become that person who serves the people in need."

We all go through our battles in our lives. Some events that happen to us are not in our control, but we can always choose to give our own meanings to these events. Meanings highly influence what we do next.

Remember, Janvi said, after all those traumatic events, she is now living a more fulfilling life. Who would have thought that?

No matter how hard our lives seem to be, it is about what meaning we give to every moment and event we face. And our lives are made up of the small decisions we make every day.

Janvi became alone. But today she lives a happier and more fulfilling life because of her new meaning and her decision to be courageous and strong.

IF YOU THINK, "WHY ME?"

If you are going through hardship, you may think, "Why me?" You may look around and feel that everybody but you—including your friends, family, and even celebrities you love—is living his or her perfect life. But hardships do not discriminate. Everybody experiences them.

Madonna got fired from Dunkin' Donuts in Times Square. Prince Harry told the Telegraph that he shut down all his emotions for almost two decades after the death of his mother. Even Dwayne "The Rock" Johnson experienced depression. Walt Disney was so broke that he didn't have money to buy food. He ate dog food.

Celebrities are not from another world. They are not immune to hardships. Often it is quite the opposite. They are just regular people whom many other people love for their work. They also go through negative events. They feel fear, anxiety, depression, and the like. They have lost their loved ones, lived in their cars, and so on. You get to know their stories because they publicly speak about their struggles. Almost all of them survived the hardships and later went on to much better lives. Many people who go through struggles and traumas come out stronger, smarter, and more fulfilled (like Janvi).

I have learned there are two main methods we use to deal with hardships. Psychologists call one of these "problem-focused coping." This occurs when you face a problem (e.g., stressing about your issue with your colleague) and try to solve it with your actions (e.g., talking to your boss or colleague). But of course, not all hardships are solvable or controllable (e.g., losing your job or someone you love). That's where the other coping method, emotion-focused coping, comes in. This occurs when you try to make sense of the event and be emotionally okay with it so you can move on.

Either way, coping generally comes down to three things: the meaning you give, the decisions you make, and the actions you take to recover.

WHAT DOES THIS EVENT MEAN TO YOU?

Whenever we experience an event in life, the brain gives a meaning to it. For example, positive events (e.g., promotions) or negative events (e.g., being made redundant at work). In both cases, your brain will make up a meaning that aligns with your belief. This means that if you believe getting promoted will give you more money and you believe that is important to you, you will be happy. But many believe getting promoted means more responsibility and stress, which might make them unhappy.

This phenomenon of the brain is called "rationalization." It happens all the time.

If you were made redundant at work, your brain could ascribe to the event a negative meaning (e.g., "Why me? I worked so hard in this job") or a positive meaning (e.g., "I might get some redundancy money and start something new"). If you are going through a divorce, your brain could ascribe to the event a negative meaning (e.g., "Why couldn't I make my marriage work?") Or a positive meaning (e.g., "Maybe I deserve someone better"). If you are going through an illness, your brain could ascribe to the event a negative meaning (e.g., "Why am I so unlucky? what do I do now?") or a positive meaning (e.g., "What is this telling me? How can I recover and live better?").

For negative events or hardships, our brains almost always default to negative meanings. That is how most of us are wired. But sometimes we have no control over an event itself (for example, someone passing away), and the only way to deal with it is to change the negative default meaning. Of course, changing the negative meaning to a positive can take a long time, depending on the person and situation, but it's possible.

If you have lost your job and all day you think about how this happened to you and you stay in pain and feel demoralized, what do you think your chances of getting another job or starting something new are?

Asking yourself this might help: "What is this event telling me to do?"

Often you will find that your problem does not need to be solved. Rather, your perception needs to be changed.

When my mother-in-law was suffering for more than three years from coughing and difficulties in breathing, we just could not see her suffer anymore. After she passed away, we were all sad. We went through difficult times. But we had to give a different meaning to her death as her "end of suffering" so she could rest in peace.

To create a new and positive meaning, you could write down your deepest thoughts about the event and what it means to you. Have a deep and meaningful conversation with someone who supports you (e.g., a friend, relative, or therapist). The person you speak with can help you see a more positive meaning. These are a few ideas supported by science.

When Janvi's dad suddenly died, she initially thought her whole world had gone black. That was her default meaning. In her journey, she asked, "Why me? What does God want from me?" then she gave a newer and more positive meaning. She said, "Through these events, I have become that person who serves the people in need." That new meaning helped her move on to a more fulfilling life.

The bottom line is that for any negative event, your brain will default to a negative meaning. Allow yourself and take your time to feel the sadness, the grief, and the pain.

But do not just stay in sorrow and do nothing. It is your job (Remember, your happiness is your responsibility) to give a more empowering and positive meaning to the negative event to recover.

I love what Anthony Robbins said: "Life happens for you, not to you."

WHAT DECISIONS WILL YOU MAKE NOW?

Once you have a more positive and empowering meaning of the negative event, you will find it easier to make strong decisions based on your meaning. For example, if you have lost your job and then your new meaning is, "I deserve a better job" or "The universe is telling me to start my own business," you might be empowered to gain some new skills and look for better opportunities with more excitement.

You must ensure that the decision to achieve your new goal is strong. Do not change it in the face of obstacles or be influenced by other people's opinions. If needed, change your approach, but do not change the goal.

Pakistan's iron lady, Muniba Mazari, said, "It is ok to be scared, it is ok to cry, everything is ok, but giving up should not be an option." She continued, "Do not die before your death. Real happiness lies in gratitude, so be grateful, be alive and live every moment."

WHAT ACTIONS WILL YOU TAKE NOW?

When you experience trauma or hardship, it might be hard to accept help or interact socially with others. But studies suggest that social support from your friends and family is one of the most effective coping mechanisms that help you navigate difficult times. But be very careful in choosing them. Not all social support is helpful. Some people can unwillingly put you down and make you more miserable. If you do not have anyone on your side, seek professional help.

Even though it may seem hard to go to a social gathering, movie theatre, or group activity (e.g., yoga, group walking), these can lighten your mood. They can help you take meaningful actions towards your new goal. Janvi's work colleagues made her laugh, and she slowly started giving new and empowering meaning to her life and recovered.

Most importantly, allow yourself to be open to new ideas.

Even if you have new and empowering meaning and have made a firm decision, nothing changes unless you continue to take meaningful actions towards your new goals. You may not see any direct results immediately. You must keep going and will see the light on the other side of the tunnel.

If you are going through hell, why stop?

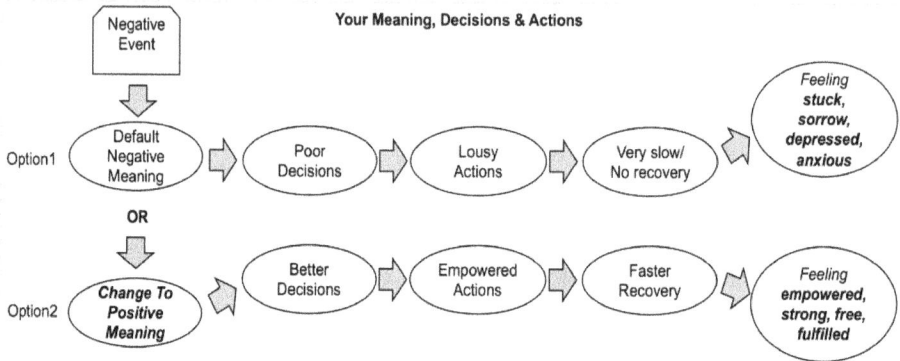

Remember, for any hardship we face, we have two options. Option one is to hold on to the default negative meaning our brain gives and stay in suffering forever. But option two is to change the default meaning to a more positive meaning that allows us to move on to better things.

Having hardships is part of being alive. But honestly, going through hardship is never easy. It takes courage, determination, and persistence, along with so many other things. But the last thing you want to do is nothing.

We wouldn't know about any Oprah, The Rock, or Madonna today if they just sat there and did nothing about their hardships. We would not even talk about them. The same goes for Janvi. They all chose to move on with new and empowering meanings. And the strong decisions and the actions they took made them who they are today.

Choose wisely. It's the meaning that you give, the decisions you make, and the actions you take every day that count. They will either break you or make you a better you.

YOUR RETURN TO YOUR GENETIC HAPPINESS BASELINE

A few days after I wrote Janvi's story, I sent the draft for her review. She emailed me and said that she loved it and corrected a few things. Then she said (exactly in her words), "I must tell you one thing that I want you to include. Before marriage, I believed I was the happiest daughter. After marriage, when I was with Pavan, I believed I was the happiest girl in the world. Even now, with lots of scratches in my heart with all my agonies and suppressed pains, I believe I am blessed and one of the happiest."

I felt so happy for her. But I was not surprised.

I was excited that she wanted me to include this part in her email, because it is probably one of the most important perceptions of all when we deal with negative events. You may remember from Professor Sonja and her team's research that we are all born with a set genetic "happiness baseline." And after any positive or negative event, you will always return to your happiness baseline. Yes, it might take some time, but you will eventually return to it.

When an adverse event happens, as human beings, we are not very good at predicting how that event will make us feel. For example, if you have lost your job or someone you love, or you have an illness or anything that threatens your future happiness, you may find yourself constantly worrying about all the potential negative consequences in the future. We typically overestimate our future unhappiness or happiness.

Many studies suggest that most people are incredibly resilient to negative events. We adapt much quicker than we initially think we will to new situations, for both positive and negative events. Think about it; when a virus or bacteria attacks one's body, the physiological immune system fights back and protects one's physical health. In the same way, we also have a "psychological immune system," as researchers call it, which is activated after a negative event. We do not even know that we have it. The activation happens on our subconscious level. It helps us make sense of the event in self-protective ways. Also, it lets us focus on other positive events, allowing us to recover slowly over time.

Professor Dan Gilbert from Harvard University says, "The truth is, bad things do not affect us as profoundly as we expect them to. That's true of good things too. We adapt very quickly to either."

Remember, Janvi believed she was the happiest daughter and the happiest girl before her marriage broke down (reflecting her genetic happiness baseline). Later, when she lost her father, mother, and brother, her happiness was the lowest. But over time, she again became "one of the happiest" (in her words). Her happiness returned to her genetic happiness baseline.

Big setbacks or wins do not last forever. Even if we predict that we will be devastated if negative events happen, most of us can adapt and return to our genetic baseline happiness.

When we bounce back, we do not live "happily ever after" lives, but we learn to deal with hardships better and smarter. The hardships make us stronger and more resilient. And hardships are not permanent; like the clouds in the sky, they also pass.

BUILDING YOUR HAPPINESS MUSCLES

Asif's phone rang at 5:00 a.m. It was his cousin.

He said, "I have a piece of bad news." Asif asked, "What happened?" he paused and said, "Rana got burnt out of an explosion." Rana is Asif's younger brother who lives in Dhaka. He asked, "Is he all right?" His cousin said, "I'm not sure. Doctors are checking him."

The previous night, Rana came back from work and went to the bathroom to shower. There was a gas leak, and a spark from the hot water system triggered an explosion. He started screaming and came out with fire around his body, and everybody inside the house became terrified. They took him to the hospital immediately.

Asif couldn't believe what had happened. He lives in the UK and booked his flight to Dhaka the next day. Asif is a kind of person who very strongly holds to his word. If he targets anything, he can achieve it with absolute focus and discipline. At that moment, his goal was to get his brother back, and he was ready to do everything in his power to achieve that goal.

On the way to the airport, one of his friends called to check on him and told him, "It's a tough time and hard to think clearly. But on your flight, you will have some time to think alone. You know, Rana believes and looks up to you. People will talk about a lot of things, but you are the one who needs to be in control and completely focused on Rana's recovery." Then he said nothing else. Asif listened but only said, "Hmm." After a long flight, he landed in Dhaka; he slept for a few hours, woke up, and then did something very unusual. He asked his parents if there was a gym nearby. They were surprised and asked whether they had heard him correctly. He said, "Yes, I need to go to the gym first." Asif runs and works out every day as part of his ritual, without exceptions. He joined a gym, worked out for a few hours, and did his usual cardio. After coming from the gym, he showered, prepared himself, and went to the hospital alone.

In the hospital, Asif couldn't recognize his brother. He only saw a man lying on the bed with his whole body wrapped with bandage. Rana had 30 per cent of his body burnt. Initially, the doctors worried about his internal damage, but his internal organs, including his stomach, lungs, and heart, were okay. He was able to speak slowly, swallow food, and digest. That was much better than what everybody had speculated.

It was heartbreaking for Asif to see his brother like that. Over the next three weeks, he went to the gym every morning, worked out, ran, and read books, and the rest of the time he spent with his brother to get him out of shock. He supported him mentally and in every other way possible. Rana slowly got better over the next few months. He seemed to handle the emotional trauma better. Asif's being there was an especially great support initially. With the blessings of God, Rana fully recovered after eighteen months.

Yes, he had a few scars, but slowly, over time, he transformed into a new person with much more energy and hope. Later, he married a beautiful girl and got back to work and his everyday life.

Why am I telling you this story?

Asif is a very happy and content person. But going through this mental trauma was a challenging experience for him. He works for a corporation and has a lovely wife and two beautiful children. He is a professional arm wrestler and marathon runner. Most importantly, he takes care of himself every day, no matter what. I interviewed him once and asked, "What makes you so content?" He said, "I operate on my schedule. I do not compare myself with others. I am very clear and focused on what I want, and eventually, I get them. Most importantly, I am very disciplined about my health and fitness, which helps me stay happy most of the time."

Everybody expected him to go directly to the hospital to see his brother. But he didn't do that. He was exhausted, his energy drained from the news and the travel. He ensured that he regained all his positive energy by going to the gym. He worked out and ran before he was ready to see his brother and deal with the situation in Dhaka.

He knew how to refuel himself—through his happiness habits.

As we discussed earlier, happiness habits are habits you do every day that make you feel good in some way. Asif's happiness habits include working out and running. Those habits give him positive energy.

Think about a situation in which you are with your best friend, and she faints, and now you need to carry her to the car. But if you do not have any physical strength or muscle to do that, you will struggle. You and I both know that if you don't have physical muscles, you can build them over time by working out regularly. And you can see them in the mirror.

But to deal with trauma like Asif's, you will need emotional muscles. If you are emotionally weak, demoralized, or unhappy, you will struggle. Your emotional energy level will be very low, and that will not help others.

But how can you build those emotional muscles?

Modern discoveries in neuroscience suggest that we all have this remarkable ability called neuroplasticity. It allows our brains to learn and rewire themselves (like flexing your physical muscles). In simple terms, if you focus on and think about negative events around you, then your brain will create more "negative wiring." That means you will be in negative emotions like worry, stress, depression, and anger.

But if you focus on and think about positive events around you, your brain creates more "positive wiring" to keep you in more positive emotions like gratitude, kindness, feeling good, and, of course, happiness. Those positive wirings of neurons are your "emotional muscles." As they are inside your brain, you cannot see them as you can physical muscles. But you can certainly feel them inside you through your positive emotions.

I like to call them "happiness muscles."

Your physical muscles come from physical workout habits. Your happiness muscles come from your happiness habits (e.g., being with your close friends, exercising, dancing, or anything that makes you feel good). In part 4, we will discuss how you can build them in details.

Over the years, Asif built very powerful happiness muscles inside his brain by doing what he loves. In this case, he was taking care of his health and fitness as his happiness habits (Yes, he also built physical muscles). And when he faced this emotional trauma about his brother, he already had strong happiness muscles in his brain to deal with the situation.

Asif's brother needed emotional support from someone he truly loved and believed in. Asif inspired his brother and made his brother believe that he was still alive, had eyes to see, and had fully functional internal organs. It could have been worse. His emotional support accelerated his brother's recovery. Yes, Asif was sad; he became worried, and he felt doubt, but during those tough times, Asif's regular happiness habits saved him from breaking down when he needed to be the strongest and at his best.

How could Asif help his brother emotionally if he was not emotionally strong himself?

Asif's daily rituals and happiness habits helped him build those happiness muscles (inside his brain) over many years. And he used them to help his brother recover when he needed them the most.

REFLECTION

Write about a negative event you already recovered from.
What did this event mean to you?
What decisions did you make at the time?
And what actions did you take to come out of that trauma?
How has this event made you stronger?
Honestly, there is no one formula to deal with adversity. But if you are going through adverse times, think about the following:
What default negative meaning have you given to this event?
What alternate and empowering meaning can you offer to replace your default negative meaning?

What firm decisions can you make now?

And what new actions will you take to progress towards recovery?

Write them down and act without stopping.

Over time, it is absolutely possible that you will get to live on your terms again. And in your journey, your happiness habits will help you build those emotional muscles and make you stronger and, of course, happier.

HOW TO PERMIT YOURSELF TO BE HAPPY

*"There are plenty of difficult obstacles in your path.
Don't allow yourself to become one of them."*
—Ralph Marston

YOUR BRAIN IS NOT ON YOUR SIDE

I learned that happiness is not something that you get. It is something that you do. You might think, what exactly am I talking about doing here? It could be as simple as having a meaningful conversation with your best friend, telling someone how much you love her, or working on your dream project. Whatever it is for you, even if you know doing these things will make you happy, you might still struggle to actually do them.

So if we want to stay happy, we must be able to do these things regularly as our happiness habits. These small but consistent things we do help us stay happy. (Remember the 40 per cent happiness in your control.) But forming any new habit will require you to do something new in your daily routine.

But what happens when we try to do something new? We feel uncomfortable. We hesitate. We may not know where to start. We may say it is not the right time, and we often come up with excuses and procrastinate. You may even truly feel motivated and do them once or twice, but a few days later, you are back to your normal routine. You may even feel guilty. We have all been there.

But why is this a struggle for most people? It is a struggle because when you want to do anything new, your brain will stop you. It does not care whether the new thing is good for you. Your brain does not like change. For example, in the morning, most people start with brushing their teeth, having coffee, checking email, freshening up, catching the train, or driving to work, and so forth. These are their automatic behaviors, and they run on autopilot, driven by their subconscious minds. You might struggle to add anything new to that routine.

You may have heard the term "comfort zone" many times before. It is the zone that your brain is comfortable operating in. Your brain has already learned that the things you do in that zone are safe and do not create any new threat. Even twenty minutes of exercise in the morning or thirty minutes of walking in the evening can seem like a big challenge for many. No matter how beneficial these things are for your health, you might still say, "I shall do it tomorrow" and end up watching Netflix instead.

For example, suppose you wish to work on your new dream project at least five hours a week as part of your happiness habit, and you know that doing the work on your passion project will make you happy. Now you will need to do something new and go out of your comfort zone.

What do you think might happen next? You may experience self-doubt. Your brain may think of your dreams as impossible and give you excuses as to why you should not chase them. Often the excuses seem very innocent. They can include things like "You are not ready yet," "when you have that money," and "When things get better, then do it." If you find yourself constantly thinking along those lines for a long time, please stop and reflect. It is not your readiness, money, or anything else that is preventing you from achieving your goal.

It is your brain that is stopping you.

Every dream requires us to go out of our current comfort zones. That's why they are called dreams. Your brain does not believe in your dreams until your dreams have become reality. Highly successful people understand this trick our brains play, but they chase their dreams anyway.

We all have been successful at something, no matter how big or small. Think about something you truly wanted that seemed very hard ten years ago and now is a reality for you today.

How did you achieve this?

If you dream about something but do not proceed because you fear what other people might think of you, remember that other people do not come to your house and stop you. Your brain does. Your brain trusts only what you have done already. Your heart, on the other hand, believes in miracles. We don't dream with our brains. We do it with our hearts.

Staying happy also requires you to form a few new habits, and your brain will likely stop you. Author Anthony Robbins said, "Your brain is not designed to make you happy. It is designed to make you survive. And that's why it's always looking for what's wrong." Millions of years ago, our ancestors used to live in caves. When they used to go hunting for food, they had to constantly look for potential dangers in the environment—for example, a tiger, a lion, or anything else that posed a threat. Over so many years, our brains evolved. However, the alertness or awareness of looking for what is wrong around us is still dominating today. Whether it is the fear of a lion, rejection, failure, or anything else, by all means, our brains try to keep us safe.

If you haven't told your partner that you love her in a while, your brain will make excuses so that you don't say it. If you want to give a hug to your teenage daughter, want to apply for your dream job, or want to speak up in the next project meeting, even if these things will make you happy, your brain can still talk you out of these actions. It does not understand what you genuinely want, and its job is to keep you where you are and run things smoothly. It does not care whether you like or dislike the situation. Liking, disliking, desire, wants or your dreams come from your heart.

That way your brain can stop you from being and staying happy.

If you truly want to stay happy, you must make some changes to your routine, and your brain will try to stop you with all kinds of reasons. But the trick is to take the smallest step at a time so you do not frighten your brain with big action items. You must keep the new thing to a minimum. For example, instead of going for a thirty-minute run, go for a five-minute walk to start. When you have done a five-minute walk for several days without failing, your brain starts to trust you because you have done those walks successfully. Then, over time, increase it to a ten-minute walk. Your brain will learn that the new activity of walking is not a threat and will add it to your comfort zone. You will eventually feel comfortable going for a ten-minute walk. By taking such baby steps, you can install any new habit.

If you blindly follow your brain, you will probably live a very static life. Your happiness or satisfaction will stay the same throughout your lifetime. But if you understand the trick your brain plays and can bypass its excuses, you will have a fulfilling life.

Your heart knows what you truly want, but your brain does not.

YOU FEEL YOU SHOULD NOT BE HAPPY

In 2010 my mother-in-law became sick from a lung disease. She used to cough and had trouble breathing. Sometimes her oxygen level dropped very low and she needed an oxygen supply cylinder system attached. My wife, Mahin, and I visited her at her place in Dhaka. During the first few nights, we noticed that she was constantly coughing during the night. She coughed about twenty times a minute and wasn't able to sleep. Imagine how hard it was for her. Towards the end of the night, she used to get tired of coughing and finally fall asleep. My wife couldn't bear it. She spent most of the nights with her mother and slept when her mother slept. Everybody, including my brother-in-law, father-in-law, and sister-in-law, was in service of my mother-in-law. As she was going through the suffering, it was heartbreaking to watch.

A few weeks later, we had to fly back to Melbourne and return to our usual routine. We were constantly in touch with my mother-in-law in Dhaka. As her condition was not improving, doctors suggested new tests. They found that the lung disease was not curable. She had only about two years to live. That was a blow to the face for all of us.

My wife was very attached to her mother. She used to talk to her every day over Skype. As she saw her mother suffer, she felt helpless.

My wife flew to Dhaka again to spend time with her mother. Doctors suggested that one hospital in Bangkok might have some treatment for this. So my wife and her brother took her to one of the best hospitals in Thailand. Doctors in Bangkok suggested a medication that might help her live a little longer. But there wasn't any sign of full recovery. Once they got back from Bangkok, her coughing got a little better. She could speak and overall felt better. A few months later, her condition again deteriorated, her coughing got worse, and her breathing wasn't improving. She became highly dependent on the oxygen cylinder. Everybody had to go through the most challenging time in their lives with nursing and financial struggle. The medication was not readily available and was expensive. Everything was going as usual, but there was no sign of improvement. We prepared ourselves to be stronger, and we were ready to do anything so she could have a chance.

We flew to Dhaka in 2012 for my sister's wedding. But during that time, my mother-in-law's condition got worse. The doctors said she had very little time to live, but they didn't know how long. All of us had been preparing for the worst over the last few years, but we kept thinking that we had a few more months, a few more weeks. To our shock, my mother-in-law passed away in December 2012, and my wife was holding her hand during her final moments.

After about three years of suffering, my mother-in-law was free and started to rest in peace. But after going through this hard experience with someone we loved and having to leave her alone in the grave, we didn't even realize that she was not there with us anymore. It was not until a few days later that we realized that she was no more, and there was no sound of coughing, no nursing was needed, there were no late nights and no medication—nothing.

Everything suddenly stopped.

Only those who have lost their loved ones will understand the pain we went through. No one else would be able to feel the same way. We all experience and react to such events very differently. Some cry out loud. Some do not cry at all; they just freeze. My wife was sad and had time to prepare herself for it. I was surprised that she didn't cry much. We came back to Melbourne, and in the next few years, she slowly recovered from the shock and became much stronger.

But what I noticed was that my wife wasn't letting herself be happy. She was not sad all the time, but she was feeling guilty, as she hadn't played a big role in nursing her mother. She had visited her in Dhaka a few times when she was suffering and had also taken her to Bangkok. But for her, that wasn't enough. She was not overly depressed and sad about that, but she couldn't concentrate on her business and life in general. She would go on holidays but not fully enjoy them, and sometimes she would not be present with people around her and would zone out. If you lose someone close, you will be sad and depressed, and memories of your loved one will keep coming back to you. For some people, it takes years to recover from trauma.

For a long time, Mahin didn't believe that she could be or should be happy, and these beliefs became voices in her head that stopped her when she wanted to get back to her everyday life. It is impossible to forget everything and move on. She felt that she shouldn't be happy because she lost her mother and hadn't been able to nurse her enough when she was sick.

Finally, she looked back and really pondered what her mother said to her during her last days. Her mother was happy to see Mahin by her side. She was happy to have her daughter taking care of her, even if only for a few weeks. She told Mahin many other things in personal conversations that I don't know about. But going through the memories of what her mother told her had a strong impact on my wife, allowing her to see life from a different perspective.

A few years later, I one day asked my wife, "If you were sitting here sad, carrying your guilt, and your mother were looking at you right now, how would she feel? Would she be happy to see you like this? Would she expect you to sit here and be sad for the rest of your life? What would she want from you if she were alive?" She replied, "My mum would not like the way I am at the moment. She would want me to be happy and be successful in what I want to do for myself."

She said that, but she couldn't turn her life around the next day. It took her a few more months before she realized it. She started focusing on herself much more than living in the past. She remembered what her mother had told her. She nurtured her good memories with her. She started developing herself and began to engage more in the things that mattered to her in the present—things like her business, relationships, health and fitness, and philanthropy work.

Since then, she has chosen to eat much healthier and has started to do regular yoga. She had never run in her life, but she finished a half-marathon in 2019. Her relationships got better. She has become much more emotionally intelligent. She has more meaning and purpose in her life. She has built a very successful online business. And the list goes on.

I'm not telling you this to impress you, but to share what is possible. We all have hard times and challenges in our lives, and sometimes the loss is never replaceable.

You may think you should not be happy. Your life will never be the same again.

You are right.

But once you ponder upon the people you still have in your life, the blessings, and everything else, you may find a different meaning. You can always start over.

Mahin is not a different person today, but she is undoubtedly a much better version of herself.

None of these things would have been possible if she hadn't realized what she truly wanted. Instead of living in the past, she focused on what matters to her today. Yes, she still misses her mother, and yes, she still becomes sad, but she nurtures her good memories with her mother.

Remembering the last few days with her mother, Mahin realized that her mother wanted her to be happy, and Mahin has allowed herself to be.

YOU ARE AFRAID TO BE HAPPY

While growing up, I heard the phrase, "Don't be very happy, as there is always sadness after that." And for quite some time, I was afraid to be happy. It feels strange that I'm still remembering and writing about this. I believed that you should always acknowledge what you have but you should not be very happy because something bad could also happen. Showing off one's happiness was a way to undermine other people, as one does not know what's going on in their lives.

It turns out millions of other people have similar beliefs. In fact, this is known as Cherophobia. When something good happens, they become fearful and don't let themselves be happy. Professor Brené Brown said, "I'm here to tell you that joy is the most vulnerable of all human emotions. We are terrified to feel joy. We are so afraid that if we let ourselves feel joy, something will come along and rip it away from us."

If you believe things like, "I'm not that happy usually," "My happiness does not last," and "There is sadness after happiness," your brain relates your beliefs to everything you experience around you. These beliefs become constant voices in your head and prevent you from being happy.

If you have such beliefs, have you ever wondered why?

I had excellent results in the year-ten exam, but I couldn't be happy about it because some of my other friends did just okay. Also, if I had let myself be happy, then there was a chance that I would do very poorly in year twelve. I believed this because I believed after happiness, there is sadness.

Guess what? I did very badly in my year-twelve exam. How could that be? I refrained from being happy after my excellent year-ten results because I thought that would save me from doing badly in year twelve.

But it didn't.

Then I thought I may have been slightly happy and proud of my year-ten results, which I felt may have caused this. I was already feeling sad because of my year-twelve results. On top of that, I started to feel guilty about feeling happy earlier.

I thought that this was a big mistake and I shouldn't have let myself be happy, not even a little bit, because it impacted the future. Slowly, I kept telling myself, "Don't be too proud, don't be happy, just do your work and keep going." So when I got into college, I did well in my first semester. Later, when I got my first job, I pretended that this was meant to happen and was no big deal. I was afraid to be happy or do any celebrating.

But over the years, I noticed that, even if I had this solid strategy not to be happy for the good things, I still had bad things happening to me. I failed two major exams during my undergraduate studies and almost dropped out of college. I got rejected eight times before I got my first job. Two of my best friends moved to another city. In all of those bad situations, I was sad. But I couldn't remember being very happy about anything before those bad events.

It didn't make any sense, because I wasn't very happy about anything, but bad things still kept happening to me.

I felt that either I was missing something or I was a loser.

Later, I looked back on the bad events and found that a logical explanation almost always existed for each. I did excellent in my year-ten exam because I studied and worked very hard before the exam. I did poorly in my year-twelve exam and then almost dropped out of college because I did little to no studying before those exams. I got rejected eight times before my first job was because I was a fresh graduate with zero experience. Honestly, eight rejections are nothing. Two of my best friends moving to another city was a very normal phenomenon of life and had nothing to do with me being happy or my actions.

Once I realized all this, I felt nothing but shame about myself.

In all those years till my mid-twenties, I had been living in fear and missed out on being happy for all the good things in my life. As I grew older, my perception of good and bad things changed. Bad things do not happen to us because we have been happy and become targets. Instead, there is almost always a logical reason. Something like someone passing away or a natural disaster can happen as part of a natural phenomenon and is sometimes unacceptable for us. But these things always happen everywhere around us but we ignore them unless they relate to us. If they are good or bad depends on our beliefs and the meaning we give to them.

If you are happy, you don't become a target for bad things.

Your brain gives a meaning based on what you believe for any event. For example, if you believe your partner is rude, and she comes home from work and goes straight to her bedroom without saying hi to you, your brain will tell you, "See, she is rude." But if she comes straight to you and smiles, your brain will say, "She must want something; that's why she is being nice." Whatever your partner does, your brain says, "She is rude."

But on the other hand, if you believe your partner is lovely, and she comes home from work and goes straight to her bedroom without saying hi to you, your brain will tell you "There must be something wrong and you should check on her." But if she comes to you and smiles, your brain will go, "See, you have a lovely partner." Whatever your partner does, your brain says, "She is lovely."

Your brain constantly rationalizes (or justifies) your experience based on what you believe. This is just how we are all wired.

Whether good or bad, things that happen to us occur not because we feel happy but because of our own beliefs, decisions, and actions. If you believe you deserve a promotion, you will apply for it, and you will have a chance to get promoted. But if you believe you do not deserve a promotion, you will not apply for it, and you will not get it.

If someone else gets that promotion (which you didn't apply for because your brain told you that you would not get it and there was no point in applying), you might think that person was lucky. But that person might have tried harder than you to get that promotion. Many blame their luck or their boss for not getting a promotion. But it highly depends on your beliefs, decisions, and actions (including asking for that promotion).

To summarize, you get what you believe.

When it comes to being afraid to be happy, this is also driven by your beliefs. If you believe (as I used to) that happiness is followed by sadness, guess what? Your brain will always look for anything that is sad around you and will justify your belief (Like the partner example earlier).

Funnily enough, sometimes a sad thing may not even directly relate to you, but your brain will still pick up on it and try to make a connection. For example, suppose you are happy today for something good in your life, and then tomorrow you hear that one of your uncle's neighbors broke his hand. Your brain might just say, "See, I told you something bad was going to happen" (even though you don't know your uncle's neighbor).

Fear is one of the most powerful manipulators of our behavior. Fear is a response that comes from your brain when it does not know how to deal with a problem. "Happiness is followed by sadness" is a belief that creates fear of sadness or something bad happening to us. The more strongly you believe that, the more bad things your brain will pick up on, and the pattern will continue throughout your life.

Feeling joy does not add to future sadness; your fearful beliefs do.

If you believe life is full of unpleasant surprises, your brain will always pick up on what's wrong around you. You will always feel anxious to be happy, in fear of future uncertainty. But if you believe life is beautiful and you deserve to be happy, then your brain will pick up on what's right around you, and if you allow this to happen, you will live a happier life.

> "Believe you can. and you're halfway there."
> —Theodore Roosevelt

Living happily or anxiously is up to what you believe, decide, and do. Remember, Your beliefs are not set in stone. You can change them.

REFLECTION

Even though you have legitimate reasons and you believe you cannot or should not be happy, then you will not be happy.

But if you believe you can, should, and will live a happier life, then you will. Your beliefs, decisions, and actions define who you are and what you feel. Your brain's job is to abide by your beliefs and make sense of what you experience every day.

Life is and can be beautiful. If you believe it is, then it really is.

HOW MUCH MONEY DO YOU NEED

"Wealth is the ability to fully experience life."
—Henry David Thoreau

CAN YOU BUY HAPPINESS WITH MONEY?

Like many of us, I thought that money could not and should not buy happiness. I felt that my happiness should come naturally and buying something like happiness with money would be evil and unfair. I wanted to find out whether money can buy happiness, and if so, how much money I need.

As I explored the impact of money on happiness, I realized that I was right, but I was also wrong.

I was never a reckless spender, but many years ago, when I used to make $50,000 per year, I couldn't cope with my bills. I remember a few times I ended up with as little as $7 in my bank. I couldn't even pay for the petrol for my car until my next pay. But having seven dollars in my bank would force me to stay at home. I couldn't go out with friends or do the things I wanted. Often, that made me very unhappy.

When my pay increased to $65,000 per year and my money habits became better, I could pay all my bills and save a little. Over time, when I started to make $90,000, I never came across that seven-dollar situation anymore. I had more money sitting in my bank and could spend on what I needed and wished for. I became happier and realized that the $40,000 increase in my pay had enabled me to "buy more happiness" with money.

Years later, in my studies, when I came across some research by the Woodrow Wilson School of Princeton University, I was surprised to find that it related to my own experience. It turns out that an annual income of about US$75,000 is the benchmark for happiness for an average American. That essentially means that for most people the lower your income is below $75,000, the unhappier you will be.

For example, if your annual income is $40,000, every dollar more than $40,000 will exponentially increase your happiness, up to $75,000. After that, the curve plateaus because you meet all your basic needs to suit your lifestyle. And more money will not exponentially increase your happiness anymore. But the curve retains the upward trajectory as you make more money. Harvard professor Daniel Gilbert says, "Money absolutely, clearly buys happiness. There is no point in which getting richer makes you sadder on the curve. Each dollar buys more happiness, but notice another thing, somewhere on this curve, it gets harder and harder to get happiness out of money." That "somewhere" is about $75,000 in the US.

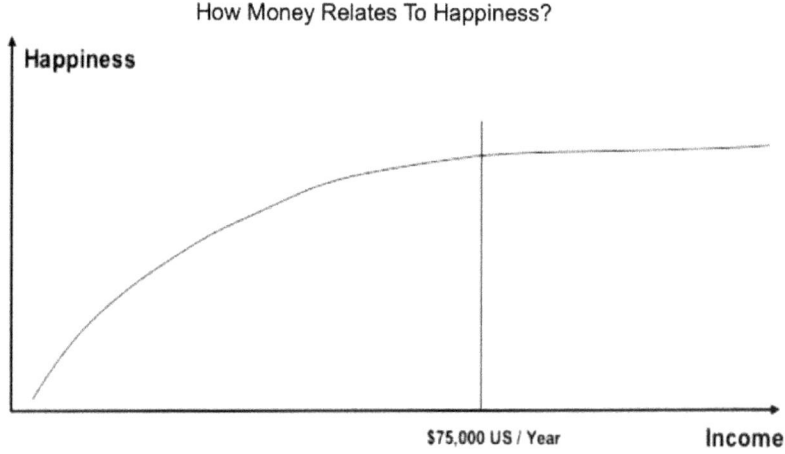

It is also essential to understand the context of this study. It was for US households. To maintain the lifestyle of an average American, $75,000 is the benchmark where one's basic needs are met. But that does not mean that number will apply to everyone in the world, and really it should not.

The definition of "basic needs" varies. If you live in a middle-class US family, your basic needs are very different than someone who lives in the Kalahari Desert. Generally, your close friends and family members with whom you spend most of your time have similar incomes and basic needs. The house you live in, the car you drive, and the holidays you go on—in other words, where and how much you spend—will be similar to what your close family and friends spend. If all your close friends make $200,000 per year and you make $50,000 per year, you will have difficulty catching up with their basic needs and will feel unhappy. Money has a strong influence on your happiness that way.

In short, there are things that you believe you absolutely need to live your life, and if you cannot afford them, that can make you unhappy.

But we all have a benchmark depending on our lifestyles. When it comes to money and happiness, once we reach that specific benchmark amount (US$75,000, or any other) and all our basic needs are met, money is no longer a strong influencer on our happiness.

The bottom line is that money absolutely exponentially buys happiness up to the point at which your basic needs are met. It gets harder and harder to extract happiness from money after that. But there is no point on the curve where your happiness declines as you make more money.

GET PAID BY DOING WHAT YOU LOVE

But where does the money come from? The money you make comes from other people. Author Robert Kiyosaki is one of the leading experts in money. He states that, legally, there are only four ways to make money: as an employee, as a self-employed entrepreneur, as a business owner, or as an investor.

That's all.

You make money by serving other people in one or more of those four ways. You can be an employee but can still have a side hustle in which you are self-employed. You can be a business owner as well as an investor. If you are an employee, your earnings are somewhat limited to your paycheck. But the money you make in the other three ways depends on whom you serve and how many times you serve them.

If you have a business that sells mangoes, and from every mango, you make one dollar, to make a million dollars, you have to sell a million mangoes. If you sell iPhones and make $100 from each, you need to sell just ten thousand iPhones.

One of my favorite teachers said the below about money.

"Money is the score of the quality and quantity of the value you bring to other people."

For example, suppose you play piano as a self-employed entrepreneur and get an invitation to play for an audience of one hundred people. In that case, you can get paid $500 for an evening. But if you play for twenty thousand people, you may get paid $3,000 for playing. You entertaining people with your piano skills is the service you provide in exchange for that money. In this case, the quantity of people you serve is the key.

But if you are an elite piano player and you play only for a high-profile audience (e.g., millionaire customers), you can get paid $10,000 for an evening but play for a very small group (e.g., fifty people). The key here is the quality.

But why is this related to happiness?

You may love teaching, trading, playing piano, or something else. But wouldn't it be nice to get paid for doing these things? If you love what you do every day, your work may not feel like work anymore. Instead, you will enjoy every bit of it and feel happy. Who wouldn't want to enjoy something and make money doing it at the same time?

If you do something with intense concentration, you can lose track of time and place. You may experience total immersion. Psychologists call this "flow." In these cases, your brain is entirely focused without distraction. You do not feel tired while or after you do it. Instead, it makes you satisfied.

Having more flow experiences not only makes you happier and more satisfied, but it also means more money in your bank.

Legendary musicians experience flow almost every day. The Greek American musician Yanni is considered a legend. He loved playing the piano. His parents encouraged him to learn at his own pace. After graduation, he dedicated one full year to music. During that time, he found himself the happiest he had ever been. And he decided that music would be his life's work. Without a doubt, he is one of the very best and most sought-after musicians in the world. He had huge success in his career.

Guess what? He is worth $50 million. How many times has he been in a flow state? And how many times has he played paid concerts? Numerous times. Every time he goes on the stage, he plays piano and goes into a flow state, which makes him happy and satisfied. But also, every time he gets paid for the service he provides to his audience, he makes more money. He says, "When it comes down to music, I have no balance. I'm 100 per cent. It is like full throttle. Five hundred miles an hour." He loves playing piano, and his music serves millions of people. And he has made millions as a result.

The author of the Harry Potter books, J. K. Rowling, once said, "And the idea of just wandering off to a café with a notebook and writing and seeing where that takes me for a while is just bliss." She also said, "I just write what I wanted to write. I write what amuses me. It's totally for myself. I have never in my wildest dreams expected this popularity." Notice she said she writes what amuses her. It keeps her happy. She may experience flow every time she writes. The books of the Harry Potter series have sold 500 million copies and counting. With every copy of her books that is sold, she makes money. She is worth $1B. Her success and the money she made are the results of what she loved doing every day, which is writing.

You can experience flow from almost any activity. But if you love doing something, it may get you to flow easily. I will explain flow in detail in part 3. Flow helps you stay happy every day. The more flow you have during the day, the happier and more satisfied you become.

In this section, I am talking about staying happy and making money while doing what you love. Many people love to play piano, as Yanni does; play football, as Lionel Messi does; and write, as Rowling does. They get into flow states, which makes them happy and satisfied. But their doings may not serve many people, and so they do not get paid for them. So they do not necessarily make a lot of money. If making money is something that you want to pursue by doing what you love, you must find ways to get paid. You can get paid in many different ways. Through a job, through a business, as a freelancer, or through whatever you do, you must get paid for the service you give to other people.

Finally, if you love doing something and want to get paid for it, you must allow yourself and your work to be seen by other people so they can love it and pay you. They are not going to pay for something that they have not seen. You may have a great talent, product, or service, but you will need to find ways to serve more people to make more money.

If Mark Zuckerberg had created Facebook but had not invited his friends at Harvard, today, there would be no Facebook. No one would know J. K. Rowling or Harry Potter if she decided to keep her manuscripts in her drawer. If Yanni played piano only in his living room, no one would know him. If no one knew or loved them, they wouldn't have gotten paid.

Remember, money is the score of the quality and quantity of the value you bring to other people.

These legends have two things in common. Firstly, they loved what they did, which made them happy and satisfied. And secondly, they let their best work (value and quality) be seen, and that served a lot of people (quantity), for which they made a lot of money (score).

BUY HAPPINESS WITH MONEY

Sometime in mid-2020, I got a message that said, "Sanju, Because of the COVID-19 lockdown, I see a lot of daily wage earners are stuck at home, and they cannot go to work. They are poor and are at high risk of losing everything." It was from my friend Anwar. He lives in Dhaka, and he is the head of IT in a big bank. But he cares for people in need—not just because of COVID-19, but always. The daily wage earners struggle because of the lack of demand for their work. During the COVID-19 crisis, this has worsened. Anwar also said, "I'm distributing small packages to two thousand families this month. My team is putting together some rice, lentils, potatoes, oil, masks, and cash for every family. I'm doing fundraising for this. Are you able to help?"

Anwar and his team's effort were not going to get those two thousand families out of poverty, but their help was a small part of the big puzzle. Of course, I said yes. I sent money to help deliver packages to at least two hundred families.

I'm not telling you this to brag or show you how kind I am. In fact, quite the opposite. I sent the money about two years ago, but still, it makes me feel good. It gave me a sense of contribution that the least I could do was send some money to help two hundred families. It also gave me a sense of achievement that I could do something that truly matters. What I essentially did was buy happiness for myself with the money I sent. Yes, it did help those families, but the money I sent also made me happy two years ago and today.

You might wonder whether I intentionally sent that money to buy happiness. You might think that one should not buy happiness with money and such acts should naturally come from one's heart. Well, some people are naturally kind, and their instinct is to act kindly in most situations. It is an automatic behavior for them, like my friend Anwar. But for many of us, these acts do not come naturally. But if you plan to do such work consciously and actually do it, you will feel happier. It is about training yourself to help others. Research suggests, that if you can consistently do such acts, they will help you stay happy.

Personally, I do not want to miss any opportunity to be kind and help someone in need, whether by contributing my time, effort, or money. To be completely honest, I do it for myself. Every time I do such acts, it makes me happy, and my consistent doing helps me stay happy. Studying the science of happiness made me realize that I have been doing such acts all my life without knowing it. But now that I know about it, I am more conscious about such opportunities and helping others in need. In the last two years, I spent money on things like dining in nice restaurants, on a jacket for myself, and on holiday trips. And I can tell you these things made me happy. But the satisfaction and sense of meaning I got by sending money to Anwar lasted much longer. That's why I'm still writing about it. I'm not writing about the jacket I bought three months ago.

Actor Denzel Washington once said, "The most selfish thing you can do in this world is, help someone else. Why is it selfish? Because of the gratification, the goodness that comes to you, the good feeling I get from helping others. Nothing is better than that, not jewelry, not big house I have, not the cars. It's the joy. That's where the joy is." When I was in my twenties, I always wondered why celebrities and rich people do philanthropy work. Why would they give away so much of their money when they can spend it on themselves? Bill Gates has given $50 billion to charitable causes. Elon Musk has promised to give at least half of his fortune to charity, and many others do the same. Now I understand why. Spending money on others gives you a better quality of happiness.

If you have a lot of money but you are not happy, you might wonder why. Social scientists and economists believe that if money does not make you happy, you are not spending it right. People do many things with money, but studies suggest buying experiences that create good memories rather than material goods make people happier. For example, going on a holiday might make you happier than buying a new fridge (as we adapt to material goods quicker than experiences). Research also suggests that we should spend money on people other than ourselves (which I have discussed in this section). Social psychologist Professor Daniel Gilbert said, "I'm telling you that if you are completely selfish human being who wants to increase his or her happiness, you might try buying coffee for the person in back of you when you go to the coffee shop next time, instead of buying a double latte for yourself."

Lastly, I want to ask you, if you were to get a million dollars, how would you spend it? Most people name one big thing, such as paying off a mortgage or buying a dream car. But according to studies, instead of spending all the money on one big thing, you might consider spending that money on hundreds of much smaller things. Professor Gilbert also said, "Happiness turns out to depend less on the size of the joy you get than on the number of joys you get per day."

Hypothetically, if I spend $10,000, I might spend $5,000 on five people I know and care about which is the most selfish thing I can do for myself with money. Maybe I spend $4,000 for a short holiday. That would be an experience to create a good memory (instead of a material good). And the remaining $1,000 I can spend on something I want to buy. That way I can spend $10,000 to buy happiness in seven different ways instead of buying an expensive $10,000 watch.

This is just one of many ideas, but the trick is to spread your money across many different things instead of just spending all on one thing.

I get it; it's your money, and you choose where to spend it. If ten years ago somebody had told me how to spend my money, I would have been annoyed. Now I feel that I'm about to do that to you. But I just wanted to give you some cues to consider when you spend money.

If you already have been doing such acts, that's great. But if you have not, you might try them out and be pleasantly surprised.

REFLECTION

Contrary to popular belief, money absolutely buys happiness.

I realized money is important to some extent (the benchmark). The science tips and tricks (some of which I have shared) on earning and spending money more efficiently help me stay happy.

Do you love your work that makes you money? Also, how would you spend money differently to stay happy? Think about it.

PART 3:
The Six Elements of Your Satisfying Life By Design

In this part, we will discuss the following:

- what a satisfying life is
- the Star of Life
- how you can find meaning
- the roles you play and the impact you make
- how to attract love
- how to get more flow in your days
- why pleasure is not the best option
- why your health trumps everything
- how your positive emotions lead to your achievements
- what not to do when you relax
- life by design
- how you design your days and live on your terms

WHAT IS A SATISFYING LIFE?

We previously discussed in part 1 what we know about a satisfying life from science, so I'm going to cut to the chase. Our physical bodies need six essentials to function correctly. They are water, vitamins, minerals, carbohydrates, proteins, and fats. We know that from the science of the body. The body must have a good balance of all six essentials to function at its best and avoid disease.

Like our bodies, we also need six essential elements for satisfying lives. They are our pleasure, engagement, love and connections, meaning, achievements, and health. We know that from the science of happiness and subjective well-being studies in the field of positive psychology.

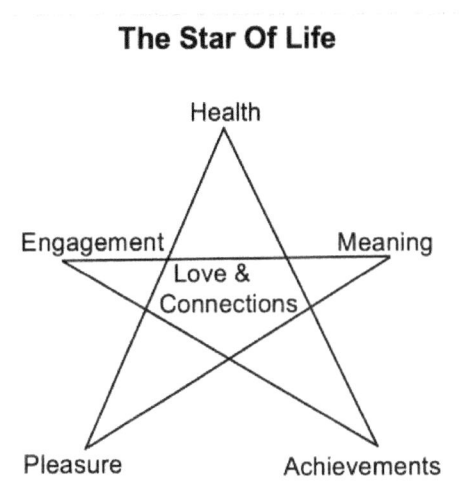

The Six Elements Of A Satisfying Life

If we have an imbalance of these six elements, we might experience unfulfillment, midlife crisis, depression, anxiety, regrets, and many other mental issues. The six elements are derived from the PERMAH model developed by Professor Martin Seligman in 2012.

The Star of Life is my representation of those six elements inspired by the PERMAH framework. In this part, I go deep into each of these individual elements. And you will identify and design them on your terms which make sense to you and your lifestyle.

MEANING

"Our prime purpose in this life is to help others."
—Dalai Lama

MEANING AND NETFLIX

A few years ago, I met Marc Randolph, the former Netflix CEO and co-founder, at a small conference in Melbourne. He told stories about how Netflix was started in 1997. He shared some of the early moments and hardships they faced. Beginning with an idea and turning it into a successful business is always challenging. At one point in their journey, they even wanted to sell Netflix to Blockbuster for $50 million, but the deal didn't work out. And Netflix eventually became one of the top companies in the world. Entrepreneurial journeys are not meant to be easy, and the journey wasn't easy for Netflix either.

But how do you navigate that uncertain road to your dream or the cause you truly believe in? Statistically, nine out of ten start-ups fail in the first two to three years. Many are passionate about their ideas and dreams but find it hard to continue their journeys and pursue their goals in the face of rejections, failures, funding issues, and the like. The few who make it are the ones who can handle the emotional ups and downs of their dreams without giving up. I always wondered how they sustain their motivation to keep going in the face of so much uncertainty and risk.

So I asked Marc, "During the course of building Netflix, when you were going through rough times, have you ever hated it? How did you keep yourself motivated during those challenging times?" He smiled and said, "During those rough times, I didn't come to work motivated every day. It was hard. Some days were not just good. But I always knew that we had a problem to solve. I knew why I started this."

At the time, Blockbuster was dominating the industry, but they were very expensive. That was the primary problem the Netflix founders wanted to solve. They believed that movie rental should not be expensive but should be more affordable and convenient for people.

That was the meaning Marc and his co-founders gave to their work every day. Their purpose was to build a system to provide better service to people and solve Blockbuster's existing expensive monopoly.

Their strong meaning kept them going.

Some time ago, I visited the Royal Melbourne Hospital and wasn't quite sure about a particular building's location. So I went to the reception area but saw a long queue. So I looked around and saw an old lady with a smaller temporary desk helping people with directions. I walked up to her, and she helped me out. But I noticed she was smiling and loving what she was doing by giving additional help to the main reception area, which was swamped. Later I found that the old lady was just volunteering and probably wasn't getting paid. But what she was doing was meaningful to her. She was helping people with directions and was loving it.

Having a solid reason to wake up every day and be motivated is a blessing. Many people from all walks of life have some kind of meaning associated with what they do every day. For example, I have a cousin who is an army brigadier general. He spent almost thirty years serving his country. For him, his meaning comes from going to work to stand up for his nation every day. It motivates him. It keeps him going. I have many doctors in my family. One of them is a sleep specialist, and he works in a hospital in Toronto. Sleep is critical for our well-being. For him, his meaning comes from helping his patients sleep better. My other brother is an eye surgeon. He gets a lot of joy and meaning every time he helps his patients see better with his surgical skills. One cousin of mine is a heart specialist. His meaning comes from helping people live with healthy hearts.

Your meaning may not pertain only to your day job. You can be a business owner or entrepreneur and believe in a certain cause or vision to make the world a better place. Your meaning is almost always the reason why your business exists in the first place. Visionary entrepreneurs believe in creating and improving things that make people's lives better. Netflix, for example, has made our lives easier by allowing us to watch movies online rather than renting DVDs from video stores.

It all comes down to why you do the things you do every day in or outside work. Whether you are an employee, a business owner, or a volunteer at a charity event, whatever your role is, it can impact you, your family, your customers, your community, your country, or even the whole world. For Marc and the Netflix team, the impact was not just limited to themselves. It was initially small, but eventually Netflix became a great success and impacted millions of customers worldwide. The strong meaning that you give to what you do every day matters.

Why is it important to you?

Many go to work every day and have no meaning associated with their roles. Some doctors just see patients because they have to pay their bills, not because they enjoy being a doctor or feel that they are making a difference. Millions do not associate any purpose or meaning to what they do every day. This is true not only in the medical profession but also in engineering, teaching, psychology, and pretty much all walks of life. If you don't have a strong meaning attached to what you do every day, your satisfaction with life can be very low. You may feel that you do not matter, that you have no purpose, and that your life is a waste. If you don't have a job, you may not feel like doing anything at all. And if you have a job, you may feel forced to go to work.

How would that make you feel every day? You can imagine.

In his TED talk, Professor Martin Seligman said that having a strong meaning and a sense of purpose is the strongest indicator of someone's life satisfaction. Meaning gives us a reason to wake up every day and make a difference in something bigger than ourselves. It makes us feel important and makes us feel that our work and contributions matter and we are needed. A person with strong meaning behaves very differently to someone without. When you talk to such a person, you will feel the difference.

When it comes to a satisfying life, your meaning is a core ingredient.

Over many years, I learned that you do not have to be a founder of a billion-dollar company or a doctor or a volunteer to have meaning in your life. You can be literally anyone and do anything that you truly care about, for which you would go the extra mile and sacrifice your own interests. Your meaning helps you be satisfied not just once but every day.

HOW DO YOU FIND MEANING?

Dear friends,

I got back from Cambodia following the Habitat for Humanity build.

We built a house for Dona, who is 65 years old. Her husband was killed by the Khmer Rouge for being educated. She struggled most of her life, selling rice cakes to provide for her family. She always dreamt that one day she would have her own home.

Thanks to Habitat for Humanity and the efforts of an amazing team of volunteers.

Dona now has a home.

> I'm blessed to have played a small part in this build. It was indeed a humbling and enjoyable experience and such a privilege to be part of the build team.
>
> Thank you very much
>
> Jack

I received the above email from Jack. He is the former chief information officer for a large corporate. He has held several top executive positions in major corporations in Australia. I was blessed to have him as my direct mentor for a few years. I learned many invaluable things from him about corporate business and the outside world, such as his travelling and philanthropy work. Obviously, he had a very busy schedule. Still, he managed to take time and travel internationally to help people in need. For example, he flew to Nepal and helped rebuild homes after the Nepal earthquake in 2015. Building a home takes physical effort and is not easy for many people. But he still does that. Also, with his wealth of experience, he travels worldwide to help companies voluntarily build their IT infrastructure.

One day I asked him, "What is in it for you?" He said, "I have been helping people out for many years. It gives me fulfilment and a sense of giving back to the community and the people in need." He works closely with Habitat for Humanity Australia. The meaning Jack gives to his philanthropy work is that his effort helps someone have a home. As he states in the email, he played a small part in the whole build. The wider team built many homes, but he played his part in the big puzzle. His role as a volunteer gives him enjoyment and purpose.

Afroz Shah is a young lawyer who lives near Versova Beach in Mumbai. He said, "I shifted to my new apartment two years back and saw plastic on the beach. It was 5.5 feet high. A man could drown in the plastic." The beach was covered with millions of kilograms of trash. Afroz told CNN, "I said I'm going to come on the field and do something. I have to protect my environment, and it requires ground action." He was shocked and couldn't believe how Versova Beach had become a dumping ground over the years. He literally started picking up plastic from it. Initially, he was alone in his personal mission, but hundreds of people from all walks of life, including little kids, middle-aged people, and Bollywood celebrities, joined him every weekend. In less than two years, it had become a movement. They cleaned the beach and made it free from trash after removing five million kilograms of plastic and filth. The hundreds of volunteers are still committed, and the work continues. Later, the United Nations called this massive cleaning operation the "World's largest beach cleaning project" and awarded Afroz with the Champion of the Earth Award. Afroz's role as a volunteer has a powerful meaning that helps keep the environment clean.

START WITH THE SMALLEST IMPACT

Jack cares for and builds homes for people in need. Afroz values a clean environment and keeps the beach clean.

See, only caring is not enough. If you care for a cause or believe in something that matters to you, it can make you motivated, but it is not enough to keep you moving every day. For example, if you believe climate change is real, you need to do something about it. You may feel bad that it is occurring, but you may not actually take any meaningful action.

True meaning comes by doing something relating to what you believe or care about. Climate change is a really big issue. You may think you are just one person and your effort will not make a big difference, so you may not actually do anything. But if you plant one tree, that is one additional tree on earth. If you believe in women's rights, help at least one woman. Many people wake up every morning and fight for it, even though one person's effort seems so small. If your effort can change one woman to have her rights restored, that is a win. It can give you a powerful meaning. You may remember former American Supreme Court justice Ruth Bader Ginsburg. She started with one court case in Boston and changed the course of women's rights and gender equality in the US.

My mentor Jack was one person who made a difference by helping build a house for Dona in Cambodia. How many of them are out there? How many plastic cans did Afroz pick up from those five million kilograms of trash? A small portion. Ginsberg, Jack, and Afroz were parts of a "big puzzle." They played their small bits by making meaningful contributions.

Caring and meaningful actions combine to give you true meaning.

What can you be a part of that you strongly care about and that makes a positive difference to someone or something?

Many people search for meaning for years and still don't find it. Your meaning, purpose, or mission, whatever you call it, is not "out there." You do not have to lead a movement or fly to another country to do that. It can literally start at home by making a positive difference to your children and family. Then you can expand your caring to your work, communities, country, and the whole world. Remember, the thousands of people who joined Afroz in his effort were from all walks of life. They also have jobs. They are not full-time volunteers either. They could have just sat at home and watched the news. But they came to pick up the plastics with Afroz, and their effort was bigger than themselves. They also connected with hundreds of people and had a sense of belonging.

Your meaning comes from what you truly care about and your consistent and meaningful actions.

American Author Neale Donald Walsch said, "There is no blackboard in the sky on which God has written your purpose, your mission in life. So your purpose is what you say it is. Your mission is the mission you give yourself." Sometimes life changes suddenly, and your priorities, focus, and meaning can change. But whatever you do, make sure you have strong meaning attached to it.

It is important that the meaning is yours and not someone else's.

People like Jack and Afroz are not full-time volunteers. But they do not just talk about caring. They take time from their busy schedules and take meaningful actions. Nobody told Jack to fly to another country to help build a house for Dona. Nobody told Afroz to start cleaning that beach. They felt a need and cared enough to make it happen.

It was them who gave meaning to their lives.

WHAT ARE YOUR EVERYDAY ROLES—WHO ARE YOU?

Ruby said to me, "The only aspiration in my life is to raise my two children properly, to give them a good education, set them up for life. I can sacrifice anything for my kids, and they mean everything to me." What role is she playing here? The role of a mother.

Can you have meaning if you play only one role? Absolutely.

Being a parent may be one of the hardest and most meaningful roles of all. Parenting is hard, but parents always feel needed and have a strong meaning for their children. Taking care of your kids is still bigger than yourself, which directly impacts your children.

You do not necessarily have to go and 'change the world' to have a strong meaning in your life. No matter what role you play or how big your impact is on the outside world, you can still have a powerful meaning if you genuinely care about and act on something. Ruby is one of the most satisfied people I personally know.

Paula is another friend. She is a mother of two, a medical doctor, a volunteer in the state nursing home, and a women's rights author. She has four roles: mother, doctor, volunteer, and author. Each role impacts people in different domains and has individual meanings and priorities. Playing the role of mother has the strongest meaning for her.

YOUR ROLES IMPACT SOMEONE OR SOMETHING

Paula plays four roles. She is a doctor, author, volunteer, and mother. She impacts her children as their mother, her patients as their doctor, older people at the nursing home as a volunteer, and women around the world as an author. Each role you play impacts someone or something. Regardless of the people you impact, the experience they get from you directly reflects how genuinely you care and how strong your meaning is. If you care and believe you are an amazing mother, your kids will experience excellent parenting. If you believe you are an excellent engineer, your company will greatly benefit from your service.

Whatever role you play, the stronger your meaning, the better the experiences people will get from you.

Your roles generally impact people in four domains:

- your family and friends
- work or communities
- state or country
- the world

The impact you make may span across multiple domains. But where and whom you impact is determined by the domain of the role.

When you wake up in the morning, you may make breakfast for your kids. If you believe and care that you are a good father, the breakfast that your kids get will be good, but if you believe that you are not a good father or that being a father is not a priority for you (e.g., over your work role or any other role), then your kids will not a get a good breakfast, as you are making the breakfast because you have to and not because you want to. That's how you impact people and things as part of your role.

Think about your work role. If you believe you are a good leader at work and that role is very meaningful to you, then your team, customers, and the company will get very good service from you. But if you believe you work because you have to pay your bills and for no other reason, then your team and customers will not have a great experience from you.

You may think, "But I'm a good father and a good leader, and both roles are equally important to me. When I'm at home, I'm a good father. When I'm at work, I'm a good leader." I agree.

Balancing multiple roles can be challenging, and we often struggle to prioritize our roles, as we have only twenty-four hours in a day. I will discuss priorities in a bit, but whatever roles you play during the day, they generally impact someone or something in four domains, as discussed earlier. Their experience is a direct result of your meaning and care about your role and how you play that role.

YOUR CIRCLES OF IMPACTS IN FOUR DOMAINS

As a parent, you may drive your kids to school, help them with homework, cook for them, hug them before bed, and do hundreds of other things. But every time you do something for your kids, it can make you feel that you are doing something that matters and that you are needed for your children. Paula's meaning as a mother is "I love my kids and would do anything for them." Paula's, circles of impacts may look like this.

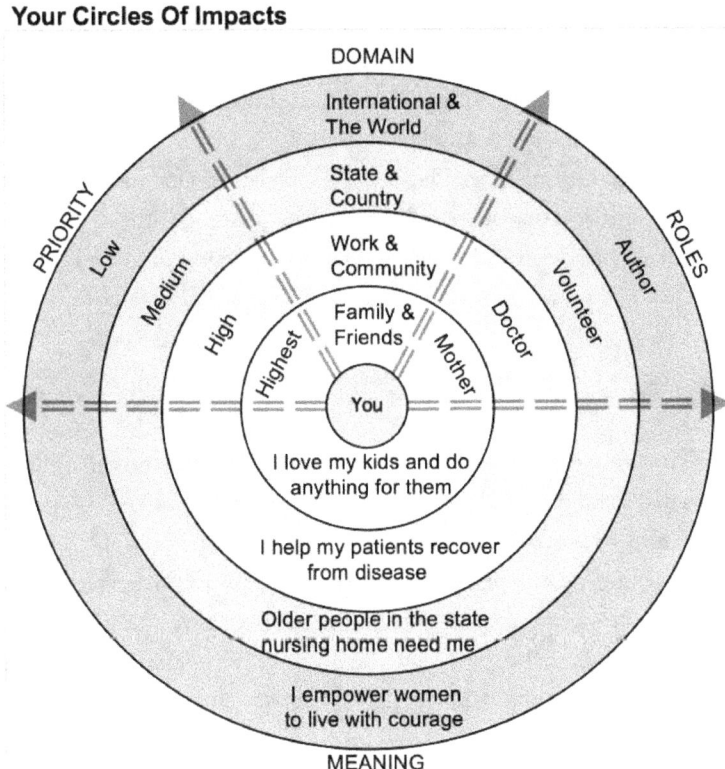

As a doctor, Paula's meaning is "I help my patients recover from disease." She feels a sense of purpose when she sends her patients home after successful treatment. As a volunteer, her meaning is "Older people in the state nursing home need me." She feels important and needed when she is there. As an author, her meaning is "I empower women to live with courage." She feels that she makes a difference when she receives a thank-you email from a girl.

You feel strong meaning when you believe, care, and do enough for someone or something. You have an emotional connection to the role, and you know exactly why you play that role.

YOUR PRIORITIES—HOW IMPORTANT ARE YOUR ROLES?

We all have only twenty-four hours a day, and our focus is limited. If you have multiple roles to play during the day, and all are important and meaningful to you, sometimes it can be overwhelming, and that's when priorities come in. Even though all or most of your roles may seem essential, deep down, you know which roles are most important. For example, volunteering at the nursing home may get a lower priority when your kid is sick and she needs you. Or, if one of your team members (that you care about) needs you this afternoon for something urgent, you may not spend the time writing about climate change.

In the circles of impacts, the roles in the family and friends domains usually have the highest priority for most people. But for many, that's not the case. It's not about what is right or wrong but is rather about what roles are important and meaningful to you at that time. The roles and their priorities can and will change over time.

IF YOU HAVE LOST YOUR MEANING

What if your role is not meaningful to you anymore? It is possible that over time something that you used to believe and care deeply about has lost its spark and does not mean much to you today.

A friend of mine, Peter, spent over five years as a project manager in a major telco in Australia. Initially, he was very excited, and his role was very meaningful to him. He was making good money. But over time, he got used to it and wasn't feeling fulfilled anymore. He lost his meaning. So he resigned and started his construction business as a developer. He'd always had an interest in the real estate industry, but after several years he got bored again. He then started to study financial education in investing and wealth creation. And now he has built his life around that philosophy. He also coaches people to be financially free using the proper investment strategies in real estate, gold, and cryptocurrencies. I have never seen him happier and more fulfilled before.

But how do you know what role will fulfil you or give you more meaning?

Honestly, you might have to try a few roles. Notice that Peter went from being a project manager to construction. Still, he was not fulfilled. He took another detour and became a financial wealth management coach to help people achieve financial freedom. He now has a stronger sense of meaning, which makes a difference in other people's lives. As you try a few roles, some will fulfil you, but some will not. If your current role has lost meaning, you might want to try something new that you care about now.

If you are a parent and your children are grown up and independent, they might not need you as much as they used to. You will always love your children, but your sense of being needed may fade away over time. Many parents start something new when their children grow up. Often, they volunteer or do something else to get meaning back into their lives.

I used to do a lot of photography. As a photographer, my meaning was "I capture beautiful moments of people around me." I still do some photography these days, but my meaning is not strong anymore. So I replaced that with my author role. I write to help people live happier and more satisfying lives. This is very meaningful for me. I used to spend many hours editing photos; now I use the same time to write.

Not only Peter and I have replaced old roles. Think about people like Arnold Schwarzenegger; he started as a bodybuilder, became a Hollywood star, and later became a politician. Or consider Bill Gates, who started Microsoft at a young age, moved to philanthropy work, and is now working on climate change. All of their roles had different meanings in different phases of their lives. Some roles may not need replacing but may rather need reprioritizing based on what matters to you the most today.

If you believe that some of your roles are meaningless to you today, you might want to honestly ask yourself whether the roles are still making you fulfilled. If not, make necessary changes so they become meaningful again, or replace them with new roles you care about now.

Whether the role you wish to change is in your relationships, work, or anywhere else, starting a new chapter in life is very common. Sometimes it is needed to have a new meaning.

BOTTOM LINE

You may have been very successful with a lot of money, status, and financial wealth. But that does not automatically mean you have also been fulfilled. Peter was making good money and held several highly desired corporate positions, but still he was not fulfilled. Meaning relates to something or someone you believe in, love, and care for, and those feelings do not come from your head but are from your heart.

You don't get any money or success by taking care of your children, but still you may play the parent role because they relate to your heart.

Whether your role is that of a mother, a volunteer, an entrepreneur, or anything else, the key is to make sure your meanings are not weak. They must be very strong and aligned with what you truly believe and care about in your heart.

Do you know which roles are meaningful to you and which are not?

Regardless of whom you impact, you will know your meaning is powerful when you feel automatically drawn to them. You are proactively going that extra mile for them, which they didn't even ask for.

REFLECTION

The best thing about meaning is that it happens in you. If you care about someone or something, you give a strong meaning and take action.

It is very simple and is up to you.

Meaning is often referred to as "contribution," "purpose," "mission," or even "legacy." These things give us fulfilment or satisfaction for what we do every day.

But the most important thing is to have a meaning that resonates with you.

If you already have strong meanings attached to your roles, that's awesome. But if you don't or have lost your previous meanings, you may brainstorm with the following questions. Be completely honest with your answers.

- What have you always believed in and cared about but took little or no action for it? (e.g., your family and friends needing more of you)
- What is the least you promise to do about it? (Only thinking about it will not help. Remember, actions create momentum, and your meaning gets stronger through them).
- What do you want to be known for? If your name is John, in two hundred words, describe who John is. (Use a separate page.)
- Now, below, list your top five roles and whom you impact (domains). Write your priorities (highest, high, medium, low) and meaning (how your role helps others live better lives) for each role.
- Do you play any role that has lost meaning and is unfulfilling for you?

(Refer to the Circles of Impacts in the previous section for examples).

My Roles	Domains	My Meanings	Priorities	Lost Meaning?
Husband	Family & Friends	My wife is my better half	Highest	No
Author	Work & Communities	I write to help people live a happier life	High	No
Photographer	Work & Communities	I capture beautiful moments of people around me	Low	Yes, review and replace this role
Your Roles	Domains	Your Meanings	Priorities	Lost Meaning?

List your *strongly meaningful* roles that you absolutely *love and care*

Remember, the more meaningful roles you have, the more satisfied you become.

ENGAGEMENT (FLOW)

"Excellence is doing ordinary things extraordinarily well."
—John W. Gardner

DO YOU LOSE TRACK OF TIME?

I hated mathematics. When I was in high school, I struggled with it. I used to scratch my head and say, "Why do I have to do this?"

But my dad loved it. He was obsessed with mathematics.

When I was little and didn't want to do maths, my grandmother used to tell me stories about my dad to inspire me. When he was about six years old, he used to solve complex maths problems for hours. He did not eat, forgot to take a bath, and did not talk to anyone, but he kept solving maths problems. Time stopped for him.

When he was in seventh grade, he solved mathematics problems from eighth grade. Whenever he solved one problem, he looked for something more challenging. The harder the problem was, the more he loved it. My grandmother told me that one day my dad was working on a math problem while sitting on the bed. He was looking at the paper and was so much into it with intense concentration that he fell off the bed without realizing it. When I was little, I heard this story many times, and I used to laugh.

But why did my dad fall off the bed?

He did so because he was in a state of mind where he became unaware of his surroundings. He had the skills to solve challenging problems. He had total immersion and satisfaction. Scientists call this state of mind "engagement" or "flow."

Years later, I realized that my dad was in "flow."

My grandmother tried to inspire me by telling those stories, but she actually scared me. I never imagined myself solving maths problems for hours, and I hated mathematics even more after hearing the stories.

My dad found what he loved to do at a very young age. He had a very successful and rewarding career as an engineer. In all different phases of his career, he could get into that flow state whenever he wanted. He loved his work so much that he didn't even know he was in flow. Sometimes, he seemed to be a workaholic to other people, but it was total bliss for him. He didn't work because he had to, but because he loved to. He was blessed enough to work on his "thing" throughout his career.

Why am I telling his story? Because he has been a very passionate and happy person with his work all his life.

Psychologist Mihaly Csikszentmihalyi recognized this particular state of mind, did research, and named it "flow." When you experience flow, you will have a meaningful time. You will surrender yourself to the experience with total immersion. You will feel that it was challenging but satisfying. You might feel a sense of great control and not feel tired after it. But primarily, two things must be present to experience flow. Firstly, you will need the skills required to do the activity. Secondly, you will also need to be challenged to the level you are comfortable with.

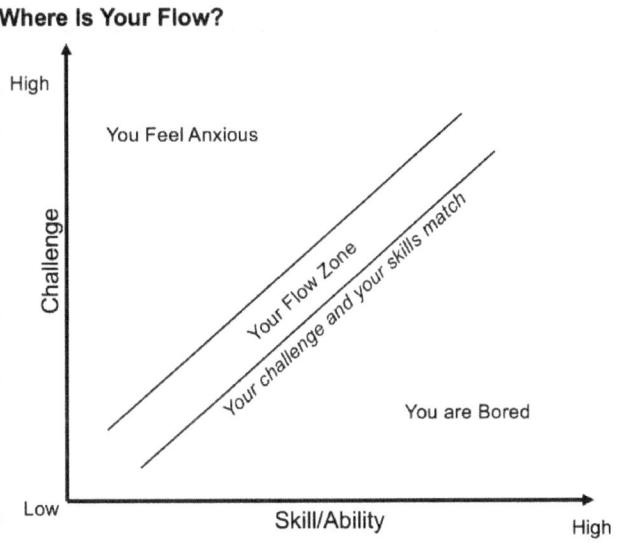

For example, if you love running and can comfortably run 9 kilometers in an hour. But if you challenge yourself to run 9.5 kilometers, which is slightly higher than your comfort level, then you may experience flow. But a challenge of eleven kilometers will be too high, and you may feel anxiety. Or a challenge of six kilometers could be too low, and you may feel bored. Flow happens in the sweet spot between anxiety and boredom, where your current skill level meets your preferred and comfortable challenge. Not too high or too low.

What do you love doing that causes you to lose track of time, love a challenge, and feel satisfied and not tired?

I asked this question to a group of people. Someone said, "I love being a mom." So she has the necessary skills of a mother and a challenge to take care of two kids.

Now, if she can handle two kids with her skills, she may experience flow. But if she has to handle five kids, she might feel overwhelmed and anxious. Or handling just one kid might be too easy for her, and she might get bored. People also said, "I love to read; no matter what, I always manage to escape to another world," "I love to spend time with my husband and kids," and "I do cross-stitch and can do it for a long time without stopping." It is possible to experience flow in most things we do in everyday life. But when we do the things we love with full attention and focus, that increases the chance of experiencing flow.

But why is flow essential to us?

After studying numerous data points, scientists, including Professor Martin Seligman (one of the founders of positive psychology), found that flow is a powerful indicator of a satisfying life. Every time you get into the state of flow, you feel total immersion and satisfaction.

Imagine being able to experience this bliss every day for the rest of your life.

How amazing and satisfying would that be?

BUT WHICH ONE IS FOR YOU?

A long time ago, I loved and used to do a lot of photography. I often went out on my own, took shots randomly, and forgot about other people. Once we went to a lovely place called the Grampians with some friends. That area has breathtaking views of the mountains in the clouds, amazing little falls, and many other things. I was taking photos, and I lost track of where everybody was. I found myself in a forest, and no one was around. Half an hour later, I found them waiting for me in the car. I felt embarrassed, and I apologized to everyone. But I know I loved the time I spent taking photos in the forest. I was in the flow.

You may have already experienced flow knowingly or unknowingly. But only you feel that mental state of total immersion, and you do not want to come out of it, because it makes you feel so immersed in the activity that you cannot feel anything. You will find that your skill and challenge meet in the sweet spot. It is that state where some people feel in the zone, forget everything around them, and lose track of time.

Maybe you spend hours talking to your best friend, spending time with your kids, painting, singing, writing, exercising, playing video games, or doing something else. The activities that can give you flow are endless.

Ask yourself, what do you love doing so much that you don't want to come out of it? The time spent wasn't enough for you on that.

You can observe your behavior. Identify what you do, where you have intense focus and a challenge, and where you feel entirely in control and "in the zone." It comes easily for you. You feel totally absorbed and lose track of time and place. Once you finish the activity, you may say, "That was awesome," "I feel great," "I feel satisfied," "I loved it," etc. Flow is so internal that many people find no words to describe it.

But can you intentionally get into flow? Yes, if you have the skills and a comfortable challenge.

According to Professor Sonja Lyubomirsky, one of the secrets to getting into flow is to be focused and pay full attention to the activity. If you love what you are doing, you will find it easier to keep your focus for the whole duration of the task.

HOW CAN YOU GET MORE FLOW?

You may have identified the activities you love to get into flow. Once you know, it becomes easier for you to escape to that world whenever you want, because the flow is often a solo activity. Things like reading, running, singing, or playing musical instruments need only you. No other person is required. If you intentionally plan to do those things that get you into flow during your day, that block of time becomes bliss for you. I personally block my time for writing, exercising, talking to my wife (yes, even with my family members, that way, I am 100 per cent present with full attention to make the best of it), and running.

Sometimes you may find that you have only one or two things, or even no activity, that gets you into flow. You may feel that flow is not for you. But honestly, everyone has skill in something. It is a matter of being more aware, paying attention, and focusing. Running was not my thing in life until 2016. I opened myself to it and tried a few times. Slowly, over time, I realized that I experienced flow from it. I have now made it a regular activity that gives me flow. Opening yourself to new activities widens the possibilities to experience more flow. If you try a new thing that does not give you flow, try something else. Also, spend more time on your existing flow activities. For example, you may love and get flow from yoga, spending time with kids, and reading. Perhaps your total "flow time" is 2.5 hours a day. If you want more flow, you may start working for two hours on a presentation of your passion project that may give you flow. You can also spend more time with your kids. And you can have more flow time of five hours in your day, and it may look like this:

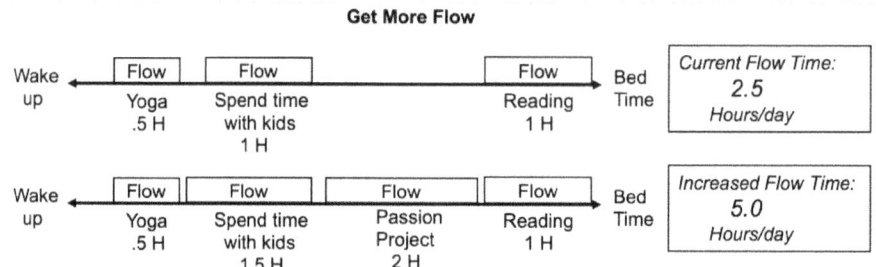

Think about how you can increase the number of flow experiences in your day. Most of us engage in conversations with others every day. Even though we do not necessarily sync with everybody, we can strive to get flow from the people we love and connect with (a best friend or family member). When I'm talking to someone, I try to listen and understand her. I notice her facial expression, ask interactive questions, and empathize. These things get me not only flow but also quality conversation.

Remember, the more flow you have, the more satisfied you become. It is a feeling that happens in your core. Only you can feel it.

HE IS NOT UNSOCIAL; HE IS IN FLOW

I was in Los Angeles, and some friends invited me to have authentic American (or Mexican) tacos. So we drove to a popular taco place near downtown LA. I sat next to a seventeen-year-old, Jay. I noticed he was playing an animation game on his phone. He noticed that I saw, and he said, "I want to show you something." I said, "sure."

He showed me the game and a few tips and tricks, then he asked me, "What do you think?" I said, "This has good graphics, and it seems to be nicely designed. Did you download it from the App Store?"

He replied, "No, I built it."

Even though I do not play such games, having a computer science background, I understand the amount of effort it takes to build such games. I automatically said, "Wow! Are you serious? You built it?"

Then he said, "Yep, it took me a year and a half."

I was shocked to hear this from a seventeen-year-old who had just finished high school. He had built that game with such great animation and graphics. I could see his expression change. He became inspired to tell me all the technical details over the next twenty minutes. I didn't understand probably half of what he said because of my lack of knowledge in physics and technology. Also, you may remember I was having awesome tacos.

To me, the seventeen-year-old has great potential. If he can nurture his interest in this area, he can be lastingly happy. Because he loves coding, it makes him excited and satisfied. He is already living a life where building games is so engaging for him that he frequently experiences flow. Remember, flow is one of the strongest indicators of a satisfying life.

When I was having this conversation with this kid, his parents were listening. I turned to them and said, "Your son is a genius. He has great potential." His mother said, "Yes, he is good, but he does not want to study hard. He is always busy with computer and phone." I knew where the conversation was going. Most parents want their children to go to school, get good grades, get a good job, and be set for life. But through no fault of their own, they fail to realize that the world has changed. Unlike old times, good grades no longer guarantee a good and stable job. But I prevented myself from getting started on this topic; I shrugged and went back into the conversation with the kid.

Achievements happen automatically from enjoyment. This kid is on a journey of enjoyment. He writes code every day, and he enters the state of flow, which is extremely rewarding for him. As a result of his daily enjoyment, he built that game, which is his achievement. If you work on something that causes you to experience flow every day, your chance to achieve a goal using that activity is very high. For example, if you get flow from writing and write one page daily, that will give you enjoyment every day. Remember to slowly increase your challenge once you get comfortable with the pace (e.g., start with 1 page a day and then increase to 1.3 pages, 1.4 pages, and so on). Three hundred days later, you can have finished a three-hundred-page book, which is your achievement (if that is a meaningful target for you).

Going back to the LA story, the kid's parents invited us for dinner the next day. During our time at their place, Jay came and said hi and went back to that game on his computer. He had his headphones on the whole time. He was there physically, but his mind was inside the game, inside a different world. He loved what he was doing. He was in flow, forgot about his surroundings, didn't attend dinner, and forgot about everything and everyone else.

Did he look unsocial? Totally. Did he care? I do not think so.

Even though he looked unsocial to most people, that was not his fault. He couldn't help it. The feeling he gets from flow outweighs the feeling he gets by talking to people or socializing. Such people choose to do what they love instead of doing something with little or no enjoyment.

Flow is addictive. Whether it is for yourself, your partner, or any other family member, people can be obsessed with it. Most people do not understand what flow is. So in a social situation, if someone is having a flow experience (e.g., even chatting to another person), it can seem rude to other people. It may seem that the person with the flow is ignoring everyone else or is lacking social skills. It is totally possible that others can get annoyed with the person having the flow.

Similarly, if you are aware of your flow activities, your flow can upset people around you. Remember, I made my friends annoyed with my flow experience with photography. When you are in flow, it might annoy others, and they might unintentionally think that you are ignoring them, but you are the one having the best time.

Just be aware that your flow can annoy others (if they do not know about it), and their flow can annoy you (if you do not notice it).

The kid I'm talking about unknowingly has this amazing experience of flow every day. He is living every bit of it. Only he knows how he feels. It is hard for other people around him to realize that. His happiness and satisfaction come from his flow. This kid may look unsocial or as if he does not fit in society, but he loves his thing. In fact, He may well be happier than most people around him.

The other day, when we were having tacos, and he was talking about his work with so much excitement, you should have seen his face.

REFLECTION

Professor Mihaly Csikszentmihalyi said, "The best moments of our lives are not the passive, receptive, relaxing times. The best moments usually occur if a person's body or mind is stretched to its limits in a voluntary effort to accomplish something difficult and worthwhile." He died in 2021 at the age of eighty-seven. Even though I didn't know him personally, I thank him for his discovery and his research on flow. I know that when I'm feeling low, my flow is my escape that I use to regain energy.

What activities give you flow? And how can you get more flow?

ENGAGEMENT (FLOW)

My Flow Activities	Average Time Spent	Current Frequency	My Satisfaction	How Can I Get More?
Writing	2 Hours	Every Day	High	Write 3 Hours A day
Talking To My Best Friend	1 Hour	2 Days / Week	High	Talk 3 Days A Week
Reading	1 Hour	Every Day	Medium	Keeping The Same

Your Flow Activities	Average Time Spent	Current Frequency	Your Satisfaction	How Can You Get More?

Activities you *enjoy and lose track of time*, you have the skills and a challenge and you feel satisfied after doing.

LOVE AND CONNECTIONS

"The best thing to hold onto in life is each other."
—Audrey Hepburn

LOVE IS THE CORE ELEMENT

Sometimes I think that if I were the only person on earth and had all the power, money, and possessions, and I could do and have anything. How would my day look like? How would I feel every day? I'm sure, after a few days, I would go crazy, and my life would be miserable.

Why?

As humans, we crave love and connections with people; it is hard-wired in our DNA. Think about what COVID-19 lockdowns did to our mental health. Even the most ruthless person craves love. He or she might not show it, but it certainly is the case.

But what do love and connections have to do with happiness?

In 1938, social scientists at Harvard University became curious about what makes people happy. They started a study with 724 men from Boston, and then they followed these men over their lifetimes. They not only measured their happiness but also took blood samples and used MRI and performed tests. The scientists also interviewed their families, friends, neighbors, and people they interacted with. They observed, measured, and analyzed their life experiences and many other things.

Over seventy-seven years later, the study continues to unfold the secrets of happiness. This is the longest study ever on human happiness. Some participants have passed away. Some are still living. As of 2015, about sixty of the participants were still living and participating in their nineties.

So what have the scientists found?

Guess what? It is not the big houses, expensive cars, or the money in the bank accounts that results in happiness. It is not even success or pleasure. In their analysis, scientists have confirmed that one thing came up over and over again,

it is the quality of their close relationships with others.

Happiness comes down to the loving, deep, and meaningful connections we make with others in our lifetimes. It is not the quantity but the quality of those connections.

That means having three very close and meaningful friends is much better than having thirty average friends.

Professor George Vaillant, who led that study for more than forty years, in his book Triumphs of Experience: The Men of the Harvard Grant Study, said, "The seventy-five years and twenty million dollars expended on the grant study, points to a five-word straightforward conclusion, Happiness is love, Full stop."

Philosophers, storytellers, filmmakers, writers, and many others have talked about love for hundreds of years. To have relationships of great quality, love is the most important element from many dimensions.

A recent study conducted in Australia suggests that one in five Australians rarely or never has someone to talk to. Loneliness is at "epidemic" levels in the US. More than three in five Americans are lonely. Even if you have family and friends, you may still feel that your connections with them are not meaningful, or you may feel isolated. These numbers are alarming and resonate with the world happiness report in 2019, which also stated that global happiness levels have declined, as we discussed previously.

The importance of your deep, meaningful, and quality relations with others is paramount. The loving relationships I am talking about do not relate only to having a romantic partner. They can be with your close family members or friends, and often work colleagues can become best friends.

Do you surround yourself with people who love and care for you?

If you do, that is the best thing for a happy and satisfying life. But if you don't, being aware is the first step. Honestly, you don't even need science to tell you that your loved ones come before anything else. But sometimes, in the pursuit of other things, we tend to take our loved ones for granted and don't give them the love and attention they deserve.

Think about just one of your favorite memories.

Are you alone?

BUT WHERE DOES LOVE COME FROM?

You might be thinking, "Okay, if love is so important for our happiness, where can we get it from? And how can we get more of it?"

You probably already know where you can get it from. Surely we do not get meaningful love and connection from our houses, bank statements, jewelry, expensive cars, or other material possessions. We feel happy for the time being, and slowly the happiness fades away with hedonic adaptation, because most material wealth is static and does not change over time. Honestly, you can love these things, but they cannot love you back. (This is only my theory.)

When people are on their deathbeds, they do not look at their lives and search for how big their houses are, how high their bank balances are, or how much other material wealth they have. They look for love and connections. We talked about these earlier. They look for people who loved them, how they contributed to making a difference, whether they were true to themselves and whether they let themselves be happy.

Your love comes from yourself and other people you interact with.

According to British anthropologist Robin Dunbar, an average person knows about 150 casual friends.

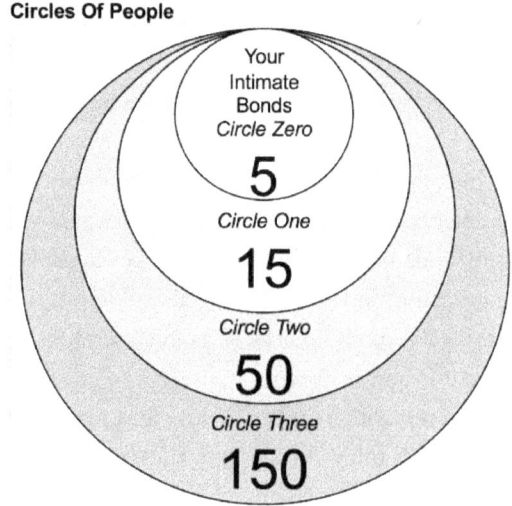

There are about 50 friends among those 150, 15 of which are likely to be close friends. Dunbar says human brains have a limit on the number of deep, meaningful relationships a person can keep track of. And that number is five. That means we can have intimate bonds with only about five people.

Your innermost circle is circle zero (5), where you have the people you love, count on, and care for the most and have intimate bonds with. Circle one (15) is for close family and friends, and circle two (50) is for friends. Finally, the people in circle three (150) are mostly casual friends, and you love, care about, and count on them the least.

Now, think about the roles you play that involve other people.

We get love by playing those roles. Whether you are a mother, father, husband, wife, friend, colleague, or leader, whatever role you play, you may interact with others. If you are a parent, you interact with your children and get love from them. If you are a business owner, you can still get love from people on your team. Many great leaders are not only respected but also loved by the people in their organizations. If you are a brother or sister, you can get love from your siblings. If you are in a romantic relationship, you can get love from your partner.

But there is a caveat, every role you play has the potential to get love from others.

Guess what? Not every parent is loved by his or her children; not every leader is loved by her people; not every person is loved by her partner. Your close people in your life have a strong influence on your happiness. They can love you but can also give you pain and worries. And people in your circles, including circle zero, can change over time. But those five people in your circle zero matter to you the most.

The people you rely on for love may not always love you back, for many different reasons; honestly, you may not know all the reasons. People (including your family members) are different and go through ups and downs. Your experience with them depends on timing. If they are going through wins and triumphs, your experience with them will be good, but you might have the opposite experience if they are going through stress and trauma.

Often we believe we know everything about our loved ones just because they are our family and we have seen them in diapers. But every day, they evolve into different people through their own life experiences. For example, many parents struggle and are fearful when their children go through their teenage years. This is true not only for one's children but also for partners, parents, siblings, and close friends in one's circle zero. Dealing with them with kindness and empathy will go a long way.

The bottom line is that the intimate bonds you create or have with your closest people on earth have the highest influence on your happiness and satisfaction. Your deep, meaningful, and loving connections with them are what you never want to take for granted; nurture them every day with gratitude.

LOVE FROM PEOPLE

Rohan is one of my friends, and he loves birds. I do not know anything about birds, but he comes and talks about his bird all the time, saying things like how adorable, cheerful, and excited she is, what she does, when she talks, the way she sings, and many other things; he loves that bird so much. He named her "Lemon." He came to our house one day and said, "Lemon is very happy by herself, but I thought she would be happier if she had a companion bird. She would be able to play with the other bird and have a great time. So we got another bird and named him Mango."

A few weeks later, I called him and asked, "What's happening with your birds?" He said, "The birds didn't get along with each other. Lemon is fine, as usual, but Mango shows a lot of attitude. It doesn't talk, doesn't sing, and doesn't do the things that Lemon does. Mango doesn't even talk to me either. He just sits in the cage, sometimes looking up and down, eating and sleeping—nothing much." After a few minutes, we hung up.

A few weeks later, Rohan came to our house and said, "I have taken Mango out of the cage and returned him." I asked, "Why? What else happened?" He said, "Mango was not just grumpy all the time. He was making Lemon uncomfortable in the cage. Lemon's behavior changed. She wasn't as happy as she used to be. Introducing Mango to Lemon in the cage was a big mistake. Lemon used to sing, but she stopped singing, she used to fly to me; now she doesn't do that often, which I do not like. I love Lemon, but for Mango, this wasn't working out."

Lemon is a happy bird, but Mango was grumpy most of the time. Rohan loved Lemon much more than Mango, which was natural. If I had to choose one of the two birds, I would surely choose Lemon, as she is a happy bird.

Who is going to look after a grumpy and angry bird every day?

It's very simple. Generally, love is always a two-way road. One-sided love does not sustain for most relationships.

Firstly, think about getting love from other people. If you are happy, you are more lovable than others. If you are lovable, naturally, people will love you more. If you receive more love, you become happier, and the cycle continues. Love feeds your happiness, and your happiness attracts more love.

But what if you are unhappy?

Honestly, even with valid reasons, if you are unhappy most of the time, it will be hard to get love from other people even though you may receive sympathy. This love is not just romantic love but includes the love from your wider family, friends, and others. If you believe you're not lovable or nobody loves or cares about you, remember that you are not alone and that, one way or the other, this is probably one of the most common beliefs many of us have. But beliefs like these can freeze you.

I cannot stress enough that you must pay careful attention to what you believe about yourself. Remember, your brain rationalizes all the time based on what you believe (as discussed earlier).

Simply put, your beliefs become your experience.

For example, if you believe you're worthy of love, even if a stranger smiles at you just for courtesy, your brain will go, "See, I told you; you totally deserved that smile. And if she doesn't smile at you, your brain will say, "She doesn't know you; why would she smile at you?" Then you feel good in both situations.

But if you believe that you're not worthy of love, guess what? If the stranger doesn't smile at you, your brain says, "See, I told you; you're not good enough." But if she smiles at you, your brain will go, "She just smiled at you for courtesy; it didn't mean anything at all." You will feel bad in both situations.

Your brain will try to make your belief "true" for you either way. Your belief becomes your experience. (It took me years to realize this about our brains) Generally, we get what we believe.

Professor Brené Brown studied thousands of people over more than twenty years. In her TED talk, she said, "People who believed they were worthy of love and belonging were the ones who had love and belonging, compared to others who thought they were not."

I'm going to reiterate. If you believe you are worthy of love, you will receive it.

Loving others also means loving the people around you in addition to your romantic partner. We have respect, honesty, empathy, kindness, forgiveness, and many other noble qualities as human beings. If you can use these qualities in the form of love for people around you, that will surely make a difference. For example, if you open the door for your wife, send a bunch of flowers to your mother without any occasion, forgive and call that friend who wronged you, or offer a ride to a friend in stress, these are very simple acts but can make someone's day.

If you give love in these forms to others, they will likely love you back.

Wouldn't you naturally love someone who loves and cares for you more than someone who doesn't? It's a no-brainer.

You do not need to be happy and high all the time with others. Your daily attitude towards others determines whether you love and care about them. It does not necessarily mean you have to go and hug everybody on the street. Or you have to dedicate your whole life to the service of others with love. The habit of treating people with love, respect, and care goes a long way. If someone smiles at you, smile back. If somebody is upset, go and cheer him up. If somebody needs a hand, go help him or her out. If somebody is ill, go visit and spend time with the person. Without giving you a sermon, I just want to make a point that you can give love in many forms to the people around you. These are a few of many ways that are very simple and easy.

You do not need to be Mother Teresa. You can just be you, who has these qualities. It is just a matter of you realizing and doing them.

One thing you can be sure of is that some people will not love you back the way you expect. Once you have accepted that, you free yourself from expectations from others.

If you show love and care to ten people, some might not love you back. They might not even say thank you to you.

But that's okay. That's just the way it is. Everybody's expression and timing about love is different. Just because some people didn't love you back, you should not stop loving the others. Most people are nice, most people are kind, and most people need love and will receive love from you. Once you start genuinely loving the people around you, you will likely receive more love from them, but you must be careful about not taking the love from others for granted.

To keep your happiness alive, love is the core element, and to keep your love alive, you must continue to love others.

> "The love we give away is the only love we keep."
> —Elbert Hubbard

How can you make more loving memories with your loved ones?

Remember, the more love you give, the more love you get, and the more love you get, the happier and more satisfied you become.

UNDERSTAND THE 5:1 RATIO WITH PEOPLE

Professor John Gottman is a world-leading psychologist at the University of Washington and probably one of the best experts on marital stability. You may have heard about his famous ability to predict whether a couple will get a divorce, which has about a 90 per cent accuracy rate. One of the primary indicators is whether the couple followed the 5:1 ratio.

The way they have explained this is as follows: "The difference between happy and unhappy couples is the balance between positive and negative interactions during conflict. There is a very specific ratio that makes love last. That magic ratio is 5 to 1. This means that for every negative reaction during conflict, a stable and happy marriage has five or more positive interactions."

The positive or negative interactions are not meant to be very big or special. For example, if you raise your voice once during a conflict with your partner, that can be treated as a negative reaction. You will need to do five positive interactions to defuse it. These positive interactions include simple things like listening to understand your partner, speaking in a warm and low voice, holding her hand, giving her a glass of water or tissue, and saying something funny.

You might think, "How can you do that when you are in a conflict?" Well, you don't have to do all five of these at the same time or one after another. Use your judgement to space them out (e.g., over a few hours) and do what makes sense to you. By now you likely realize that the people you love and care about the most have the highest influence on your happiness. Deep down, you know that the person you are in conflict with may be in your circle zero (intimate bond circle) and matter the most. Doing five positive interactions for each negative one is a skill you can build over time with awareness and actions.

The best thing about this ratio is that it was originally intended for couples to strengthen their marriages. But it turned out that this ratio can be used in any of your relationships, including your work and business relationships, to make meaningful connections. If you are a leader, don't you think your team members will perform better and create a more meaningful connection with you if you provide five warm and helpful interactions for each bit of constructive feedback you give them? (I don't know if you got the joke, but that means one negative reaction.)

But yes, whether it is with your partner, parent, children, friends, or colleagues, conflicts will surely happen. Having a negative reaction during conflict is normal for most people, but that's why building that deep and meaningful connection takes conscious effort and is one of the simplest things you can do to be intentional about the 5:1 ratio.

Tell your loved ones, friends, and work colleagues about this ratio. It's not only you who has to do five positive things for each negative one; they will also have to do the same with you.

How nice would that be?

LOVE FROM YOURSELF

I had a friend in college, Mohit. Mohit was a very talented computer programmer. His passion was to spend most of his time coding. Whenever I went to his place, I found him working on something remarkable. He was a few years older than I and had long hair like musicians. He was calm, spoke in a soft voice, was very humble, and was very kind.

One day, I went to his house and asked what he was doing. He showed me some of his work. It was amazing. I asked him, "How was your week?" He smiled and said, "Yesterday was my birthday." He kept his smile on his face but didn't say anything else. I was like, "Really? Wow, sorry, happy birthday." He said, "Thank you." I expected him to continue talking, but he didn't. He was still smiling. I became a little impatient and asked, "And then?" He shrugged and said, "Nothing. I kept working for a few hours and got these done," and he pointed to the work he had shown me before.

I asked, "That's it? You didn't have a party?" He smiled again and said, "Nope." He didn't seem upset or sad at all for not having a party on his birthday. But I insisted on doing something with our other friends on his birthday. He became a little shy and said, "Don't worry about it. I'm good; I'm really good. I enjoyed my time yesterday with myself." I asked, "What did you do? Do not say you worked on your computer all day on your birthday." He replied, "That! I surely did. I love it. But I also did another thing." He paused, then stood up from his chair. He went to his bookshelf and picked up one of the books, gave it to me, and said, "Open it and read the first page." So I opened the book cover, and on the first page, I saw something handwritten. I read,

> Hi Mohit.
>
> Today is your birthday.
>
> I want to tell you that you're an amazing person.
>
> You're not perfect, but you are awesome.
>
> I love you so much, every bit of you, for who you are. I'm in love with them all. This day is yours, make the most out of it, and many happy returns of the day.
>
> With love
>
> - Mohit

I looked at the book and then looked at him. While I was reading, he started working on his computer again. But he felt that I was looking at him, and he turned and smiled. I thought he was going to say something, but he didn't. He kept working. After a few moments, he said, "It was my birthday. I didn't have a party, but I got a few presents from my family. But I still bought this book for myself and wrote to me." He paused. "This was the best one I got on my birthday, as it was from me to myself."

He smiled again.

Was that weird? Maybe. We call things weird when we do not understand them. But just because we do not understand something doesn't mean that thing is wrong.

It is just different.

That was a simple conversation, but twenty-five years later, I'm vividly remembering this because that was the first time I experienced something remarkable about self-love. Mohit didn't wait for his friends to come up with many presents (which he probably got as a bonus) and make him happy. Instead, he celebrated the way he wanted to. He loved himself for who he was. He loved his ability to code. He loved his long hair. In other words, he was just content with himself.

If you love yourself, you know what I'm talking about, but if you don't, you are not alone. Many don't.

You may think, "I don't like my body, I don't like my voice, I don't like my hair, I don't like my …" See, you cannot change a few things about yourself, such as your height, hair, skin color, and how you look. But if you count those things, you will find that they are very limited. This applies to all of us. But there are so many things that you can improve in yourself, such as how you present yourself to others, how you treat others, your physical body (to some extent), learning any new skill you love, and hundreds of other things you can change the way you want about you.

Over the years, I realized that the more I grow as a person, the more I love myself. Look around and notice the people you admire and aspire to be. Do you like them because they live in a mansion or drive the most expensive car? Or are they Miss or Mister Universe? Or are they the most powerful? If you ask yourself and are honest, you will find that you like them not because of what they have but because of who they are.

Think about your favorite teacher, favorite actor, or the coolest friend. Now ask yourself, do you like this person because he or she has the best look, hair, or skin color? These are important but are probably not the only reasons. You probably like the person because of things like how she talks, how she presents herself, and how she is uniquely beautiful in her own way. Also, maybe the person is nice, humble, kind, and has many other qualities that have made her who she is today. And you probably like her because of all of these things.

The qualities you like you can also develop over time in becoming the best version of yourself. There is no perfect person on earth. Literally everybody has shortcomings. But most people we like are the ones who believe in and love themselves.

Even though I designed this section for love and connections with other people, I couldn't resist myself and talked a little about self-love.

Whoever you are and whatever you do, regardless of the things you hate about yourself, you can be sure that there is someone else out there who doesn't have what you have.

It is never too late to fall in love with yourself. The easiest and most reliable way to get love is from you.

REFLECTION

- Write five things you love about your partner or best friend and why you love this person?
- Identify three people you can count on in an emergency and why?
- What is the most important thing you want your best friend to know about you?

I believe that if you are blessed to have intimate bonds (circle zero) with people who love and care for you, then they are your most precious on earth. They are the heart of your happy and satisfying life.

At the end of the day, if you want love, it is essential to give first.

Who are the people you love and care about the most and have intimate bonds with (circle zero)?

Who are the people in your life in your outer circles—circles one, two, and three?

I have mentioned a few of mine from each circle below.

People In My Circle Zero	Circle One	Circle Two	Circle Three
Mahin	Mother	Father	Jason
	Sister	Asif	Nick
	Bec	Mili	Casual Friends
	Phil	Sheryl	Work Colleagues

People In Your Circle Zero	Circle One	Circle Two	Circle Three

People In your life whom **you love, trust, rely, care** the most (circle zero) and the least (circle three)

PLEASURE

"Enjoy present pleasures in such a way as not to injure future ones."
—Seneca

WHAT IS PLEASURE?

This is where I got stuck. I had been staring at the blank page for a while, stood up, had some water, and walked back to my study, hoping I would know how to start this section. I wrote a few words and then removed them, stood up again, walked around the house for a bit, looked through the window, and came back to study again.

But guess what? Nothing.

Then I thought I would put this section off for later and get some work done in other areas, but I procrastinated on this section for a few weeks. Then, one day, I decided that I would start writing this section no matter what. So I closed my study door, removed all the distractions, and sat at my desk to start on this, and I wanted to keep writing until I finished.

Then I thought, "Let me quickly put some music from YouTube on in the background to help me concentrate more." So I started browsing through my playlist. Some of the new songs YouTube recommended caught my attention. I found some awesome remixes and covers in my all-time favorite list of old songs by new artists. It is amazing how talented these new artists are. It always feels good to have a more recent version of the songs I love. Then I also came across some amazing people that I listen to: Author Simon Sinek, Jim Rohn, Brené Brown, and a few others.

But wait, didn't I set myself up in my study room (without distraction) to write this section I had been putting off for weeks? Before realizing it, I had spent more than three hours in my study, during which time I listened to probably more than thirty songs and ten speeches.

And surprise!! Surprise!! I didn't write a single word.

Now, I'm frustrated and not feeling great about myself.

But I was having a good time listening to the music and speeches on YouTube for four hours. Why am I frustrated now? Well, I was having a good time earlier, but I didn't make any progress on this section of my book. Where did I spend my time? On YouTube, which is always very easy and fun for me, and very addictive.

Instead of writing, I was listening to music and speeches. It was just passive enjoyment. It did not require me to do anything on my part. As I was listening, the experience made me feel good in a way. The songs were amazing. The singers were awesome. I felt good as I was enjoying the process of listening to the music. But soon after I finished listening, I realized that I hadn't made any progress on my book, and I felt frustrated. I felt good while listening to music, but once those moments were gone, the good feeling was also gone. Generally, the good feeling does not last in these activities. Either soon after finishing the activity or after a little while, the enjoyment subsides.

This is pleasure.

These activities give us momentary enjoyment. We feel pleasure as this happens. The activities can be simple things like having a cup of tea, watching a favorite TV show, drinking, listening to music, having sex, dining at a favorite restaurant, clubbing, or partying. These are raw enjoyments. Some of these activities give us longer enjoyment than others, but generally the enjoyment does not last for a long time. Pleasure is different from flow, which requires you to have skills and a level of comfortable challenge. When you are in flow, you cannot feel anything. You may get pleasure from drinking, but you can get flow from painting.

As human beings, we crave pleasurable things because they are relatively easier to do and give us instant gratification. We have been conditioned to believe that only these activities make us happy as a society. I discussed these earlier. That's why it is very hard for most of us to find that lasting happiness—because most people focus on pleasurable activities (e.g., partying on the weekend or celebrating only on special days). They make people happy in the moment, but after a little while, the enjoyment is also gone (e.g., the Monday morning you hate comes about). There is no denying that these pleasurable activities make us happy. It is essential to have them, but they should never be the focus for one's lasting happiness.

Most people link happiness with pleasure.

I became stuck in my progress in this section because I struggled to pick one of the thousands of examples of pleasure that we seek in the pursuit of happiness, and I didn't know where to start. So I decided to use my own and speak my mind.

WHAT TO WATCH FOR

You may think, "If pleasure is the easiest and the most fun thing to do, then shouldn't we all go for more and more pleasure in life?"

The answer is not that black and white.

PLEASURE

Most people link happiness with pleasurable activities, and that's how we have been conditioned to believe. But remember that the world's happiness has been declining in recent years. Also, about 80 per cent of people in the global workforce are not engaged at work. There must be something wrong with our approach. Under the umbrella of positive psychology, scientists have been studying what makes a life worth living, what makes a good life, and what a fulfilled life is. Professor Martin Seligman is one of the world's leading experts in psychology and the founder of positive psychology. He summarized three types of lives that relate to living a satisfying life. First is the pleasant life, where you pursue pleasurable activities and try to amplify them as much as possible. Second is the life of engagement, where you focus on more and more flow experiences. And finally, there is the meaningful life—living every day with a true purpose and mission to serve others.

So what type of life should you design for yourself? This highly depends on what you believe and value. It also relates to the type of person you are. For example, if you are introverted and have excellent skills to engage in flow, such as being an artist or a chess player, you can choose a life of engagement. Or if you overcame poverty and have become financially abundant, then you might decide to help other people come out of poverty and live a very meaningful life. Or, finally, you may love to party and can't wait to have a drink with your best friends on the weekends. You live a pleasant life where you amplify the raw pleasure and instant gratification as much as possible every day.

Many people live only the pleasant life. They do not have a strong meaning or engage in flow in their days. The problem with that is that they are aiming only for raw pleasure to make them happy for the short term, which does not give strong meaning to their lives. Regarding the pleasurable life in his TED talk, Professor Seligman said, "It turns out that the pursuit of pleasure has almost no contribution to life satisfaction. The pursuit of meaning is the strongest, and the pursuit of engagement is also very strong. Where pleasure matters is if you have both engagement and meaning, then pleasure is the whipped cream and the cherry."

Now you may think, "Can you have all three lives?" Yes, absolutely. And that is called a "full life." That's one of the primary reasons why I wrote this book. Most people choose pleasurable activities, as they are easier to do and result in enjoyment almost instantly. Going on a good holiday, staying in a luxurious hotel, renting a nice car, and dining in nice restaurants are all pleasurable activities. In other words, they are what rich and famous people do in movies. Most people want to be like them. It is not a surprise that many pursue only pleasurable activities.

But what most people do not see is the years of hard work rich and famous people put in to become who they are today. For example, Arnold Schwarzenegger is rich and famous. He wears a nice suit, dines in a very expensive restaurant, drives a nice car, and so forth. But what most people do not see is how Arnold became the person he is today.

When he was young, he was into bodybuilding. He might have had strong engagement (flow) from that activity, and with his determination and hard work, he became a bodybuilding champion. Then he began acting in movies and conquered that world. After that, he went into politics and became the governor of California in the US. Also, he is actively involved in a lot of philanthropy work that facilitates a better future in education, energy, the environment, health and human wellness, and political reform.

So does he live a meaningful life? Absolutely. Has he got flow? I'm sure he has. You can read and watch about him living a pleasurable life, but his life as a bodybuilder, actor, and politician—all three roles—was engaging and meaningful. Yes, he also has a pleasant life, but that is in addition to the life of engagement and the life of meaning he has.

Remember, Professor Seligman said the pleasurable life matters only if you already have both engagement and meaning in your life. Then the pleasures become the whipped cream and the cherry. Most people just see the whipped cream bit and miss the engagement and meaning. They can say that Arnold has millions of dollars, and so he can do charity. This is true, but he didn't inherit the money. He did years of hard work to build that wealth. And honestly, you can have strong meaning and flow without millions of dollars, which we will discuss in part 8, "Stay Happy at Work."

You already know that, according to studies, if you are focusing only on pleasure in your life, even if you amplify it as much as you can, it has almost zero contribution to your life satisfaction. What's the point of focusing on only short bursts of pleasure that don't last? Remember, the world happiness 2019 report finds that as a society with the traditional pleasurable life approach, we are becoming increasingly unhappy and unfulfilled. A possible solution would be to focus on more engagement (flow) and meaning.

But yes, I also engage in pleasurable activities. They are essential. But if you spend most of your time on pleasure, you will miss one or more core elements, such as meaning, flow, love, health, and achievements. For example, watching six hours of Netflix (which I used to do), partying the whole weekend, or drinking will give you pleasure, and you will feel good. But they are not going to fulfil you or satisfy you. As human beings, we not only want to feel pleasure but also want to feel that we are needed, engaged, and satisfied.

At the end of the day, no one wants to live an unfulfilled life. With the aid of science, we now know what it takes to be more engaged and live a life with strong meaning.

And the pleasurable life? It will follow you if you want the whipped cream and the cherry.

REFLECTION

As human beings, we crave things that are easy and fun to do. There is no denying that. You do it; I do it. Everybody does. With our daily routines, we all get tired, and at the end of the day, we just don't want to think about meaning or engagement, and it feels that pleasure is the easiest thing to do. This can include things like watching a movie, having a drink with your gang, partying or browsing social media.

We all do these things.

Think about your typical day. How much time do you spend doing things that are easy, fun, and pleasurable? They can be very addictive, and before you know it, you may have spent hours of your precious time on raw pleasure that has no meaning or flow. Make sure you work on strong meaning, flow, love, and health on most of your days. Pleasure takes a backseat for good reasons you already know.

But surely, always plan something pleasurable to look forward to in the coming weeks or months, such as going for a holiday or attending a party, a celebration, or some event that excites you.

Think about this,

- Where would you love to go for a nice holiday? Whom would you take with you, and why?
- What pleasurable events are you looking forward to in the next three months, and why?

What can you do daily, weekly, monthly, or yearly as your pleasure activities? What can you look forward to? I have outlined a few of mine.

My Daily Pleasure Activities	Weekly	Monthly	Quarterly	Yearly
Watch Netflix for 2 Hours	Explore a new restaurant	Attend one event of interest(i.e. A show, concert)	Going away for a few days holiday with family	Travel to a new city to explore and enjoy with family.
Listen to Music	Hangout with close friends	Go to the beach	Buy something I love for myself.	Participate in one long distance running.
Something that makes me laugh (i.e. comedy, refreshing memories)		Going for a photography session		

Your Daily Pleasure Activities	Weekly	Monthly	Quarterly	Yearly

What do you *love and look forward to?*, Daily, Weekly, Monthly, Quarterly And Yearly as **pleasurable**

HEALTH

"He who has health, has hope, and he who has hope, has everything."
—Thomas Carlyle

THE JOURNEY OF A FORMER COUCH POTATO

I woke up in the morning and brushed my teeth with a frowning face. I felt that I needed to sleep more. I didn't feel rested but went to work. I felt fatigued all day. I came home and ate something and went straight to the couch. I turned the TV on, sat there for hours, fell asleep, woke up again at 9:00 p.m., watched some more TV, and finally went to bed at 2:00 a.m.

On the next day, it was the same story.

I needed to catch up on my sleep and woke up at 12:00 p.m. on the weekend. And then I was always tired, frustrated, grumpy, didn't feel good, and didn't feel like doing anything, let alone any physical activity. The same cycle repeated for several years.

Fourteen years ago, that was my typical week.

I heard, "Health is the greatest gift." I thought I had that because I was not overweight and did not have a health condition. I had no reason to focus on my health. I assumed that I was well because I didn't have any issues. Feeling tired and having low energy was normal. But when I look back on my life and think about those times, I realize how foolish I was. I had no idea about what that greatest gift of health actually meant. According to the WHO, health is "A state of complete physical, mental and social well-being and not merely the absence of disease or infirmity."

Over many years in my health journey, I have realized that true health is not about just surviving or the absence of disease but rather about how much energy you have, how vibrant you are, and whether your body and mind can perform at their optimum.

In other words, do you feel truly alive? Fourteen years ago, I didn't.

So what changed for me? And how? It was sparked with a one-line conversation with my colleague and started with my awareness of eating.

EAT

Many years ago at work, I ordered a pack of chips for my "quick lunch" before my next meeting. I opened it and offered it to my colleague. He said, "No, man, thanks," then he smiled and said, "I do not put unhealthy stuff in my body." I shrugged and went to my desk. Even though I wanted to ignore what he had just said, I couldn't. It may have hit my ego, as I believed there was nothing wrong with chips, and I had offered them to someone who had rejected them. What he said kept coming back to me. I thought my colleague was showing me an unnecessary attitude about food, which made me really annoyed. How could anyone say that to me, especially when I had the greatest gift of health (so I thought)?

I couldn't ignore what my colleague said for days. I asked myself, "Why should I care about eating healthy?" But I started to notice my eating habits. I continually skipped breakfast and had unhealthy lunches and dinners. And as I mentioned, I used to feel tired and fatigued, and I had very low energy all the time. I spoke to my wife about the whole thing, and she was very supportive. We decided to make some changes to our eating habits, but we didn't know where to start. We had no idea what "healthy eating" really meant. But from a little research, we found that a few things like reducing carbs and avoiding bad fat are common across all healthy eating advice. We adjusted our grocery purchases accordingly and made conscious choices when eating out, such as avoiding fried food and sugary drinks. I must admit that the first few weeks were hard, and we even had a few days of junk food. We felt guilty and frustrated, but we never stopped. As we progressed, the percentage of junk food in our diet started to decrease, and we got better over time. I began to sleep slightly better and felt a little more energy during the day than before.

I caught up with an old friend at dinner after a few days. He had bought an expensive car, and he said, "I'm going to only put in the best fuel in my car from now on. That helps the engine run smoothly." I'm not into cars and don't know much about them, but that statement made me think about our physical bodies. We live in our bodies, and the food we eat is the fuel for our bodies. Shouldn't we be putting the best food in our bodies? That was a paradigm-shifting question for us.

Fourteen years ago, I started with cereal with milk for breakfast as a healthier choice than skipping it or having a donut. Over time, we made simple but small changes to all our meals. We made conscious choices every time we ate at a restaurant or anywhere else. Your food choices will likely evolve as you continue to explore, learn, and pay attention to permanent healthy eating. But yes, rest assured there will be days when you just won't want to eat healthily, and that's okay. But always bounce back to your version of healthy eating. That's the key wherever you are in your healthy eating journey. The most important question of all that we kept asking ourselves was, "What is our next level?"

Over the years, every level we have been in has made us feel better, stronger, and lighter, and has also given us a sense of achievement. If you honor your body by eating healthier (putting in the "better fuel"), it will pay off. You will never regret eating healthier.

It does not matter where you are in your healthy eating journey. You can start with the smallest step possible, taking one baby step at a time. Don't worry about super-strict diets and exercise routines at the start. For example, if you took one spoonful of sugar in your coffee yesterday, commit to taking a half spoonful today and onwards (you may think that's a 50 per cent reduction and you can't do it). Trust me; you will not even notice the difference after three to four weeks. You will most likely adapt to it. It is what you believe about yourself. If you believe you can, you will be able to do it. But if you believe you cannot, you will never be able to do it.

The trick is in what you honestly believe and tell yourself every day.

WALK

A few years into our healthy eating journey, I went to a doctor, and he found that my blood pressure was high. It was kind of a blow to the face. As I thought we had started eating healthy, which was a big deal then. So the doctor told me to monitor my blood pressure for two weeks, and I measured it twice a day and I created a chart. We found that the average was not too high, and the doctor did not advise any medication, but he asked me about my physical activity, which at the time was zero.

He advised me to start walking briskly. Even though I was scared at first, I still did not take any action for at least two months because, with the chart, I saw my pressure was not too high, and the walking was only "recommended." A few days later, my wife said she wanted to join a yoga class at the gym. I thought I might join as well and try some walking and potentially a little bit of running. On my first day, I tried to run instead of walking, but I couldn't. Twenty seconds later, I was breathless. I had no idea that I couldn't run for even twenty seconds. I decided to just walk for ten minutes every day.

To make a long story short, over the following eleven months, I gained the ability to run 4.5 kilometers in thirty minutes without stopping. After a few years of running, in 2019, both Mahin and I finished a 21.1-km half-marathon at Melbourne Marathon Festival. Prior to joining the gym, we had never run in our lives. We had never thought of going such a distance. It was an amazing experience, and we had never felt happier and more satisfied with ourselves in our health and fitness journey.

If you are not a runner (like I wasn't), just start walking for five minutes (remember the smallest step to start), then build on that over time. You may miss a few days, but never stop. Some days are hard for running, but I put in a genuine effort to run at least three days a week as my ritual, and this gives me more energy and makes me satisfied every day.

SLEEP

Generally, I can fall asleep very quickly. But in 2018, we came back from Singapore, and my body clock couldn't revert to Melbourne time for a while. Since then, I have had intermittent sleep issues whenever I have travelled or had a stressful week. I have struggled with falling asleep and experienced sleep deprivation.

I do not know about you, but this was a very big deal for me. I must have at least eight hours of sleep no matter what. According many studies, sleep deprivation increases the risk of high blood pressure, diabetes, heart disease, and other health issues. It can cause issues with the central nervous system, digestive system, respiratory system, and many other systems in the body over both the short term and long term. Many sleep only five hours a day, and they say they are fine with it. The impact may not be evident now, but they may experience issues later in life. I could list study after study about the benefits of proper sleep. But at the end of the day, sleep allows our bodies to rest and recover.

I have had to repair my sleep rituals over the years to get back on track, doing things like lowering the room's temperature, slightly increasing my carbohydrate intake, increasing my exposure to sunlight, and exercising. Also, minimizing my screen time before bed and adopting a few more strategies helped me get back to my regular sleep routine. A good night's sleep almost always makes my day and allows me to perform at my best. And 99 per cent of the time, my sleep is non-negotiable.

According to many studies, at least seven to eight hours of sleep is absolutely mandatory for our bodies to function at their best.

Sleep makes one's waking hours more enjoyable and worthwhile.

DRINK WATER

700ml was my daily water intake for many years. I never paid attention even after Mahin and others in my family told me to drink more water. I kept ignoring them. It wasn't until I attended a seminar in 2016 and it explained why staying properly hydrated is important and what are the potential consequences of dehydration for a long time.

Something shifted in me.

To simply put, the physical body you live in is a collection of 37 trillion cells. Each cell needs oxygen, food and water to function. All three things must be present for each cell to keep you alive.

Your body can survive without food for weeks, but without water only 2 - 4 days. You can imagine how important water is for your body.

Over the years I have increased my water intake to at least 2.2L every day. Measure and increase your water intake to at least 2L a day, keep a bottle of water 'Visible and around' you throughout the day.

Stay hydrated & stay alive.

EXERCISE AND MOVE

When I was studying positive psychology at Harvard in 2017, one of our assignments was to engage in physical activity. Part of the challenge was to do ten consecutive push-ups. I thought that was not a big deal, but I got stuck at six. That was my best. I registered six in my activity assignment. Later, I found that a person my age should be able to do four sets of ten push-ups.

I could not take the fact that I was stuck at six. I committed to doing seven a day, and then eight, and so on, and in the next twenty months, I was able to do five sets of ten—that is fifty push-ups—every morning. I also incorporated three types of planking, standing up every hour for five minutes when working at my desk, moving as much as possible, increasing my daily steps, and other activities. I also dialed down the push-ups to thirty a day as my everyday ritual. These rituals help me stay motivated, replenished, and energized, and they give me a sense of achievement every day.

When I started with just seven push-ups a day, it took me less than one minute a day. Would you give your body one minute a day? What is the easiest exercise you can commit to every day?

THE SIMPLE DAILY HABITS

When I was a teen, I had no discipline for eating, walking, sleeping, exercising, or studying. I was very spontaneous, and I used to do almost nothing on time. My dad used to tell me in his exact words, "You must be a regular in your life in what you do." Of course, he meant the good things—in other words, discipline.

I never bothered paying attention to that. Almost thirty years later today, I'm writing this section of my book and remembering how true that statement is.

My grandmother lived till 92, and Mahin's grandmother lived till 103. They didn't have the perfect diets, didn't have access to any scientific studies or the best medical facilities. Yet they made it to their nineties and lived very active, happy, and healthy lives. They woke up early in the morning, ate a fresh and limited amount every day, were physically active during the day, surrounded themselves with their loved ones, went to bed early, and had good sleep every night.

I noticed that both Mahin's and my grandmother had one thing in common, and that was their simple daily habits.

Living a healthy and fit lifestyle is NOT complicated. It is much simpler than you might think.

YOUR BEST RETURN ON INVESTMENT

I'm not telling you about our health journey to brag, but rather to share our first-hand experience in this element of life. Remember, I used to have poor sleep, low energy, and fatigue during the day. I used to fall asleep at odd times and was frustrated and grumpy. Over the last fourteen years, paying attention to and nurturing our health and fitness has made us happier and more satisfied than ever before.

We both have become much more health-conscious about what we eat every day. Our sleep patterns have been in rhythm. The way we feel during the day couldn't be better. We feel much more vibrant and far more energetic than before. We understand what it takes to sustain that level of energy throughout the day. Wherever you are in your health and fitness journey, remember to ask yourself, "What is my next level?" And then start taking the smallest action possible, and never stop evolving.

I thank my colleague today for saying he did not put unhealthy stuff in his body. That was a defining moment for me. I wouldn't be talking about it fourteen years later today if it wasn't. I used to be a couch potato and sit for hours. But today, when I eat healthy, when I sleep well, when I do my push-ups, when I run five kilometers, and when I move as much as I can, these things give me a sense of achievement and respect for my health, because fourteen years ago, I couldn't do any of them.

My life is not perfect, but my rituals have surely made me a better version of myself. Your body is where you live. It is always there for you, and you will need to take care of it regardless of other things. Your heart, lungs, eyes, brain, and everything else work for you 24/7 without stopping. Are you grateful to your lungs? Your eyes? Your brain? Your heart? Every organ of your body is part of a team that takes care of you, keeps you alive, and allows you to do everything else.

Any time, money, and effort on your body has the highest rate of return. Whether you realize it or not, health is truly the greatest gift of all. It is simple; the healthier you are, the happier you become.

I could have given you hundreds of science-backed facts, but it wouldn't matter unless you make a solid decision to act on your health and fitness. What solid decisions would you make to take your health and fitness to the next level? Do you commit to acting on your decisions every day? Remember, our motivation does not last, but strong decisions do.

WHAT NOT TO DO TO RELAX

My day was swamped with meetings, presentations, and a few client sessions. I had a quick five-minute lunch during my busy day. When I finished, I thought I would just relax and do nothing as I deserved it.

In the evening, I sat on the couch and let myself lie down a little. For the first few minutes, I felt that I so needed this. I turned the TV on, and then I thought, "What can I watch?" I started browsing the channels, but none of them was interesting. So I kept browsing, and then I found an old movie that I had seen many times before. I thought it might be a good refresher, so I started watching that. A few minutes later, I felt bored again.

I kept thinking and started browsing Netflix. There were so many movies. It was really hard to decide which one to watch. I started playing a few but couldn't continue with any of them. Then I remembered a meeting I had the next day, and I thought I might do some preparation work. But then I felt I deserved to rest for a bit, as I'd had a very busy day. I looked at my phone and found we needed to attend a birthday party on the weekend. Guess what? That reminded me that I needed to book accommodation for our upcoming holiday. I was thinking all of this as I was browsing Netflix to watch a good movie to relax.

But an hour later, I ended up deciding on nothing on Netflix.

Later, I thought, "Why couldn't I watch something I love?" I sat on the couch for an hour and did nothing. All I was doing was mind wandering. Instead of feeling rested, I felt a little stressed about the fifty different things I needed to do in the next few days.

I wanted to understand why I couldn't rest.

It turns out that our brains have two modes. First is the focus mode. In this mode, your brain is engaged in one activity only. It has intense concentration and focuses on the activity. Professor Amit Sood from the Mayo Clinic College of Medicine explained this phenomenon very nicely in his TEDx talk. About this focus mode, he said, "When your brain processes something very interesting, very novel and very meaningful, for example, playing with a little baby gets you into focus mode. Our brains love to be in this mode, but we do not give ourselves enough doses of that." It is about being fully focused and attentive to one thing at a time as we experience life (i.e., flow).

The second mode is the default mode, where our minds wander. We are distracted by many different things and are not focused on one thing. This mode is essentially the opposite of focus mode. Professor Sood said, "An average person has about 150 undone tasks at any time. We are like that about 50-80% of the time during the day." In default mode, we become distracted and start to think about things, such as having to cook dinner, call a client, watch a film, or help your kid with her homework. This is similar to the things I was doing the other day when I was trying to relax.

Two researchers, Matthew A. Killingsworth and Daniel Gilbert of Harvard University, analyzed two hundred fifty thousand data points on a subject's thoughts, feelings, and actions about mind wandering in the default mode. They wrote, "A human mind is a wandering mind, and a wandering mind is an unhappy mind. The ability to think about what is not happening is a cognitive achievement that comes at an emotional cost." They also found that people were happier when making love, exercising, or engaging in a conversation. But they were least happy when working, using a home computer, or resting (Surprise!).

The idea of relaxing or resting, for most people, means doing nothing. Studies suggest that when we do nothing, our brains are not at rest. In fact, our brains are actually very busy wondering about many different things. Most of the time, those things are the ones we worry about. Sometimes they can be not only stressful but also frustrating.

You might wonder what you can do to get your brain into focus mode. Firstly, you can make a firm decision on what you want to do (preferably something you love to do with full focus—for example, talking to your best friend or cycling) and not change your decision.

When you think to yourself, "What should I do? What movie should I watch? Is it a good one? is there a better one?" Having many options will keep you in the default mode of mind wandering. Instead, if you just decide to do one thing and not change your mind, your decision gives you a better chance to get your brain into focus mode and keep it there. Another study by Professor Dan Gilbert with a group of photography students found that making a decision and sticking to it helps our happiness, as opposed to having many options and not being able to make a decision, which adversely impacts us. You might think having one hundred movies to choose from is better than choosing from five. True, but many of us struggle to choose and get stuck in a state in which we cannot make a decision. Being in that state makes us unhappy. This does not mean you should not have preferences, but it means that to feel happy, getting your brain into focus mode by making a decision helps you relax and enjoy instead of wandering to find the "best option."

That day I was constantly trying to find a good movie to watch, I could not rest and ended up being stressed out. But another day, I firmly decided to watch The Queen's Gambit and finished the episodes in one go (Yes, all of them) without browsing other things. It was very satisfying.

Making a decision and sticking to it is the first step. Having options is good, but not to the extent that it makes you unable to make a decision. About this, Professor Gilbert also said, "The real risk in happiness happens when people overrate their choices. Allowing the mind to conjure dozens of this or that scenarios that keep the brain in a constant search, when our ambition is bounded, it leads us to work joyfully."

Secondly, after making a firm decision, pay 100 per cent attention to the activity. For example, be mindful of what you are eating, pay full attention to the person you are talking to, and really listen to your kids. Also, strive for flow with your skills and in challenges. Flow requires our brains to be in focus mode. The more you stay in that mode, the more satisfied you will feel.

Doing just one thing with 100 per cent attention to relax may sound counterintuitive because, socially, you are not supposed to do anything when relaxing. But studies suggest that idea does not really let us relax. What makes us enjoy the time is keeping our brains in focus mode as long as we can by doing a single thing with full attention. Remember, our brains love focus mode, which lets us enjoy our relaxing time. The last thing you want to do to relax is let your mind wander by doing nothing.

REFLECTION

Everything falls apart if the body you live in is not livable anymore. Your happiness and satisfaction matter only as long as you live.

My Decisions & Habits	Eat	Drink Water	Walk	Move & Exercise	Sleep	Rest
Current Habit	I'm on **6/10** to choose a healthier option (i.e. 2 spoons of sugar in tea)	1.3 L	7000 Steps	30 Pushups 3 X 50 Sec planks	7.5 Hrs.	Browse Facebook, Netflix
What 'smallest' change I committed to make it better?	I decided to be **7/10** to choose a healthier option (i.e. 1 spoon of sugar in tea)	1.5 L	9000 Steps	35 Pushups 3 X 60 Secs planks	8 Hrs.	Look at old photos, Go to park, talk to an old friend
Your Decisions & Habits	Eat	Drink Water	Walk	Move & Exercise	Sleep	Rest
Current Habit						
What 'smallest' change you have decided to make it better?						

What **smallest** change **you have decided** to make when you eat, drink, walk, exercise, sleep and rest to live better?

When you decide and commit, it's never too late to start a ritual.

ACHIEVEMENTS

"The biggest adventure you can take is to live the life of your dreams."
—Oprah Winfrey

MEETING RICHARD

I was at a conference; Richard had just come off stage after his talk and stood with a few people outside the hall. My wife and I wanted to ask him about a product he had just launched on the stage. He seemed very approachable, and we went and asked him about the product. He didn't know my wife or me, but he was very humble and kind. I initially thought he was just trying to sell his new product. I got side tracked a little and engaged in a conversation with another person. Twenty minutes later, I noticed my wife was still talking to Richard, and she looked very engaged and excited. So I got closer to them and joined their conversation. They were not talking about the product at all; rather, they were discussing philosophies of life. I was intrigued.

Honestly, I didn't know much about Richard until that day. But later I found out that he was the CEO of one of the largest event organizers in the world, which he founded in 1992. It is a platform that has organized more than five hundred world-class events, such as seminars, workshops, and conferences, worldwide in seventy cities and in thirty countries. His life's work and his company's mission have helped millions of people achieve success worldwide. That's why he named his company "Success Resources." His platform brings not just good but the best to people who have a proven record of producing extraordinary results. These people include former US president Bill Clinton, former British prime minister Tony Blair, Sir Richard Branson, Robert Kiyosaki, Anthony Robbins and the likes. Success Resources is valued at more than $100 million today, and Richard is the man behind all this.

But it took Richard more than twenty-seven years with his enormous passion and determination for personal development. As he was building his business in the early years, he also went through cancer treatment. Even during that time, he climbed stairs and went to every floor of a high-rise building to sell seminar tickets, but nobody bought any. He survived cancer, and he became a phenomenal leader in bringing his company to where it is today. His mission and his achievements are remarkable.

Why is it important to have achievements, goals, and dreams? Honestly, I can talk for hours about why your dreams are important and why you should go for them. But to cut to the chase, no matter how small it is, every human being has a dream.

If you are an average person, you may have a goal of getting a job, getting married, or being a parent, or perhaps you are an entrepreneur who wants to change something in the world for the better, or even a homeless guy who might just want to have his next meal. Whatever it is, almost everybody has some kind of target or goal. And when our goals seem too big, we often call them "dreams." I have been talking about living on your terms throughout the book. To be able to do that, you will need to have dreams and goals of your own.

Without dreams and goals, we don't feel alive.

But what types of dreams or goals should you have? We use the terms "dreams" and "goals" interchangeably all the time. But in short, dreams are usually a complete picture that you see (not while sleeping, obviously) of something you want to experience. For example, your dream may be that you want to build a home with a green lawn where you are having tea with your wife and children. But a goal towards that dream can be a small target you set with a time frame to achieve it. For example, you may be saving to put down a deposit for a home within two years, or to buy the land to build a home in six months.

Dreams and goals come in various forms. But there are three basic types. Firstly, extrinsic goals are goals set by other people for you, and they are not really your true goals (although you may think that they are yours). For example, if you are an employee, you may get a sales target to meet, or if you are the company's CEO, your investors may set a revenue and profit target for you. These goals may or may not excite you. In fact, they will likely make you stressed out, and you will feel anxious about meeting them.

Secondly, there are intrinsic destination-based goals. These are your own goals. For example, you may want to hit a revenue of X in your business or buy a beach house. But these are destination-based goals. That means you may or may not love the journey (maybe you don't love what you do in your job to make money). When you achieve that goal, you will feel excited for a little while. Then your burst of excitement will go away (because of hedonic adaptation, which you already know). Then you will set another goal (e.g., buy a bigger beach house), and the same pattern will continue.

As you are reading a happiness book, I want to highlight the third type of goal. This will help you be lastingly happy. The third type of goal is the intrinsic journey-based goal. That means you actually love the process involved in hitting your target. For example, if you love sales conversations and feel a comfortable challenge with them, you will experience flow and will be more likely to make sales. You will actually enjoy the process of selling every day. And in your journey, over time, you will likely hit your sales targets. Strive for the intrinsic goals where you feel strong meaning (as previously mentioned) or where you are passionate about something and experience flow. These journey-based goals make you feel happy as you work on them more often without hitting your target. That way you will be drawn to the process instead of something you have to do to hit your target. You will achieve your goals, but you will also enjoy the ride.

You get the most enjoyment and meaning from the intrinsic journey-based goals because they are your own and are close to your heart.

I talked about Richard earlier to share the two most important things about goals I learned from him. Remember, he is the man who brings the world's best to his stages so people can learn from them. These two things are not just theory but have been proven by the world's best achievers (e.g., former US presidents and highly successful businesspeople).

Firstly, whatever you want to achieve, the primary step is to decide on and stick to your goal. It is all about decisions. Richard said, "It was from Bill Clinton when we had lunch together. I asked him, do you think it is right or wrong for America to be in Afghanistan? To which he replied, 'It is not whether it is right or wrong for America to be in Afghanistan. It is about making it right.' From that, I realized that it is not about making a right or wrong decision because who knows what might happen in the future. But if you decide to commit to something, do it to the best of your abilities."

But yes, of course, be flexible with your approach and change the small decisions to pivot if needed, but never change your big decisions to your dream.

Secondly, think big. All my life, I have always been a dreamer. But I had boundaries created by the people I surrounded myself with for many years. We all have that, but it is essential to break free and not limit our potential based on the opinions or decisions of others. The conversation that my wife and I had with Richard on that day was a defining moment for me. Remember, my wife was talking to him for about twenty minutes about the philosophies of life, and then I joined them. I also realized that one is never too big to be humble and kind to a stranger. Since that day, I have met Richard a few more times, but on that first day, my wife and I were complete strangers to him, and he didn't know us, but he literally spent thirty minutes with us where he owns a business that is worth $100 million. His time is valuable (also in a business sense). So make sure you think big and respect your own decisions to act consistently on them.

Do you know your "bucket list?" I want to finish a full marathon in New York City. I finished a half-marathon in 2019. My wife and I both love travelling, and we want to visit 150 cities in the world; We have travelled to 54 so far. I love good conversations and would love to meet former president Obama one day. These are a few items from my "bucket list."

Write your own bucket list. Remember, "Achievements" is one of the primary elements of your satisfying life. Take the time to decide on the things on your bucket list, and start doing them without procrastinating so as not to regret not having done them later.

You define the experiences and achievements you want to have. Don't let other people or circumstances dictate your direction. If you don't give up, you will eventually achieve what you truly want from your heart.

Over the years, I have learned, in life, except for birth and death, your destiny is the creation of your thoughts, decisions, and consistent actions.

YOUR ENJOYMENT LEADS TO YOUR ACHIEVEMENTS

Facebook has a Facebook Live feature that allows you to broadcast your live video for people to watch and comment on in real time. Since its launch, as of 2018, there have been 3.5 billion total Facebook Live broadcasts, with more than 150 billion reactions to live videos. The way people consume media and do live broadcasts today can potentially make the traditional television network "a thing of the past." It is a massive success for the Facebook Live project. But you might be surprised how it started in a broom closet.

One of my favorite mentors is Randi Zuckerberg. She is the founder and CEO of Zuckerberg Media. She was the director of marketing for Facebook for many years and one of the very few people who joined Mark Zuckerberg when he started Facebook. As you may have guessed, she is Mark's older sister, and she is also the creator of Facebook Live.

I was blessed to have learned many things directly from Randi. It started in Sydney a few years ago with very few people in an intense workshop. Randi shared and taught us invaluable insights from her success and how companies like Facebook operated as start-ups.

Randi was among the few people who joined Facebook in its early days. Over time, they have introduced the idea of a "hackathon" within their team, where employees were encouraged once a month to spend some time on their passion project, which is unrelated to their everyday roles at Facebook. Randi came up with the idea of Facebook Live. She created a special project. She was always very passionate about television and media, and she decided that she was going to start a program called Facebook Live with Randi Zuckerberg. It was going to be like CNN but inside Facebook.

She set up a little studio in a broom closet and interviewed a few people live. Only a handful of people tuned into her broadcast. Of course, it was a pilot, and not many people knew about it. But she was very passionate and kept going. But not many people liked her idea. A few weeks later, singer Katy Perry's manager contacted Randi and said that Katy Perry would like to go on Facebook Live and announce her world tour. Even though they were not ready, Randi convinced her team and worked days and nights to prepare for Katy's broadcast. They had a few million people tune in. That was a launch for Facebook Live, and people started to understand what it was and how to use it. Later Randi hosted a chat with President Obama via Facebook Live as well. The rest is history.

Why am I telling you this story?

Because Randi loved and believed in media for everyone, her passion was to give everybody a voice through the Facebook platform. When it comes to achieving goals, if you treat them just as targets in your day job, you may not be internally or emotionally driven. There might not be any sense of meaning or presence of flow. You may just be doing it because you have to pay your bills, then you might find it very hard to achieve the goals given to you at work.

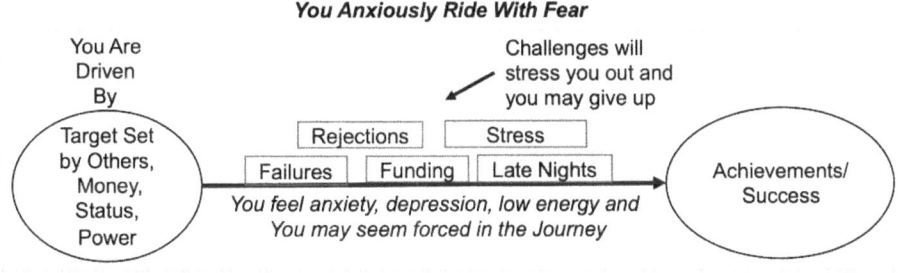

Even if you achieve your target, it might result in anxiety, depression, or drainage of your energy. Many people struggle to continue and sometimes give up. On the other hand, if you are driven by mission or passion, it does not mean you don't have challenges, but you are likely to deal with them better than if you are not.

But when you relentlessly work on your passion, you are more likely to experience strong meaning and flow. As you make small amounts of progress on your project, you will get momentum, it will drive and motivate you every day. It can make you believe in yourself in the face of challenges.

You Enjoy The Ride With Faith

You Are Driven By
Passion + Meaning + Flow

→ Rejections | Failures | Funding | Stress | Late Nights

You will handle challenges better and won't give up

You feel enjoyment, satisfaction, flow, high energy and you are drawn to the cause in the Journey

→ **Achievements/Success**

If your meaning is strong enough, it will help you keep going no matter what. It will certainly lead you to success if you never give up. Your meaning and passion link to something you love, care about, and strongly believe in. If you work on something meaningful and experience flow, you will not only find enjoyment but also eventually achieve your goals.

Remember, initially, only a few people tuned in to Randi's Facebook Live, and not many people supported her. Also, when they were working on getting the platform ready for Katy Perry's broadcast, they faced technical challenges related to broadcasting to millions of people. The same occurred with the interview with President Obama. All eyes were on her team, and the delivery needed to be spotless. In the journey of making this happen, Randi and her team had a mission. They had strong meaning and experienced flow. Overall, it was a great team effort with excitement and enjoyment for most of them. She and her team overcame those challenges because her mission and passion drove her every day.

Passion comes from the heart; it is an uncontrollable emotion. If you have a strong passion for something, generally, you can barely stop thinking about it, and you find it very hard to resist doing it. Robert Vallerand from the University of Quebec at Montreal and his team found that working on your passion can add eight hours of joy to your week.

Who doesn't want that?

When you are engaged with your passion during the day, you will be more fulfilled, and your chances for success will be higher than if you are forced to work on something.

Achievements do not occur only in business or work. Make sure you always have something to look forward to. Whether you want to win someone's heart in a relationship, get into shape or run a full marathon, climb a mountain, build a school, take a holiday, or whatever else, you will achieve your goal with passion, with purpose, and by not giving up.

My dad loved electronics all his life. His passion was to work on them every day, which he did. At the age of eighty-two, he is retired, but he still plays with electronics. He was so passionate that he had to learn Japanese to study electronics when he went to the University of Tokyo in the 1960s (they used Japanese to deliver lectures at the time instead of English). Dad learned a whole new language to pursue his dreams.

In 1965, his research publication at the University of Tokyo made such an impact that his paper became a case study for the students of engineering. He was also featured in TIME magazine (LIFE magazine at that time). During his thirty-plus-year career in Dhaka as the director of research for the Bangladesh Telephone Board, he was awarded Best Engineer in Fifty years in Telecommunication by the Engineers Institution of Dhaka. He led the project to introduce digital telecommunications from the old analogue systems for his country. He had been featured in national television and newspapers for his valuable contributions to his country. These are a few of many of his achievements.

But I can say the main reasons for his achievements are two. Firstly, his mission was to modernize the telecom system of his country, and secondly, his passion was electronics and engineering.

Don't just chase achievements; instead, focus on excelling on your mission and passion.

My dad did not chase being featured in TIME magazine and did not chase engineering awards. He had a very strong mission and excelled in his passion over many years, which automatically resulted in those successes. Honestly, that is the natural phenomenon for success. Remember, Randi started her little Facebook Live project in a broom closet, and her mission and passion, with relentless execution, resulted in a huge success that eventually impacted billions of people.

If you work on your mission with passion without giving up, it is an unstoppable combination. You will not only enjoy the journey, but it will also help you stay happy and you will also better deal with the inevitable challenges. And your achievements will naturally happen.

LETTING YOUR LOVED ONES SUCCEED

One of the most incredible things I learned from Randi was the parenting style within the Zuckerberg family.

Randi told CNN, "Both of my parents are doctors, it would have been very easy for them to encourage their children to go into medicine. But they never once pushed any of us into medicine. I think somewhere inside, they knew that the careers that we would have did not even exist yet." Being open-minded, Randi's parents took a courageous step for their children.

She continued, "I think that was a huge thing that they did for us, leaving us open for that curiosity. You can see Mark did some pretty great things. I always loved theatre and music. I wanted to sing on Broadway. That was my life passion. Mark, he was always talented in a lot of things. He developed a passion for computers and writing codes really early on, he always was building games and building little things and testing things out."

You might be thinking, "Yes, that is Mark Zuckerberg. Of course, he is a creative genius, and not everybody is like him. He is gifted, talented, and exceptional." I agree. He is super talented, but he had to be nurtured at a very young age. He had to be given the freedom to create and fail. Jim Kwik is one of the world's leading experts in speed reading and memory, and he said, "You don't have creativity; you do creativity."

When they were growing up, Randi, Mark, and their siblings had an environment in which they were always creating, inventing, collaborating, filming things, writing songs, and basically trying anything that they felt interested in. The experience of failing and learning gave them the belief in their abilities to do something meaningful and better that the world hadn't seen before.

Years later, when Mark started his project called Facebook, he moved to California and called Randi to join him. She was not very intrigued at first, because Mark was always working on something when he was very little, so she thought it was one of Mark's little projects. But Mark insisted on her flying to California and seeing what they were working on, and she did. And she was blown away to see that "little project." Today, we call it "Facebook."

They didn't find their passions when they were ten years old, but they were allowed to think and play with the things they loved at the time. For example, Star Wars was one of the things that almost all of them were into, which highly influenced them. Most parents would not allow their children to spend a lot of time playing with and creating things based on the Star Wars trilogy, but their parents did. And the results? Everybody knows. Not just Mark, with Facebook, but all the Zuckerberg siblings are successful in their own ways.

The point is, if you encourage your loved ones (e.g., children) to be creative, give them the environment to create, let them fail, and encourage them to never quit on their ideas, they will eventually become successful in what they are passionate about. They will enjoy their journey not only when they become successful but every day. It is critical to have an environment in which your children can not only learn and study but also flourish in their passion and in which they are not afraid to fail towards their dreams.

It gives me immense pleasure to talk about someone very special and close to me. Areeb is the son of one of my close friends, Ashraf. I still remember the day when Areeb was born at the Sunshine Hospital. Seven years later, this little one made history.

Areeb was just seven years old when he completed his 21.1km half-marathon run in two hours and thirty-four minutes on July 30, 2017, in Melbourne. He became the youngest Australian to do so and put his name in the national record book of Australia. He was featured in leading newspapers and interviewed by reporters from radio and television media. He was the topic of talk during that time.

I have seen him in diapers, I have seen him learning to walk, and I have also seen him run, but I never thought he would aim for a half marathon at that age. One night, Ashraf and his son Areeb came to our place back in 2016, and Ashraf told me that Areeb loved running and was preparing for a half marathon. I was like, "Are you serious?" Both of them smiled back. I said, "Nice, I'm happy for you guys, but is he allowed to run?" He was just seven years old. The minimum age for participating in a half-marathon was fifteen.

Then Ashraf told me the organizers had not yet approved Areeb to run, as he was too young, but they were talking to Athletics Victoria about it, and they would need to seek special permission for Areeb. Over the next few weeks, Areeb had to go through a few medical tests, and the doctors thoroughly checked his overall fitness. It wasn't an easy process. The authorities also arranged special medical assistance in case he needed it during the run. Areeb trained for more than a year before the half-marathon. His dad, Ashraf, is also a marathon runner. He was the primary trainer for Areeb during the whole year, and Areeb made it, to everybody's surprise.

But Areeb couldn't have done this without the support of his parents.

When I talk to parents, 99 per cent say they want their children to be successful and happy. That is great, but many parents also impose and define the success and happiness of their children. They put their children in races with other children. They want their children to excel at what they like without paying attention to what their children like. When your child does what you want, you become happy, but that does not mean your child also becomes happy.

For example, suppose you want your child to get good grades in school. For that, your child needs to excel in physics. But perhaps your child doesn't like physics. Often, children are put into race situations in school or sports competitions where they do not like the activity or are not very excited about it. But parents and society put unbelievable pressure on them to succeed. The students' stress levels are constantly high because of their obligation to succeed, and failing is not an option.

Under pressure from parents and teachers, the poor kid might work the hardest to achieve good grades, but that journey will suck all of his energy out, and he will feel drained. His good grades will be a result of his stress and anxiety. Can you imagine what happens to his happiness? And when you interact with him, what will your experience be? Instead, for example, if your child loves chemistry or photography, he will enjoy studying it and get good grades as a result of love and happiness. His chances of being successful will be much higher.

Most parents fall into this trap. Their children suffer and blame them later. But it is not the parents' fault either. It is how we have been programmed to think. We want our children to have what we know the best. But we are living in a new era of a constantly changing world. The opportunities for children are unlimited and somewhat affordable for most households. Children define their own success. Often our children know, anticipate, and dream about things much more than we can imagine. Imposing our old ideas of success or happiness on our children has become obsolete. If you want children to be successful or happy, you will have to give them the environment to create, fail, and innovate, and set them free to live their purpose, passion, or anything else. That's the only way a human being can become truly happy—by living on her terms.

I'm not here to give parenting advice. Every house is different, every parent's situation is different, and every kid is different. But there is one thing very common across almost all parents: they want their children (or loved ones) to be successful and happy. Your loved ones must be able to choose and get the support they need on their journeys.

Yes, they might not exactly know what they want right now. It is like going to a new restaurant where you are not familiar with the menu and wanting to try a few items before saying, "I love this." The things your loved ones might choose initially might not be a hit for them, and it takes time, but not trying and following the crowd will stress them out later in life when they realize that they couldn't even try.

The Zuckerbergs' parents wanted the best for their children, but they also let them live their passion.

In short, live your own passion and let your loved ones live theirs.

REFLECTION

Spanning across your career (job or business), sports, wealth, pleasure, relationships, or any other thing, list your top five greatest achievements in your life so far.

1. _____
2. _____
3. _____
4. _____
5. _____

Now take a piece of paper and think about your next-level dreams or goals on each area of the six elements of life (i.e., The star of life).

ACHIEVEMENTS

For the longer term, what goals do you want to achieve in the next five years, three years, and one year?

In the short term, what do you want to achieve in the next six months, three months, or one month so these goals align with your long-term goals?

Below, I have outlined some of my goals. You want to ask yourself, "Where am I?" "Where do I want to go?" and "What will I do every day or week to achieve my goals?" in all six elements, plus anything else you might want to pursue.

Be as honest as possible with your answers.

Achievements and Goals	Health	Meaning	Love & Connections	Engagement	Pleasure	Others Goals
Where I am?	I finished a half-marathon in 2019	I do zero volunteering at the moment.	I spend 3 hours a week talking to my parents	I can get flow from writing, reading and talking.	I spend 2 hours on Netflix	My Business Revenue is $ XX
Where I want to go?	I want to finish a full-marathon next year	Volunteer at least twice a month to make a difference.	I want to spend 4 hours a week on them.	I want to try getting flow from running and exercising	I want to spend 1 hour on it.	My Business Revenue needs to be $ YY
What will I do everyday/week to reach my goals?	I will run 30-40k a week	I shall actively look for opportunities to volunteer every week	I will make time and intentionally schedule an additional hour	I will make time and *pay full attention* to these activities to get more flow	I will use a timer to make sure to reduce Netflix time	I will make more strategic *decisions and actions* every day to make this happen

I have identified *where I am?* and where *I want to go*. In all six areas of *the Star of Life*

Achievements and Goals	Health	Meaning	Love & Connections	Engagement	Pleasure	Others Goals
Where you are?						
Where you want to go?						
What will you do everyday or week to reach your goals?						

Honestly identify *specifically* where *you are?* and where *you want to go?* In all six areas of *the Star of Life*

Whether it is for you or your loved ones, focus on excellence in what you love, and success will follow you automatically

YOUR LIFE BY DESIGN

"If you don't design your own life plan, chances are you'll fall into someone else's plan. And guess what they have planned for you? Not much."

—Jim Rohn

DESIGN ON YOUR TERMS

Remember, our goal is to design and have all six elements of the Star of Life and live extraordinary lives on our terms. By now, you will have identified and planned the individual elements for yourself—things like what roles are strongly meaningful to you and how and whom you impact by them. What activities give you engagement, or flow, and how can you do more of them? Who are the people you love, care for, and have intimate bonds with? How can you create beautiful memories with them? Who are the people in your outer circles?

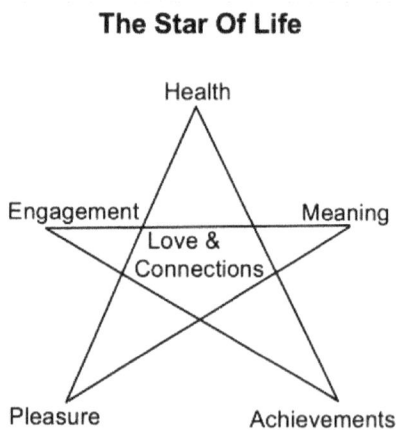

The Six Elements Of A Satisfying Life

What activities give you pleasure, and what do you look forward to in the coming days, weeks, and months? What dreams and goals do you want to achieve, and by when? Do you know exactly where you are and where you want to be? What have you committed to doing daily or weekly towards your goals? And finally, the most important element is your health. How do you honor your body? What minimum will you commit to getting to the next level when you eat, drink, move, exercise, sleep, and relax?

But designing and writing these things down is not enough. You must be able to do them as your habits to get results. Nothing changes in your life unless you take consistent and directed actions.

DESIGN AND LIVE YOUR DAYS

Life by design is nothing but living your days by design, because your life is a collection of days. You must change your days to change your life.

So how do you actually incorporate the six elements in your days?

Before I started to study the science of happiness, my days were very spontaneous. Over the years, my wife and I redesigned our days and weeks to include all six elements. For example, Mahin wakes up in the morning and does yoga, which helps her health. Then she will have her morning coffee (it is a big deal for her), which is her pleasure point. She runs her online business and has small goals, so her daily progress helps her achievement point. She is very analytical and loves to do research and crunch numbers to get into flow. In the afternoon, she spends half an hour in her small garden, which gives her flow again. Then she runs for thirty minutes, which again helps her health point. At night she spends time with family, which gives her meaning, love, and connection points. Most nights, she watches Netflix for an hour or does something pleasurable.

She also helps other women to live more empowering lives in and outside her wider family on Sundays. This is strongly meaningful to her. A portion of the profit she makes from her business goes to that cause.

Mahin's design of her days is not perfect, but that works for her. And this is just an example of how anyone can design have all six elements in a week. Of course, yours will be different to suit your own context. Mahin's schedule wasn't always like this. She did a lot of tweaks and tricks to her schedule to see what works for her, and over the last few years, she optimized her schedule to make it sustainable for her lifestyle.

Take a piece of paper and design your perfect day. Remember, you don't need to have all six elements in a single day. You can spread them across your whole week. But make sure you have all six elements,

What does that look like from morning till night for you?

USE POSITIVE EMOTIONS FOR MOMENTUM

You can use those specific activities that give you positive emotions more intentionally, and they will give you momentum throughout the day. Professor Barbara Fredrickson's research on broaden-and-build theory suggests that our positive emotions help us succeed in micro activities. For example, Mahin's morning coffee gives her pleasure, which boosts her mood to help her work better. When she makes a little progress on her business, it makes her feel good, which encourages her to push more boundaries in her business. After she finishes work, she is excited about her small garden, which gives her flow, and she is more likely to go for a run and feels stronger and lighter. That helps her spend quality time with her family, and then she watches Netflix or something she likes. Positive emotions will create positive ripple effects in our daily activities.

But where you get your positive emotions from is important. For example, Mahin gets positive emotions from Netflix, but she also gets them from gardening. Both activities give her positive emotions, but in gardening, she has to earn the positive emotion (from flow) by "doing" it. She generates positive emotions by gardening. Watching Netflix does not require her to do anything on her part to get a positive emotion. Focus on the activities in which you can actively do something to have positive emotions (e.g., as opposed to waiting to watch your favorite TV show passively). That way you will always have the key to your happiness whenever you want.

The amount of time Mahin spends purely on pleasurable activities is only about one hour a day. Things like drinking coffee and watching Netflix make up about 6.25 per cent of her waking hours. But she gets deep satisfaction (and positive emotions) from the other 93.75 per cent of her time, which is spent on health, engagement (flow), achievements, meaning, or love and connections. So Mahin lives by design on her terms. Has she become happier and more satisfied?

Absolutely.

Can you do the same or better? Why not?

IF YOU DON'T HAVE TIME

When you feel you don't have time for something, that essentially means the thing is not a priority for you. Almost anyone would agree that a US president is one of the busiest people in the world. If President Biden, President Obama, and the likes of them can make time to go for a run, exercise, spend quality time with family, play golf, and engage in what they love to do, most people (including you and me) don't have an excuse.

See, time is not a problem. We all get twenty-four hours a day. But still, we end up being, doing, and having different things in life. It is your life, and you decide how you want to live, but if you think you are too busy to redesign and live your days, maybe living on your terms or living by design is not a priority for you. As previously mentioned, if you want to live a satisfying life led by science, you will need to make your heart a priority, value your time, and make a strong decision to live an extraordinary life on your terms.

The only way you can do that is by living your days by design—not when you get some time, but by making time every day.

SCHEDULES, SPONTANEITY, AND HARMONY

You may already be doing some activities to get a few elements of the Star of Life. That's awesome. But designing your days or weeks and living by them requires you to consistently follow a schedule and make that part of your habits to suit your lifestyle. And if you follow that ritual long enough (usually at least thirty to ninety days), you will start to see results.

Think about it. If you have a great body, that is a result of your eating and exercise rituals. The money you have in your bank is a result of your money habits. If you have a deep and loving connection with your partner, how did that happen? It is possible that your partner didn't fall in love with you because you got her a present on her birthday (or on any special day) but because of the little things you do every day for her as your loving rituals (e.g., you hold her hand when walking, you listen to her with empathy, you bring her a glass of water without her asking).

Living a satisfying and extraordinary life on your terms also results from your daily rituals. Scheduling and following a pattern led by science ensures we have all six elements of a satisfying life every day or week.

Yes, sometimes we all get derailed from our schedules. It is expected that you design your perfect day but you miss a few things or forget about them, as they are new additions to your schedule. Remember, we are all human beings and not machines. Often, we forget that we run on our emotions more than our schedules. But schedules help us stay on course to improve the quality of our lives.

You may or may not like schedules and prefer to deal with one day at a time with spontaneity. That's fine, but make sure you have all six elements done. For example, perhaps you didn't have time for pleasure (e.g., watching a movie) or didn't get a chance to get flow (e.g., by playing guitar). Maybe you were swamped with meetings, and you didn't get to exercise or couldn't take your kid to football as you promised the other day. We all have those things. Make sure you do them as soon as you get a chance, and do not procrastinate.

> "We are what we repeatedly do. Excellence, then, is not an act, but a habit."
> —Will Durant

But if you constantly find yourself catching up on things, you may have to work on your priorities and schedules. Don't fill up your days with back-to-back appointments (not just work appointments, but personal appointments as well [e.g., yoga, getting into flow, calling your best friend]). You might think, "Seriously! Schedule for personal stuff?" Yes, until such appointments become automatic habits in your days. Remember, most of us have been programmed to schedule "work stuff" so we do not miss or forget meetings with our bosses, colleagues, teams, or clients. That way, corporates ensure that their employees get things done on time. Think about it; how many work appointments have you forgotten, missed, or procrastinated on compared to your personal commitments? For most people, procrastination at work is much lower.

Also, do not overestimate your schedules. If you can comfortably do five items a day, don't schedule eight. Always have 30-40 per cent (Yes) room for adjustments and rest. That way you will not feel overwhelmed, and most importantly you will get things done instead of putting them off for tomorrow. Often, saying "No" to things with lesser priorities is the key.

If you design your days and then fail to follow them, don't worry. But always get back to your desired schedule. Every time you miss one thing (e.g., your yoga class, spending time with your kid, your flow activity), you will miss out on that little bit of satisfaction for the day,

and if you keep missing those little bits of satisfaction for weeks or months, guess what happens?

Your life doesn't change.

And you don't become happier or more satisfied. You may fail over and over again to stay on your schedule, and this is normal. I failed numerous times too. But you must get back to your schedule, make adjustments, and make them your lifestyle. And over time, you may not need a schedule anymore as they become your automatic behavior. But if you don't give up, you will find the harmony that works for your lifestyle.

In anything you do, you want to be satisfied.

Otherwise, what's the point?

REFLECTION

Remember the default life of assumptions? Many people chase that and end up regretting it later. But the science of happiness and satisfaction gives us the ability to live extraordinary lives by design on our terms.

Yes, you may still have regrets, but they will be fewer.

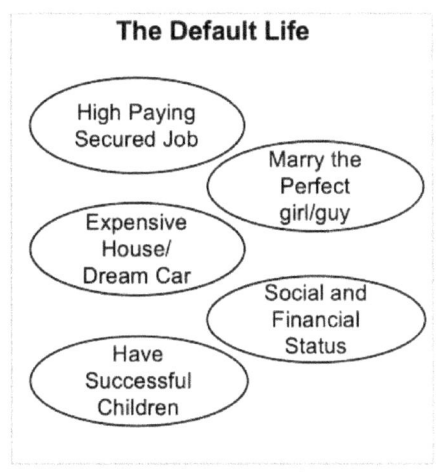

What Most People Chase

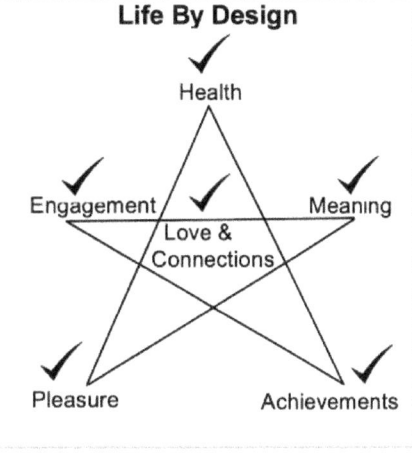

What Science Tell Us

To live a satisfying life, science does not tell you to get a high-paying job; it tells you to get a job that fulfils you. It does not tell you that money cannot buy happiness; instead, it tells you how to use money wisely to be happy and satisfied. It does not tell you to build an expensive house; it tells you to build a loving home. It does not tell you to marry the perfect and the most beautiful girl; it tells you how to build a loving relationship. It does not ask you to chase success to be happy but gives you the tools to be happy so your success can happen naturally.

And, of course, it tells you to take care of your health, which allows you to do everything else.

I sincerely believe that you will live your life by design and have an extraordinary life on your terms.

PART 4:
Your Skills to Live a Happy Life

In this part, we will discuss the following:

- what a happy life is
- why your happiness is your responsibility
- what the three lanes of happiness are
- what you can and cannot control
- where to focus on and what to avoid
- how to be happy
- how to stay happy
- your happiness and emotional habits
- your DAD
- eleven happiness habits to make you happy
- seven emotional habits to protect your happiness
- what to do the next time you are angry, frustrated, or scared

YOUR HAPPINESS IS YOUR RESPONSIBILITY

"Life is not about how fast you run or how high you climb, but how well you bounce."
—Vivian Komori

WHAT IS A HAPPY LIFE?

If you live till ninety or more, you will have 32,850+ days.

But if you had only one day, how would you like to live? How would you want to feel at every moment?

I was talking to one friend and asked her this question. She is a food lover, and she said, "Oh my god, really! Well, I will go to my favorite restaurants and eat. I have so many on my list." I was stunned and said, "Are you serious? You would be eating?" she said, "Yeah. I guess when I'm not here, eating is what I will miss." Then we both started laughing. But with all seriousness, she has a beautiful family. She loves her family more than anything in the whole world.

There is a saying that states, "Airports see more sincere kisses than wedding halls. The walls of hospitals have heard more prayers than the walls of churches."

Would you agree?

Most of us want to spend our precious time with our loved ones and create loving memories. We want to feel relaxed, peace, calmness, love, excitement, and, of course, happiness. No one wants to feel the opposites. We are hard-wired to seek pleasure and avoid pain. All of our feelings happen in our brains and cause us to feel good or bad in some ways. We don't always call the good feelings "happiness" but give them many different names. Professor Dan Gilbert from Harvard said that when we feel happy, the neurons in our brains are in a "certain dance."

But the line between feeling good and bad is very thin. You may remember my day in San Francisco. I was excited to see the Apple garage, but I felt frustrated being stuck in the traffic on our way back. I was having a great time at the Golden Gate Bridge, but ten minutes later, I was very annoyed with the guy at the petrol station.

We all have similar moments in our days when we feel good in one moment, but the next, we feel the opposite. Feeling happy or unhappy is like the clouds in the sky or like the wind at the beach. They keep changing. Even when you have a happy special occasion, you may still feel frustrated about your cake on your birthday, your best friend for being late for your graduation, or even the flower guy at your wedding.

You see, just because those special occasions are supposed to be our "happy days," they are not guaranteed to be. There is almost always something or someone screwing things up, which can make you angry, frustrated, or unhappy. Yes, feeling low, sad, or angry about someone or something is okay, but staying that way does not make sense.

The most important thing to realize is that your happiness always fluctuates and is very susceptible to internal (your own thoughts, actions, and behaviors) and external factors (other people and things around you). You may also remember our genetic happiness set point from Professor Sonja's research. Every one of us has a baseline happiness set by our genetics, and that is our default level of happiness. After an unhappy event or any setback (e.g., the loss of a job), we feel unhappy, or after a win (e.g., a promotion), we feel happy. But over time, we adapt to both situations, and our happiness always returns to our genetic default happiness.

Our aim is to have our happiness levels to be and stay higher than our default genetic happiness.

How often? Well, most of the time.

As I said before, the difference between feeling good and feeling bad is very small. That essentially means you have the power to change the way you feel very quickly.

But how do you do that? You do so by developing that skill.

Feeling low or unhappy is normal. We all feel those ways. But your ability to change the way you feel from being angry to being calm, feeling frustrated to feeling grateful, judgmental to non-judgmental, or unhappy to happy is determined by your skill to change the way you feel.

In this part, I will explain why we feel the way we do and how to change that by developing the skill of being and staying happy.

When you keep your happiness level higher than your default genetic happiness by creating more happy moments than unhappy ones, you have a happy day. And a happy life is about creating more happy days.

YOUR RESPONSIBILITY

Earlier, we discussed the satisfying life. You must have the six elements in your life to feel fulfilled and satisfied.

But happiness is not like that.

It is more about how you feel in your moments. Do you have the skills to feel good more than bad? Or are you just going with the flow and reacting to events around you?

Just knowing about the happiness skills is not enough. But your ability to develop them as your habits and apply them in your days makes all the difference. It is your job to create more happy moments every day. Also, to guard your happiness, you need to notice and act on someone or something that makes you unhappy. That's why when it comes to being and staying happy, the first thing to understand is responsibility.

If you want to live a happy life, whose responsibility is that?

I have a number of families, friends, and business contacts in New York. When COVID-19 hit hard in early 2020, I wanted to check on them. I called one of my contacts, Sarah. She works for an insurance agency. I asked her how she was doing. She looked very distressed and said, "I was doing good until this surge in COVID numbers. I'm stuck at home and cannot go out. A lot of people are hospitalized, suffering and some are dying. Everywhere I look, I see sad news. So not good, really. Can't wait for this to be over."

I asked, "You haven't contracted Covid, have you?" She rolled her eyes and said, "No, but I hope not. Things are already very bad here." I was actually in New York for some work just about a month prior. I empathized, and I couldn't imagine the rough times they were going through. I asked her, "How do you spend your days?" she said, "I wake up, check my messages, then watch the news. I order some food. Sometimes I like to cook, but these days don't feel like it. I worry about the future. The government isn't doing enough. I'm not sure how we get out of it."

A few days later, I spoke to one of our business relationship managers, Mark, at a major bank in New York. He helps us with our banking needs for our online businesses in the US. Mark picked up the phone and said, "Hello, Mr. Ahmed. So good to hear your voice." He said it in a way that sounded as if he were talking to his best friend after a long break, even though I had met him only a few times in person during our visits to New York over the previous couple of years.

So I asked him, "How have you been?" He said, "You know things are tough here, but I'm good. Even though I have Covid, I'm recovering now." Then he laughed. I was surprised and asked, "Are you doing all right? Do you have any sickness?" He said, "Yeah, I had a fever for a couple of days but getting better now. All of my family members have Covid, but most of them are recovering. My main goal is to take care of myself and my family right now, which is the only thing I can do. But I'm going back to work in four weeks." Then he laughed again.

I asked, "How do you spend your days at home?" He said, "Well, I spend most of my time with my family. We play board games, cook what we like together, watch movies, order Uber Eats, and sometimes play video games. Other than having Covid, we are actually doing really good. In fact, it allowed us a lot of family times that we never had before."

Sarah and Mark are both New Yorkers, about the same age, and have similar jobs. But yet they see the world around them very differently. Sarah didn't even get COVID, but she said she was not doing well because of the COVID numbers in New York. She was stuck at home, and everywhere she saw sad news.

On the other hand, Mark and his whole family had COVID, and he had every right to complain about the whole COVID situation and how they were impacted, but instead, they were doing their best to recover at home and actually enjoying their time together.

My intention in telling you about Mark and Sarah is not to persuade you to take COVID lightly. In the last six months, I lost one of my sweetest aunties and another uncle in my close family, as well as several others in my wider family and friends circle. Most people were directly or indirectly impacted by it. This pandemic has taken many lives and created a lot of mental health issues. Think about Sarah; even though she didn't have COVID, she was constantly worrying about it. It is hard to ignore such worries, especially when you fear that you could be the next on the line.

And what does it do to your happiness? You can imagine.

There was life before the COVID, and there will be life after COVID, just like the world saw with the Spanish flu in 1918. But we get impacted by our surroundings all the time. When the COVID pandemic is over, there will be hundreds of other things we will be worried about.

It was not COVID that made Sarah unhappy. It was more the way she dealt with worries that determined her happiness. Worries are part of our lives and will always be there. The question is, how can you deal with them so that they minimally impact you? If you are always worrying about the future or regretting the past, then you may not have been responsible for your own happiness.

Let me unfold that. Think about a few things that give most people pleasure—things like enjoying a delicious meal, having a great conversation with a best friend, watching an amazing film, or having sex. Notice that for you to have pleasure, you are the one who has to eat that delicious meal, have the great conversation with your best friend, watch the film, or do the sex. No one can do these things for you.

The enjoyment of a meal, a conversation, a film, or sex happens inside your brain as you do the activity. It is impossible for other people to do the activities for you. In simple terms,

if you are not doing these things, you are not getting any pleasure. That's it.

And whether you actually do those things that make you happy or sit there and worry is really up to one thing. And that is your responsibility.

For example, think about just one thing you are proud of in your life. You may have built a great body, earned a lot of money, built great loving relationships with your loved ones, or some other such things. Did your achievements just automatically happen? I'm sure you must have taken full responsibility for them.

If you truly want to be and stay happy, that is also your responsibility. Your happiness is and will be highly influenced by the people around you, whether they are your loved ones at home, colleagues at work, or friends at social gatherings. But if you are always dependent and waiting for them to make you happy, you have given the key to your happiness to them. When they act in your ways, you feel happy; but when they do not, you become unhappy.

That is conditional happiness.

While the people around you love you and support you, it is not their primary job to make you happy all the time.

It is yours.

Remember, Sarah was complaining about the COVID situation and the government, and she was not letting herself be happy because of them. But being in the same city, Mark, even after having COVID, was not complaining and was doing whatever he could to deal with the situation and make the best of his time at home.

Sarah was not responsible for her own happiness, but Mark was.

Think about it, if you are a house owner and something breaks in your house, who is responsible for protecting or fixing it? It is your house, and you are responsible for what happens inside it.

Whether it is COVID, laws, the news, the people around you, or some other influence, its impact will always be there and make you either happy or unhappy. But how you deal with that and respond is what matters.

Your happiness is not someone else's responsibility.

It must be yours.

Nothing in this book (or any other book) will matter to you unless you take responsibility and focus on your own happiness.

Where exactly does your happiness or unhappiness happen? Inside your brain. And who is responsible for what happens inside your brain?

You are.

REFLECTION

If you are feeling low for any reason,

- When you are alone, pay attention to your thoughts.

- When you are with other people, pay attention to how they make you feel.
- When you are doing something, pay attention to how the activity is making you feel.

These are a few things I learned. If you are curious, give it a try.

THREE LANES OF HAPPINESS

"If you want to be happy, set a goal that commands your thoughts,
liberates your energy, and inspires your hopes."
—Andrew Carnegie

You might say, "Okay, I have now taken ownership of my own happiness and am fully responsible for it.

What's next?"

Think about driving. As a responsible driver, you must understand the controls of your car, such as the steering, brakes, and accelerator, and you must know when and how to apply them on the road. As you take responsibility for your own happiness, it is important that you clearly understand and realize what and who makes you happy or unhappy and what level of control you have over them.

We derive happiness from many different sources. A sunny day, a nice cup of tea, falling in love, getting a promotion, or going on a holiday can make us happy. But the irony is that the same sources often also make us unhappy, as we can see with things like stormy weather, awful tea, breaking up with someone, getting fired, or maybe losing your wallet on your holiday.

As you know, the difference between feeling good and feeling bad is small. And your mood and feeling can change in an instant. That's why you must be in control' of your emotions all the time (or at least most of the time).

Generally, in almost any situation, you have two options. The first is to complain about it and expect it to be fixed by others, and the second is to take responsibility and actually do something about it. But no matter how hard you try, that something may not be in your control (such as the weather). Sometimes you may have partial control (such as getting a promotion), and often you have full control (such as you love singing).

I have put those sources and controls into three general categories.

Combinedly, I call them the "three lanes of happiness."

Firstly, in the outer lane, the sources could be weather, government, news, and the like, where you have no control. Secondly, in the people lane, the sources could be your family, friends, and people you spend time with, and you may have partial control over them. And finally, in the self-lane, the sources are your own thoughts, actions, and behaviors, and you have full control over them. All three lanes of control have the potential to make you happy or unhappy.

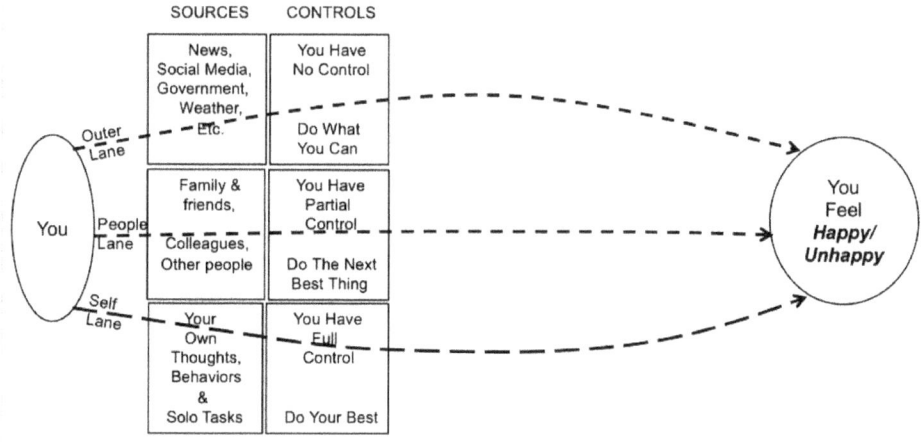

THE OUTER LANE

It was March 2020. We had just landed at LAX airport in Los Angeles. It was the week when COVID-19 started to become a big deal and the WHO declared it a pandemic. We flew from Melbourne to LA, as my wife and I had previously planned, for a few weeks of business work in the US. Neither Australia nor the US had any travel restrictions at that time.

So we were at the gate, waiting for our next flight to Dallas. I looked at the TV screen and saw that they were talking about declaring a state of emergency. With the uncertain situation unfolding rapidly, it looked as though everything was about to close. We had a few conferences to attend, and some of them sent us emails straightaway saying they had been postponed. I sensed that most of our plans in the next few weeks were going to be either cancelled or changed.

I was very tired following our long flight already and was witnessing that things were changing every minute, and almost all of them were not in our favor. I was stressing out and felt completely helpless.

So we decided to go to a cafe nearby, went over our original plan, and then started reprioritizing. We had to drop several things (probably more than twenty) and decided to do only the two most important items and go back to Melbourne as soon as possible.

In the next few days, we were able to go to New York as planned, and with some pivoting and rescheduling, we got our work done.

Well, thank God, and we were relieved a bit.

The next challenge was to go home as soon as possible. We didn't want to get stuck in the US while most countries were shutting their borders. The prime minister of Australia declared that anyone entering Australia must self-quarantine for two weeks at home. And we thought that wouldn't be a problem when we returned. But our return flights were another two weeks out. Our airline had also mentioned on their website that they would allow passengers to modify the flight dates and times with no additional fees. But the challenge was to get through to their customer service phone number. The waiting time was about five to six hours before someone picked up. I tried a number of times every day for three days with no luck. We even tried going to the actual airline counter at LAX, but they couldn't change our flight to an earlier date. After exhausting all possible options, the only thing we could do was to buy another one-way ticket home with an earlier date.

We did that and flew back to Melbourne after spending only nine days in the US instead of three and a half weeks.

RESISTANCE TO CHANGE

The things outside your control have the potential (and good chance) to upset you. Becoming upset and complaining do not necessarily make things better for you. In fact, the system (that you are annoyed about) does not change, but the neurons in your brain change and make you unhappy. If that is a pattern for you, you are the one suffering, not that system or people you are complaining about.

Things like weather, government rules, and companies do not wait for you. They change whether you like it or not. Everything changes. Your best friend can change, your loved ones can change, and you will change. In fact, the body you are currently living in is constantly changing. Change is the only constant in life. Your inability to cope makes your life harder and makes you unhappier. The opposite makes you happier.

DO WHAT YOU CAN

Things don't always go according to plan. Government rules, weather, pandemics, traffic conditions, and such things will always be part of our lives. They literally create the environment that we live and operate in. But we have almost zero control over them, and there is not much we can do about any impact we directly or indirectly get from them. And, of course, these impacts can make us uncomfortable, stressed out, or unhappy in general, even though sometimes they do make us happy.

We may not be able to do our best or even do the next best thing. But we can do what we can.

For returning home from the US, the best thing would have been to change our return flight to an earlier date, which we couldn't do. Well, the next best thing, which we did, was actually go to the check-in counter at LAX airport and talk to them, which we did, but it didn't help. The last thing that we could do, which was somewhat in our control, was buy another ticket and go home, which we eventually did.

When we came back home, the lockdowns and restrictions started. We had to operate within the rules and regulations set by the government. That was the right thing to do. But within those rules, I shifted my face-to-face group workshops online. We couldn't dine out at a restaurant, so we did Uber Eats. We couldn't meet our family and friends, so we regularly chatted via video calls. We couldn't share meals with them, so we drove to their homes and dropped food at their doors, and they did the same for us. I personally reconnected with many old friends and families after a long time during the lockdowns.

It was not only us; many people did similar things during lockdowns. Singers and musicians from various parts of the world got together and played and started singing on Zoom calls. Early in the pandemic, New Yorkers began cheering for the frontline essential workers every evening at 7:00 p.m. from their windows, balconies, and streets. They clapped, yelled, and blew horns to support each other, and that ritual lasted for months.

These things didn't make the pandemic go away, but as human beings, these rituals helped us come together and be stronger than ever to fight it. When things are hard, you may not be able to do what you want, but instead of complaining, you can always do what you can.

MAKE YOUR TIME COUNT

Another time, we were flying from Melbourne to Bali, and at the airport, just an hour before the boarding, the crews announced that they needed to do an urgent repair of the aircraft and that boarding would be delayed. They didn't mention how long that was going to be. So most people, including us, thought it would be a minor repair that would take an hour or so. But we ended up waiting for about four hours.

That day, I noticed something as all the passengers on our flight were waiting; some people got very impatient and were walking back and forth for a few hours. They were calling people and complaining about how bad and unprepared the crews were. They were not making a lot of fuss about it, but they seemed very unhappy. Some people were looking at their phones or laptops almost the whole time as they were waiting.

They seemed very calm and in control. And finally, there were some who started chatting with other fellow passengers, having some snacks, having a few drinks, and playing games with their kids, and they made their waiting time very enjoyable.

You may find it a little weird, but I love observing other people. My wife and I were watching other planes taking off. We talked to some other passengers and had a few snacks, and, of course, I did some work on my laptop. (That's just me.)

The reason why I'm telling you this is that people react very differently to the same events. The flight delay was for everybody that day, but some became impatient and unhappy, some were calm, and some made the most out of their time at the gate.

Sometimes you literally just cannot do anything but wait. But the last thing you want to do is complain and do nothing. The things in the "outer lane" are not in your control.

If you believe that you are going through things (including the pandemic) where you feel stuck and helpless, please don't feel that way. Rather, ask yourself and do what you can to make this time more enjoyable and meaningful for you and your loved ones.

THE PEOPLE LANE

Many years ago, Simon was my manager at a big corporate. One morning he asked the team, "Is any one of you available to review the design document for the blueline project?" I was the only one from our team involved and already working on the project. (Just to set the context, I had led several projects successfully in the past for Simon.) The most logical thing would be for me to review the document. There was no need to ask someone else on the team. So I said, "This is my project. I would be happy to review." Simon pretended that he didn't hear me and said, "Jeremy, can you review the document and send me your comments this afternoon?"

Jeremy said, "Yes, no problem."

Simon's behavior made me very annoyed and frustrated. It was just one of many examples I experienced during his time as my manager.

Ideally, I would give you more context of the conversation and why I was annoyed, but just for this section, I just want to highlight that you will surely come across people like Simon—whether they are at your work, at home, or anywhere else—who will make you feel unappreciated, unheard, disliked, or generally very unhappy.

Earlier, I had another manager, Richard, for a couple of years. One day, Richard came and said, "I just heard that Paul resigned yesterday, and there is a vacant position in the SME team. I thought you guys might want to know." And then he left. Ideally, Paul's vacant position would be my next-level role. Richard knew that. But originally, I thought I needed another year of experience, and then I would think about the next level. And I felt that I was not ready for my next role. So I said to Richard, "I have been thinking about my next role, but I don't think I'm ready to take Paul's role just yet. What do you think?" Richard said, "Well, opportunities don't always align with your readiness. If you are serious about your next role, you should apply for it now." That statement pushed me out of my comfort zone and kind of mandated me to shift my thinking. Then I asked him, "What if I don't get it?" Richard shrugged and said, "You will never be 100 per cent ready for any role. No one will. Some things you will have to learn on the job, and I think you have what it takes." Then he said, "If you don't get that role, you will still have your current role. You have nothing to lose but an opportunity to level up."

As Richard suggested, I did apply for my next role. But I didn't get it at that time. But about ten months later, they created a new role in the SME team and promoted me automatically.

The reason why I'm telling you this is that some people believe in you more than you do in yourself. People like Richard are blessings, and they push you to move forward, inspire you, support you, and give you good and honest feedback when needed. If you genuinely ask yourself, you will almost always feel energized around these people. They give you a feeling of comfort. You will automatically feel that these people can understand you. Generally, they make you feel happy.

The people you regularly surround yourself with (usually family, friends, and work colleagues) have a much stronger influence on your happiness than a stranger at the cafe. Some of them will regularly make you feel good and happy, while others will do the opposite to you. I highly encourage you to take an audit of the people you usually hang out with.

A very simple way to do this is to select a person and ask yourself, "How do you usually feel after you spend time with this person?"

Take a moment and really ponder upon the people who make you feel important, valued, appreciated, and generally happy. For me, Richard was one of them.

Who are they for you? Spend more time with them.

Also, identify the people who make you feel bad, guilty, annoyed, or generally unhappy. For me, Simon was one of them.

Who are they for you? Be aware and protect yourself by spending less time with them.

The closer the person is to you, the harder it is to be aware and protect yourself. On the flip side, though, the closer the person is to you, the easier it is to spend more time with him or her.

YOUR PARTIAL CONTROL

Once you have identified and decided to spend more and more time with the people who make you feel good or happy, whether they are your partner, children, parent, close friends or colleagues, or whoever, you must realize an important aspect of them. Even if they or their doings make you feel good and happy,

You cannot fully control them.

For example, when your children excel at school, your partner brings you a flower, your boss gives you a nice compliment, or your best friend arranges a surprise birthday party for you, all these will make you happy. However, what if your children didn't excel at school, your partner forgot to bring you flowers on your anniversary, your boss didn't give you a well-deserved compliment or your favorite team member didn't perform as you expected. All these things will make you unhappy.

You see, with them, there is always a condition attached to your happiness. You may not have many expectations from the people who make you unhappy, but you do have expectations from people who make you happy. When your expectations are not met for whatever reasons, you might be upset about it.

That is your conditional happiness from people you spend time with. And that includes the people you expect and cherish the most. Whenever there is a condition attached, you have only partial control.

SO DO THE NEXT BEST THING

You may have planned the next weekend with your son to spend some quality time, but perhaps your son does not look very interested on the day. You cannot get him to enjoy the activities you planned.

He is bored.

You have every reason to be unhappy, but you realize that even though he is your son and you know what might be best for him, the older he gets, the less influence you will have on him. As a separate human being, your son will have his own mood swings, interests, choices, and passions (different from yours).

As his parent, you might find that his disengagement makes you unhappy.

Ideally, the best thing for your happiness is your son enjoying what you planned for him. But often that does not happen with other people (including your family). What you can do in such cases is do the next best thing. If you can "encourage" or "inspire" your son to enjoy the activities you planned, or help him choose what he loves to do, then he might enjoy them. Spending quality time with your son is an activity you planned and depends on your son's engagement and enjoyment (The condition).

Suppose you want to go to a party with your best friend but she doesn't want to go or you were expecting your partner to take you on a nice holiday but he doesn't want to or you have been expecting a promotion for a long time but your boss does not seem to be interested. The best thing for you to be happy would be all these events happening as you wish, but again, they are all dependent on other people and can make you unhappy.

The next best thing (which may or may not work) you might do is encourage your best friend to go with you, convince your partner to go on that holiday, or prove yourself to your boss to get promoted, and then leave the rest of them, which are not in your control.

Even if you do the next best thing, people can still incorrectly judge you, reject you, or tear you down unknowingly (sometimes knowingly). You will have to accept the risks and conditions when it comes to being and staying happy with people around you.

Yes, when you are going through tough times, a simple and warm chat with your best friend can help you. While you can highly rely on them, you cannot blindly expect them to do all the right things for you. Even if they genuinely want to, they might not be able to because of their own situations, including lack of understanding, skills, time, or even money.

The bottom line is that it is critical to realize that while people around you may love and support you, they may often fail to meet your expectations and can make you unhappy. Your individual experience may differ, but generally, the people you get the most love from have the potential to give you the most pain. Not that they will, but they can.

Keep in mind that while people around you can and will make you happy, at the end of the day, you are responsible for your own happiness.

In the people lane, you have partial control, so do the next best thing.

THE SELF LANE

When I first started my business eleven years ago, I had to reconcile all the business transactions at least a couple of times a month to keep the accounts up to date and have accurate business reports. But that task took a lot of energy out of me and used to make me stressed out. I understood its importance, but I just didn't like to do it myself. Over time, I realized that the task of bookkeeping was not serving me personally. So I outsourced it to a bookkeeper. Even though it was hard for me (as I was starting out) to pay for a bookkeeper, it actually helped me reduce my stress and allowed me to focus on what I actually loved in my business.

At home, I don't like cutting grass in the backyard, which I also outsourced. But there are things that I love doing, like writing and running. Whenever I write or run, I get engaged and lose track of time and experience flow. After I finish writing or running, I do not feel tired; rather, I feel good and satisfied.

Bookkeeping, which makes me unhappy, and writing, which makes me satisfied and happy, are both solo tasks. No other people are involved. Only I am. Every time I write or run, I feel good. I can do these things whenever I want, as often as I want, in the way I want. I have full control over them. Sometimes when I feel low or stressed, I run or write something. Doing so helps me escape to another world and gain more energy to deal with difficult situations and manage stress.

People journal, read, exercise, cook, listen to music, meditate, and do all kinds of solo tasks to feel happy and satisfied.

We do hundreds of tasks every day, some we like and some we don't. The idea is to identify what you do not like and minimize it or outsource it while maximizing what you like. The things you like are your solo tasks. You do not need to depend on anyone or anything to be happy. (Note: Personally, this is one of my favorite "hacks" to be happy.)

YOUR SOLO BEHAVIOR

"I will do it tomorrow" had been my mantra for many years. I used to be a big procrastinator (I still am, but I have improved a lot over the years). A few years ago, I embarked on a journey to lose some belly fat, and I wanted to start a ketogenic diet. But I couldn't get started on it. I kept planning to begin next week or the first of the next month or on the day after my birthday, and so forth. I changed the date to start the diet several times. I procrastinated for more than two months. I noticed that every time I pushed the start date out, it gave me temporary relief, but my guilt and frustration for not starting were piling up inside me. That temporary relief didn't help me reduce my belly fat. I was not making any progress. And that feeling of being stuck was not serving me any longer. One day, I decided that I would not wait for the following week. I would just start that very day and would continue for at least two weeks, no matter what.

I was able to start my new diet and continued for about five days until my regular habit kicked in. I failed to continue, and I went back to my regular diet. In those five days, I didn't lose all my belly fat, but I felt that I made a little progress, which actually made me very happy. In a few days, I restarted my ketogenic diet, and this time I was able to keep going for about ten days and then failed again. The similar on-and-off pattern continued for about three months. But eventually I could stick to my diet and lose my belly fat to the level I wanted, and I continued the diet for nearly two years after that.

The reason why I'm telling you this is that behaviors like procrastination, overthinking, social comparison, or any such self-sabotaging pattern are actually based on the small decisions you make all day. You are the one who is in control of these behaviors, and these patterns can make you and keep you anxious, sad, and frustrated for a long time. No one can control them but you. They are primarily driven by your small decisions.

The opposite of procrastination is taking immediate action. The opposite of overthinking is making decisions quickly. The opposite of social comparison is working on yourself. Even though these skills come with practice and take time, once you learn them, you will find them very fulfilling, and they will help you stay happy.

YOUR THOUGHTS

It is probably impossible to find someone on earth who does not worry. All of us, including you and me, worry about many things every day. But worries and happiness both happen inside our brains. One moment you are happy, and the next, you are worried about something. And that worry steals your moments of happiness, and if it is a chronic condition, it can lead to many other mental issues.

There is an interesting phenomenon called "medical students' disease," a condition frequently reported by medical students who think themselves to be experiencing the symptoms of a disease they are studying, even though, in reality, they are not. This is just one example of our worries. There are hundreds of things we worry about that are never going to be real in the future.

But where do the worries originate from? Our own thoughts.

According to a recent study, an average person has about six thousand thoughts a day. Research varies, but there is no doubt that most of them are negative thoughts. Things like regrets from the past, guilt, worries, and anxiety about the present and future can keep our brains pretty busy during the day and also can keep us up at night.

YOUR FULL CONTROL AND DOING YOUR BEST

Perhaps you have noticed that your thoughts, behaviors, and tasks that we have been discussing are all solo, and you have full control over them. (Yes, you may not be able to completely control your thoughts, but with practice you can get better at managing them by being more emotionally intelligent.)

Our solo thoughts, behaviors, and tasks can make us happy, but they can also make our lives miserable. Nurturing more positive thoughts and discarding negative ones sounds pretty simple, but it is one of the hardest things to do. Using mindfulness is a healthy practice. But developing that awareness and skill to filter your thoughts is the best investment you can ever make when it comes to being and staying happy.

One technique I learned over the years is to ask myself, "How am I feeling?" At 10:00 a.m., 3:00 p.m., and 8:00 p.m. (at least three times a day). Usually, If I'm alone and still feeling low, it is because of my thoughts, and I'm in the wrong thought pattern (either I'm regretting about the past or worrying about the future and not being present). Once I catch myself, I take three deep breaths and refocus on the task in hand to get busy.

Sometimes, you may come across situations where it may feel that your negative thoughts are literally controlling you and stressing you out. No matter how hard you try, you may feel stuck and helpless. Honestly, when I go through such situations myself, I find being engaged in a solo activity (e.g., getting into flow by going for a run or writing) helps me stay away from the negative thoughts in my head and regain my energy.

Remember, you may have a very nice car with full control, but your ability to drive safely in the ever-changing traffic conditions still depends on your good driving skills, which come from years of practice. Likewise, when you are responsible for your own happiness, even in the self-lane, you have full control, but it still requires you to master your own solo tasks, behaviors, and thoughts by practicing every day.

In the self-lane, you have full control, so do your best.

SO WHICH LANE TO FOCUS ON?

My mother is very social and loves hanging out with her family and friends. My dad, on the other hand, is introverted and doesn't mind being by himself. He loves his own company. Before the pandemic started in 2020, my parents used to travel back and forth to visit us in Melbourne and to Toronto to visit my sister and her family. Mum loves to travel. It doesn't matter where or when; she is almost always up for a trip.

But when the COVID-19 pandemic started, they were in Dhaka, and as of this writing, they have been at home over the last year and a half. Also, we put a "family-imposed lockdown" on them and kind of took their freedom away for their own safety.

While my mum understands and realizes the importance of these measures, as a naturally outgoing person, it was very hard for her to cope with the change and stay at home for such a long time. I talk to my mum a few times a week and try to alleviate her worries and help her go through this difficult time. My wife and sister do the same. Before the pandemic, mum spent some time with her four-year-old grandson in Toronto. She misses him a lot, and obviously she cannot travel, as most international borders are closed. She is very upset, but she does video chat with him almost every day. As the situation around the pandemic unfolds, she does not see a way out until most people are vaccinated, and that is going to take at least another year. She cannot stand the fact that she might have to stay at home until that happens.

One of my aunts (mother's younger sister) used to live very close to my parent's house in Dhaka. She was very close to my mum, and they used to talk almost every day. A few months into the pandemic, she contracted COVID-19 and was taken to the ICU, as she had asthma for a few years. Five days later, she passed away. She was not even sixty. Because of the government restriction, no one was allowed to see my aunt after her death except for her son and husband. As you can imagine, this was a big blow for my mum, her other siblings, and the whole family. My mum broke into tears on the video chats during those days as she was going through the trauma of losing her younger sister. It was heartbreaking for my wife and me as well. The auntie we lost was one of the kindest, most empathetic, and sweetest human beings we knew.

A few weeks later, mum was losing interest in many things and was constantly worrying about the things that were not in her control. During my positive psychology studies at Harvard, one of the most important tools I learned from Professor Martin Seligman's talk was journaling the "Three simple good things." That means, before going to bed at night, finding and writing down three good things that happened during the day, along with why they were good for you. They do not have to be very big events. They can be as simple as having a nice tea, your best friend calling you, reading a nice book, and so on. I have also learned that this journaling method rewires the neural network inside your brain and trains your mind to see more positive events that happen during the day for you (you will do this intervention later in this book).

I spoke to my mum and encouraged her to start journaling in this way. For the first few days, she was a little hesitant and made excuses so she wouldn't have to do it. My sister, my wife (they both do regular journaling), and I insisted my mum do it. So she started. For the first few weeks, she missed a few days, but after about two months, she felt a lot better, and I could see that in her facial expressions on our video chats. I asked her, "Do you think that journaling the three good things has helped you see things differently than before?" She said, "First few weeks, I didn't get any notable result, but over time, I could see that not only did it help me come out of the trauma, but in everyday life, I see more positive things." I was very glad to hear that.

Two months later, one of my uncles (my mother's brother-in-law) in Toronto suddenly got sick with a cough and fever and was taken to hospital. After testing, they found that he was COVID-19 positive. He was taken to the ICU as his condition deteriorated. After about nine days, he also passed away. He was about eighty years old. He left behind his wife, three children, and a big family, all of whom live in Toronto.

What can I say? In six months, I had lost one auntie and an uncle in the pandemic. The whole family got their hearts broken and went through trauma. After a few days, I was talking to my mum and asked, "How are you coping?" In normal conditions, when someone dies, the whole family gets together to support each other, but at this time, that was not even possible. She said, "I was hoping that I would be okay in a few days, but two deaths in the family and the pandemic is not getting any better. Also, I had to stop journaling the three good things over the last few days. I just couldn't find anything that I could write as positive." She looked very upset.

I said, "I understand."

I was on LinkedIn the other day and saw that someone from India had posted a picture of a ninety-three-year-old man sitting on a hospital bed. He was getting released from a hospital after being treated for COVID-19. He had already paid his bills. As he was about to leave, the hospital staff stopped him and said he had more bills to pay. The old man asked, "What is the additional bill for?" The staff said they forgot to charge him for one day's oxygen supply. The old man asked, "How much is it?", They said, "13,000 Indian Rupees." Then the man paused for a bit and started crying. The hospital staff thought he didn't have any more money, and they said, "Ok, you already paid a lot, don't worry about it." But the old man didn't stop but kept crying and said, "I have the money. I will pay you now. But I'm crying because, for 93 years, I have been getting oxygen from nature for free. How much do I owe to her?"

I told my mum the old man's story. She didn't say much. After a few minutes, we hung up.

A few days later, I called my mum and asked how she was doing. She said, "I have been thinking about journaling the three good things and how it has changed my life over the last four months. But because of the recent death of my brother, I stopped writing and feeling very low. But this cannot be happening to me. I must bounce back. So I decided to start journaling again." And then she smiled.

A simple five-minute journaling session cannot solve all your problems, but it can certainly train your mind to see more blessings and positive things that happen around us all the time. She shared some of the things she wrote in her journal with me. She said that she watched a nice movie, cooked something that she liked, spoke to her grandson (who gave her a virtual kiss via video chat), called her older sister and had a nice chat, had a good night's sleep, and so on. No matter how hard things look on the surface, we always have something to be thankful for as long as we live.

Remember, COVID-19 takes the "breathing" away for most who die of it. The simplest but most important blessing is our ability to breathe. You can always start with that. Be thankful for every second of your life.

I was so impressed with my mum that I couldn't resist but share this story with you. I didn't even ask her to restart the journaling after her brother's death. I thought she needed some more time to process it. But she did realize how powerful the journaling was for her, and even though initially she found it hard, she started loving it in a few months. She was able to pivot and refocus on the things in her control in her self lane.

Yes, when the pandemic started, she had to stay home for more than a year. When her sister and brother died of COVID-19, she was upset and was going through emotional trauma, but none of these things were in her control. The only thing she could do was pray for them and share the grief with the rest of the family. Yes, she did some other things to engage and take her mind off worries, but the most powerful and reliable thing she did during this time was the solo journaling.

Your brain defaults to picking up on what is "wrong" around you. It is not designed to make you happy. Rather, it is there to help you survive. Most people are wired that way. My mum's solo journaling helped her retrain her brain, which allowed her to see and realize more of what's going right than what's going wrong.

Where does journaling fall? In falls in your self lane as a solo activity.

Through this journaling, my mum became more aware of where to focus than before.

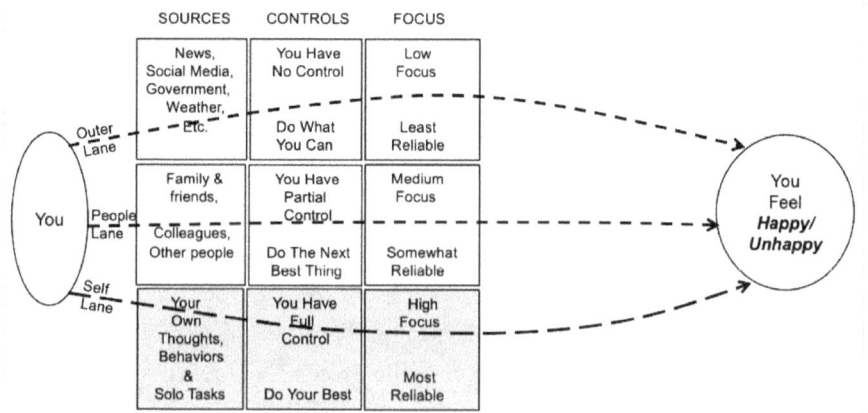

I know. I get it. It's not easy to focus on the bring side all the time. In fact, it is very hard. But this is a skill that comes with practice. Worries are part of our lives. There is no switch to turn off worries. When someone you love, even if in another country, is fighting for his life, you will be worried, no matter how much control you have. We will always have past regrets, present issues, and future worries. But we will also have good memories from the past, blessings in the present, and hope for the future.

REFLECTION

Feeling good or bad, our happiness or unhappiness keeps changing as we live every moment. But our ability to keep our happiness levels higher than our default genetic happiness in those moments is what matters.

How do we do that?

We do so by focusing the least on the outer lane, having a medium focus on the people lane, and, finally, focusing the most on the self lane.

For many years, I have been learning to worry less about the things that are not in my control and focus on the things that are in my control. Author Anthony Robbins summarized this beautifully, he said, "What you focus on is what you feel. What you feel is your experience of life."

Anything you think or do in your self lane is the most powerful to your happiness, and it is the most reliable source you have.

HOW TO BE HAPPY

"Happiness is not something ready-made. It comes from your own actions."
—Dalai Lama

BEING HAPPY IS ABOUT DOING

If I ask you, "What is the most important thing in your life that will make you happy?" Most people say just one word, and that is "Family." Some might say "Health," "Money," "Service to others," or so forth. You may want to spend good quality time with your family (that is doing). If your answer is "Health," what would you do with your health? Maybe you will live longer and spend more time with yourself and your loved ones (also doing). If your answer is "Money," what would you do with that money? You might mention a bunch of things that you want to spend your money on (spending is also doing). There are countless examples of things we do that make us happy.

Remember, happiness is not about getting. It is about doing.

In the past year and a half, because of COVID lockdowns, I personally couldn't do a lot of things that make me happy. For example, I love dining outside, hanging out with friends and family, running face-to-face workshops, travelling, going out for movies, and such. Not only I but millions of other people had similar issues.

Why? Because we couldn't do the things that make us happy.

But even without lockdowns and restrictions, we do not do those things enough or are not very regular in doing the simple things (e.g., getting wet in the rain, giving a random hug to our partners) that make us happy every day. We are so into our daily routines that we forget to do them. Or we don't feel like doing them because they are just too simple and feel ordinary. We postpone being happy and save our happiness for special occasions like celebrations, birthdays, or anything special. Often, we do not allow ourselves to be happy because of past regrets, guilt, present issues, or future worries.

I heard the phrase "Every day is a new beginning" many times over the years but never paid close attention to it. I realized that no matter how bad or frustrating your past has been, and no matter whether you are going through a tough time in the present or worrying about the uncertain future, with a new day, you always have a choice to be that person you have never been, do something you have never done, and have anything you never had.

You might be thinking, "Can you be more specific?"

If you have never taken a walk along the beach, kissed your partner without reason, bought food for a homeless guy, given your teenage son a random hug, or something similar, just do it. These simple but powerful acts will make you (and them) happy today. They will help you navigate the tough times, create good memories, and give hope for the future.

Being happy is about doing numerous things you love. And that essentially means creating happy moments whether by yourself, with your loved ones, or somewhere else. Doing spans across all three lanes we talked about earlier. In the self lane, people lane, and the outer lane, you can choose to do based on your mood and situation in one or more of these lanes. But make sure you do these things every day and do not postpone them for later.

DOING IN THE SELF LANE

As mentioned previously, in the self lane, everything you think or do is solo, and you will do things on your own. You have full control without any dependency. The solo tasks I personally love to do are writing, running, listening to music, reading, planning, and things like them. I am an optimist, and often I live in the future. My thoughts about a better tomorrow get me excited. I'm also an activator; that means I do not just think, but also that I act (behavior) on my thoughts to make progress. Whenever I do a task, thought, or behavior, I feel good, engaged, and energized.

Other ideas are journaling, cooking, meditating, playing musical instruments, playing video games, swimming, exercising, singing, and so on. You want to ask yourself which solo tasks, thoughts, and behaviors you love doing. List them and intentionally do them more often.

The best thing about the self lane is that I can do these things anytime, almost anywhere, and as many times as I want. When I feel low, I seek refuge in this lane. I do my best with my highest focus in this lane, and this is the most reliable lane for my happiness.

DOING IN THE PEOPLE LANE

Almost everything you do in this lane involves other people. So there is dependency, and you have partial control. Some of the tasks I love to do with people are having deep and meaningful conversations with my wife, close family, and friends; running workshops with my students; working with my team; meeting interesting people and making new friends; and so on. These activities with people are meaningful for me and give me a sense of purpose and belonging.

Other ideas are talking to your best friend or someone you trust and emotionally rely on, going to movies or travelling with others, spending time with your family, playing soccer, playing board games, acting, and teaching. You want to ask yourself about and list the activities you love doing with other people. Do them more often with the people you like.

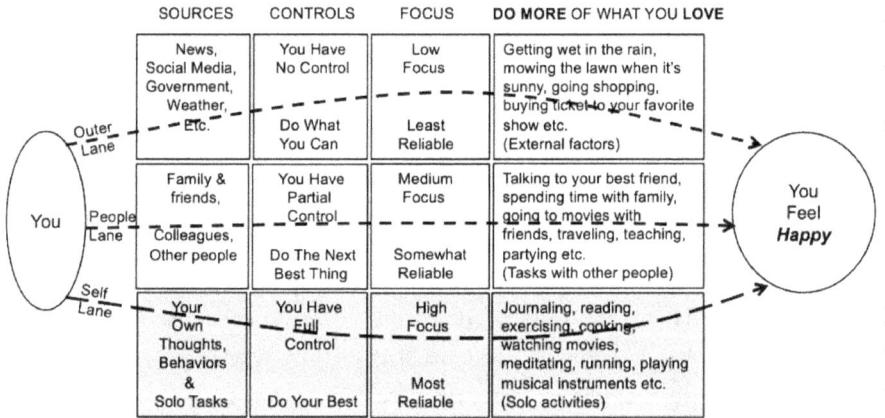

With a bit of a caveat, watch out for the people or activities that you do; sometimes they can make you happy in the moment, but they can be destructive to your life (e.g., hanging out with friends and people who drive you to smoking, using drugs, or doing any other self-destructive behavior).

With people, I may not be able to do my best (e.g., I may want to talk to my best friend, but she may not be available at the time). I try to do at least the next best thing (e.g., I leave her a message to call me back or drive to her place to have a chat whenever she is available next).

The people and tasks in this lane have my medium focus, which is somewhat reliable for my happiness.

DOING IN THE OUTER LANE

Things in this lane are not in my control, so my focus on them is the lowest. The tasks I personally love to do are buying tickets for my favorite show or game, watching a long-awaited movie on Netflix, sitting on the swing with Mahin on a sunny day, driving to our favorite places, and so on. What we do in the outer lane is highly dependent on external factors, so I try to make the best out of every opportunity. Sometimes this strategy does not work, but there is no harm in trying. But when I get to do the things that I truly want, I feel good, accomplished, and generally happy.

Other ideas are getting a tax break from the government; getting out of the pandemic lockdown or restrictions; having the best weather for skiing, swimming, or even mowing the lawn; and buying tickets and actually attending a game of your favorite team. You want to ask yourself what you would love to do if or when possible. List these and intentionally do them whenever you can.

As I don't have any control over external factors, I do what I can and do not sweat it if I cannot make it work. Almost everything in this lane is the least reliable for my happiness. If I have to wait for something, I focus on the things in my control, usually in either the self lane or the people lane.

When things in the outer lane or people lane seem far-fetched or not possible, where do you focus? On the self lane.

As I was going through the pandemic lockdowns, I wanted to focus on my self lane and people lane, which were somewhat in my control. So, in the people lane, I had a lot of deep and meaningful conversations with my family and friends, which made my relationships much better. After many years, I reconnected with some old friends and cherished some old memories. And in my self lane, I optimized my health and fitness rituals, watched more Netflix in the last year than what I watched in the last five years, and finished this book that you are reading.

PROTECTING YOUR PRECIOUS HAPPINESS

One night we went to watch the movie The Fast and the Furious. It was amazing. We loved it. Later, we had a nice dinner. My wife and I were still talking about the movie. When we came home, our eyes caught the news on the TV. A man in his fifties had been found dead in his apartment, and the cops were investigating. Twelve people had been killed and forty-one were missing as the result of a landslide in another country. We saw the images on TV, and they were heartbreaking. I couldn't watch it, and I had to change the channel.

The next day, one of my close friends called at lunchtime. After talking to him, I found out that his cousin slipped in the toilet and injured herself. His neighbor lost his job, and then he started complaining about his business. Five minutes later, he hung up.

You might think, "What's the relation between watching a movie or TV news and then talking to a friend?"

After watching that awesome movie, I realized that I enjoyed the movie more than I thought. It felt really good. But when we came home, the news of the dead man in his apartment wasn't good. Even though the landslide had happened in another country, seeing those images made me sad. And the next day, talking to my close friend and finding out about his cousin, his neighbor's loss of job, and his complaints about his business didn't make me feel any better. My emotional states on every news quickly changed from happy to unhappy.

The TV news I watched and the conversation I had with my friend seemed harmless and would be very normal for most people. While I feel bad and have sympathy for the dead man in his apartment, the people affected by the landslide, and my friend's neighbor who lost his job, consuming that information simply does not serve me. In fact, it made me feel sad, helpless, and unhappy. I shall forget these things in a few days, and the next time I watch the news, I will have more negative news to make me feel bad, and the same pattern will continue every day or week. Imagine what will happen to my happiness.

I will be always in an endless cycle of consuming negative news, which regularly makes me unhappy (and I'm not even aware of it!!).

In this age of technology and information, we are constantly being bombarded with articles, TV news, social media posts, emails, and so on from many different directions. It is only natural to feel overwhelmed and low. Most people are not even aware that these sources are constantly impacting their emotional states.

You may feel that you need to be informed, but that comes with an emotional cost to you—and often you are not even aware of it. This is like someone offering you a meal, and you pay for it. Then later you realize that you didn't really want that meal. For me, the TV news and the conversation with my friend were like meals I didn't want to eat. I didn't want to or didn't need to feel sad or bad.

Our emotions keep changing all the time. You see, the sources of our happiness and unhappiness are the same. They are either the things in the outer lane that we do not have control over (TV news); people in the people lane (e.g., my friend's news and complaints); or our own thoughts, behaviors, or tasks in the self lane (overthinking, self-doubt, and such).

If you are trying to be healthy and fit, only eating healthy foods is not enough. You must also avoid junk food that is harmful. Similarly, being and staying happy is not only about doing the things that make you happy but is also about avoiding the things that make you feel bad or unhappy. By avoiding these things, you will protect your happiness.

Like doing, avoiding also spans across all three lanes. In the outer lane, anything that makes you unhappy and over which you have no control. In the people lane, think about those people who annoy you, make you feel low, and drain your energy. And finally, in the self lane are your own thoughts, tasks, and behaviors that make you frustrated and unhappy. Make sure you avoid them when appropriate and needed.

AVOIDING IN THE SELF LANE

In 2018, my friend Ashraf finished a full marathon for the first time, and I was very happy for him. He actually inspired me. On that day, I decided that in 2019, I would finish a half-marathon. But a few weeks later, I realized Ashraf was a regular runner and had been running for many years, and that was why he could finish a full marathon. But I had only about two years of running experience. I decided that finishing a half-marathon might have been too far-fetched for me. I thought I may not have what it takes.

When I started training, my belief became stronger. I ran less than ten kilometers, never had gone more than that. And during training, I realized that long-distance running is a very different game. I started doubting myself. A few weeks into the training, I thought it was not for me, and I stopped. I was beating myself up for not being able to progress. Every time I thought about restarting the training, I felt scared and started procrastinating.

For two months, I felt terrible. I told myself that no one had forced me into this—that I had chosen it. I had made a decision for myself. But I was not respecting my own decision. I couldn't take it anymore. Then I thought, "I still have eight months to go. I will start with the smallest step possible and then work my way up." To make a long story short, after about five months of training, I was able to finish my first half-marathon in 2019. I couldn't run the whole time, but I ran most of it, and I finished it. But my self-doubt before my training made me question my own decisions. I was scared, and I was skeptical about my own abilities.

And who was responsible for that? Only me.

Often, we—not the TV, social media, or other people—are our own enemies regarding our progress and happiness.

In the self lane, everything you think, do, or act is solo. You have full control. But negative thoughts or behaviors automatically kick in. As human beings, many of us overthink and have self-doubts. We feel terrible about ourselves, and that's normal. As

I mentioned earlier, I am an optimist, and I often live in the future, but that sometimes triggers a lot of worries about the future. Even though I'm not an overthinker, I used to suffer from procrastination, which did not serve me. I felt worried, anxious, and scared, and I used to beat myself up for not taking action.

But if you find yourself constantly trapped in those thought patterns, you may feel stuck, frustrated, or even angry with yourself. You want to ask yourself, what are the solo things (tasks, thoughts, and acts) that make you feel bad? Identify and list them. They do not serve you. With awareness and practice, you will be able to minimize them.

Remember, your thoughts and behaviors can make you super unhappy, but still, they happen inside your brain and are in your control only if you own them.

When you decide to avoid self-destructive thoughts, solo acts, or tasks that make you feel bad, it is absolutely possible (sometimes with professional help) to develop those skills and protect your happiness. Over the years, I got better. But I learn and try to improve every day.

There is no final point to reach; it is a continuous process.

If I can do it, so can you.

AVOIDING IN THE PEOPLE LANE

Remember my struggle with my own thoughts and behaviors during my half-marathon training? I spoke to a few people about that, and some of them said things like "I don't know why you are doing this," "What will you achieve by finishing a half-marathon?" and "You are not a runner; you will need five years of training."

All of the above came from my close family and friends. Whether it is chasing your dream, working on your passion, building a business, or anything that you cherish doing or being, some family and friends might actually support your journey, but most of the time, it will not be the stranger on the street whose voice will stop you, but the voices of the people closest to you.

And how do those negative voices make you feel? Ask yourself, when you try to do something new or challenging that nobody has ever done in your known family and friend circle, whose voices are supporting you? And ask yourself whose voices are stopping you or pulling you down?

It is essential to identify those who support you and those who do not.

The unsupportive behavior from your close family and friends may well be because they do not know how you will achieve your goal because they have not tried themselves. So they try to protect you from being hurt or failing by questioning your journey. My friend Ashraf (who inspired me to do the half-marathon) said it beautifully:

"First, they ask you why you do it. But when you succeed, then they ask you how you did it." People, including your loved ones, only see results.

But yes, It's not just about families and friends. You might find similar people at work or in social gatherings. And honestly, not everybody will question you out of care. They might be jealous or scared of your success and, in fact, intentionally try to pull you down or make you feel bad. For example, being unappreciated at work is one of the most common things that make people unhappy. You might find it impossible to meet some people's expectations at work. No matter how good or perfect you are, it is never enough for them. Every time, there is something missing. Well, this is a pattern of their behavior, not yours. They make you work the hardest and stress you out to the maximum to meet their own expectations. While that may make you push your boundaries every day and make you efficient, but this will make your life miserable, and your happiness will go out the door.

And there are other people who actually are good-hearted. They don't wish any harm to come to you. But they are worried and stressed out themselves, and when you talk to them, they unknowingly transfer their worries to you, as in the case of my close friend telling me that his cousin injured himself and his neighbor lost his job, and then complaining about his business. People share their worries and pains with you. That's how most people behave. But you will notice that some people unintentionally provide you with information you do not really need to know. You can listen to them and help them whenever you can, but you must stand guard at the door of your happiness. This is a skill that you will build with awareness.

Being aware of and identifying these people in your life is the first step. You can do this by asking yourself how you usually feel during or after spending time with a person. Do you feel energized, or do you generally feel low? If you have not thought about this, select one person and try it out.

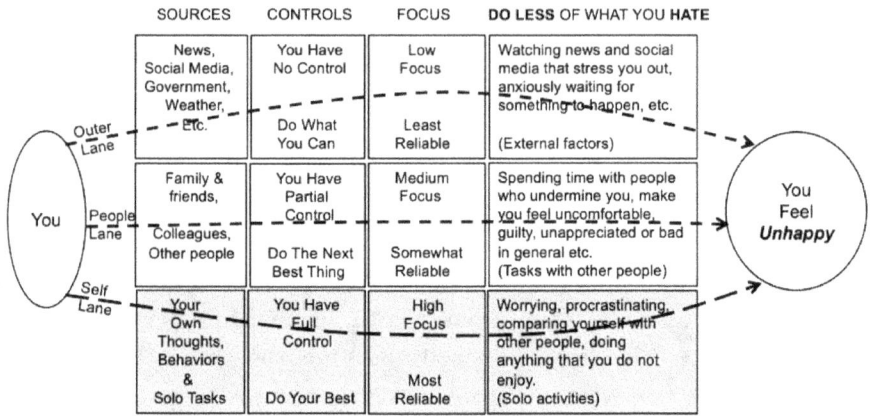

You will likely have people around you whose energy makes you feel low. I do. Everybody does. You may not be able to cut them out of your life, but if you truly want to be and stay happy, you must rethink their opinions and voices in your head (like a bad renter in your head), pay less attention to them, and stand by your own beliefs, values, and decisions.

I personally try to minimize my time spent with such people, whether at home, at work, or anywhere else, because they do not serve me. You might find it hard to identify and avoid them in your circle of close family and friends, but once you create that boundary with them, slowly, over time, you will create your own space where you can invite others who genuinely love and support you. It is not always easy to do, but it is totally worth doing to protect your happiness.

I do not know about you, but after dealing with various people from many walks of life for over thirty years, I have realized that some people just do not serve me, and it is not worth spending time, effort, or money on them. But there are others who totally deserve my attention, appreciate me, and don't take me for granted, and for them, I have a lot of time.

Your ability to identify these two types of people and then deal with them accordingly with awareness will help you protect your happiness. As author Paulo Coelho said, "Be kind, but don't be stupid."

AVOIDING IN THE OUTER LANE

Even though the things in the outer lane are not in your control, they can absolutely make you unhappy. For example, perhaps you can't wait to go to your favorite show, but the tickets are not yet for sale; perhaps you want to travel, but the borders are closed because of the COVID-19 pandemic; or maybe you are in lockdown and want it to be over soon.

None of these are in your control.

Any situation in which you have zero control—whether it relates to government rules, weather, or anything else—makes you feel unhappy. You must refocus and redirect your attention to the things in your control, most likely in the people lane or the self lane.

I learned to intentionally minimize my attention from the mainstream news from all directions, such as TV and social media. But still, during the COVID-19 lockdowns, I followed the government's public health advice. For example, if I'm going out, I check the restriction levels regarding what I can or can't do. I look for this information online, and it shouldn't take more than five minutes instead of being glued to the mainstream news for three hours and being informed about every bit of news related to COVID-19 out there around the world.

Another example might be Facebook. If I find anyone's content is regularly not making me feel good, I will unfollow the person, and her posts will no longer show up on my newsfeed. That way, I try to keep my news feed clean by allowing only the content that I like to see instead of the default. The same goes for other social media platforms. In short, not only on social media but really anywhere, you must clean up any content you intentionally or unintentionally consume that makes you feel uncomfortable, sad, or unhappy, to protect your happiness.

FACE IT WHEN NEEDED

Sometimes it may not be a very healthy practice to keep avoiding the things that make you stressed out. If you are constantly worrying about something that may not be real (or is never going to be), then it would be very hard for you to be and stay happy. Often instead of worrying, it is easier to face the issue. For example, if you know that someone who tested positive for COVID-19 visited a shopping mall you were in around the same time, you may worry about it and may find yourself unable to decide whether to get a test. That state of indecision can keep you up at night. Instead of worrying about it, get tested. For any reason, being in a state of indecision may lead to unhappiness.

Although there might be something or someone that you have been avoiding, deep down, you know that you cannot avoid that thing or that person forever. Avoidance will temporarily give you comfort, but for long-term happiness and peace, you really need to face the issue to permanently resolve it. Instead of avoiding it, you might want to do something about it. You may seek professional help if needed, but don't let it pile up inside you. Whether the issue is your own worries, your desire to forgive someone, guilt, regret, or whatever else, your worries will be alleviated when you face them.

REFLECTION

Do more of what you love and avoid what you don't.

This is the simplest way to be happy.

Someone told me during the pandemic, "How can I be happy when I look at the COVID-19 case numbers in the US, UK, Europe, and everywhere else? It is devastating."

Well, your happiness does not happen "out there" in another country.

It happens inside your head.

HOW TO STAY HAPPY

"Motivation is what gets you started. Habit is what keeps you going."
—Jim Ryun

STAYING HAPPY IS ABOUT HABITS

For most people, being happy is not a challenge but staying happy is. When I was in college, I studied hard, worked hard, and focused only on exams and assignments to get them submitted on time to get good grades. I couldn't wait to graduate because I thought that when that happened, I would be free from those assignments, late nights, the anxiety of exams, and that my life will change and I would live happily ever after.

But that never happened. After graduation, I did become happy for a few weeks, but being a graduate became a part of my life very quickly, and it didn't excite me anymore as much as I thought it would.

In short, the graduation didn't help me stay happy.

Getting a promotion, moving to a new city, having a holiday or your wedding day—events like these are special events in our lives. You will likely have a spike of happiness on those days (and remain happy for a little while), and you will also adapt to the new thing and get back to your default genetic happiness. You may work so hard to make your special days perfect so you can feel the happiest possible on them. Most people look for these special days to be happy as if our ordinary days don't matter. But these special days simply don't have the expected return on investment of happiness to allow you to stay happy forever.

Our lives are collections of days. If you have a life of ninety years, that is 32,850 days.

How many special days are there? Yes, they vary, but hypothetically, just to put a number on it, maybe six per year? That is 540 special days. Yes, of course your happiness on those special days lasts longer than just one day. Let's just say we make them fivefold. That would be 2,700 days, which is about 8.2 per cent special days for a ninety-year-old.

I will be happy when I get promoted, but now I need to work hard, or I shall be happy when my kids excel in school, but now I have to push them to study hard, or I shall be happy when my business hits that revenue, but now I have to stay up all night to make that presentation. We put almost everything else first but don't allow ourselves to be happy, because we reserve being happy for our special days. If you are always postponing being happy for special days, which means postponing for 91.8 per cent of your life, you are not allowing yourself to be happy.

How can you live a happy life?

Our lives are made of our ordinary days. As human beings, we all look forward to our special days, but they do not make us lastingly happy. Our ordinary days do. Staying happy really means being happy on the ordinary days, which are not so special. And that's where our everyday habits come in.

Let's say you want to stay happy for the rest of your life. Technically, that is the result you want. Almost any result you achieve comes from your habits. If you want to have a great body, you must work on it every day. To have a great relationship with your partner, you will need to work on it every day (yes, every day), through little things like sudden hugs or kisses on ordinary days, holding her hand when walking, opening the car door for her, and so on. Small things like these take less than a minute to do, but they make a much longer-lasting impact than only taking her to a nice dinner on her birthday.

Suppose you have a presentation due for a client but you started working on it only the night before. Can you imagine what the quality of the presentation will be? But if you had worked at it consistently, a small bit at a time, over a week, you would have created a great one. Think about your best friend (or a very close friend).

How did that person become your best friend? Did it happen in a day, in a month, or over a long time?

Your habits towards your best friend and also her habits towards you determine how great your friendship is.

Ask yourself what great results you have achieved over the years, and think about your everyday habits for them. If you have lousy results, it is because of lousy habits; but if you have great results, it's because of great habits.

That's it.

Your loving connections with others come from your habits with them. Your health and fitness come from your daily eating and exercise habits, your income comes from your money-making habits, and so on.

When we talk about the result of staying happy, that result also comes from your habits on ordinary days.

So exactly which habits are we talking about here?

Think about it. If you want a good bank balance, you will need two solid money habits. Firstly, you need a habit of earning more, and then, to protect your money, you will also need a second habit of spending less. Likewise, if you want to be and stay happy, you will also need two habits. Firstly, you need the happiness habits of doing what makes you happy, and secondly, you need your emotional habits to protect your happiness.

FIRST HABIT: YOUR HAPPINESS HABIT

You already know happiness is about doing—that is, doing more of the things you love doing or spending more time with people you love that make you feel good, excited, energized, and appreciated. In other words, these things are where you come alive or are happy in your ordinary days.

SECOND HABIT: YOUR EMOTIONAL HABIT

Protecting your happiness by avoiding or doing less of what you don't like, or spending less time with the people who make you feel uncomfortable, sad, unappreciated, unworthy, or generally unhappy, we discussed this earlier.

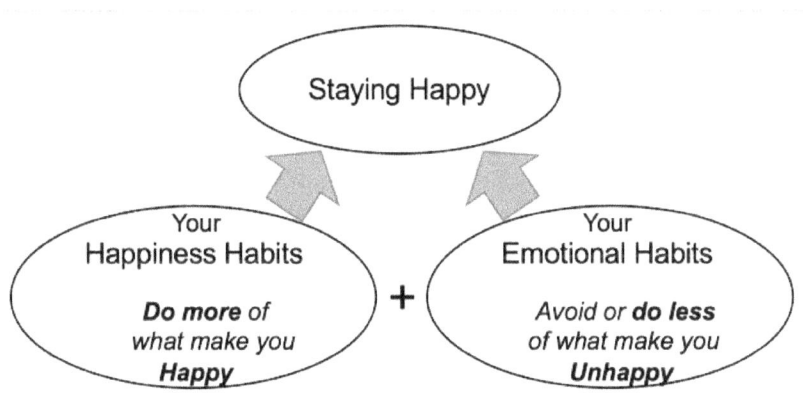

When you do what you love and avoid what you don't as your rituals on your ordinary days, you will build the skills of happiness and will also protect your happiness from outside forces. Slowly, your happiness habits and emotional habits will form and stay with you.

Remember the 40 per cent of happiness that is in your control, as determined from Professor Sonja Lyubomirsky's research? We need to capitalize on that using our happiness habits to create small (and easier to do) happy moments every day as our rituals. Also, to protect those precious happy moments, we need to avoid or minimize the things that make us unhappy, using our emotional habits.

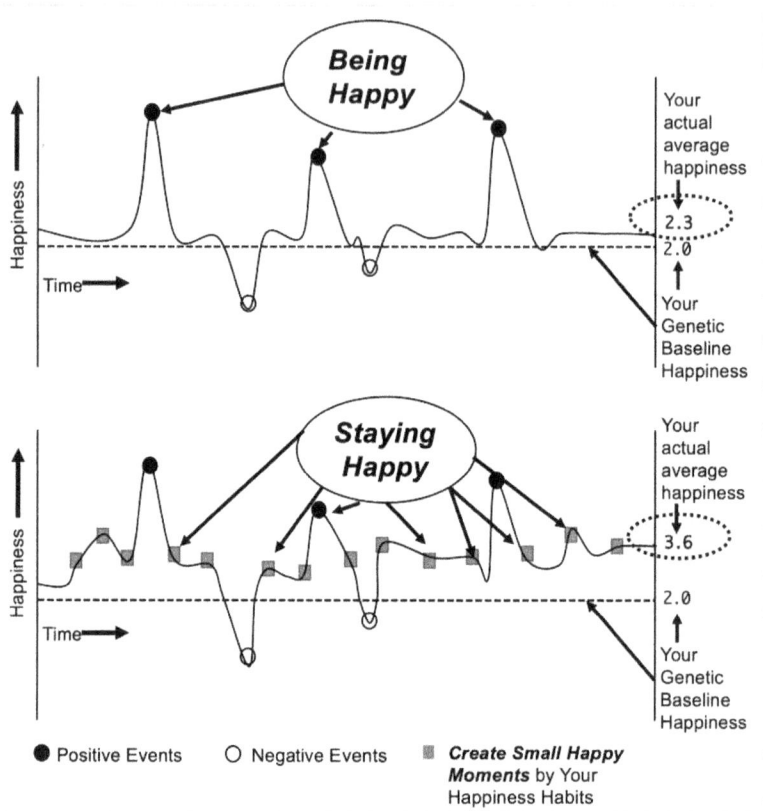

So, for example, if your genetic happiness set point is 2.0, then with your happiness habits and emotional habits, your happiness over time may be 3.6, as above, which will be higher than your default genetic set point.

Once you have both happiness and emotional habits as part of your lifestyle, then you will automatically do and avoid the things that make sense to you to stay happy.

FIVE THINGS TO CONSIDER

As you form your happiness habits by making conscious choices to do what you love doing every day, you will need to be aware of the below five things (or secrets) I have learned from Professor Sonja Lyubomirsky. She writes about them in her book The How of Happiness. For details, please refer to her book.

Firstly, recall that we discussed the broaden-and-build theory of Professor Barbara Fredrickson earlier. We know that the more positive emotions or pleasures you get from various activities, the more likely it is that you will succeed in your endeavors. For example, if I have a nice conversation with my best friend, it will generate positive emotions that might inspire me to go for a run. When I finish my run, I feel good and more energetic, then I work on a piece of writing in a good mood that enhances the quality of my writing and helps creative thinking, and so on. Positive emotions can create a ripple effect on everything we do in a day.

That's why the more positive emotions you have, the more likely it is you will create, enhance your productivity, feel happier, and have many other benefits. I have touched on this before, but I think it is worth refreshing this idea. The sources of your positive emotions are important. For example, you will get a positive emotion or pleasure by watching Netflix, but you can also get positive emotion by being kind to your partner (e.g., helping her with her presentation). Both give you positive emotions, but being kind actually makes you go the extra mile by doing something, and it is in your control. If you can generate positive emotions by your actions (e.g., being kind or even having a great conversation with a friend) as opposed to passively experiencing something that is dependent on an external factor (e.g., watching TV), you will have the key to generate as much positive emotion as you want, as many times as you want, and whenever you want. The control of that emotion must be with you.

Secondly, as I have mentioned in part 1, hedonic adaptation is the phenomenon that dictates that once we get a promotion, get a bonus, hit our business goals, or achieve anything else, we adapt to the new settings very quickly (much more quickly than we originally expect). But if that is the case, are we not also prone to adapt to the activities that we do as our happiness habits over time? For example, if you count your top three blessings every day for five days, on the sixth day, you may just say, "Yeah, I know my blessings, and I do not need to write them anymore." You get bored (or adapted). Or maybe buying the same flower for your partner every day seems like a crazy idea. That's why you may not want to do the same activity every day but instead watch the frequency of your happiness acts. For example, you might want to refrain from counting your blessings every day but do it once a week instead. Studies suggest that doing this once a week is more effective than doing it every day.

Thirdly, variety can help fight adaptation if being kind comes naturally to you. If you do an act of kindness for your partner today, next week you may not want to do the same act for your partner. Try something new or do something for someone else. You want to vary your activities as much as you can by changing different parameters, such as person, place, blessing, days, and the activities themselves. Try different things and see which timings and varieties work best for you, but do so regularly (e.g., weekly).

The fourth point is about connections. Research suggests that happy people are very social. They usually have stronger social support systems around them than other people who are not so happy. Having more quality social connections makes it easier for you to be kind, grateful, and engaged. This may also help you recover from setbacks.

The benefits are countless. In the next section, we will talk about one happiness habit—staying connected in meaningful ways with the people you love and care about. I personally think this is priceless.

The final and fifth point is about your desire and commitment. I have been talking about these two items throughout this book. I cannot stress enough that if you are not genuinely committed to being and staying happy, you will never be so, because staying happy requires you to do the happiness habits consistently. That is the only way to stay happy. At the end of the day, it is your life, and how happy you want to be is up to you. But if you genuinely want to live a happy life, no one can stop you.

As I keep saying, your results come from your habits in almost every area of your life. As you form your happiness habits, you want to consider these five things (we just discussed) in them. These five things will make your happiness habits sustainable.

YOUR DAD

I'm going to be blunt with you. You see, just because you have desired and designed your happiness habits and emotional habits, that doesn't mean you will be able to do them on your first attempt.

There is no doubt that you will fail, procrastinate, and be hesitant and doubtful about them. You may not even believe in them, as they might seem too simple or easy. Also, your happiness and emotional habits will need to be formed in your ordinary days. Maybe you had a busy day at work, your kids gave you a hard time, your relationships aren't looking great, and you are worried about paying your bills. Or maybe you hold on to past regrets, have present issues, or have future worries. There could be countless valid reasons why you may struggle to form those habits.

But you are not alone. We all have them.

When you experience a negative event or feel low in general, you have two choices. Usually, your brain almost always chooses the default negative meaning, which puts you in a negative mental state, and the decisions and actions you take in that state are also lousy.

So what do you get? A lousy result.

You don't do what you love, and you don't spend time with the people you love. Instead, you do the opposite. You may feel tired, low on energy, anxious, and depressed, and you may go to bed and wake up the next morning, and the same pattern continues today, tomorrow, and every day.

That's a survivor's life.

But I am sure, you are not reading this book just to live a survivor or average life. As I said earlier, you owe it to yourself to live a good or extraordinary life on your terms. You don't live life because you have to, but because you love to.

The second choice is to change the default negative meaning of your brain towards any negative thought, event, or situation. This was discussed in the resilience section earlier in detail. (Please refer to that chapter.) Your heart, time, and decisions were also mentioned previously. Your heart sings a song. Make sure your song aligns with what you do every day within your precious time on this planet.

To live an extraordinary life on your terms, what you have to do is break your old patterns of thoughts and actions.

This is where your DAD comes in. No, not your parent.

These are your decisions, actions, and discipline (DAD).

But how exactly can they change your days and life?

In 2021, all Melbournians spent most of their days in lockdown because of COVID-19. In fact, Melbourne was one of the most locked down cities in the world. Mahin and I enjoy each other's company, but we also love dining outside, travelling, spending time with our close family and friends, and other things. Not doing these things for a long time slowly impacted us, and we didn't even realize it, even though we kept telling ourselves that the restrictions didn't or couldn't impact us.

That wasn't true. We realized that we were lying to ourselves.

Mahin had some tough times handling her online businesses, as did many other business owners. Products were out of stock because there wasn't enough supply, there were shipping issues, and the market was uncertain. Before the lockdowns, she used to do group yoga, and she loved the experience. She naturally is not very demanding or outgoing, but simple things like having a nice coffee in a cafe or going for a drive are important for her. All of that stopped because of the restrictions. Doing group yoga, having a nice coffee outside, and hanging out with friends were a few of her happiness habits, and most of them were impacted by lockdowns.

She was stressing out. She was not anxious but had trouble falling asleep and had low energy. I also felt a similar impact. Millions of other people were impacted directly or indirectly by COVID-19. Life was not easy during the pandemic.

But one day, Mahin and I discussed what we could do about it. She couldn't do the group yoga classes, but she had a few health and fitness goals. She decided to start Pilates, a physical fitness system developed by Joseph Pilates in the early twentieth century. But she had no experience with it. She found an expert personal trainer online and decided to work with her one on one, three days a week.

In the next three months, Mahin worked with her personal trainer and was able to get her sleep in rhythm. She adjusted some food habits and timing and started doing advanced-level Pilates and high-intensity interval training (HIIT), which she had never done before. Also, she hit some of her health and fitness goals.

The reason I'm sharing this with you is that when she felt stuck and frustrated in the lockdowns, she knew she needed to do a lot of things, but she didn't feel like doing it and started procrastinating. She was living a very static life with not much progress. Her frustration only increased because she let her negative emotions drive her for a few months. And she was not getting any better in terms of her health, fitness, or business.

But after working with her PT for three months, she became much more in control. Her online businesses picked up. She became physically and mentally stronger, felt more energy, and became happier.

So what changed? Well, remember DAD? She made a strong decision (D) to start Pilates to take her fitness goals to the next level. She took directed actions (A) by booking sessions with her personal trainer. And she committed to three sessions a week with her trainer with discipline (D) for a few months and continued.

Doing Pilates and HIIT with her trainer three days a week has become a part of her life. In her HIIT sessions, she feels good and energetic, and she gains a sense of a small achievement every day. She enjoys the experience. In a few months, she had formed her new happiness habit, and that's how she stays happy every day.

No matter how hard or tiring your days are, if you strongly decide with commitment and take everyday actions with discipline on what you love doing or enjoy, you can totally form your happiness and emotional habits to stay happy. There is no doubt about it. It was not the Pilates or HIIT that made all the difference, but it was Mahin's DAD.

WHEN YOU DON'T FEEL LIKE IT

I have just talked about decisions, actions, and disciplines (DAD). But you know we are all human beings and mostly operate on our emotions. Our feelings are like clouds, in that they change very quickly. Think about it; if you let your feelings (especially negative feelings) dictate your decisions and actions, where would you end up? You would be stuck in a circle of negative thoughts, feel stuck, and go nowhere. The DAD we just discussed keeps you on track not only to achieve any goal but to be and stay happy and to live a satisfying life.

Living a happy life and living a satisfying life both require you to have DAD in your days. It's your habits that determine the quality of your life.

But what if you don't feel like doing it?

Often, you know you should do exercise, you know you should call your old friend to catch up, and you know you should work on the project that you are so passionate about. You know you should do hundreds of other things that will make you happy or satisfied. You may even have added them to your Star of Life designs and to your happiness habits.

But yet, when it is time to do them, you may not feel like doing them, and you may end up watching Netflix or doing something else.

Writing is in my happiness habits. It is also among my flow activities in the Star of Life design. I know it gives me flow and satisfaction. I know I feel good and have a sense of achievement every time I finish a piece. But sometimes when I write, I don't know where to start. Staring at a blank page is one of the hardest parts. Many writers often experience writer's block when they are not able to write anything. I experienced that for a few months last year.

Before I wrote the first draft of this section, I was feeling very low energy. I didn't feel like doing anything. But I remembered my decision to finish this section of my book that night. But then I thought, "As I'm not feeling very good, it may impact my writing. Maybe I will finish tomorrow." But guess what? I noticed that my procrastination behavior kicked in. I didn't want to frustrate myself with another "I will do it tomorrow" story. I came to my study and finished this section.

I was letting my negative emotions dictate my actions, and I almost lost it. You might think, "Not a big deal." Yes, a few days don't matter, but if you lose and surrender to your negative behaviors for many days, you have lost big time. Your life slips away from you, and the gap between you and your dreams gets wider. That feeling of frustration is devastating.

So how do you deal with it?

There are several things you can do to fight procrastination, but the most effective I find for myself is to start with the smallest action possible. On that night, when I felt low, I went to my study and decided to write anything for just ten minutes. That's all. And then, if I didn't feel well, I would stop. But after I started writing, 1.5 hours passed by. I didn't even notice, and I finished this section. I also experienced flow. And as a result, I felt good and had a sense of progress.

In fact, I ended up working on it for about three hours.

See, your brain gets scared when something feels like a lot of work, it just does not want to start on it. It finds all kinds of reasons why you should not get started. For example, if you decide to exercise for thirty minutes today and don't feel like it, just do five minutes. If you have planned to work on your passion project for two hours and have lots of great ideas, you may feel overwhelmed and may not actually get anything done. Just work for ten minutes or whatever feels the smallest to you.

Even if you don't feel like it, remember Nike's slogan and just do it.

Then you will see the magic.

You may end up doing a whole lot more than your "smallest" target. If you are genuinely not feeling well or have any sickness, this might not be the case. But most of the time, it will be.

I talked in part 1 that your brain is not on your side. Anything you intend to do in the micro-moments during the day—going for a walk, calling a client, sending an email—you might struggle to actually do it because your brain will try to keep you from doing or experiencing that which is not part of your regular habit. Your brain is not there to make you happy, but to help you survive. If you listen to your brain always, you will have a survivor life or average life, but if you listen to your heart, you will live a good life or an extraordinary life.

Author Mel Robbins talked about a brain hack she used to change her life, and she wrote the book The Five-Second Rule. She said that if you intend to do something during the day, when it's time to do it, you have about five seconds to get into action before your brain comes up with all sorts of reasons why you shouldn't do it (including that you don't feel like doing it). Mel said, "There were moments all day long where I knew what I should do, and if I didn't move within that five-second window, my brain will step in and talk me out of it. Every human being has a five-second window." Refer to her book for more details.

It is your job to "skill up" on how to bypass your brain and do what you love anyway.

Remember, courage comes by taking action.

Another thing I learned—this one from Neil Pasricha, the author of the book The Happiness Equation—is that motivation comes by doing. That means that though you may not feel motivated to do something, if you start to do it anyway, regardless of what you feel, your motivation will come later in the process (e.g., after five minutes of doing the task).

In short, motivation does not cause action. Rather, your actions cause motivation.

As I said earlier, I set myself up for ten minutes of writing and then ended up writing for 1.5 hours. Well, I didn't feel motivated to start writing. I decided on the smallest amount I was willing to do (ten minutes) and went to my study and started writing (even though I didn't feel like it), and my motivation and momentum came only after I started writing.

Even the smallest amount of progress is still progress. I love how author Anthony Robbins said, "Progress equals happiness."

When you do things as part of your happiness habits or emotional habits, even when you make the smallest progress toward your health, relationships, business goals, or whatever else, you will feel good. As you continue, you will feel the momentum, and if you don't stop or give up, that will create a habit loop and help you stay happy.

REFLECTION

I was going to name this chapter "The Secret Recipe for Happiness," but I later realized that people always look for shortcuts or the secrets to happiness. But the more I learn and ponder upon the science of happiness, the more I believe that there is no secret to happiness.

Rather, there are just fundamental principles.

As I said earlier, do more of what you love than what you don't every day as habits. Being and staying happy is really that simple

THE ELEVEN HAPPINESS HABITS CREATE HAPPY MOMENTS

"Progress equals happiness."
—Anthony Robbins

THE COOL THING ABOUT THE SIX ELEMENTS

We know from the science of physical bodies that for good physical health, growth, and disease prevention, the body needs six essential nutrients. They are fat, protein, carbohydrates, vitamins, minerals, and water. These are the must-haves for the body to function at its best.

And where do you get the nutrients from? Various food groups. But one food can contain multiple nutrients. For example, an avocado can give you both fat and vitamins. A chicken can give you protein, fat, and vitamins. So if you eat just one avocado, your body can get two essential nutrients. Chicken can give your body three of the nutrients.

If you get that, now think about this. This chapter outlines eleven happiness habits that social scientists discovered from various studies that make people happy. We are going to explore each one of them. But here is the best part: each happiness habit links to either one or more of the six elements of your satisfying life.

This is pretty cool.

The six elements (meaning, engagement, love and connection, pleasure, health, and achievements) are like the six nutrients of your physical body. And the eleven happiness habits are like various foods. Each happiness habit can link to one or more of the six elements of satisfaction. So if you make just one happiness habit a part of your day, you can get one or more of the six elements of a satisfying life every day. That way you get two birds with one stone.

But how do you form happiness habits to do that?

There is no one way to form your happiness habits. Every one of us is different. We come from different backgrounds, places, genetic dispositions, and circumstances. As happiness is very individualistic, our tastes, aptitudes, and interests are different. There is no one set of habits that will work for everybody. You may already have a few happiness habits. One habit may work for me, but that does not mean it will work for you. And the ones that you like may not work for me.

So what are the eleven happiness habits?

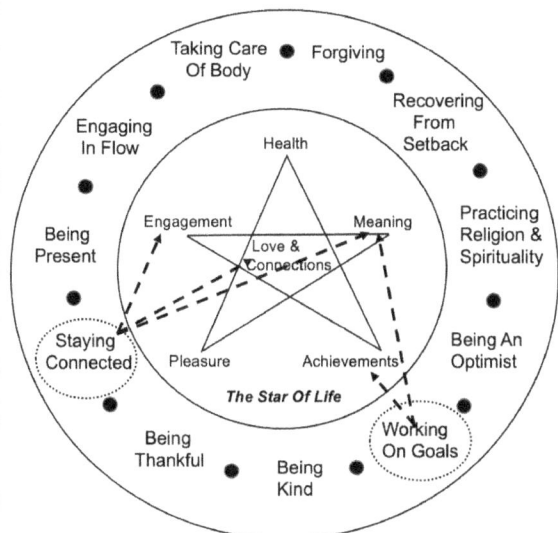

11 Happiness Habits & The **6** Elements Of Satisfaction

Above, I have outlined the eleven happiness habits that make people happy, according to studies. As stated above, one happiness habit can potentially link to one or multiple elements of the Star of Life. For example, if you spend some good time with your son to stay connected, you will likely strengthen your loving connection, you may experience flow, and it can be very meaningful to you. That way, your "staying connected" happiness habit can give you three elements of satisfaction. Or, if your goal is to build a school for underprivileged kids, when you work on your goals, it can link to your achievements and be very meaningful to you.

But you may not want to do all eleven of them as your happiness habits. Everybody is different, and so are you. Therefore, you do only the ones that suit you best. In the next part, I will explain about a tool to discover your habits that are best suited to your personality, beliefs, and values. Happiness is about doing more and more things that suit your individual personality and character as your happiness habits. You may not believe in doing or enjoy doing some habits (e.g., being an optimist or being thankful), and you might find them hard to do, but there are habits that you may believe in and enjoy doing (e.g., being kind or working on your goals), and you will find them very easy and enjoyable. This tool will give you your top five habits. They will come naturally to you more than the others. This will not require you to change who you are, and you will be more of who you already are by forming your happiness habits.

Next, as you read these eleven happiness habits, notice the ones you believe you might enjoy doing. Notice how they can potentially link to the six elements of your satisfying life.

FIRST HAPPINESS HABIT: STAYING CONNECTED

I was taking some rest, as I had a little headache. I hadn't slept very well the previous night. But then I got a phone call. It was one of my old friends, Ripon. We have been friends since 2001. Literally, it has been over twenty years. He is a corporate consultant in Sydney, and he came to Melbourne for two days for work. He asked, "Are you free for dinner tonight?" Even though we have been friends for a long time, we do not talk every week or month, because of our busy lives. The last time I caught up with him was more than a year ago. So I said, "Yes, absolutely," even if I had plans for some writing. He drove to our house, and we went for a nice dinner and spent some time together. It was very relaxing and refreshing after a long time. My headache went away.

I'm talking about this because this is one of my rituals that helps me stay happy. Whenever I go to Sydney, I do the same with Ripon. You may think, "Yes, sure, this is a no-brainer," but I actually plan and execute this ritual intentionally and make time for it. Not only in Sydney, but anywhere in the world, whenever I'm visiting, I connect with my family and friends so that I stay connected; this habit helps me stay happy.

In our lifetimes, we meet many people. As we discussed before, an average person has about 150 connections, or casual friends. There are about 50 friends, and 15 of them are likely to be close friends. And from British anthropologist Robin Dunbar, we know that human brains have a limit on the number of deep, meaningful relationships a person can keep track of. And that number is five. That means there are about five people we can have intimate bonds with. You may remember this already.

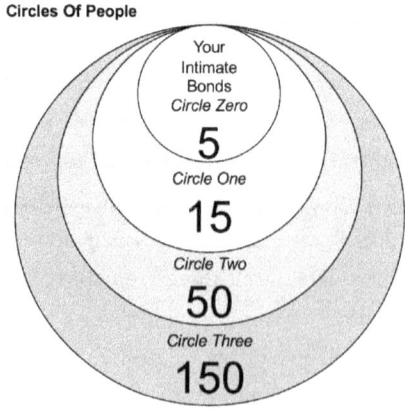

COVID-19 had enabled me to reconnect with many family and friends around the world. The sense of connection with them has made me happier (but sure, stay away from people who suck your energy out). Remember, a very simple way to assess a person is to ask yourself, "During or after spending time with this person, how do you feel?" Do you feel good in some way? Or do you feel down? If you feel good, keep the connection to this person and make a conscious effort to keep it alive. If not, you know what to do. I stay connected only with the ones I truly care about, and they make me feel good. Ripon is one of them in circle two.

Over the years, I have created a small and private mastermind group where I spend time with a very special group of people who share the same ideals and values. Everyone is expected to treat each other with respect and trust, have an attitude of gratitude, see life as beautiful, not play the role of a victim, and be open and honest to oneself and others. These people take and give feedback with an open mind, keep sensitive and personal information about others to themselves and do not discuss it with anyone outside the group, and, most importantly, are non-judgmental. These dynamics create a safe place for everyone in the group, including me. Every member of this club is extraordinary in his or her own ways and genuinely endeavors to bring his or her best every day. We call it the "Best of Me Club." No matter what, we try to hang out every two weeks. If anyone is travelling, she will join via zoom. Spending time in this group helps me stay happy. You may or may not be part of such a group, but many people are part of groups where they hang out with their close friends and share their life stories with them and count on them.

In the Dunbar circles, they would be in my circle one.

I must revisit here the longest study of happiness, which started in the 1930s in Boston and continues today. Professor George Vaillant, who led that study for forty years, wrote in his book Triumphs of Experience, "The seventy-five years and twenty million dollars expended on the grant study, points to a straight forward five-word conclusion,

Happiness is love, Full stop."

Guess where am I going with this?

Yes, into my circle zero, the innermost circle, where I have very few people from family and friends. Only I know who they are. And no, I'm not going to name them. After me, they have the most impact on my happiness. They are the ones who deserve the highest level of respect, love, kindness, and every other noble behavior from me over anyone else on earth. And I make sure that I stay connected and go that extra mile in loving and meaningful ways with them every day.

People in your innermost circle are the ones who have the greatest access to your happiness, after yourself. The love and pain you get from them are the most impactful to your happiness or unhappiness. It is critical to nurture these people regularly, make time for them, and create loving and lasting memories with them every day. Tell them and show them with your actions how much you love and care for them. Be nice and kind to them. When they do something wrong, forgive them, and give them your best support with your money, time, and genuine effort so they can (and will) also bring the best out of themselves. Yes, they are also human beings and can take your love and care for granted and may not acknowledge these things as much as you expect them to. But it is not just them; and the same phenomenon applies to me and my own inner-circle people too. It applies to almost every person on earth. But it is not their fault. It is how we are all wired. Take a moment and keep all your worries away, then close your eyes and imagine you are getting on a plane to escape from a crisis, knowing you can never come back. Who would you take with you on the plane if you can have only five people with you. (I know this might be clichéd, but it totally works!)

You may or may not have a partner, children, or a family member; those five people in your intimate circle can be from among your friends or even your coworkers. Keep in mind that people can move between different circles. As life changes, a very close friend can become just a casual friend, or a new friend can become one of your closest and move into your innermost circle.

This is normal and, in fact, expected.

In any situation, believe it or not, your friends are your psychological support system. We all need them, whether they are our family, friends, or both. We are all social animals. It is hard-wired in our DNA that we crave love and connection. There is no confusion or denial of this fact. And when it comes to our happiness, if we stay connected in deep and meaningful ways to the people we love and care about the most (usually in circles zero and one), we stay happier. It is that simple.

Pleasantly surprise your loved ones on your ordinary days. Try to genuinely listen to them; tell them and show them how much they mean to you; celebrate good news together; schedule an activity together, such as going on a holiday, to the gym, or to a movie; and so on. Also, support them in hard times. There are literally hundreds of ideas.

Remember the six elements of a satisfying life? This habit of "staying connected" can potentially link to four elements of life satisfaction: meaning, love, flow, and pleasure.

For example, if my partner loves gardening and I help her water the plants every day, it will strengthen my loving connection with her. Also, this will be meaningful for us. I may experience flow, and maybe we can have coffee together in the garden as pleasure.

I intentionally stay connected in meaningful ways with my circle zero (the intimate bond circle) almost every day, with my circle one every two weeks, and with my circle two every few months. No matter how busy I am, I make time to stay connected with the people who matter to me the most.

You do not have to do what I do. You decide what works for you to stay connected in loving and meaningful ways to people that matter to you. I personally believe this habit of staying connected is one of the most powerful of all happiness habits.

Pick one person from your intimate bond circle and write five things you have in common with this person.

Try it out.

I stay connected as my happiness habit; that helps me stay happy.

SECOND HAPPINESS HABIT: BEING PRESENT

When I talk about living every moment or being present, it always reminds me of my good friend Bec. She brings a lot of energy and joy into our lives. She is very passionate about food. She owns two restaurants in Melbourne and Perth. In addition, she runs two other businesses, and she has an amazing husband and three beautiful children. As you can imagine, she is a very busy person. When it comes to food, she is an explorer. She loves tasting all kinds of foods. She is skinny and takes care of her health regularly. What is so special about her is that whenever I see her eating something, the only thing she is doing is eating—nothing else. It doesn't matter how many times she has eaten the same food. Even if she is in a rush, she is still a mindful eater. It's a delight to watch her eat.

One day, I asked her what she thinks when she is around food and how she stays present when she eats. She said, "I just think of the person who cooked the food for me. Even if I do not see her, it may be in a restaurant or outside, and I thank her in my mind. Then I think about myself, that I'm so blessed that I have this food. Not many people can afford to eat three times a day. Whenever I'm in front of a meal, it doesn't matter if I'm in a rush; I still remind myself to do that.

"Secondly, when I'm eating, I try to fully enjoy it. I try to notice the color, flavor, and texture of the food in my mouth to the level that I can possibly tell the ingredients. Sometimes, the food may not be cooked very well; it may not taste as good, but I do that anyway because I'm thankful that I'm privileged to have it."

That day, I learned something new from Bec. I'm not passionate about food like Bec, but I had never looked at my meal and thought about the person who cooked it for me. That was a different perspective. The whole idea of eating changed for me. I did not become a fully mindful eater the next day, but I understood that eating is not just about eating; it is also about being grateful. Since then—not every time, but as much as I can—I have tried to remind myself that I'm blessed to have food on my table. Over a few months, I have developed an awareness of savoring the moment while eating, and my experience has been great. It was just a slight shift in my perception of food and eating.

But it was not all about food or mindful eating. Bec is generally a person who gives 100 per cent to pretty much everything she does: taking care of kids, running multiple businesses, handling people in her business, spending time with her family and friends, or even doing laundry. She is a great leader, and the people on her team love her. You will never see her on her phone during these times. She said to me once, "I don't think I have time. I want to enjoy every moment I have on this planet, and I do not want to miss anything."

She is one of the happiest people I personally know. We hear all the time about living every moment of our lives and being mindful. But really, it all comes down to what you believe about yourself and your time.

What do you believe about your moments? If you believe that the moments you are living are limited and that one day all of those moments will run out, you will treat them differently than if you think you will live forever. You will savor them, be present, and live as much as you can. But if you do not value your precious moments, you will do the opposite.

Some ideas are practicing mindful photography (we shall do an intervention in the next part), eating, and mindfully talking to someone. In fact, if you are putting all your attention on anything you do, you will experience the magic of being in the moment.

Remember the six elements of the Star of Life? This "being present" activity can potentially give you four life satisfaction elements: pleasure, love, health, and engagement (flow).

For example, If I go for a mindful photography walk for thirty minutes, I can get into flow. It will help me focus on my surroundings and be present to savor the moments. I can get a lot of momentary pleasures (e.g., having a nice coffee) The walk can help my health, and if I go with my family or friends, it can help strengthen my loving connections with them.

Many of us live either in the past, regretting the things that didn't work out well, or in the future, worrying about what may go wrong. We may even think about how glorious the past was or how exciting the future could be. But in those endeavors, our present moments slip away. To make more glorious memories, we have to create them in the present. Also, the "exciting" future does not just happen automatically. The creation of the future also happens in the present. Our time on this planet is limited, and one day the present will become past, and we will have used it all. The past moments are gone; you cannot do anything about them. And the future moments are yet to come. What truly matters are the moments right here, right now.

Being present is in Bec's daily happiness habits. It helps her not only be happy in the moment but also stay happy as a person.

THIRD HAPPINESS HABIT: TAKING CARE OF YOUR BODY

When Ashraf was growing up, he was an active person. He loved sports and wanted to be a cricketer. Later, when he became more focused on his study, work, and career, he slowly moved away from sports. Over many years, he slowly became physically very inactive. He stopped playing and exercising. He started neglecting his health to the point that he would eat anything and everything and became thirty kilograms overweight. One day, he went to a doctor and found that his blood sugar level was very high and he was prone to diabetes and heart disease in the future. At the time, he was constantly feeling lazy, didn't have a lot of energy, and found it very difficult to keep his weight under control.

A few years later, his daughter was born. "When she was born," he said, "I decided to take care of my health, but nothing really worked for a few years. I was only getting frustrated, as none of the diets I tried actually worked. Why? Because I wanted to have a very quick result and was only trying to lose weight. I forgot that my unhealthy body resulted from many years of an unhealthy lifestyle, which would not be fixed in a few weeks or months. I was desperate to keep my weight under control and wanted a quick fix for it.

"Later, I shifted my focus from weight loss to a health-first approach. I completely stopped standing on the weighing machine every morning and concentrated on healthy eating and started to work out. I became very strict with two things. First, my routine for working out. I allocated one hour at a specific time five days a week. No matter what, I made sure that I worked out. Secondly, I gradually controlled my sugar intake to the point it became almost zero. I promised myself and was so disciplined that some days when my wife and two kids were asleep, I worked out in my garage. I never skipped that.

"Some days were really hard, especially when I had to wake up early in the morning for work. For the first few weeks, I wasn't getting a lot of results. I was 110 kilograms at the time and had many self-doubts. But I remained committed and never gave up. After a month or two, I started to see some results, and I also started to feel better. I started to gain more energy from healthy eating and working out. I understood the process by doing it myself. I realized what I needed to do to become a healthier person.

"In a couple of years, healthy eating and working out had become my lifestyle. The ketogenic diet I followed was not an occasional diet to lose weight. I have lost weight and brought my weight down to seventy-eight kilograms again, which perfectly aligns with my optimal BMI. My everyday food is what this diet allows me to eat. Over the years, my metabolism also changed, and honestly, I like my diet better than anything else, because it not only helped me lose weight but also gave me energy, and I have never felt so good in my life before."

Ashraf's journey inspired many people around him, including me. Some ideas to take care of your body are as simple as going for a nice walk, meditating, joining a fitness class, participating in a running festival, sleeping, eating fresh and healthy foods, trail walking, having a massage now and then, or doing anything that you love to take care of your physical body. Basically, with anything you do at the moment for your body, think about how you can take it to the next level. If you cannot run, walk fast. If you cannot walk fast, walk slowly. If you cannot walk slowly, stand for a while. If you cannot eat super healthy food, eat something less unhealthy. If you normally drink one bottle of Coke, drink only half a bottle and progress slowly.

Lay one brick at a time without stopping.

You can eat whatever works for you, and you can do whatever you can, but with anything you do, take the baby steps with commitment and consistency. Surely, there will be times when you will feel down in your journey, feel alone, and surely fail, but the key is to never give up and to trust the process.

The habit of taking care of your body can potentially link to three elements of life satisfaction: health, engagement (flow), and achievements. For example, if I run for twenty minutes, I can get into flow. It will help me achieve my fitness goals and help my health.

Ashraf mentioned he was very strict with his exercise routine and sugar intake initially, and he slowly built up his habit over a few years. He also mentioned he had never felt so good in his life before. Taking care of the body is one of the happiness habits that makes people live and feel better. It may not relate only to eating healthy foods or doing exercise; it can relate to having a massage or going to a spa, playing sports, running, or anything else that nourishes your body and can make you happy every day. No matter how minor your progress may seem, taking care of your body is something that you will never regret doing.

Taking care of the body is a happiness habit that helps Ashraf stay happy every day.

FOURTH HAPPINESS HABIT: PRACTICING RELIGION OR SPIRITUALITY

I first met James a few years ago at a seminar in Melbourne. He had just finished speaking about a new product launch. After his talk, we had a chat, and somehow, we started talking about happiness. Suddenly he stopped, looked me in the eye, and said, "I must tell you that I'm the happiest person in the world."

Who says that to a person you have just met?

I was hooked. He lives in Brisbane. He is in his fifties and has a beautiful wife and children. His company designs and builds cities around the world. He travels, exploring new places and opportunities. He is very successful in his field. He is in good health and shape, and he loves his life the way it is right now.

A couple of months later, he was coming to Melbourne from Brisbane for some work, and we invited him and his family for dinner. At the table, he was telling the amazing story about how he met his lovely wife about thirty years ago. He had fallen in love with her and finally got married. He is a phenomenal storyteller. He loves his wife so much that, even today, he makes coffee for his wife every morning and cooks for the family and children despite his busy schedule. The energy he brings to his family and the people around him is incredible.

You might think that if a person has a beautiful family, makes a lot of money, is healthy and fit, and lives his dream travelling around the world. he essentially has pretty much everything someone could possibly ask for in this life. It is a no-brainer. He must be very happy.

It certainly looks like that, but remember, happiness is about doing. What does he do? What are his happiness habits? I caught up with him to find out.

His answers may surprise you.

He said, "The reason why I'm truly happy is the way I look at things. One of the greatest sources of my happiness is contentment. When I was little, every time we had a victory, no matter how small it was, my parents celebrated it. Being brought up in a Christian family, seeing happiness from God's point of view is a big thing. I cannot run away from God even if I try. We can choose how we look at things. It is learning to be contented with God. Contentment leads to happiness."

I asked him, "What are the main sources of your happiness?"

He said, "Knowing every day when I wake up that I'm enjoying something from God that is beyond what an average person will have. It is unique to me. I have a unique relationship with him which is quite special and tangible to me. I always expect an unmerited favor from God every day—the unusual manifestation of the power and love of God. Knowing this, how can you not be happy about it every day? Love is the most powerful thing. I trust in God's provision. I wait when I have to wait."

James has a successful business, a beautiful family, health, financial freedom, and many other things. I asked how he would feel if some of it were taken away from him. He said, "If any one of these is taken away from me, I would be content with whatever I have remaining. But I will prepare myself to achieve in a natural way. Whatever I do not receive, I shall strive for. I can be somewhere where there is no food, no water. I would just look for it, not only for me but also for others. For me, the word of God also reminds me that you are the son of God. If you know who you are, nothing worries you."

I asked how he finds time to make coffee for his wife every morning. He said, "One of the things that give me a lot of contentment is helping others. If you cannot serve your wife, how can you serve the whole world? It has become a bit of a routine. It starts at home. I serve the kids, teach students, and have developments in Canada as well. Serving, serving, serving—it is fun doing that. I live a very blessed life."

But it was not always rainbows and colors for him all the time. In 1999, he and his wife lost one of their children during birth. I asked him how they had gotten through that tough time. On that day in the hospital, he and his wife were going through immense mental stress when they heard the news. But they gave a very different meaning to the situation, sought refuge in God, and started singing to God with teary eyes (yes, in the hospital room). He said, "Yes, we were sad, but it wasn't long. Something happened after we started singing because we were in the presence of God. Giving thanks is very important. We thanked God for our other children we already had. We thanked for everything that we had at that time." Slowly, over some time, both of them recovered from it. I asked for his permission to share his experience about losing their child. He didn't mind at all. He said, "Maybe someone is going through this right now and can learn from my life experience."

His belief in God and his religious rituals help him stay happy every day, and that happiness fuels his success.

This habit of practicing religion or spirituality can potentially give you three elements of life satisfaction: meaning, engagement (flow), and achievement. For example, If I spend an hour praying to God, I can get into flow. It is meaningful for me. Depending on what I choose to believe, it may also give me a sense of achievement (e.g., I serve God by helping people).

If you believe in God and follow your religion or any other spiritual practice, that will help you be happy and content every day.

Practicing religion is in James's happiness habits, which helps him not only be happy every day but also stay happy as a person.

Remember, when I first met James, he said he was the happiest person in the world. Honestly, after all these years of knowing and seeing him closely, I don't disagree with him.

FIFTH HAPPINESS HABIT: BEING AN OPTIMIST

"Mr. Watson, come here, I want to see you" were the first words ever spoken on a telephone by Alexander Graham Bell, the inventor of the telephone, on March 10, 1876. He was talking to his assistant, Mr. Watson. He also opened the first long-distance call, from New York to Chicago, in 1892. If you were born in the 1700s and you were talking about speaking to someone in Chicago from New York over a telephone line or having a live video chat with your brother halfway across the world, people might have called you crazy. But today, these things occur in our everyday lives. If you are not willing to get on a plane, do not have a smartphone, or do not use Google, people might still call you crazy but for not using these things (see people might call you crazy either ways).

Everything we use in our everyday lives today is the result of someone's dream.

I want to point out two things. Firstly, you do not have to have a dream to change the world. You can just have a dream of what most people have: a house that is paid off, a good car, a nice family, maybe a dog, good health, and stable financial ability. Those are what most people's dreams are. Secondly, dreams come from imagination. We have been given this higher faculty to imagine the future for ourselves. No other animal on the planet can do that as we do. That literally means dreams are free. You do not have to pay for dreaming. You can dream about dating the most beautiful girl in the world, you can dream about having a few billion dollars in your bank account, and you can dream about having more success than even Steve Jobs. You can go as wild as possible.

You might just say those dreams are unrealistic.

Maybe, but really?

Everything seems unrealistic until it is done.

Not everybody can think at the level of Steve Jobs. Everyday people do not think about changing the world. Back in 1976, when Steve Jobs, Steve Wozniak, and Ronald Wayne started Apple in his parents' garage, they were everyday people, and nobody knew them. Forty-four years later, I'm writing about them because they have changed the world. At the time, all of Apple's inventions looked impossible and unrealistic. In fact, reportedly, Ronald Wayne sold his share of 10 per cent for $800 within twelve days. Later he said, "What can I say? You make a decision based on your understanding of the circumstances, and you live with it." Even being a co-founding member, Wayne did not (or could not) believe in Steve Jobs and Steve Wozniak until they made it happen years later. But they were all everyday people. We know about them because they were the ones who dreamed about something crazy and made their dreams come true.

If you dream about something that is too good to be true in the future, people will call you crazy. Anything you say which does not align with their beliefs will cause them to have a tough time believing in you, because you see something that they do not see or are not capable of seeing at your level. Historically, humans have invented one thing after another for hundreds of years. Someone thought of something new, but others didn't believe it until he or she succeeded; that's just the natural phenomenon of people (this must be understood when your goals are big).

Even the most pessimistic person you know, the most skeptical person you have ever seen, has a dream. His dream may not be as big as yours, but it is still a dream because he can see how he is going to achieve it, and it is realistic for him. But he may not be able to see your dream and how you will achieve it. He has no idea. That's when he says your dreams are unrealistic or crazy (and that's ok).

Some dreams are so big that they look impossible even to the dreamer. You are meant to come across some doubts about your dream or idea. You will surely feel doubts about the idea itself (idea doubt), and you will also feel self-doubt about whether you are the one capable of achieving that dream. Either way, both of these doubts are normal and expected for almost any dream that you may have. There is nothing wrong with that. Scientists call these "barrier thoughts," and you need to identify them and then replace them with more empowering thoughts towards your dream.

I want to simply say that your belief in your dream must outweigh your fears and doubts for the whole duration of your dream journey.

You will feel doubts about yourself and doubts from other people around you. The time when no one believes in you, including yourself, are the hardest, especially when your progress is slower than you expect or you feel stuck and are not making progress towards your dreams.

Remember, it is not other people's (including your family members) job to believe in your vision.

It is yours.

Also, people will not believe or trust your vision unless you have results, no matter how minor they are. This is how we are all wired, but you have to trust yourself and keep going. When some doors close, new doors will open (that's how it works), but you must be open to seeing them. In almost every success story, the founder or the dreamer goes through self-doubt and idea doubts; there are literally thousands of stories like that.

But if you do not trust your dreams, no one will.

Your dreams and hopes do not need to change the world or result in an invention. They can be literally anything that matters to you. Some ideas are having a great life partner or finding your soul mate, having a fit body, swimming in the Olympics, going on a holiday you always wanted to go on, moving to a city you love, recovering from an illness, or getting out of an abusive relationship. Whatever they are, your dreams are possible only when you believe and work on them without giving up.

But always remember that dreaming alone will not give you results. Your directed and consistent actions will.

This habit of being an optimist can potentially give you three elements of life satisfaction: meaning, engagement (flow), and achievement. For example, If I spend an hour dreaming and writing my plan to run a half-marathon, I can get into flow. If I can raise some money for charity, this run can be meaningful for me, as it will help other people, it will help me visualize my success, and it will help my achievement.

Personally, I am an optimist. I dream about a lot of things. I believe our lives can be beautiful and abundant. I believe everyone has unique talents of her own and deserves to live a life true to herself. I believe everyone can live a happier and more satisfying life no matter what. There are so many people in the world; I may be a small raindrop in the storm, but I still dream about making someone happier through my book. Every time I think about it, it feels good, and I do it many times during the day.

At the end of the day, everyone has a dream. They might not talk about it because they are fearful about their dreams. Almost everybody wants to be, do, and have something better than what they currently are, do, and have. Our dreams may not be as big as Steve Jobs's or Alexander Graham Bell's, but we still dream no matter how small our dreams are.

Dreaming and hoping for a brighter future is among my happiness habits. In fact, it is one of my favorite acts. It helps me stay happy every day.

As our dreams keep us alive, they give us hope.

SIXTH HAPPINESS HABIT: WORKING ON YOUR GOALS

Nancy was preparing for a world tour with some friends. She had saved some money and planned out the whole year for it. She had been waiting for that for a long time. It was on her bucket list; she had always wanted to achieve it. She booked the air tickets, hotels, attractions, and so forth. At the time, she was about twenty-eight years old and working in a major bank in Australia. She was the kind of a person who would stay in the most luxurious hotels, wear only branded clothes, drive a BMW, and so on. For example, she told me that she once went to Queenstown in New Zealand, one of the best places for skiing. Even though she was not a regular skier, she spent over three thousand dollars on ski gear for a few days of skiing. In short, she used to spend a lot of money on luxurious things (just to set the context).

A few weeks before her flight to her first stop, she was talking to her mother. Her mother said, "You're going on a world tour for the whole year. Why don't you visit Vietnam for a few weeks and include that in your itinerary?" Her mother is from Vietnam, and she wanted her to spend some time there. She was like, "Why? there isn't much to see there." She didn't want to spend a couple of weeks somewhere she didn't find interesting. But her mum insisted, and a few days later, she decided to go and visit Vietnam for a week. So she flew to Vietnam. Before going, she booked one of the best hotels in the city.

She had no idea what was waiting for her.

Nancy wanted to explore the areas near the hotel, and she was told that there was an orphanage she could visit. So she went, and she found out there were about twenty orphan kids, and fifty children were attending the charity school. The classrooms were made of wood and were unstable, with no proper school supplies or blackboard. A fourteen-year-old orphan child was the teacher. The children were malnourished and very ill. She was shocked and could not believe that those kids were so underprivileged and there was just not enough support.

During my interview with Nancy, she told me, "The more I explored, the more I realized that the suffering was not necessary for those kids. something shifted in me." She came back to the hotel, but she didn't feel good at all. She was sitting by the swimming pool and thought about how she could help. She had planned the world tour with her friends already, but at that time, she was so shocked that she became confused and began wondering whether she wanted to go on a world tour at all. The next day, she went back to the orphanage again and started helping those orphan kids, they were very sick, and there were not enough medical supplies for them. They were suffering from malnutrition and didn't have access to clean water.

Over the next few days, she decided to put all her savings into the orphanage and cancel her world tour with her friends. She helped with what needed immediate attention. Later she ran a nutrition program for the kids, which provided multivitamins for children and babies, freshly produced vegetables delivered from the local market, clean water, fruits, and decent meals instead of rationed rice in congee with a bit of salt. She also started a baby program, a first aid program, and a medical treatment program over the next few years. She showed me a picture of a three-year-old girl who, in 2010, had suffered a second-degree burn. Nancy's medical treatment program helped the little girl and other kids recover. There are more water pumps for them to access clean water now.

In the past eleven years, she has helped make this orphanage a better place. Nancy and her team of volunteers built proper classrooms instead of wooden structures. They hired proper teachers, matched primary school curricula to government schools, and built decent toilets. They also have built a second floor to save kids and people from floods. They now have fifteen water pumps instead of one. There are 160 children attending school instead of fifty, with a high school scholarship program.

Nancy has her own family and commitments and a full-time job, but still she saves money for the orphanage, and every September, she goes back to the orphanage so the orphan kids and the people in the area can live better lives. She plans the whole year and has all the improvement programs she created reviewed. She pays the school fees for the kids willing to enroll for the next year and many other tasks in that couple of weeks every year. With proper planning, limited money, and minimal help from others, she has been doing it successfully with flair. She literally changed the lives of many kids for the better. She is still going and is showing no sign of stopping any time soon.

Remember her original goal of a world tour? Nancy said that after visiting the orphanage, something shifted in her, and her goal changed to making a difference to the kids. This new goal is very different from the goal of touring the world. Nancy's goal of making a difference for the kids has been an intrinsic journey–based goal for her. You may remember this type of goal from the earlier "Achievements" section. These goals are more meaningful and fulfilling than others. Working on your goals close to your heart is one happiness habit that can help you stay happy.

No one told Nancy to cancel the world tour; she decided to put her money, effort, and hard work towards the orphanage, and it was her decision. She has put a lot of focus on the orphanage in the last eleven years. Over this long period, she planned, saved money, sold her BMW to fund her projects in the orphanage, spoke to hundreds of people, and organized and executed thousands of things for the orphanage. When she works on these small tasks linked to the orphanage, they are very meaningful to her. She sometimes experiences flow. She feels that she is needed for the kids, and she is always drawn to them no matter what.

Regularly working on her goal to help those kids as her happiness habit results in progress and helps her stay happy every day. Whatever your goals are, make sure they are truly yours and intrinsic journey-based goals rather than destination-based goals. Whenever you spend any time, effort, or money working on your goals close to your heart, they will help you stay happy.

This habit of working on your goals habit can potentially link to three elements of life satisfaction: meaning, flow, and achievement. For example, when I write for two hours a day, I can get flow from it, and that will make me happy and satisfied every day. It is meaningful for me, as it has the potential to help someone live on her terms. The little progress I make can also give me a sense of minor achievements.

Nancy told me that one of her colleagues in Australia recently went to volunteer at the orphanage. When she came back, she said the place had everything and didn't look poor at all, and that it was probably not worth helping there anymore (that is Nancy's success). But it doesn't matter to Nancy what other people think or see. She knows what she has done for the kids over the past eleven years. So Nancy just smiled.

Because the place today has a new face and does not look poor anymore, this gives Nancy a lot of fulfilment and true happiness.

SEVENTH HAPPINESS HABIT: ENGAGING IN FLOW

The other day, I went to a family party. I walked in and saw two of my nieces, one eight years old and the other nine. Usually, whenever they see me, they will come and give me a hug. I am probably one of their very few uncles who actually listens to what they say without judging them. After entering the hallway, I saw both of them talking intensely. They were not fighting. They were just so excited, and they were discussing something I had no idea about. They didn't notice me, so I got closer to them. They were still talking and were completely ignoring their surroundings. People were walking past them, and other kids were yelling at them. I was waiting for them to notice me, but they were so engaged in their conversation that they were in a zone that no one else had access to. They seemed to be ignoring everything around them.

So I didn't say anything and walked past them. Ten minutes later, both of my nieces came to the living area where I was sitting with others. One of them said, "Sanju uncle, when did you come?" I said, "About ten minutes ago." She said, "Really? I didn't see you. Where were you?" I smiled and said, "I just walked past you guys, but you didn't notice me." The other one said, "No way. I would have, but you sneaked in."

They didn't notice me because both of them were so engaged that they forgot their surroundings and experienced total immersion. It is possible that they were experiencing flow. The only reason I walked past them was that I didn't want to interrupt their flow experience by saying hello to them. I love watching people in flow.

You might say, "They were just having a conversation." You can get flow from almost anything. Everybody engages with different activities in their own ways, and the level of flow they experience may also vary. Some people find flow in parenting, reading books, cycling, speaking, praying, and countless other things.

When I was as little as my nieces, I grew up reading a lot of books. I read stories of Tom Sawyer, Huckleberry Finn, and many others. Later, when I was in my teens, I picked up some Sherlock Holmes stories and other thrillers. Over the years, I have noticed that my interest in reading books has always been there, but my taste has changed over time. I was so obsessed with reading that every night, at least three to four books used to be at my bedside when I went to bed.

When I was in sixth grade, I remember one night picking up a storybook that I had just bought. I started reading, but I could not finish it at night. The next morning, at my desk, I was supposed to be reading my textbook for my exam, but I couldn't resist reading the storybook. And I was scared that if my dad saw me reading the storybook, he would be very upset. I had my textbook on the table, and on top of that, I had that new storybook. The sizes of both books somehow matched. So it looked as if I were studying the textbook, but in fact, I was reading the storybook. I thought that was very clever of me. I was so absorbed in the storybook that I forgot what was happening around me. I lost myself inside the storybook. I don't know how long it had been, but suddenly I noticed someone standing next to me,

and guess what? It was my dad.

He is one of the kindest people I know, and he would rarely become angry. In my whole life, he has probably been very angry with me only a few times. And that day was one of those days. He didn't say anything; he just took my storybook and said, "I can't believe it," and he then walked away.

I felt that I was the stupidest person on earth.

How did I not notice him coming to my room? At the time, I had no idea. I was in the zone. I forgot about my surroundings, time, and everything around me and lost myself in that book. I had a flow experience.

Remember, flow requires you to have a certain skill, and you must be challenged in that activity you are doing. Your comfortable challenge must match your skill in the sweet spot; your challenge level cannot be so high that you feel anxious or so low that you get bored. Even though you can get flow from almost anything, it is likely that you will experience flow from doing the activities that you love and being challenged to the level you are comfortable with. The secret is your 100 per cent focus on the activity and your ability to maintain it for the whole duration.

Every time we experience flow, we feel nothing. We hardly feel any emotion; we just have total immersion, and when we get out of that zone, we feel satisfied. Many people define that feeling in their own ways and words. The more flow you have in your daily life, the happier you become.

This habit of engaging in flow can potentially link to three elements of life satisfaction: engagement (flow), meaning, and achievement. For example, if you love painting, you can experience flow. When your audience see and love your work, it is meaningful for you. If you have an exhibition, that can be an achievement.

You can experience flow from almost anything you do: reading, having a conversation, playing musical instruments, singing, dancing, and many other things. The question is, what are you obsessed with? Do you forget about the time? Do you forget about your surroundings?

What do you do that you lose yourself in?

My nieces got flow from their conversation. I got it from reading. Flow is part of my daily happiness habit, which helps me stay happy.

EIGHTH HAPPINESS HABIT: BEING KIND

I was at a New York airport and was flying to Toronto to visit my sister. I bought a cricket set for my three-year-old nephew. As I had only a carry-on bag, I could not fit everything in it, and I decided to carry the small plastic bat in my hand. I was in the queue for security check, where you have to take your stuff out and put it on the trays for scanning. One of the officers saw that yellow bat I was carrying, and she came forward and said, "Sir, you cannot take that with you unless you put that in your bag." I didn't quite know the rules and regulations about this unique situation.

I said, "I have already tried to put that inside my bag, but it wouldn't fit in." She said, "Well, then there is nothing we can do. You have to leave it behind." I was like, "Really?" It was just a small bat for kids. Even the couple in front of me said, "They should just let you take it. It is just a bat." I didn't want to make a big fuss about it, so I stepped out of the queue and opened my bag, and I wanted to give it another try to see if it fits inside, and without any luck, I figured that it was not going to fit in.

After a few minutes, the manager of the security team came up to me and asked, "Who is this bat for?" I said, "It is for my three-year-old nephew. He lives in Toronto," She said, "Oh, poor kid." Then she paused and thought for a second and said, "Can I see your bat? Have you tried putting that bat at an angle inside your bag? I think it might fit in that way." I said, "I actually tried that too, but it didn't work," She insisted, "Bring me your bag. Let me see myself." So I opened my bag again, and she said, "Here is the bat. Try putting it at an angle and see what happens." I took the bat and tried putting it in at various angles, and it would look like it would fit, but it was just a little too long. The manager saw this, and she said, "I'd really like to let it go, but the airline would not allow this to carry in hand. I'm so sorry. What do you want to do?" I could see the genuine desire to help in her face, her body language, her words. She was very nice and kind. I thought, "She didn't have to make me try again to put that bat in at an angle. She could have just said, 'Sorry, cannot help,' as the other officer said earlier." She actually went that extra mile to help, and she wanted to see for herself whether there was a chance for this bat to fit in.

Being nice, being kind, and putting in the extra effort took her less than two minutes. Initially, I felt bad that I wasn't able to take the bat with me for my nephew, but after she insisted, I tried again, and she was there to help. I thought, "At least she genuinely tried to help me, and that gesture was very kind. She didn't really have to do that for me." I shrugged and said, "Thanks for trying. Rules are rules. I might just leave the bat behind." She said, "Sorry, I understand how it feels for the little one." I thought, "I shall buy my nephew another bat later. No big deal." But the effort the manager put in made me feel good. When I reached Toronto, I didn't have the bat with me, but I had a kindness story to tell.

Another time, we had just finished our grocery shopping, and I noticed that a man was sitting right next to the supermarket door. It was a cold winter night in Melbourne. After unloading the groceries, I came back to return the trolley, and the man was still sitting there. He looked like a homeless person, and I thought he might need some help. So I walked up to him and asked if he was okay this winter night and needed any help. He said, "No thanks, man. I'm good. I'm fine. I don't need anything." I noticed that he had a piece of paper, and he was drawing something on it with a pen. It was really good artwork. So I asked him, "Do you sketch?" he said, "Yes, I do sketching all the time. I love it." I said, "Those are really good works, not that it is any of my business, but I wasn't sure if you needed anything, as you are just sitting outside in this cold winter?" He looked at me and paused for a bit, then said, "I actually got out of prison today, and I don't have a place to spend the night. I spoke to a lady, and she said she would give me a job tomorrow. So I have to wait until that time and find some accommodation then. But if you want to help, you can buy me some pencils to sketch. I do not like sketching with a pen."

I was thinking, "Should I judge him and walk away because he was in prison?" Then I thought, "I do not know the full story and do not need to know at this point. Who am I to judge him after a thirty-second conversation? This man didn't ask me for anything." I'd reached out to him, wanting to see whether he needed help. He was authentic. He didn't have to tell me about getting out of prison. He could have just asked for some money, which he didn't. I didn't have a lot of time to go and look for the pencil in the supermarket for him. People who sketch with pencils are very particular, so I thought it would be easier just to give him some money so he could buy it himself. So I did.

Then two things happened for me. First, I felt that I had done the right thing by not judging him. People who go to prison must have done something wrong, and that's why they go to prison, but I didn't know his back story. Honestly, I didn't want to know. I just wanted to play my part to be kind and helpful to others. Secondly, I felt really good that even though that man had no place to stay at night, I did not know whether he had eaten. I didn't know whether he had any money at all, but I was able to help him with what he asked for, and that was buying a pencil. With the money I gave him, he was able to do that.

That manager at the security check at the airport was kind to me. That made me feel good. After I spoke to that homeless guy, I also felt good. The person who is being kind and the person who receives the kindness both feel good. It is a win-win for both sides. A study by Professor Barbara Fredrickson from the University of North Carolina and her colleagues revealed that happy people become happier through kindness. The study also suggests that happy people perform more acts of kindness and feel more gratitude when on the receiving end of kindness. Many studies have been done on the relationship between kindness and happiness, revealing similar results.

But acts of kindness are not reserved for strangers. It is most powerful for our happiness when we are kind to the people we love and care about the most. Often, we take them for granted and do not pay them much attention. But we must be kind to them, surprise them, and do things randomly for them that they do not expect us to do. Even simple things like making tea, cooking dinner, and giving a random hug can change someone's day. If you can consistently be kind to people you love and care about, I can tell you that it will only make your loved ones love you more. It is a no-brainer. You do not need science to tell you this.

For other people, look for opportunities to be kind. For example, offer someone your seat on a train, help someone load groceries in her car after you come out of the supermarket, or smile when you make eye contact with a stranger.

This habit of being kind can potentially link to three elements of life satisfaction: flow, love and connection, and meaning. For example, if I can be nice and kind to my partner and help her prepare for a presentation, I may get into flow. That will strengthen my loving connection with her. I may feel that I am needed, and that is meaningful.

While there are many acts of kindness, make sure to vary your acts so you do not get bored. And don't forget to be kind to yourself.

Honestly, the money I gave to the homeless person was more for myself than for him. I truly believe and admit that. Every time I perform a random act of kindness, it makes me feel good. It helps me stay happy.

NINTH HAPPINESS HABIT: BEING THANKFUL

Nathan is a middle aged homeless person on the streets of London. He lost his way a good few years ago. He became involved with heavy drugs. He was a heroin addict for about fifteen years and was in and out of jail. Even though he has a rough past, he seems to be a kind person.

One day, he saw a little dog with a beggar and found he had a strange connection to the dog. So he bought the dog off the beggar for twelve pounds. Even though he was homeless, he took him to the vet the next day, and the vet advised that the little dog was just four weeks old and the beggar (who owned the dog before) may have doped him with Valium so that the dog would not cry for his mother. Nathan kept the dog with him and looked after him for a long time. He said, "I had to get him off the drugs. I had to get off the drugs. I weaned him, I have had him since, and I haven't touched a class-A drug since."

He named the dog Pluto. Over time, the dog has gotten bigger and more mature. Nathan struggles to buy his own food, but he manages to keep Pluto with him. He loves Pluto so much that he said, "When you're homeless, it can be a pretty unforgiving world. More than anything, it's company. It's about having another heartbeat that's on your side." Being homeless is not an easy life. Nathan lost his family and friends. There was no one by his side but the dog. Being frustrated with life for such a long time, Nathan even contemplated suicide. One day, he even went to a bridge (which he pointed out) to throw himself off of it. But he had Pluto with him, and he thought about what he would do with him. Would he jump with Pluto? Then he thought, "Who am I to choose when his time is up?" He ended up staring at Pluto for a few hours. He felt that Pluto looked at him and there was communication. Nathan felt that Pluto had convinced him to live. Nathan couldn't throw himself off the bridge.

He said, "When you're stood there hungry and no one's noticing you, just walking by as if you do not count, in your mind, it convinces you that you're worthless and that you do not count. But with Pluto, he looks to me for his food. He looks to me for love. He looks to me to play with him. It gives me a role—it might even be a tiny role, but it is a purpose. It's a purpose to get up and behave. If I get arrested and go to prison, I lose my dog. They will put him in a home, and I will never see him again. I don't want to be homeless. I don't want to be in jail. But it's the extra incentive to do good. I still wake up and think about drugs. As an addict, whether drinking or gambling, it's always there. But I take my dog for a walk, and it changes my mindset. It's all about love. And through him I have learned how to give love—and most importantly, how to receive it—and he loves me unconditionally. And it's wonderful. I count my blessings every day."

I watched Nathan's story on TV, and I still remember the look on Nathan's face when he said, "I count my blessings every day," and he kissed his dog. There was peace, serenity, and love all in one expression. He was holding Pluto as if he were his baby. That day, I realized that a person might not need many blessings. If you acknowledge and nurture, you can be fulfilled and happy from just one blessing in your life. And that feeling of gratitude can allow you to notice and nurture your other blessings.

Regardless of the situations that we are in, we can still find blessings around us, whether they are our health, relationships, wealth, careers, or anything else. As humans, we are meant to adapt to our blessings and take them for granted because of hedonic adaptation (as we learned earlier). We get a boost of happiness for any new blessing, and then slowly, that blessing begins to not excite or make us thankful anymore.

However, according to studies, practicing gratitude induces positive emotions, helps with stress, helps us recover from setbacks, and strengthens relationships. Thankful people are more likely to help others and have moral behaviors. These are some of the many benefits of being thankful. Some ideas for being thankful are journaling three new blessings (no matter how small) as a habit (which research suggests is more effective when done once a week rather than every day), and partnering with someone and talking about your blessings.

This habit of being thankful habit can potentially link to two elements of life satisfaction: love and connections, and meaning. For example, writing a gratitude letter and reading it to my partner will strengthen my loving connection. Also, this will be meaningful for me, and I may even cry out of joy.

Nathan got off the drugs, and he started to behave. He refrained from throwing himself from the bridge. He started to give love and learned to receive love, and he found a role of a guardian for Pluto, regardless of how minor it was. He found a purpose for his life. All of these things happened as he realized Pluto was his blessing and nurtured him over time.

When a person like Nathan can find blessings, most of us don't have any excuse not to.

What are your top three blessings? How can you acknowledge and nurture them as a habit? Remember, we all have blessings. Whether we notice and are thankful is up to us. Why is this important? Because just this one habit can help you stay happy every day.

Counting his blessings and being thankful for them is part of Nathan's happiness habits, which help him stay happy and at peace every day.

TENTH HAPPINESS HABIT: FORGIVING

Eva and Miriam were born in 1934 as twins in a very small village in Transylvania, in Romania. During World War II, at the age of ten, they were taken to the Nazi concentration camp Auschwitz. They got down from the cattle car. People were being selected to live or die. People were crying and pushing others, dogs were barking, and the twin sisters were trying to make sense of the place. One Nazi came and separated the twins from their mother. That was the last time the twins saw their mother. In just thirty minutes, Eva and her sister lost their whole family. The two little twin sisters were holding hands and crying.

That camp was run by a physician, Dr. Josef Mengele, known as the Angel of Death. His mission was to discover how to increase the birth rate of an Aryan master race. He counted all the experiment subjects (people) every morning and performed experiments on them. Eva and her sister became some of these subjects. Eva said, "They would put me naked in a room with my twin sister and many other twins, up to eight hours a day. They would measure every part of my body, compare it with my twin sister, and then compare it to charts." On alternate days, they would take both sisters to a blood lab. They would tie both of their arms to restrict the blood flow, take blood from Eva's left arm, and give her a minimum of five injections in the right arm. After one of those injections, she became very ill with a high fever. Her legs and arms were swollen and very painful. She has only one clear memory from the following two weeks, which is of crawling on the barrack floor because she could no longer walk. She would crawl to the other end of the barrack for water. As she crawled, she faded in and out of consciousness. She was telling herself, "I must survive." Dr. Mengele performed many such experiments on them over a year, and in 1945 both twin sisters were liberated by the Soviet army.

Later, in 1963, when Miriam got pregnant for the second time in Israel and had some complications, an Israeli doctor studied her and found out that Miriam's kidneys had never grown larger than a ten-year-old child's. After a long battle in 1993, she died even though Eva donated a kidney to her early in the process. Eva and her sister carried bitter memories for a long time, and Eva could not forget and forgive Dr. Mengele from Auschwitz.

Many years later, Eva received a telephone call from a professor in Boston. He invited her to go to Boston and speak, but he also said it would be nice if she could bring a Nazi doctor. She was stunned at such a question, but she managed to invite a Nazi doctor from Auschwitz. The Nazi doctor (Dr. Munch) told her that he was unwilling to go to Boston but was willing to meet Eva at his house in Germany. In August 1993, Eva arrived at Dr. Munch's house in Germany. They started talking about the Auschwitz camp and the stories of their experiences there. She wanted a signed document from the doctor about the gas chamber operation he had witnessed, which had killed many people. Surprisingly, the doctor agreed to sign one for her. She said, "I wanted to thank this Nazi doctor for his willingness to document the gas chamber operation. I didn't know how to thank a Nazi."

After ten months, one morning, she woke up, and a simple idea popped into her head. She said, "How about a letter of forgiveness? From me to Dr. Munch?" She immediately thought that he would like it, as it would be a meaningful gift—an Auschwitz survivor giving a letter of forgiveness to a Nazi doctor. She said, "What I discovered for myself was life-changing. I discovered that I had the power to forgive.

No one could give me that power. No one could take it away. It was all mine to use it in any way I wished. That became an interesting thing, because as a victim of almost fifty years, I never thought I had any power over my life."

She started to write a letter, but she didn't know how to write a letter of forgiveness, and it took her four months to write it. Her diction was good, but not her spelling, so she sought help from her former English professor, and she finally finished writing that letter.

The professor told her that forgiving Dr. Munch would not resolve her problem with Dr. Mengele (the doctor who performed experiments on her and her twin sister). Eva was not quite ready to forgive Dr. Mengele. The professor told her, "I want you to go home and pretend that Dr. Mengele is in the room, and you forgive him. Because I want to find out how it would make you feel if you could do that." Eva thought that was an interesting idea. When she got home, she did something else. She said, "I picked up a dictionary and wrote down twenty nasty words, which I read clear and loud to Dr. Mengele in the room. And at the end, I said, 'Despite all that, I forgive you.' It made me feel very good that I, the little guinea pig of fifty years, even had the power over the Angel of Death of Auschwitz."

She said, "I felt free. I felt free from Auschwitz, free from Mengele. So now that I have forgiven him, I like it. It is an act of self-healing, self-liberation, and self-empowerment. All victims feel hopeless, helpless, feel powerless. I want everybody to remember that we cannot change what happened, that is the tragic part, but we can change how we relate to it."

Dr. Mengele died a long time ago. He was dead, but the bitterness that Eva had been carrying for fifty years relating to Dr. Mengele was only within herself. It was the memory within Eva that was bitter. It needed to be softened. It was more for her than for Dr. Mengele. She would not have been able to set herself free without forgiving him.

Some ideas for forgiving are writing a letter of forgiveness or forgiving someone who gave you only a small amount of pain, which may be simpler and easier for you. Also, remember times when others forgave you. Be empathetic to the other person, and modify the meaning of that person's actions to you (e.g., "She was mentally unstable, so she did it; she was struggling with X at the time").

The act of forgiving can potentially link to two elements of life satisfaction: meaning and achievement. For example, writing a forgiveness letter to a friend who wronged me will free me from bitter memories. That could be meaningful for me. I may feel like the bigger person for forgiving her. I may even feel a sense of freedom or achievement.

Forgiving someone like Dr. Mengele is hard and can take years to do. You may not have experienced what Eva did, but we all, in one way or another, hold grudges against others, and they stay within us for a long time to make us feel bitter. They all need to be softened—not for them, but for us. Those memories of others are in our brain cells, and they only give us pain. If we don't forgive or make peace with them, it is like part of our houses catching fire and us letting it burn without extinguishing it. The fire then might extend to other areas in our houses.

The Buddha said, "Holding on to anger is like grasping a hot coal with the intent of throwing it at someone else; you are the one who gets burned."

Forgive once, as everybody deserves a second chance, but don't be fooled into forgiveness if the person repeats the wrongdoing and you keep forgiving him or her every time. Learn from the first instance and decide wisely.

Forgiving others for minor things as a habit can help us not sweat the small stuff, make us happy, and build muscles to deal with bigger issues if needed.

ELEVENTH HAPPINESS HABIT: RECOVERING FROM SETBACK

Maddy is a very successful business executive and has held several prestigious positions in a few large corporates. She is also a mother of two children, a wife, a philanthropist, and a friend to people who love her energy and passion. They look up to her and get inspired by her as their leader.

A few years ago, she lost her husband in an accident while they were on holiday. Her life changed in a day.

Her husband died suddenly, and it was unimaginable for her to live through. She said that it felt as if there were a void closing on her. She thought her kids' happiness would just be wiped out. She wasn't sure how to navigate that difficult time. She said, "So I turned to my friend Andy, who was a psychologist, and I said, 'What do I do to get me and my kids through this?' What he taught me is that we are not born with a fixed amount of resilience. It is a muscle everyone can build."

Her loving husband was the go-to person for her and her kids in many ways for love, support, and companionship. But when he died, her preferred option was no one. She also said that one way or another, we all live in some form of second option. People go through divorce, go to prison, lose someone they love, have illnesses they have to live with, don't have enough money, and experience many other challenges. It is never easy for someone to go through such trauma in life. For Maddy, it wasn't just the grief but also the isolation. When people know that someone suffered a loss or is going through some type of trauma, they become overly careful of what they should or should not say. We become too conscious about what is the right thing to say. Most people tend not to say anything and keep quiet. This can happen in a social gathering or a workplace situation.

Maddy was going through a similar situation, and after some time, she finally opened up. She shared her feelings through a Facebook post, which allowed her to express herself at that moment. She became vulnerable, and people around the world started to support her and her journey through her situation. She felt that it was necessary to speak out and that her experience would help others go through similar situations.

Going through this journey, Maddy learned a few important lessons in life. One of them she mentioned is permanence. When someone goes through trauma or any kind of adversity in life, we feel low, sad, and unhappy, and we grieve for some time. But eventually, as you probably remember, we are very resilient. Our happiness, most of the time, comes back to our default genetic baseline. After any positive or negative events that happen to us, it is important to understand and remember that any negative feelings we have as we go through any adversities are not permanent.

Maddy wrote a book on her journey and said, "Knowing that I will not feel that way forever, when I lost my husband, I thought the early grief—there were days that felt like every day was a month—would never get better, and you know what? The grief is still there. I still miss him, but it is not what it was like two years ago, and I am hoping this book helps people believe that in a way that I didn't."

She was not alone. She has a daughter and a son. She was also worried about how they were going to miss their dad and how they were going through the situation. It must have been devastating for them. She said, "I tried to tell my kids to respect their feelings. It is okay if you cry. It is okay if you feel sad or jealous of other children who have fathers. It is also okay to laugh and be happy, because Daddy would want that for you."

The other thing she learned was to avoid personalization—blaming ourselves for things that are not even our fault. Initially, she started blaming herself, and she felt guilty. She didn't allow herself to be happy for a long time. She was not compassionate to herself. She said that self-compassion is huge for recovery and that you should not be too hard on yourself during these times. The key here is to stop blaming yourself and live life with gratitude.

Support from friends and families is vital in the recovery process. If someone you know is going through trauma and you want to help, sometimes the person might not be open to you; if you ask the person she might not want to be helped. But it is important for the person to know that you are there for her. Helping can be as simple as buying dinner for them, offering them a ride to work, or even just spending time with them, visiting them, and staying a little longer with them. There are many ways to do that. It is up to you how you do that and what's appropriate. Instead of saying, "How can I help you?" most people going through trauma will not tell you how you can help them.

So does Maddy have joy and happiness back in her life?

After a few years, she said, "I do, and I try to notice it. One of the best suggestions is to write down three moments of joy every day, no matter what hardship you are facing. There is a moment. Coffee tastes good. My daughter gave me a hug. Someone gave you a smile, and we focus on joy." (You may remember, this is the 3 good things exercise we explored).

As Maddy's friend Professor Andy said, we are not born with a set amount of resilience. It is a muscle we can all build which helps us recover. Most people have remarkable power to do that. Hardships in life come in different shapes and forms. You can be going through a divorce or having an illness that you are recovering from, having a tough time in your business, losing a job, or being in a relationship that is not working. Whatever it is, it is always hard. But you are not alone. We all go through tough times.

An idea for recovery is writing down three moments of joy, as Maddy did, modifying the meaning of the situation you are going through as discussed earlier. For example, instead of saying why it happened to you, think about what this event means to you in an empowering way. (You might not be able to do this straight away, and it might take you a number of attempts over a period of time, but eventually you will be able to do it.) Also, seeking social support can be very helpful. There can be many ways to recover from a setback.

The act of recovering from setback can potentially link to three elements of life satisfaction: pleasure, flow, and meaning. For example, spending five minutes writing down three moments of joy every day can give me momentary pleasures and flow. I can eventually find a better meaning for the setback and move on.

You may or may not see that right now, but there is hope. There is something you can do about it. Maddy didn't have the option to fix it, but she learned and built that muscle of resilience over time to live with it in peace. I hope you are not going through any trauma, but if you are, this is not permanent, and you will eventually get out of it.

Maddy wrote those three moments of joy every day. That would have been one of her happiness habits that helped her be thankful for life and move on. If you are going through a tough time, like Maddy, you can also bounce back.

REFLECTION

Remember, you don't want to do all eleven happiness habits. Rather, do the ones that resonate with you. In the following part, we will discuss a tool that will help you discover your own style.

Your happiness habits are the secrets that will help you stay happy.

THE SEVEN EMOTIONAL HABITS - PROTECT YOUR HAPPY MOMENTS

"In the midst of movement and chaos, keep stillness inside of you."
—Deepak Chopra

Our emotions go up and down all the time. One moment, we feel good, but the next, we may feel the opposite for whatever reason. These fluctuations can be triggered by external things, people, or our own thoughts. We have been focusing on various happiness habits that make us happy, but our emotional habits help us protect that happiness.

There are many tools and strategies that can help us be more emotionally intelligent. In this section, I have shared seven emotional habits I have learned over the years that are simple and easy to do every day.

FIRST EMOTIONAL HABIT: WHEN YOU JUDGE TOO EARLY

I was entering a clothing store when I saw a middle-aged man coming out of the door, pushing a pram with a baby in it. I stopped for him to get out, but as he rushed out, one of the pram wheels rolled over one of my toes. I got a little hurt, but he did not stop. He did not say thanks as I stopped for him or say sorry as his pram rolled over my toe.

I was a little surprised and annoyed, as it seemed very rude of him. I got into the shop, and in my head, I was thinking that it was very mean of that guy to have acted that way. I felt that he had no respect for others, and so on. Ten minutes later, the guy came back to the store and anxiously asked the girl at the counter, "Have you seen a little girl? She is about six years old. She was just here in this store." He was breathing heavily, and his eyes were looking everywhere for the little girl he had lost.

I was speechless. I was just standing there with a blank head. My wife asked me, "Do you want to help him find his girl?" I said, "Huh." I was not thinking clearly. It took me more than five seconds to say, "Yes, sure. Yep, I'm on it."

In that five seconds, I was thinking, "How have I completely judged this man?" Ten minutes ago, he had lost his little girl. I felt so ashamed of myself that I had been hesitant to help him find his girl. It felt as if he were looking through my mind, even if I did not say anything to him. Anyway, as I started walking toward him, I saw that his wife had already found his little girl outside the store, and the little girl was very scared and was crying. She jumped into her dad's lap.

I thought to myself, "Thank God."

Years later, I'm still remembering this and writing about it because it made an impact on me. I have learned that everyone has a story behind why people do or say something. At times, their behavior can annoy us or make us angry, but whether they are our loved ones or a stranger, often we see only the tip of the iceberg of their story.

When I misjudged the man at the shopping center, I learned not to judge anyone or anything too early and to let their story unfold, if it matters to me, before I get upset.

SECOND EMOTIONAL HABIT: WHEN YOU FEEL ANNOYED

I landed at an airport in South East Asia after a long flight and wanted to take a train to Berges, where I booked our hotel. I wasn't very familiar with the train system and was too tired to figure out the exact train and platform, so I found a customer service booth nearby with only one counter open. A man was sitting behind the counter with a not-so-welcoming face. But I had no choice, so I asked him, "Hi, how's it going? I need some help." The man said nothing and looked at me with a frowning face and then looked down at the paper he was reading, and then he nodded.

I said, "Could you please tell me which platform I go to, to catch a train to Berges?" I wasn't sure whether he heard me, as he kept looking down at the paper. After a few seconds, he said, "You want to go to Berges?" I said, "Yes." Then he raised his hand and pointed and said, "Buy the ticket and go to Berges." He directed me to the ticket machines, but he didn't answer my question about which platform I needed to go to. So I thanked him and asked him again, "Which platform do I go to?" He looked at me and replied in a raised voice, "Buy the ticket and go to Berges." He made clear with his hand gestures that this was the end of the conversation.

I was like, "Seriously? Is this really customer service?"

This time he completely lost me. I was already tired and didn't feel like arguing with him. But I thought to myself that clearly, he was not present. He was not even making eye contact, was ignorant, and—I could go on and on. I have no idea why this person behaved like this. He might have had a bad day, might have just been fired, might have had an argument with his partner, or was a mean person. Whatever it was, his behavior was a reflection of his own feelings. He seemed very unhappy, and I had a poor customer experience.

Honestly, as you interact with people, sometimes you don't have time or patience to let their stories unfold, or perhaps their stories do not concern you. But still, their behavior can make you feel annoyed or angry.

For me, it was one of those moments where I couldn't be bothered.

I learned the trick of asking myself, "The person or event that is making me upset right now—will it matter to me in a year?" If the answer is no, I make up a meaning for that event and move on. On that day at the airport, I made up "This guy at the counter was mean because he may have lost his job and didn't care about customers anymore."

You might say, "But that meaning may not be true."

Well, who cares? Your made-up meaning doesn't have to be true, because it is made up and does not concern anyone but you. The meaning is only in your head. No one needs to know about it, but it will help you stay calm (suddenly you will feel a little sympathy for this person).

See, you have two options. The first option is that you can remain annoyed with this person for a long time, which may impact everything and everyone else around you. The second option is, with your made-up meaning, to feel sympathy for this person. You are not going to see this person again, and this made-up meaning is not going to impact anyone else.

It is a choice.

Remember, your annoyance and sympathy both happen in your brain, not in someone else's brain. Which one bothers you most? Annoyance or sympathy? Of course, annoyance (or any similar emotion) does. Who is feeling bad? You or the other person? Of course, you are. Will you forget this event in a year? Most likely.

Then why not forget it now? Creating a new meaning (which does not need to be true) helped me get this man out of my head. Give it a try when you are annoyed or angry with a stranger.

But what if you have someone annoying at home, at work, or in your friend circle and you are going to see this person regularly?

Honestly, there is no one way to deal with it. The trick of the made-up meaning can help temporarily. However, you will need to think about your long-term solutions and make a firm decision about the person in question. For example, if you have been in an abusive relationship for a long time and the other person makes you unhappy every day, well, sometimes it is a much healthier option to replace the person. If replacement is not an option, you must think and act on alternative options in which you will not have to deal with this person. If you let yourself be hurt, be abused, or be a victim of anything or anyone, how can you live an extraordinary life on your terms?

The control of your life must be with you at all times. And that's where your decisions and actions will come to the rescue (your 'uncomfortable' but strong actions will set you free).

The experience I had at the airport was a small interaction with a stranger. When you learn to deal with the small interactions, it will help you build a muscle that will allow you to deal with the bigger ones.

Remember, your time is the most precious thing. My time was too precious to remain upset with this man I didn't even know or care about.

THIRD EMOTIONAL HABIT: YOU FEEL SAD BECAUSE OF REJECTION

Many years ago, I received an email saying, "Thank you for your application. But after careful review of your experience and qualifications, we regret to notify you that on this occasion, you have been unsuccessful." Earlier, I had applied for a job and also attended the interview, which I thought went well, and the employer had even been negotiating salaries and benefits. After receiving the email, I was shocked and very upset.

But over the years, I built a perception around rejection. I thought I would share it with you. If you decide to buy a watch, you might think of its brand, functionalities, look, and so forth. If you purchase a dress, you will check the fit, look, size, and so on. Or if you are buying a house, you will consider the number of bedrooms, location, price, and the like. These are only a few factors of many to consider, and it can be overwhelming to make up your mind. When that happens, we can easily get in a rut of a constant search to get "the best." I know someone who inspected seventy-nine houses before they chose "the one." I know a manager who interviewed seventeen candidates before he found the "perfect fit."

There are two things to think about when you are making a buying or hiring decision. Firstly, if you don't know exactly what you want, you will have a hard time selecting one. Secondly, even if you know exactly what you want, you may not be able to find the right fit for your criteria. In both cases, you will likely browse through many options before you make a final call.

But in the process of browsing in the above scenarios, you will reject many watches, dresses, houses, or people. The person who inspected seventy-nine houses, in fact, rejected seventy-eight houses before finally choosing one. The manager rejected sixteen candidates before he hired one. I'm sure that before making a final buying decision, whether it is for a watch, dress, or anything else, you must have said no to plenty of options and rejected them all.

Your own criteria must match before you say yes.

I realized that when we apply for jobs, university admission, business deals, positions on basketball teams, or whatever the case may be,

there is always someone on the other side browsing for the right fit for his or her own criteria.

They will not say yes to you unless their criteria are met. It is much like when you say no to many things before saying yes. You may believe you have what it takes (and you actually may), but it is not about whether you deserve the job or have the best experience; rather, it is about matching the criteria of the person who is deciding for you. Often the person's decisions are emotionally influenced and are not so logical.

No one likes to be rejected, but think about the times when you said no to a dress, a watch, or anything else, or you said no to a person or a proposal. You rejected that thing or person, and the thing or person had no say in your decisions.

Likewise, if you got rejected from a job you applied for, you didn't get a promotion, you didn't get accepted to your favorite university, you didn't get a business deal, you got rejected from a marriage proposal, or a guy you went on a date did not call you back, whatever it is,

there is always a person who is browsing, and he has not yet found someone who matches his criteria.

He may have said no to you, just as you said no to other people. But if you keep going, you will eventually match with someone else's criteria. And you will be "the one." Rejection is a standard phenomenon attached to every decision-making.

The bottom line is that it must match the criteria of the person making the decision.

Remember, it is not about you not being good enough or falling short of anything. It is always about the decision-maker. Sometimes it is you making that decision, and sometimes it is the person on the other side.

FOURTH EMOTIONAL HABIT: WHEN YOU FEEL ANGRY

After we had dinner at a restaurant, my wife and I got out and started walking towards our car. Earlier, I parked the car on the street, but now I couldn't find the car. We walked back and forth a few times, but nothing.

Ten minutes later, I was like, "Where is the car?"

We were really surprised. After a few minutes, we figured that the place where I parked the car was actually a tow-away zone between 4:00 p.m. and 6:00 p.m., which I had overlooked because I was in a hurry. I realized that our car had been towed away, and it was my fault. So we took an Uber to pick the car up. We had to pay $350 to get our car back.

That was the first time I experienced such an event, and I couldn't believe it. I was very angry with myself. In my head, I was thinking, "How could I let this happen? How could I have missed the road signs?" But I had almost no expression on my face. My wife was sitting next to me, and she said, "Are you okay?" I said yes with a big smile, and then I suddenly started laughing. She frowned and asked, "Why are you laughing?"

You might think I had gone crazy.

As I was very angry, I remembered one thing I had learned but never tried before, and that was using laughter to slow down anger. I quickly decided to give it a go. It felt a little forced at first, but without letting my brain stop me, I started laughing without much thinking. I tried to think of something that I had laughed about before and recalled a joke I love. We started to talk about some funny scenes from the TV show Big Bang Theory (which we both love). Eventually, my wife and I both started laughing.

You might think, "How can you laugh when you are angry?"

It still may sound counterintuitive, but as I said, when you feel angry or upset and you keep thinking about laughing, your brain will talk you out of that idea. That's why you must bypass your brain and start laughing without much thinking. The window for this is usually five seconds. Laughter therapy has existed for many years. In the short term, laughter stimulates many of your organs, including your facial muscles, heart, and lungs, which help you take in oxygen-rich air, and increases the release of endorphins, which are considered part of the "happy hormones." It reduces the stress response too. In the long term, it improves your immune system, relieves pain, and improves your satisfaction and mood. Laughter can go a long way in fighting anger and can result in many remarkable returns for your body and mind.

I like what author Judy Carter said: "Laughing about anything gives you power over it, instead of it having power over you."

Next time you are angry or upset, give it a try.

FIFTH EMOTIONAL HABIT: WHEN YOU FEEL LOW

When I feel low for whatever reason, I know the underlying reason is most likely my thoughts. I have read, seen, or heard something upsetting; someone made me annoyed; or I'm worrying about something in the future, and those things may have triggered a series of negative thoughts in my head.

Some things are not in my control, but some are.

For many years, I overlooked the idea of taking three deep breaths and power posing, but I realized that, no matter what the situation is, those are two things I can do instantly without much effort. What that means is that when I feel low, I instantly focus on taking three deep breaths and change my physiology immediately from passive to active. (If I'm standing, I fix my posture and stand straight; if I'm sitting, I sit straight—in other words, in a "power pose" (similar to how Superman and Wonder Woman stand). I change my body language so that I physically feel powerful.

Does that take my worries away? No.

But changing in physiology or power posing actually helps us change our mental states, and we can then feel more powerful and confident. Social psychologist Amy Cuddy was one of the first to do research in this area, and she released a TED talk related to that in 2012. This phenomenon allows us to better deal with challenging situations. If you are in a positive state (including power posing physically), your decisions are much better than those you may make while in a negative state. And the decisions you make every day basically shape your life, including your happiness. There is no one rule book that works for everybody in every situation.

But taking three slow and deep breaths and moving to a power position is what everybody can do in almost every situation.

Don't wait to feel low. Give it a go right now as you are reading.

How does that feel?

SIXTH EMOTIONAL HABIT: AWARENESS OF PEOPLE AND THOUGHTS

In any given situation, whether you become happy or unhappy really is influenced by your outer lane, your people lane, and your self lane (as you may remember from previous chapters). This emotional habit is not related to anything in particular, but be generally aware of those three sources and the level of control you have.

In your outer lane, be aware that the things like weather, laws, and governments are not in your control. Anything in the outer lane can still make you happy or unhappy, but there is not much you can do about it. If you keep your focus on the outer lane to be happy, your happiness is based on chance.

In your people lane, understand that you have partial control over people (including your close family and friends) and that, through no fault of their own, they may fail to make you happy. We are all wired this way. Some people are narcissists and will try to make you unhappy intentionally. Well, that's part of the game. So make sure that people who make you unhappy or cause you to feel bad don't have any power (or less power) over your happiness.

You must be in control.

In your self lane, you have full control. Be aware of your thoughts, feelings, and behaviors. If you find yourself constantly in a low mental state even when alone, it is mainly because of your thoughts. If you regret or feel guilty about the past, worry about the future, or think about today's problems, how do they make you feel? While you may not be able to control all your thoughts, over time, with practice, you will get better.

Whatever happens, remember your decision to live an extraordinary life. Live with passion, and live with courage.

The things and people that are making you unhappy today may not even exist in your life in a year.

SEVENTH EMOTIONAL HABIT: FEAR DOES NOT LIKE GRATITUDE

We took a flight from Sydney to Melbourne after attending a seminar in 2016. The hour-long flight was not too bad, but when it was time for landing, we experienced some turbulence. Most people are scared of turbulence, including me. But I also felt that my ears were slightly blocked and were causing me some pain. That was a new thing for me, and I got scared. There might have been some change in the cabin air pressure, or perhaps the plane was descending a little too fast. As more time passed, the pain in both ears started to increase.

I went from scared to very scared.

In the seminar we had attended, one cool thing I learned was that you cannot be fearful and thankful at the same time. Also, you cannot feel anger and gratitude at the same time. Our brains cannot process positive and negative emotions at the same time.

I thought I might just give it a try and see what happened.

As I was literally counting the minutes for the plane to land with a lot of pain in my ears, I started to think of three things I was thankful for at the moment. Firstly, I was thankful to have attended the seminar, where I had learned a lot. Secondly, I focused on my own breathing and tried to feel my own existence, and thirdly, Mahin was next to me, and I was holding her hand and was thankful for that.

Do you know what happened after that?

My feelings started to flip between fear and thankfulness. It went something like scared, scared, thankful, scared, thankful, thankful, and so on. And after a few moments, as I tried to focus more on being thankful, I felt more gratitude and had a sense of calmness. (Yes, the pain was still there, but my feeling changed from very scared to little scared).

As I had seen a little result straight away, I intentionally focused more and more on my blessings and felt much better. When the plane landed, the pain in my ears was also gone.

I realized that my ability to completely focus on being thankful exactly at the same time I was scared made all the difference. Since then, I have used this technique on several occasions and have gotten better at focusing on my blessings.

But the key is that you will have to somewhat force yourself to think about and feel what you are thankful for at the same time as you are fearful or angry.

The next time you feel fear or anger, give it a go.

Remember, you cannot feel anger or fear when you are thankful. It would be an injustice and an unfair thing if I didn't mention whom I learned it from. He is one of my most favorite people on earth—Anthony Robbins. In the past forty-four years, he has helped change the lives of millions, and I am one of them.

REFLECTION

I believe your ability to control your emotions with intelligence is probably the most important skill of all. You can earn a lot of money, but if you don't know how to keep it, your money will be gone. Likewise, you can be happy by doing the happiness habits, but protecting your happiness is just as important (probably more). And your emotional habits help you build those skills. Your moment-to-moment emotions shape your life experiences.

PART 5:
Building Your Happiness Habits on Your Terms

In this part, we will discuss the following:

- how your happiness and emotional habits make a measurable difference in your lifetime
- what it is like when you put your satisfying life, your happy life, and the protection of your happiness together all on one page
- how you discover your own happiness habits
- a six-week intervention program for you to try, during which you will measure your happiness levels
- how to build your own happiness habits on your terms and live them

JOHN OR MIKE - WHO WILL BE HAPPIER AT NINETY

"Do what you have always done, and you'll get what you have always got."
—Sue Knight

HOW CAN YOUR HAPPINESS HABITS MAKE A DIFFERENCE?

John was twenty-four when he bought his first two-bedroom apartment and a new Toyota. He worked very hard for these. He was over the moon for a little while. Then he saw his boss drive a BMW. In a few months, he forgot about his Toyota and set a new goal for a Lexus. Again, he started working very hard and bought a brand-new Lexus after a year. He sent pictures of his new car to his friends. He was very happy. But he thought his two-bedroom apartment, which he bought earlier, wasn't big enough, and it really didn't go with his new Lexus. So, again, he started working very hard and bought a four-bedroom house. He invited all his friends to his new house, posted photos on social media, and he was one of the happiest until he found that one of his friends earned more money than he did. He started looking for another job that paid at least the same amount as his friend's. After a year of trying very hard, he landed his dream role, and he told everybody about his new job and celebrated his achievements.

Over the last twenty years, he has changed seven houses, taken nine different jobs, and bought eight new cars.

Do you see the pattern?

John is not a greedy person, but he is very competitive. He strives to be better than everyone else around him. But his happiness does not seem to last on anything he achieves, whether it is a house, a new car, or a new job. He is a very target-oriented person. For anything he focuses on, he will do anything in his power to achieve it. He spends most of his time at work and comes home late. But when he is at home, he is almost always on the phone.

He barely spends any quality time with his family and friends.He sacrifices his health and time with his children and partner. He does not take holidays or go to the movies but saves money everywhere possible. In a social gathering, he is not present and does not genuinely engage with his friends.

But every time he achieves one of his goals, he invites everybody to celebrate. But until that special day comes, he sees nothing but his goal.

Mike is about the same age and income group as John. Over the last twenty years, Mike has bought only one house, where he lives with his family; has changed jobs twice; and has bought two cars. Every day, Mike comes home from work, goes for a walk with his wife, and spends quality time with his children at home. They watch Netflix together, chat, and have a little fun. He also helps his children with their studies. They have a dog, and they all play games with the dog almost every night, just for ten minutes. They do not need an occasion or a special day to invite their friends over. Mike spends a lot of time on his health and builds quality relationships with his family and friends. He also has goals, but he must make sure his health and family are okay before anything else.

Mike is also very kind. He checks on his neighbors to see whether they need anything. For him, every day is precious, and he does not want to miss his family time. Even if that is for only an hour a day, he makes the best out of that time. Mike is generally a happy and fulfilled person. John is also happy, but only on or right after his special days of achievements.

But can their happiness and emotional habits make a difference?

JOHN'S HAPPINESS AND EMOTIONAL HABITS

John does not have any happiness habits on his ordinary days. He postpones being happy until he achieves any success and celebrates only on his special days, and those occur only when major events occur (e.g., when John bought a new house).

John's happiness formula is "I will be happy when X happens. Until then, I will do anything to make that a reality." But when the X finally happens for John, he becomes very happy, and when that short-term boost of happiness fades away, he sets a new target and postpones being happy until he achieves his next goal to be happy again. He does not see or allow himself to be happy with the little things that happen during his ordinary days (e.g., he has not seen the picture his son drew, and he didn't notice when his daughter made pasta for the first time).

John does not have any emotional habits either. His only focus is to achieve his goals, no matter how hard he has to work, and no matter how many sleepless nights he has, how bad he feels during the day, or how mean people are to him. Usually he deals with people he does not like and does the things he does not love to make his goals a reality. All of his endeavors keep him in a state of worry and anxiety on his ordinary days until he achieves his goals.

MIKE'S HAPPINESS AND EMOTIONAL HABITS

Mike does the opposite of John. He also has goals. He loves surfing and is a state-level runner-up. He has also won various awards for running. His goals and special days are different to John's. But Mike does not wait for his special days to be happy. Rather, he celebrates the little things on his ordinary days (e.g., Mike's son playing a nice piece on his piano, or his wife dressing nicely for a party).

Mike's happiness formula is "Y happened today, and I'm happy about it now, no matter how small it was." Instead of one big X, Mike focuses on those little "Y things" (e.g., Mike's daughter making coffee for him) to be happy. Small but good things always happen around us. And each Y gives Mike only a small amount of happiness, but that occurs reliably and almost certainly every day. Mike and his family have learned to see and celebrate the little things on their ordinary days, as their happiness habits.

Mike is also emotionally intelligent. He tries not to worry about what he does not control and focuses more on what he can do in his self lane. His philosophy is doing fewer things efficiently rather than doing many things inefficiently. He spends quality time with the people he loves and carefully filters those who do not serve him as his emotional habits.

Who do you think is a happier person? John or Mike?

Even though John and Mike are from the same age, background, and income group and have similar family structures, their perceptions of happiness are very different. John's happiness does not happen in the present until his special days. Mike is quite the opposite and can be happy for little things in the present moments on his ordinary days.

> "Doing what you like is freedom. Liking what you do is happiness."
> —Frank Tyger

Generally, happy people do not chase the best of everything. They make the best of everything they have on their ordinary days.

HOW HAPPY WILL JOHN AND MIKE BE AT NINETY?

Remember the research by Professor Sonja Lyubomirsky from UC Riverside? Our genetics contribute about 50 per cent of our happiness; only 10 per cent comes from various life events, and 40 per cent is actually in our control (our intentional actions and behaviors).

So, hypothetically, if John and Mike both have the same genetic contribution to their happiness and have the same life events and then we know Professor Lyubomirsky's research says that any positive life event that makes us very happy (e.g., buying a house or getting a promotion) or any negative life event (losing a job or having a chronic illness) that makes us unhappy is something we adapt to over time, and our happiness always comes back to our default genetic happiness.

So genetics and life events for both John and Mike will be the same.

If you just live a default life and have no happiness or emotional habits on your ordinary days, your average happiness will be very close to your default genetic set point. But if you intentionally build your happiness and emotional habits, your average happiness will be higher than your genetic set point.

The question is whether John or Mike are capitalizing on that 40 per cent happiness that is in their control.

Assuming both John and Mike are forty-five years old, if both live up to the age of ninety and we measure and record their happiness regularly, how happy will they be in the next forty-five years till age ninety?

On the next page, the black dots are positive life events, and the white dots are negative life events. This assumes that both John and Mike have the same life events and experience the same levels of happiness and unhappiness from these events. And it also assumes both of their genetic baseline is about 2.0. That way, the contributions of their positive and negative life events (10 per cent) and their genetics (50 per cent) will be the same for both John and Mike. Therefore, the only difference in their happiness will be determined by the remaining 40 per cent, which is actually in their control and determined by their daily actions.

As you can see, as John does not have any happiness or emotional habits on his ordinary days, he is not doing anything intentionally to make use of the 40 per cent of happiness. But Mike, with his happiness and emotional habits, creates small happy moments (the little black squares in the second graph) that make him happy on his ordinary days.

JOHN OR MIKE – WHO WILL BE HAPPIER AT NINETY

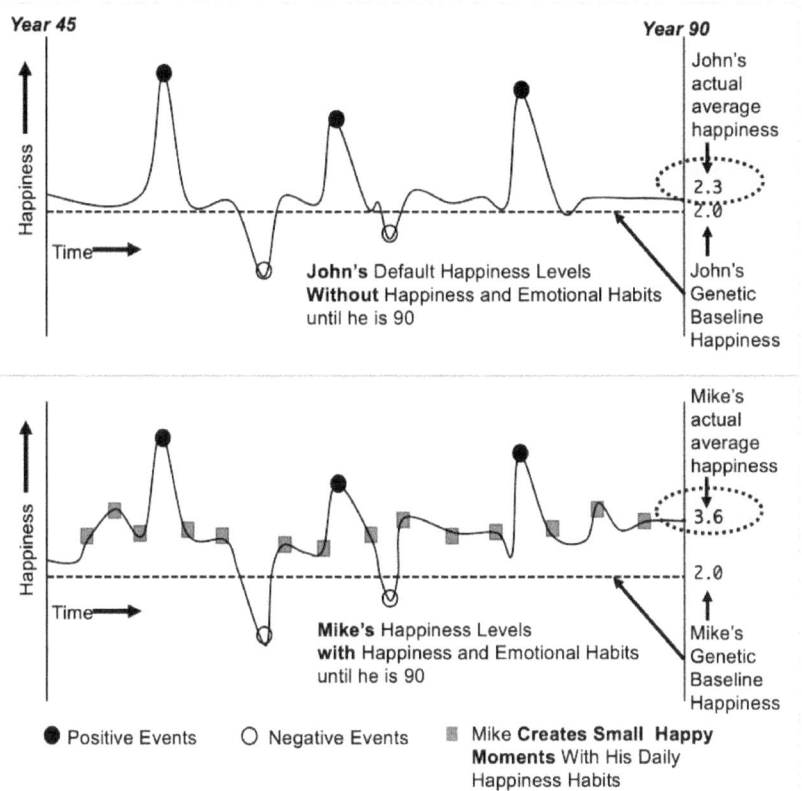

So, in the next forty-five years, John will likely have a life with an average happiness of 2.3 (which is very close to his default 2.0 genetic set point). But Mike's actual average happiness might be much higher, at 3.6 (which is 1.6 points higher than his default 2.0 genetic set point). The 1.6 on a scale of 1 to 6 does not look very significant, but over forty-five years, it will be a huge difference. These numbers can vary widely and depend on many factors, and I have used them only as an example and demonstration.

Whether you are more like John or Mike or someone in between, I do not know, but what I do know and hopefully I made my point, is that regardless of who you are, your past, or your current situation, you can live on your own terms and be happier with your happiness and emotional habits (like Mike over many years).

The question is, will you settle for your default genetic happiness, or will you live a happier life than that?

REFLECTION

Many things in life are not in our control, but many are. Whether you brush your teeth or not, eat junk food or healthy food, go on a holiday or not, take an opportunity or not, or love your partner or not,

are your choices.

The difference between being happy once in a while and staying happy every day is also about small choices you make every day.

Our special days often make us happy and that happiness is not meant to last long. Our lives are mainly made of our ordinary days and your habits on your ordinary days help you to stay happy.

Remember your decision to live an extraordinary life on your terms and stay happy with your happiness and emotional habits for the rest of your life.

How amazing would that be for you and your loved ones?

ALL ON ONE PAGE

Remember, my primary goal of this book is to empower and inspire you to live such a life that you will have a satisfying life, have a happy life, and protect your happiness.

If you choose to do that, this is what it comes down to.

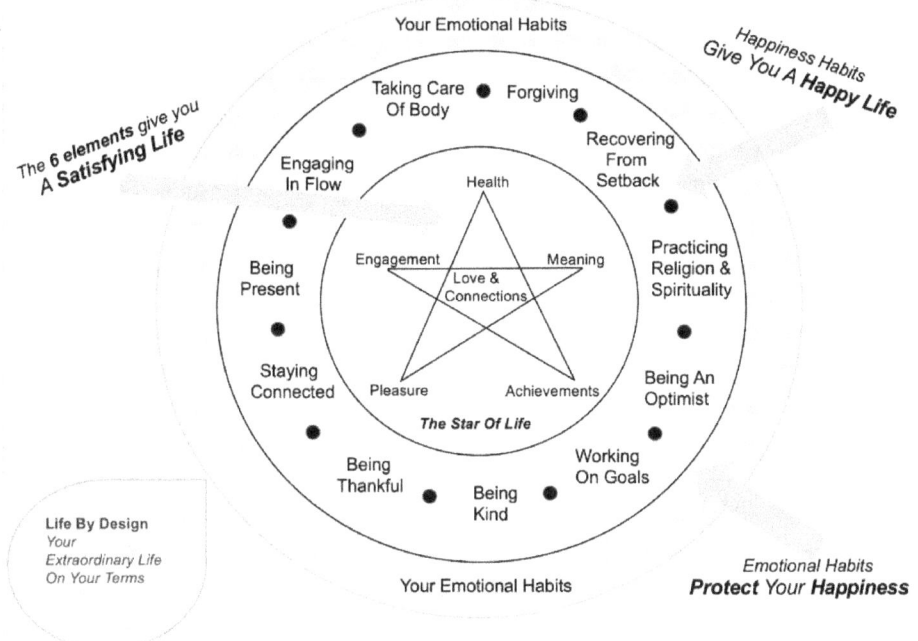

If you have read up to this point, you will have realized that

- six elements in the Star of Life give you a satisfying life by design,
- your happiness habits give you a happy life, and
- your emotional habits protect your happiness.

You see, if you genuinely desire and commit, it's easy to design and live your life on your terms. And for that you will need to tap into the things that come naturally to you. So I have a little gift for you to try in the next section.

DISCOVER YOUR NATURAL HAPPINESS HABITS

"You are one of a kind — Gallup research finds the possibility of two people having the same top five talents in the same order is one in 33 million."
—Gallup Research

WHAT ARE YOUR NATURAL HABITS?

If you have ten good friends and you are asked to pick only three, even though you like and want to pick all of them, deep down, you know whom you can count on as your real friends. You will likely pick whom you trust, love, and care about the most. We all do that. From the science of happiness, we know that there are eleven happiness habits that make us happy.

But you may not want to adopt all of the happiness habits, as everybody is different and not every happiness habit is suitable for all. What I like is not necessarily something you will also like. What you like is not something your partner will like the same. You are more likely to sustain the happiness habits you love that suit your own personality, beliefs, and values. For example, if you are not naturally grateful, practicing gratitude will not last for you, or if you are not goal-oriented, forcing yourself to create and pursue your goals might not be a good idea. Following is a simple tool for you to discover the happiness habits that are best suited to your personality, beliefs, and values.

COMPLETE YOUR HABITS DISCOVERY TEST (HDT)

By now, you are already familiar with the eleven happiness habits. In this test, there are eleven sections, one for each habit, and there are five statements in each section. For each statement, you score yourself between 1 and 10 (1 is no, not at all; 10 is yes, absolutely). Once you have scored all five of them, calculate the total for each happiness habit.

Here is an example:

Happiness Habit—Being an Optimist:

You genuinely believe that life can be better, and you are excited about it. You love imagining and planning your better future. Every time you do that, you feel satisfied, and you want to do it again and often. Score the below statements for yourself.

- I truly believe in it. _____8_____ (1–10)
- I am excited about it. _____8_____ (1–10)
- I love doing it. _____8_____ (1–10)
- I feel satisfied after I have done it. __7__ (1–10)
- I want to do it again. _____7_____ (1–10)

Total score for being an optimist: ___38___ (5–50)

So, for the happiness habit of being an optimist, you score 38/50. Take the test below and do the same for each happiness habit to score yourself.

1. Happiness Habit—Being Kind:

You genuinely believe that you are a kind person, and you are excited to show kindness to yourself and others. You love being kind to someone. You feel satisfied after you have done an act of kindness, and you can't wait to do it again. Score the below statements for yourself.

- I truly believe in it. _____ (1–10)
- I am excited about it. _____ (1–10)
- I love doing it. _____ (1–10)
- I feel satisfied after I have done it. _____ (1–10)
- I want to do it again. _____ (1–10)

Total score for being kind: _____ (5–50)

2. Happiness Habit—Working on Your Goals:

You genuinely believe you will achieve your life goals and are excited about them. You love actively working on your goals. Once you have made a little progress towards your goals, you feel satisfied, and you can't wait to work on your goals again. Score the below statements for yourself.

- I truly believe in it. _____ (1–10)
- I am excited about it. _____ (1–10)

- I love doing it. _____ (1–10)
- I feel satisfied after I have done it. _____ (1–10)
- I want to do it again. _____ (1–10)

Total score for working on your goals: _____ (5–50)

3. Happiness Habit—Being an Optimist:

You genuinely believe that life can be better, and you are excited about it. You love imagining and planning your better future. Every time you do that, you feel satisfied, and you want to do it again and often. Score the below statements for yourself.

- I truly believe in it. _____ (1–10)
- I am excited about it. _____ (1–10)
- I love doing it. _____ (1–10)
- I feel satisfied after I have done it. _____ (1–10)
- I want to do it again. _____ (1–10)

Total score for being an optimist: _____ (5–50)

4. Happiness Habit—Engaging in Flow:

You genuinely believe that you can experience flow in your favorite activities, and you feel excited about them. You love the total immersion, and time stops for you. Once you are out of flow, you feel satisfied, and you want to do it again. Score the below statements for yourself.

- I truly believe in it. _____ (1–10)
- I am excited about it. _____ (1–10)
- I love doing it. _____ (1–10)
- I feel satisfied after I have done it. _____ (1–10)
- I want to do it again. _____ (1–10)

Total score for engaging in flow: _____ (5–50)

5. Happiness Habit—Staying Connected:

You genuinely believe that staying connected to people around you in deep and meaningful ways brings you joy. You are excited about creating quality relationships with them. You love spending time with them. Once you have spent time with them, you feel satisfied, and you want to do it as much as possible. Score the below statements for yourself.

- I truly believe in it. _____ (1–10)
- I am excited about it. _____ (1–10)
- I love doing it. _____ (1–10)
- I feel satisfied after I have done it. _____ (1–10)
- I want to do it again. _____ (1–10)

Total score for staying connected: _____ (5–50)

6. Happiness Habit—Forgiving:

You genuinely believe that forgiving yourself or others sets you free and make you happier, even though it can be very difficult sometimes. But you genuinely want to give it a try and move on to better things. You see true values in forgiveness, and you feel that forgiving others is more for yourself than for them. You may love the process of forgiving yourself or others. Once you have forgiven someone or yourself, you feel satisfied, and you believe you have learned the lesson and can do it again if needed. Score the below statements for yourself.

- I truly believe in it. _____ (1–10)
- I see value in it. _____ (1–10)
- I may love doing it. _____ (1–10)
- I feel satisfied after I have done it. _____ (1–10)
- I can do it again if needed. _____ (1–10)

Total score for forgiving: _____ (5–50)

7. Happiness Habit—Taking Care of Your Body:

You genuinely believe that taking care of your physical health is absolutely necessary, and you see value in it. You love taking care of your body, whether eating healthy, exercising, or anything else. Once you have done this, you feel satisfied, and you can't wait to do it again. Score the below statements for yourself.

- I truly believe in it. _____ (1–10)
- I am excited about it. _____ (1–10)
- I love doing it. _____ (1–10)
- I feel satisfied after I have done it. _____ (1–10)

- I want to do it again. _____ (1–10)

Total score for taking care of your body: _____ (5–50)

8. Happiness Habit—Being Thankful:

You genuinely believe that life is a blessing and you have a lot to be thankful for. You are excited about it. You love counting your blessings and saying thanks. Once you have done this, you feel satisfied, and you want to do it often. Score the below statements for yourself.

- I truly believe in it. _____ (1–10)
- I am excited about it. _____ (1–10)
- I love doing it. _____ (1–10)
- I feel satisfied after I have done it. _____ (1–10)
- I want to do it again. _____ (1–10)

Total score for being thankful: _____ (5–50)

9. Happiness Habit—Recovering from Setback:

You genuinely believe that life can be better after a setback, and you look forward to it. You also understand that a recovery process can take time but can transform and make you stronger. Once you have made a little progress, you feel satisfied and look forward to the next step. Score the below statements for yourself.

- I believe recovery gives hope. _____ (1–10)
- I believe life can be better again. _____ (1–10)
- I value the process of recovery. _____ (1–10)
- I feel satisfied after I make progress. _____ (1–10)
- I look forward to the next step. _____ (1–10)

Total score for recovering from setback: _____ (5–50)

10. Happiness Habit—Practicing Religion and Spirituality:

You genuinely believe that practicing religion and spirituality fulfils you, and you value it. You love the process of practicing religion or spirituality. Once you have done this, you feel satisfied, and you want to do it often. Score the below statements for yourself.

- I truly believe in it. _____ (1–10)
- I am excited about it. _____ (1–10)
- I love doing it. _____ (1–10)
- I feel satisfied after I have done it. _____ (1–10)
- I want to do it again. _____ (1–10)

Total score for practicing religion and spirituality: ___ (5–50)

11. Happiness Habit—Being Present:

You genuinely believe that you love living every moment of your life, and you are excited about it. You focus on the present and enjoy each experience. This nature of you makes you feel satisfied, and you can't wait to experience the next occurrence. Score the below statements for yourself.

- I truly believe in it. _____ (1–10)
- I am excited about it. _____ (1–10)
- I love doing it. _____ (1–10)
- I feel satisfied after I have done it. _____ (1–10)
- I want to do it again. _____ (1–10)

Total score for being present: _____ (5–50)

Once you have scored each element of the eleven different happiness habits, add the individual numbers to get a total score for each, and sort them on the below table.

Your highest-scoring happiness habit is no 1	Your Top Five Happiness Habits	Score
1		
2		
3		
4		
5		

These are your top five happiness habits. They come naturally to you. You believe in them, see their value, feel excited by them, love doing them, feel satisfied after you do them, and want to do them again and often.

YOUR SIX-WEEK INTERVENTION PROGRAM

WHAT IS IT?

This is a program designed for you inspired by the scientific evidence. Now that you know your top five happiness habits. You can proceed with implementing them on a weekly basis. The commitment would be about one to two hours a week of honest, consistent participation, and completion of the program's activities for six weeks. At the end of the sixth week, you will see your results. Then you will evaluate, adjust, and continue with your happiness habits.

BUT WHAT RESULTS CAN YOU EXPECT?

You may remember Glenn and Amy. Earlier, I shared the results and graphs of these two-real people from my six-week intervention program in the "Results" chapter of part 1.

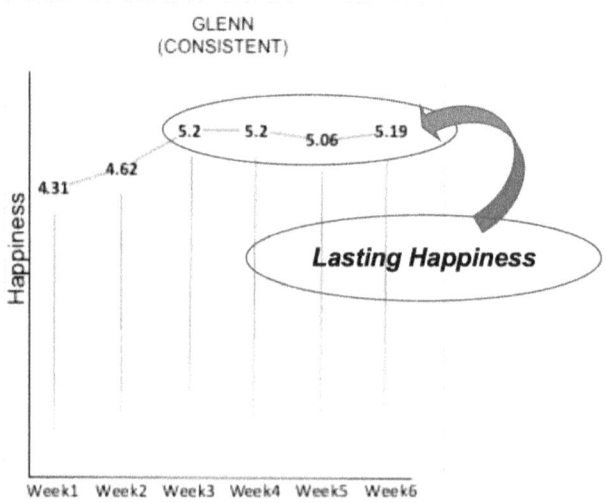

Glenn was very consistent and completed the happiness activities on time every week.

YOUR SIX-WEEK INTERVENTION PROGRAM

The first one is for Glenn. He completed the activities every week on time, and you can see that his happiness levels increased and lasted in the final four weeks of the six weeks.

But the second one is for Amy. She was not consistent and did not complete the happiness activities every week. You can see she had little spikes of happiness, but they did not last because she didn't do the happiness activities for some weeks (weeks 2, 4, and 6).

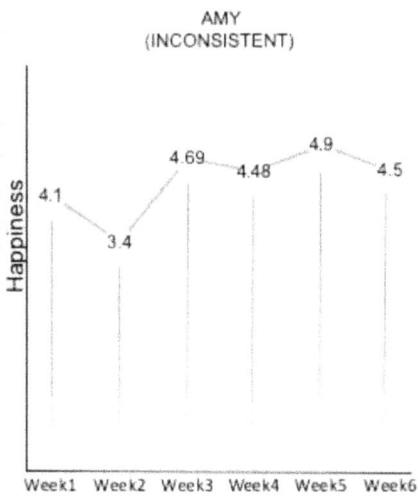

Amy was not very consistent and did not do the happiness activities on time every week.

If you schedule and do the happiness interventions (activities) every week for at least six weeks, you will not only feel happier and more satisfied but you will actually see your results on paper. Whether you will be better than Glenn or worse than Amy is up to your actions.

I know it might sound a little strange to record your happiness levels every week. But think about it; an average person probably will not do this, but you are not average.

Remember the decision we talked about to live an extraordinary life on your terms? If you have made the strong decision to live that life, then this six-week intervention will help you realize that you can surely be happier and track your progress over time, and you will get a head start.

WHY SCHEDULE AND TRACK?

Everybody is different. Some people are spontaneous and will find it strange to schedule something about their happiness activity in their calendar—for example, you are scheduling to spend quality time with your wife, watching Netflix, or even calling an old friend on Sunday at 5:30 p.m. These may seem counterintuitive. If you find this strange, the only thing for you is to make sure you do them as your habits.

But if you like to plan and stick to your schedule, this program will help you stay on course and track your progress over time.

We often forget, get distracted, and do not do things even if they are on our calendars. For example, if you have already scheduled spending time with your friend, a work call can stop you from doing that; or if you promised your son that you would take him to basketball, one of your clients could request a meeting at the same time.

What do you do?

Whatever you do, reschedule your happiness habit activities and make sure you do them that week. To do otherwise is akin to scheduling a gym appointment because you want to build muscle and procrastinating because of hundreds of reasons. Would you be able to build that muscle? You know the answer. The same goes for your happiness habits.

Finally, measuring and tracking allow us to see progress. If you want to live a happier life, scheduling, doing, measuring, and tracking over time will give you confidence that these happiness and emotional habits actually work for you. When these habits become part of your life, you may want to stop scheduling or tracking them.

The actual tasks in each week are inspired by science and sample only. However, they can vary based on several factors, such as people, blessings, and situations in your specific circumstances. If one activity does not apply to you, please feel free to modify it accordingly to suit your situation. There is no right or wrong; do whatever works for you as long as this habit makes you happy.

At the end of the day, it is your life, and you are responsible for your happiness and satisfaction. You can be lastingly happy only by your happiness and emotional habits.

SO HOW DOES IT WORK? MEASURE YOUR HAPPINESS IN WEEK1

In the first week, measure your current happiness to understand where you stand. Record it. Do not do any happiness activity in your first week, but check the eleven happiness habits in detail (in the next section) and pick the five happiness activities based on your top five (HDT, Habits Discovery Test, in the previous chapter) and skip the other six. If you like, you can plan your six weeks or pick the happiness activity you wish each week from your top five.

From 2nd week, Follow The Weekly Intervention Steps Below

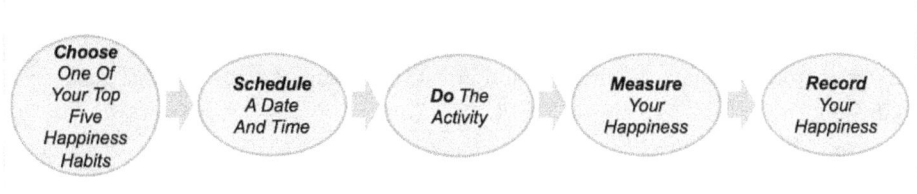

CHOOSE

Every week, you will pick one of your top five happiness habits and do the activity. For example, if working on your goals is in your top five, you can pick this for your second week, "Being Present" in the third week, and so on.

SCHEDULE

You will schedule one to two hours a week whenever it is convenient for you to do the activities. For example, every Sunday, from 4:00 p.m. to 6:00 p.m., you will do these activities for six weeks.

DO

In the next section, I have outlined the instructions for each of the eleven happiness habits. Just follow them to suit your context. Improvise accordingly based on whatever is appropriate for you. For example, if it states, "a loved one," you can pick your partner, parent, children, or anyone else you love; or, if it states, "one of your flow experiences," choose an activity that gives you flow. But remember to do only those happiness habits (or activities) that are in your top five. For example, if practicing religion or spirituality is not in your top five, you will skip that and move on to the next one which is in your top five from (HDT).

AVOID

We have been examining various emotional habits which can help you become emotionally intelligent and protect your happiness. These include overthinking, social comparison, judging others, failure to stay calm, procrastination, worrying about the things that are not in your control, and any self-sabotaging behavior that makes you unhappy.

When it's time to do the happiness activity (or even at other times), please make sure you are not in the trap of any such behavior that stops you from doing the activity. Usually, procrastination and overthinking are such behaviors that have high impact on sabotaging your good intentions.

MEASURE, RECORD, AND REFLECT WEEKLY

Once you have completed the happiness activity, right after that, take the Oxford Happiness Test and measure your happiness score (Refer to Part 2, "Measure your happiness chapter") for that week. You can record your results below or anywhere you feel like and write how you felt during and after the activity in a journal.

Week	Date	Happiness Activity Name	Completed?	Happiness Level (score)
1			No Activity	
2			Yes / No	
3			Yes / No	
4			Yes / No	
5			Yes / No	
6			Yes / No	

In the next section, I have outlined all eleven happiness habits (sample) and instructions on how to complete the interventions.

> **BEING PRESENT**

Is this habit in your top five? If not, you may move on to the next habit. But if yes, schedule this activity below.

Week no._____ Date: ___/___/___ Time: From _____ To_____

Do - A Mindful Photography Session

Understand that it is not about the camera or the photos, but the process. It is about training your brain to focus on your surroundings. (This will help you escape negative thoughts.) Secondly, don't just take photos but be selective and intentional about the things that capture your attention. Limit the number of photos (e.g., a maximum of twenty photos in thirty minutes).

Thirdly, don't worry about the type of camera or settings. Just use your phone camera by default. Don't worry about showing the photos to others. It is for you and training your brain to be more mindful. And finally, you can take multiple photos of the same object from different angles. (This will help you be aware of perspectives.) You can choose to photograph colors or anything that interests you.

The key here is to pay attention.

Schedule about thirty to sixty minutes for this session.

Avoid

You can go for a photo walk alone or in a group. Be careful if you have a phone camera that you do not end up scrolling on the phone instead. Complete this activity without procrastination or avoidance.

Measure, Record, Reflect

Once you have completed at least thirty minutes of mindful photography, measure your happiness using the Oxford Happiness Scale (Refer to Part 2, "Measure your happiness chapter"). You want to record your happiness level for this week for tracking. Also, reflect on how you felt during or after this activity, and write about your experience in a journal or wherever you feel is appropriate.

STAYING CONNECTED

Is this habit in your top five? If not, you may move on to the next habit. But if yes, schedule this activity below.

Week no._____ Date: ___/___/___ Time: From _____ To_____

Do - Telling Your Loved Ones

Pick the three most important people you love. On a paper, write their names, and for each name, write down why you love them, what they mean to you, and how would you feel without them?

Once you have written, without distraction, connect with them face-to-face (most preferred), via video call, or via phone call (least preferred). Tell them at least two specific things that you love about them. Then tell them how much they mean to you. Be specific, genuine, and vulnerable in your words. For example. Instead of saying, "I love you, and you mean the world to me," you may say, "When things are hard, I look up to you. You inspire me to do better. Because of you, I never lost confidence, and I went for that job and got it. You are my candle of hope."

Do this for at least one or all three people you picked. You don't need to be poetic or perfect, but express your feelings genuinely and honestly.

Avoid

It can be hard to acknowledge the blessings we get from our loved ones and harder to tell them. Start by telling them a little thing you love about them; then you will break the ice and open up. Avoid overthinking.

Measure, Record, Reflect

Once you have told these three people how much you love them and what they mean to you, measure your happiness using the Oxford Happiness Scale (Refer to Part 2, "Measure your happiness chapter"). You want to record your happiness level for this week for tracking. Also, reflect on how you felt during or after this activity and write about your experience in a journal or wherever you feel is appropriate.

TAKING CARE OF YOUR BODY

Is this habit in your top five? If not, you may move on to the next habit. But if yes, schedule this activity below.

Week no._____ Date: ___/___/___ Time: From _____ To_____

Do - Engage in Thirty Minutes of Physical Activity

There are literally hundreds of ways to take care of your body, but whatever your routine is at the moment, I humbly request you to ask yourself, "What is my next level?" If you already walk ten minutes a day, can you do twelve minutes? If you do ten minutes of meditation, can you do twelve? Basically, anything you do now, think about how you can take it to the next level (e.g., just a 5 per cent increase). No matter how small that is, remember, the smallest increase is also progress, and that will give you momentum, and you will feel good. Engage in a physical activity for 30 minutes that you are comfortable with a five percent increase (i.e., go for a walk, run, meditation, horse riding, swimming, weight lifting).

Avoid

If you do not normally engage in physical activity at the moment (as was the case for me when I was a couch potato fourteen years ago), just go for a thirty-minute walk (that was my next level at the time). Any movement is better than no movement. Whatever you do, identify your next level and then do that. Do not overthink it; just do it.

Measure, Record, Reflect

Once you have completed at least a thirty-minute walk or whatever your "next-level" activity is, measure your happiness using the Oxford Happiness Scale (Refer to Part 2, "Measure your happiness chapter"). You want to record your happiness level for this week for tracking. Also, reflect on how you felt during or after this activity and write about your experience in a journal or wherever you feel is appropriate.

PRACTICING RELIGION AND SPIRITUALITY

Is this habit in your top five? If not, you may move on to the next habit. But if yes, schedule this activity below.

Week no._____ Date: ___/___/___ Time: From _____ To_____

Do - Pray for Thirty Minutes

If you believe in God and are a practicing person, you will not need guidance from me or science. However, the most common thing believers usually do is pray. Praying comes in different shapes depending on the religion or practice. If you truly believe in God but do not regularly pray, you may try praying or start going to religious worshipping places to keep your practice going. If you have any other spiritual practices, you may want to try them out. If you experience love, flow, and strong meaning, that might be the best outcome from this.

Avoid

Whatever your religious or spiritual practice is, the idea here is that you consciously schedule thirty minutes without distraction and, with your complete focus, do it without procrastination or avoiding.

Measure, Record, Reflect

Once you have completed at least thirty minutes of praying or spiritual practice, measure your happiness using the Oxford Happiness Scale (Refer to Part 2, "Measure your happiness chapter"). You want to record your happiness level for this week for tracking. Also, reflect on how you felt during or after this activity and write about your experience in a journal or wherever you feel is appropriate.

BEING AN OPTIMIST

Is this habit in your top five? If not, you may move on to the next habit. But if yes, schedule this activity below.

Week no._____ Date: ___/___/___ Time: From _____ To_____

Do - Write about Your Best Self

Whether it is your health, relationships, career, or anything else, pick an area of your life in a quiet place, allow twenty to thirty minutes, and imagine what your best self looks like in this area. Who would you be, and what would you do or have, in the future as your best? (For example, perhaps you want to sing in a competition, make $2 million in revenue in your business, or run a half-marathon.) Dream as best as you can, but your dreams should be believable to you.

Now take a pen and paper and write what you want to achieve in six months, one year, and three years in this area of your life. How could you possibly get there, and by when? You do not need to figure out everything, but allow yourself to get there in your heart first (and later in your head). Visualize that you have already achieved your dreams. When all your dreams in that area come true, how would that make you feel? Write them down.

Avoid

If being an optimist comes easily for you, you will know what to write, but don't get stuck in figuring out how to get there. This exercise is about just imagining and writing down your best self. The "how" part will manifest as you work on them without giving up, so avoid overthinking.

Measure, Record, Reflect

Once you have completed writing about your best self, measure your happiness using the Oxford Happiness Scale (Refer to Part 2, "Measure your happiness chapter") to record your happiness level for this week for tracking. Also, reflect on how you felt during or after this activity and write about your experience in a journal or wherever you feel is appropriate.

BEING KIND

Is this habit in your top five? If not, you may move on to the next habit. But if yes, schedule this activity below.

Week no._____ Date: ___/___/___ Time: From _____ To_____

Do - Intentionally Being Extra Kind

Pick one person in your circle zero (people with intimate bonds), which usually comprises family and friends. Ask yourself, "What does this person love?" Do something you do not usually do to pleasantly surprise this person. This person will not expect this extra kindness from you. For example, if you know your son loves painting, surprise him by taking him to a painting exhibition. If you know your partner's dream is to participate in a cooking competition, pleasantly surprise her with the entry form and pay the fee. Avoid buying things you want others to have. Rather, do something that they love and is meaningful for them.

Avoid

Please do not procrastinate on this, as this exercise is about being kind to your loved ones. It is very easy to think, "I will do it when I get some time." Well, make time. As I said earlier, the acts of kindness are not reserved only for strangers. In fact, you will be amazed at how powerful these acts are to the people you love and care about the most.

Measure, Record, Reflect

Once you have done the act of extra kindness with your loved one, measure your happiness using the Oxford Happiness Scale (Refer to Part 2, "Measure your happiness chapter"). You want to record your happiness level for this week for tracking. Also, reflect on how you felt during or after this activity and write about your experience in a journal or wherever you feel is appropriate.

ENGAGING IN FLOW

Is this habit in your top five? If not, you may move on to the next habit. But if yes, schedule this activity below.

Week no._____ Date: ___/___/___ Time: From _____ To_____

Do - Engage in Flow for Thirty Minutes

Ask yourself, "What activity makes me forget about time and causes me to not want to stop doing it?" Pick one of those activities (e.g., talking to someone, reading, writing, painting, or almost any activity that gets you into flow). The secret is to achieve 100 per cent focus on the activity and maintain it for the duration of the activity. Once you have identified such an activity, schedule thirty minutes without distraction to engage in that activity and complete it. Remember, this activity should have some level of challenge that you are comfortable with (not too high or too low for you), and you should also have the skill to do it.

Avoid

If you don't know what gives you flow, try something you love doing with your full attention for thirty minutes and see if that gets you into flow. Avoid too much planning and procrastination. Just do it.

Measure, Record, Reflect

Once you have completed at least thirty minutes in flow, measure your happiness using the Oxford Happiness Scale (Refer to Part 2, "Measure your happiness chapter"). You want to record your happiness level for this week for tracking. Also, reflect on how you felt during or after this activity and write about your experience in a journal or wherever you feel is appropriate.

WORKING ON YOUR GOALS

Is this habit in your top five? If not, you may move on to the next habit. But if yes, schedule this activity below.

Week no._____ Date: ___/___/___ Time: From _____ To_____

Do - Work On Your Intrinsic Journey-Based Goal

Pick a goal that truly matters and is close to your heart. Whether in health, love, career, pleasure, or whatever it is, it can be a goal you want to achieve in the next three to six months. For example, you want to participate in a two-hundred-kilometer cycling event, you would like to have a romantic relationship with the girl you like, you want to pass an exam, or you want to holiday in Hong Kong. Whatever it is, work on that goal to make progress for at least an hour without any distraction. (Schedule a time for this in your calendar.)

Make sure the activity is meaningful to you (e.g., it impacts you or someone else in a positive way). You may not achieve the goal in one hour, but a little progress towards it will give you momentum.

Avoid

As long as this goal is an intrinsic journey-based goal (which we discussed earlier) for you, you will enjoy it, and it will be meaningful to you no matter how little progress you make. We often give our passion projects the lowest priority, as they are nice to have and not musts. So make sure you do not fall into that trap to procrastinate and do it without overthinking.

Measure, Record, Reflect

Once you have completed working on your intrinsic journey-based goal, measure your happiness using the Oxford Happiness Scale (Refer to Part 2, "Measure your happiness chapter"). You want to record your happiness level for this week for tracking. Also, reflect on how you felt during or after this activity and write about your experience in a journal or wherever you feel is appropriate.

BEING THANKFUL

Is this habit in your top five? If not, you may move on to the next habit. But if yes, schedule this activity below.

Week no._____ Date: ___/___/___ Time: From _____ To_____

Do - Write a Gratitude Letter

Grab a notepad and pen, close your eyes for a second, and try to remember someone who did something extremely important for you in the past that positively changed your life but whom you have never properly thanked. This person has to be alive. Now write a three-hundred-word letter outlining what she or he has done for you, why it impacted your life, and how it has changed your life for the better. Once you finish writing, catch up with this person without distraction and read this letter to her or him. Most people end up weeping and stay happier over a long time after this.

Avoid

If you struggle to find someone to thank, you may want to look at your close family, a parent, a partner, a child, a close friend, a mentor, or a coworker. Schedule a catch-up with this person, but don't explain why. Don't just give the letter to the person, but read it to her or him. Avoid being shy, being hesitant, or procrastinating on it.

Measure, Record, Reflect

Once you have written the letter and read it to this person, measure your happiness using the Oxford Happiness Scale (Refer to Part 2, "Measure your happiness chapter"). You want to record your happiness level for this week for tracking. Also, reflect on how you felt during or after this activity and write about your experience in a journal or wherever you feel is appropriate.

FORGIVING

Is this habit in your top five? If not, you may move on to the next habit. But if yes, schedule this activity below.

Week no._____ Date: ___/___/___ Time: From _____ To_____

Do - Write a Letter of Forgiveness

Find a person who has wronged you that you have not forgotten or forgiven. This person may or may not be in your life now.

In the letter, write down what she did and how you suffered because of her actions. Describe how she should have behaved instead. Be honest with yourself and your feelings. Finish the letter with a statement that directly forgives her. An example is, "Over time, I have realized that you have acted based on your values and beliefs, and you injured me emotionally. I hope you have grown since, but your bitter memories in me do not serve me anymore. I have better things to do, so I forgive you."

Avoid

I know this can be hard, and you don't have to send the letter to the person. Just write it, and you may choose to keep it to yourself. Be the bigger person for yourself and not for the person who wronged you. If you are not ready to write the letter, don't despair. Try writing a letter for another person who also wronged you but against whom you hold a smaller grudge. Avoid overthinking or procrastinating. Forgiving this person will set you free.

Measure, Record, Reflect

Once you have written the letter, measure your happiness using the Oxford Happiness Scale (Refer to Part 2, "Measure your happiness chapter"). You want to record your happiness level for this week for tracking. Also, reflect on how you felt during or after this activity and write about your experience in a journal or wherever you feel is appropriate.

RECOVERING FROM SETBACK

Is this habit in your top five? If not, you may move on to the next habit. But if yes, schedule this activity below.

Week no._____ Date: ___/___/___ Time: From _____ To_____

Do - Write Down Three Moments of Joy Every Day

At night, before going to bed, spend five to ten minutes writing down in a diary a joyful moment that occurred during the day. Give it a title (e.g., "John Smiled at Me"). Next to it, write what actually happened. And then write why was it a joyful moment for you and how it made you feel. (Just one sentence is fine. Feel free to write more if you feel comfortable, no matter how small or insignificant the moment was. For example, perhaps someone smiled at you, you watched a good movie and loved it, or you called an old friend and had a nice chat.) Write down at least three new such moments every night for at least a week.

Avoid

If you have never done journaling before, it can be hard for you to find three joyful moments in the first few days. But the key here is not to give up. This method rewires your brain to pick up on and notice more positive things around you. So avoid overthinking, procrastinating, or any other behavior that may stop you from doing it. Remember, it is only for you to read.

Measure, Record, Reflect

Once you have completed at least five days of journaling, measure your happiness using the Oxford Happiness Scale on the fifth night (Refer to Part 2, "Measure your happiness chapter"). You want to record your happiness level for this week for tracking. Also, reflect on how you felt during or after this activity and write about your experience in a journal or wherever you feel is appropriate.

REVIEW YOUR RESULTS

Congratulations!!

Once you have completed the six-week happiness activities, you can see the progress of your happiness by putting your numbers below to see how far you have come. (You can also put them in Excel and generate a graph.)

Week	Date	Happiness Activity (Habit) Name	Completed?	Happiness Levels (Score)
1			No Activity	
2			Yes / No	
3			Yes / No	
4			Yes / No	
5			Yes / No	
6			Yes / No	

As discussed earlier, after every activity, reflect on how you felt during or after the activity and write your experience in a journal. If you have done that, you will know what activities are best suited for your individual personality and situation. That way you will be able to do the necessary tweaking and adjustments when you do them again.

Remember Glenn? He was one of the participants in my six-week program a few years ago. In week 1, his happiness level was 4.31, and it had increased to a sustained level of around 5.10. Your six-week graph should at least look like his or better, provided that you have consistently done the activities and measured on time every week with determination, persistence, and honesty.

Glenn did not do anything extraordinary, but he spent one to two hours every week regularly on his happiness activities with seriousness and persistence. In fact, he was going through some struggles during these six weeks, including the loss of one of his very close friends. He said that the happiness skills he had developed (happiness muscles) by doing these activities during that six weeks helped him deal with the loss.

Yes, Glenn was part of my in-person six-week program. The experience in the program is not the same as reading my book, even though the interventions are similar, but that should not stop you from doing the interventions. If you are determined to be happier and live that extraordinary life on your terms, you can absolutely just use this sample program (adjust to your individual needs and situation) and do it yourself.

We all go through different phases of our lives, some of which are great and some of which are not. But it is always worth mastering the skills of happiness and satisfaction regardless of who you are and the situation you are going through.

I hope the six-week intervention has made you happier and more satisfied and you are one step closer to your extraordinary life on your terms.

BUILD YOUR OWN HAPPINESS HABITS

"I don't design clothes. I design dreams."
—Ralph Lauren

YOUR CUSTOM DESIGN

Now you know your top five happiness habits (or activities for now), and you know how to measure your happiness using the Oxford Happiness Scale. (And yes, you also feel it inside.) By now, you may have also put in the genuine effort to complete the six-week intervention, and I believe you have been happier and more satisfied.

But what if you want to build your own happiness habits and not follow any program?

The six-week intervention program was just an introduction, and the purpose of it was to give you a glimpse of what is possible. If you have felt good, been excited, and experienced joy and happiness during this program, don't just stop there. I highly recommend you build your own happiness and emotional habits and make them part of your daily life.

We already know there are six essential elements we must have to live a satisfying life. In this book, I represent these as the Star of Life. Remember, each of your daily happiness habits will link to one or more of the six elements of your satisfying life.

SAMPLE HAPPINESS HABITS DESIGN

I have shared three of my happiness habits on the next page. The first column is the name of the happiness habit (from my top five). In the second column, I list what I do and the things I avoid (negative behaviors, such as procrastination, self-doubt, and making excuses) which can stop me from actually carrying out my habit. Finally, in the third column, I have listed elements of satisfaction this happiness habit can potentially link to.

My Top 3 Happiness Habits	What I Do and Avoid	Elements I Get Every Day (Life Satisfaction) from the Star of Life
Being Kind	**I Do:** Every two weeks, I call an old friend and have a twenty-minute chat, and I listen to this person with kindness and empathy and offer encouragement. **I Avoid:** Procrastination or cancelling.	This happiness habit strengthens my love and connection element. This is also meaningful for me because I can potentially help friends if needed. I experience flow (engagement) from the conversations with my friends.
Engaging in Flow	**I Do:** Every Week, I schedule ten hours for writing, and I ensure nothing distracts me from doing that. **I Avoid:** Excuses, procrastination, cancelling	This happiness habit gives me flow as I write. My writing can make someone's life better, so this is meaningful, and if the writing makes a difference in someone's life, it gives me a sense of achievement.
Being an Optimist	**I Do:** Every week, on Sundays, I review and track my twelve-month, six-month, monthly, and weekly goals. I review the previous week and create a to-do list for the following week. This activity gives me hope and keeps me on track to my dreams and goals. **I Avoid:** Self-doubt, idea doubt, limiting myself, procrastination	This happiness habit gives me flow as I review weekly goals. Most of my goals are intrinsic and meaningful for me, and as I tick or hit a goal in a week, it gives me a sense of achievement.

I use a white paper and keep it in front of my desktop computer. You can use similar methods or even keep a diary. For best results, keep it visible so you do not forget to do your habits, which is the whole point.

DESIGN YOUR HAPPINESS HABITS ON YOUR TERMS

Below, I have provided a form for you to write down your happiness habits from your top three (you can use a paper to do five). Feel free to adjust, add to, or remove from the habit list as you get used to it. You will know what works for you and how efficient your happiness habits are.

My Top 3 Happiness Habits	What I Do and Avoid	Elements I Get Every Day (Life Satisfaction) from the Star of Life
	I Do: I Avoid:	
	I Do: I Avoid:	
	I Do: I Avoid:	

DESIGN YOUR WEEKS

You can design your days and weeks the way you want. Feel free to adjust the activities, frequencies, intensities, and durations to what suits your schedule the best. Remember, it is a continuous process.

If you are committed enough, you can redesign the same six-week program to suit in a week. For example, see below:

Day	Time	My Happiness Habit
Monday	8:30 a.m.- 9:00 a.m.	Being thankful
Tuesday	5:30 p.m.- 6:00 p.m.	Being kind to my family
Wednesday	10:30 a.m.- 2:30 p.m.	Working on my intrinsic goals
Thursday	6:00 p.m.- 8:00 p.m.	Being present with my kids
Friday	9:00 p.m.-10:00 p.m.	Planning my dreams and goals
Saturday	10:00 a.m.- 2:00 p.m.	Spending time with my family
Sunday	3:00 p.m. - 5:00 p.m.	Making someone else happy

The duration of the activity depends on you. If you do an activity weekly, you can start with thirty minutes (or even ten minutes) every day and then build on that over time. People design their weeks in many different ways. When it comes to building the happiness habit as a skill, as we have been discussing, it takes your conscious effort and requires that you do it consistently over time.

You may be tired of me talking about "doing" so much. It is your life, and you choose how to live your days or weeks. But if my book and the sample program design can slightly help you become happier, all my efforts (and, of course, yours in reading and doing the activities) will be worth it.

REFLECT AND CONTINUE

If you have been happier after six weeks, Why stop? You may want to be happier for the rest of your life, Not just for six weeks, right?

Take the sample program, make modifications, share it with others, and adjust it to make it the way you love it. Make sure you have all the elements of a satisfying life in the Star of Life. Your Happiness habits make you happy, and your Emotional habits protect your happiness.

PART 6:
Stay Happy by Yourself

In this part, we will discuss the following:

- how you can be happy when you are alone
- how you can be true to yourself
- how you can live as your better self
- how you can escape to your flow activity
- what type of happiness you should choose, and why

STAY HAPPY WHEN ALONE

> "The more you like yourself, the less you are like anyone else, which makes you unique."
> —Walt Disney

We have talked about the concept of the science of happiness and satisfaction. Also, by now, you know what it means to live an extraordinary life by design on your terms using the Star of Life framework. I hope you have had a chance to measure your happiness over the six weeks in the intervention program. I sincerely believe that has given you a glimpse of what is really possible when living a happy and satisfying life.

But when you are alone, what do you think? How do you feel? What do you do? Do you love your own company?

How can you be and stay happy by yourself?

Over the years, I have learned a lot about myself—how I operate as a person and what it takes to be and stay happy. I also realized that the more I develop and grow as a person, the more respect and love I feel for myself.

I have shared a few of mine here.

YOUR TRUE SELF

When I first decided to write this book, I thought of two of my favorite authors, Louise Hay and Dale Carnegie. Their books changed the lives of millions, including me. I have a lot of respect and love for them. Then I thought, "How did they write those world-changing books? How do you know that this is going to change someone's life? Is there a formula? Is there a secret they knew that other people didn't?" I thought I must be like them to make an impact. It was natural for me to aspire to be like them.

Then, over time, I realized that neither Louise Hay nor Dale Carnegie tried to change the world. They never thought their books would change the lives of millions of people. They didn't write those books to sell millions of copies. They didn't want to be famous or rich. Dale Carnegie originally wrote How to Win Friends and Influence People as a textbook for a small group of his students in his course on human relations and public speaking. But it took a place in publishing history as one of the all-time international bestsellers. In 2011, it was number 19 on Time magazine's list of the one hundred most influential books. The truth is that Dale Carnegie did not originally want to write that book. He was persuaded by his publisher, Leon Shimkin.

In the thirtieth-anniversary edition of the book You Can Heal Your Life, the author Louise Hay wrote, "I would never have imagined that while I was photocopying the first pages of my book that one day it would be read on phones, computers and distributed electronically in the blink of an eye." Her book was published in 1984, and by 2008 it had sold 35 million copies worldwide.

Both Dale and Louise had one thing in common: they genuinely cared for their readers and trusted themselves with their messages. Their messages were nothing but the expression of their true selves, which resonated with millions of other people, and that is the secret.

According to a survey of millennials, 80 per cent of them want to be rich, and 50 per cent of them want to be famous. We aspire to be like the people we like, they are primarily people who are rich and famous. Where do we find famous people? An easy pick is in the movie industry, which most people can relate to. Will Smith is one of my favorite actors in Hollywood. If I were in the acting industry, I would want to be like him. See, I just wanted to be like someone else. There is nothing wrong with liking someone, but when we try to be like someone else, we lose our own selves. If you truly think about it, is Will the best actor in Hollywood? No. Is he second to none? No. Has he got the best body? No. Is he the best-looking? No. But I still like him. Millions of other people like him. Why? Because there is no one like him in Hollywood. He is not the best in everything, but he is authentic and brings the best out of his true self.

The same goes for George Clooney, Sean Connery, and Meryl Streep, who are all legends in their own ways. Many people do not like them but like other actors. For example, I believe Sean Connery was the best actor to portray James Bond in all the James Bond movies. My wife does not like that. For her, it is Pierce Brosnan. Does that mean Sean is not good enough? Or that Pierce is the best? Absolutely not. The definition of "best" or "perfect" is subjective to the person saying it.

When Will Smith, Sean Connery, Pierce Brosnan, Meryl Streep, and other great actors were just starting, no one knew them. No one cared about them. They had struggled, faced a lot of rejections, and had to ignore the naysayers, but most importantly, they had to believe in themselves. If they had tried to be someone else, today there would be three Will Smith–, five Sean Connery–, two Pierce Brosnan–, and ten Meryl Streep–like actors. But that's not how it works, and there is no one like them. They are all unique and shining in their own ways as stars. That's why we love them. In fact, I'm writing about them because they trusted their true selves and never gave up.

When Barack Obama was running for office for the first time, many people didn't believe in him. It was an impossible dream. What was he thinking? What were the voices in his head? "You're not good enough. You're not white. You are not smart enough. How can you become the president of the most powerful and predominantly white nation in the world when you are not even white?" It was very easy and a no-brainer for him to talk himself out of it.

But he didn't.

Even if you think the first time was a chance occurrence, he got elected a second time. He made history, set examples, and inspired millions. He is one of the coolest and smartest presidents the world has ever seen. Obama trusted in his true self and went for it without giving up.

Again, there is no other person like Obama.

We love others not because they are like someone else but because they are true to themselves. Every one of us is unique in his or her own way. But often, we do not trust or love ourselves. We believe we are not good enough, we do not deserve what we have, our work does not matter, we are too fat, we are not good-looking, we will not be loved, and so many other made-up stories we all tell ourselves. They are all inside our heads.

Relax. You are not alone. This is the case for everyone.

Being your true self is nothing but the fearless expression of your heart.

Babies are best at expressing their true selves. They are fearless and genuine. They are not afraid of what other people think. They are not worried about being themselves. They are 100 per cent authentic in their lovely expressions. That's why we love babies.

Remember that we were all babies at one time. But what happened?

How many times does a baby hear the word "no"? You and I probably heard it thousands of times. As we grow up, we continue to hear things like "Don't do this," "Don't go there," "Be quiet," and thousands of other things. Our curiosity, creativity, determination, and most noble qualities that make us human beings become chained. We start to fit into society and learn to suppress the true feelings of our hearts.

Your heart does not like to be suppressed; It must be expressed.

Anything you love or care for comes from your heart and is very personal to you. No one, including your loved ones, will truly feel why you love something or why you care for someone. Remember the unique song your heart sings? Only you know what it is. For many, this song is private.

This notion is good but also bad. It is good because you have no limitation in your thinking; you can feel anything inside your heart, and no one will see, feel, or judge you. You can be as creative as you want. It is bad because if you are scared and don't express yourself, you will be unfulfilled.

When did you last sing to yourself or with others?

Most of us can sing to some level. It doesn't matter if our voices are like Lady Gaga's or an owl's. We love singing. You may not want to admit it, but deep down, you know you do. Whether at a concert, while listening to music, while on a bus with friends, or even while in the shower, chances are, at least once or twice, you had a singing episode in your life, no matter how small it was. If you had one and can remember it, how were you feeling then? Excited? Thrilled? Happy? If so, it is because you truly expressed yourself. But if you haven't had one, the next time you are alone driving, walking, or in your study, try solo karaoke with your favorite song.

Remember the top five regrets of the dying? They said, "I wish I'd had the courage to express my feelings" or "I wish I'd had the courage to live a life true to myself, not the life others expected of me."

The song of your heart must be released. Singing, dancing, presenting, playing, and writing are all forms of the true expression of your heart.

Studies suggest that people who scored higher on a measure of authentic living reported greater happiness, more positive emotions, and higher self-esteem than people who reported being less authentic. More authentic people also reported better relationships with others and more personal growth.

So what does it mean to be your true self? How can you be and stay happy if you are constantly trying to fit into a society where you are afraid to express your true feelings from your heart? One of our deepest fears is that we are not enough, so we don't express ourselves. This can lead to regrets about something you always wanted to do but never did, the song you wrote but never released, the girl you loved but couldn't say so to her, or whatever it is that is close to your heart but you never let yourself express. If you hold yourself back by thinking you are not enough or are not perfect because others are better than you, you will never be able to express yourself, and you will regret it later.

The idea of perfection is a myth. Literally no one is perfect.

The truth is that it is not about perfectionism. It is about authenticity. It is about what is inside you, who you are, and what you do as you, not as someone else. If you are constantly trying to be someone else, that will make you stressed out and unhappy for a long time.

Remember Will Smith, Barack Obama, Sean Connery, and others? They do not have everything perfect either, but still they have let others see their true selves, and people love them for who they truly are. They had doubts and insecurities, and they felt negative, disempowering thoughts, but they expressed themselves anyway.

If you want to do something, be someone, or have something, don't wait, because your time will never be more right than now. Also, you will never be perfect so being true is your only option.

Now think. What is close to your heart? What do you want to express? You don't want to regret it when you become old.

Is this the best happiness book on the market? No. Is this book perfect? No. My book is a representation of myself. The way I write, the way I talk, and the way I create distinction are totally mine. They are not like anyone else's. Being yourself does not mean not caring about anything or anyone. Instead, you love and care about your true self more than what others expect of you.

My book is part of my world. Some people will judge me from every angle. Some may not like it, but I also know some would love it. My passion, what I truly believe and genuinely care, must be expressed.

Am I afraid? Yes.

Am I scared to be judged? Totally.

But am I stopping myself? No.

I'm being my true self, and my book is one way to look at me.

> "Tension is who you think you should be. relaxation is who you are."
> —Chinese Proverb

LIVE AS YOUR BETTER SELF

During my teen years, I did outdoor sports, but when I finished college and stepped into my career, I phased them out and replaced them with playing pool, video games, and mostly indoor activities, which didn't require any physical effort. I used to sit on the couch and spend a lot of time watching Netflix. I always thought, "Why would I go to the gym if I can spend my time in the comfort of my own home and do what I love?" I avoided any physical activities with limitless excuses.

I slowly became a very lazy person.

Being built skinny, I never had to worry about keeping my weight under control. We ate somewhat healthily, slept well at night, and generally felt good, and there was no reason to pay attention to physical activities. Then I went to a doctor for a general check-up. He checked my blood pressure and said, "How do you feel?" I shrugged and said, "I feel all right. Why?" Then he said, "Your pressure is high. Do you have headaches sometimes?" I said, "Not really." I asked the doctor, "Are you sure? could you check it again?" He did, and it was the same. He asked if I used to smoke or drink, but I didn't at the time. He suggested monitoring my blood pressure for two weeks and getting back to him.

I came out of the doctor's room in disbelief. I knew I could have had an issue much more serious than high blood pressure, but it was a big blow to the face for me. I had never thought there was anything wrong with my physical health. I became completely stressed out and was thinking many other unpleasant things.

I checked my blood pressure for two weeks, and surprisingly, it wasn't too bad. It was very close to the normal range. The doctor was satisfied and advised that I didn't need any medication but advised me to do brisk walking and increase my physical activity as a habit.

Even though I initially got scared, as my blood pressure readings were close to normal and the doctor didn't give me any medication, I felt at ease and didn't take any meaningful action for a few weeks. Every time I thought of brisk walking, I came up with excuses to avoid it. And then I thought I might have high blood pressure in my future, as it runs in my family. I became scared again. But it was winter in Melbourne, and it would be impossible for me to go out for a walk on a cold and rainy day. I asked myself, "What is the least I can do?" and I started to walk inside the house. I know it sounds funny, but trust me, even that was very hard for me as a start. But I had no option but to try.

After a few weeks, walking inside the house felt really stupid. At the time, my wife wanted to join a yoga class, so we both joined a gym. As I had been walking inside the house, the idea of walking on a treadmill made me excited. I thought I could walk on it, but maybe I could also run.

On the first day at the gym, I started to walk, and after a few minutes, I started to run. Twenty seconds later, I became breathless and couldn't continue running. So I slowed down and was back to brisk walking again. But I noticed next to me an Asian lady, probably in her late sixties, who was running away without stopping, while I had not even imagined myself running up to that time. I kept walking for another thirty minutes, but the Asian lady was still running. I was like, "Are you serious? How much longer is she going to run for?" I couldn't believe she didn't look tired and wasn't showing any sign of slowing down.

I was driving home, and I felt so low that I began questioning myself again. "I could not even run for twenty seconds. What am I doing? Why can't I even run for one minute? How could I have let this happen?"

At this point, I want to say that for almost all my life, I have loved myself. No one is perfect, and neither am I.

So what? I love the way I am. That is the mantra I always had.

But on that day, I was focused on the part of me that could not run even for a minute. I did not love it and couldn't take it.

It was as if I had found a bug in my current self, which needed an upgrade. So I asked myself, "What would be my best version's ability to run?" I was thinking about this as I was driving home. I came to my study, and I wrote down on a piece of paper that I did not want to be a sprinter, even though I ran only twenty seconds today, but I certainly should be able to run smoothly for at least thirty minutes without stopping, and that would be my best version in this area of life.

Basically, I redefined my internal standard of who I was as a runner.

Then, the next morning, I woke up and looked at the piece of paper, and it seemed so impossible. I thought I was crazy, and my brain was doing everything to talk me out of it. The doctor had told me just to do "brisk walking," so why on earth would I want to run for thirty minutes? "I'm not going to a competition. I could not even run for twenty seconds, and that seemed an unnecessary struggle for an ambition that did not make any sense. But I just could not take the fact that I am someone who cannot even run twenty seconds." It made me question who I was as a person and what my abilities were. Twenty seconds was just not good enough for me. In other words, that could not be my standard.

I made a strong decision to hit my best self's target and not quit. So I committed myself to running on the treadmill every week. I took baby steps and increased my running time by twenty seconds per week. Yes, sure, there were days I didn't feel like running at all. I didn't think it was worth the effort, and I injured myself once, but I had to remain committed because I needed to reach that standard of thirty minutes of running. I needed to be that person. Eleven months later, I reached the point where I could run 4.7 kilometers in thirty minutes without stopping.

I know that for many of us, running for thirty minutes is not a big deal. Maybe some can run for two hours nonstop, but that is their best self, not mine. I compare myself only with my best self: "Am I doing better as a runner than yesterday? Am I a better person than yesterday?"

Think about how you can bring a better version of yourself into your roles. For example, if you are a mother and come home from work every day and tell your kids that you love them, that is your current version as a mother. But could you do a bit better? Maybe you could say you love them and hug them, doing a little bit more than what you already do.

We hear about pushing boundaries and coming out of comfort zones a lot, but you do not necessarily need to go and do bungee jumping or anything that scares the hell out of you to push your boundaries.

Simply doing just a little bit more of what you already do is sufficient.

When I started to walk inside the house, then walked on the treadmill, and then ran for only twenty seconds, then for one minute, and eventually for thirty minutes, each of those milestones was a boundary for me, but I pushed past them one at a time over eleven months.

Your standards (or versions) define who you are. Your body is a reflection of your eating and physical activity standards. The quality of your relationships with your loved ones is the reflection of how you treat them every day. The amount of money you make comes from your financial knowledge and standards and so on.

And all of your standards are set by you and your habits.

In any role you play, your standards are driven by your habits. For example, my running standard was twenty seconds, which came from my couch habit. But a year later, I was able to upgrade (by modifying my habits) to thirty minutes of running, which became my new standard.

If you could upgrade one thing about yourself, what would that be?

I realized the best thing is once you have become better (or upgraded your standard) in one role and feel happy with it, you will feel the urge to do better in your other roles. For example, I bring out the best of myself in the running, which motivates me to eat more healthily and do better in my business and loving relationships.

Don't feel that you could never do what I did. You can do better. Check your current standards in your daily roles and ask yourself what your best version (or slightly better version) would look like. Then work on them with baby steps without quitting. The first few steps are the hardest, but slowly they will become part of you, and you will think, "How did I live my life without these new standards?"

I can tell you that, generally, I'm a happy person, but being at my best as a runner, has made me happier. It feels like I have increased my internal wealth. Honestly, every time I run, I feel much better than if I were sitting on a couch. I feel stronger because I make progress as my better self. I feel a sense of accomplishment, and I felt that I needed to share this with you.

I believe that the more you develop yourself, the better you become, and the better you are, the happier you feel.

GET INTO FLOW

We planned a trip to Lorne. This is a place both my wife and I love. It is about a two-hour drive from Melbourne. We were supposed to have lunch at an amazing seafood place. We wanted to start at 9:00 a.m. But, in the morning, my wife told me that she needed to sort something urgent in her business and we might not be able to have lunch at that seafood place.

I was not surprised. As she is a business owner, the nature of her work is like that. But I was a bit disappointed. I cleared my calendar for this, and I had nothing to do as I was waiting for her. I came to my study and thought I could finish a piece of writing I had worked on earlier. I started to write with my headphones on. I kept writing until

I heard a knock on the door of my study. It was my wife. She said she had finished her work and we could go now. I was like, "Are you serious? What's the time?" She said, "It's been more than two hours." I didn't even realize it had been that long. I had been completely immersed and had lost track of time. I couldn't wait to finish what I was doing. I said, "Ten more minutes. I promise I will be ready by then." I knew we were already late, but I just could not exit from the writing as I was enjoying it so much, only because

I was in flow.

Professor Martin Seligman (I already mentioned him a few times) shared a story of his friend Lane in a TED Talk. Lane was an introvert. He was a champion bridge player and extremely successful in the stock market as a broker. He earned millions of dollars. But in his love life, especially when it was about dating girls, he didn't have a lot of success. The girls he dated didn't like him.

On the surface, it would appear that he worked all day at the stock exchange and then played bridge with boring people, and that he had no fun in his life. In other words, he seemed to be a miserable person.

But in reality, Professor Seligman mentioned that when Lane walked into the stock exchange or played bridge, he experienced intense concentration. He had skills, and he loved the challenges of playing bridge and trading. In both cases, time stopped for him. Lane was highly capable of flow. Professor Seligman said that Lane was one of the happiest guys he had ever seen.

Flow is unique to you. Only you know how you feel as you experience it. Each one of us loves doing something. Anything that we love to do makes us happy for the duration of the activity and afterward. Many of us are not even aware that we are good at something and that something is our uniqueness. For instance, if you love acting and that is your uniqueness, every time you act, you may experience flow because it is natural for you.

Do you know what activity gets you into flow?

One of the easiest indicators is losing track of time on an activity. Do you feel so engaged that you forget to do other things? Do you feel satisfied and fulfilled after you finish? Do you have the necessary skills to do that activity? Do you feel a level of challenge? If, for any activity, all the answers to these questions are yes, you may have experienced flow from that activity.

Think about Michael Schumacher, who holds seven world championship titles in Formula 1 racing tournaments. He once said, "The more precisely I can drive, the more I enjoy myself." Driving more precisely requires driving skills, and the difficult tracks he had driven were the challenges that he was comfortable with. It is possible that he experienced flow many times while racing Formula 1 cars.

You can experience flow in any activity during the day, either as a father, a mother, an actor, a pilot, a runner, a driver, and so on.

When you are by yourself, getting into flow is one of the best ways to be happy and satisfied. Look for the activities that get you into flow. The best thing about flow is that it is in your control. Flow can be something like escaping to another world whenever you want and staying there as long as you want. That way, you will have the keys to your happiness without depending on anyone or anything else.

Lane didn't need the girls to make him happy. He made himself happy by getting into flow every time he played bridge or traded on the stock exchange.

Personally, when I need to recharge myself, I seek every opportunity to get into flow, either by writing or running, where I lose track of time and surrender to the experience. The other day as I was waiting for Mahin, I chose to write.

The next time you are by yourself and want to be happy, you know what to do.

CHOOSE BETTER QUALITY HAPPINESS

We love exploring new restaurants. My wife was browsing through some pictures of desserts and found a cafe with great reviews, and it was not too far from our place. So we decided to drive to this new cafe. She was very excited about it. On our way, she wanted to drop something at her friend's place, so we stopped. She went in, and I was waiting in the car. She was going to be only a few minutes, but she came back after half an hour and said that they were having a chat when suddenly her friend broke into tears, as she was having some relationship issues which Mahin did not have any idea about. Mahin couldn't just leave her there. So they chatted for a bit. I asked, "Is she okay now?" Mahin said, "Not really. Maybe I should stay with her a little longer."

I said, "No problem, go for it." She went in again, and I waited and did some work in the car. Half an hour later, she texted me, "I think I might need some more time. We might not be able to make it to the café on time. Are you ok with it?" I replied, "It's your call. I'm fine with it. Take as long as you need." She came back after an hour with a smile on her face. I asked, "How is she feeling now?" Mahin said, "I think a little better, but she needs to stand up for herself and build that courage over time slowly." I asked, "So, are we good to go?" She said, "Let's go."

Mahin is not a professional relationship advisor, but as her friend had a little meltdown, she could not leave her there. She needed to comfort her during this period of struggle.

That day, we could not make it to the cafe and have dessert. We went to another one. On our way back, I asked her, "We couldn't go to the cafe for the dessert you were so excited about. Are you okay?" She shrugged and said, "We can go on another day, but I feel that I have done the right thing. I needed to be with her, but she might need professional help. I just did my part to comfort her. In fact, I feel that I made very little difference today. She actually texted me." As I was driving, she read her friend's text: "'I do not know how to thank you, Mahin. I'm so sorry that I ruined your plan today, but I promise I will rise again.'"

I nodded.

Mahin was excited about that cafe, but she didn't feel bad. Rather she chose to stay back for her friend and had that meaningful conversation that her friend needed at that time. She felt that her words mattered to her friend, which made a difference, no matter how small or temporary. She chose to have that conversation over having that amazing dessert in the cafe and didn't become sad or regretful.

Instead, she became much happier on the day.

Why am I telling you this story? If you remember the six elements of the Star of Life satisfaction? Mahin initially chose to have the dessert, which would have been a pleasure point, but she decided to stay with her friend, which is the meaning point or love and connection point for her.

Both having a dessert and having a meaningful conversation with someone you care about can give you some kind of good feeling. One comes from pleasure, and the other comes from meaning, but they are not the same. You already know pleasure is very short-lived. Usually, the good feeling is gone when the pleasurable activity is finished. But the good feeling you get from meaning or love & connection is much stronger and longer lasting.

You may ask yourself, "Should I watch a movie or spend time with my kid? Should I go to the gym or call a friend to help?" In a day, our time is limited. Every day, we make choices like these.

Every time I personally come across a situation, I use the lenses of the Star of Life. I often ask myself, "Should I choose meaning, pleasure, flow, or a combination of these?" And I have learned that doing things in meaning, love and connection, flow, or health is much more satisfying than experiencing raw pleasure.

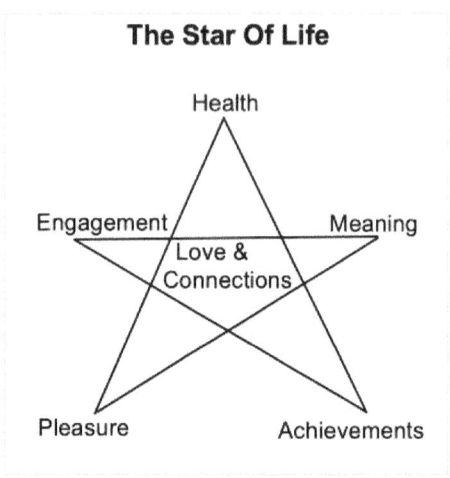

The Six Elements Of A Satisfying Life

A few months ago, as we were driving around the Great Ocean Road, a beautiful scenic drive in Melbourne, Mahin was telling me, "We have been blessed to travel to so many places, but one thing I regret not being able to do is to show my mum this beautiful drive." Her mother passed away about eleven years ago. She was very close to Mahin, but she couldn't visit her in Melbourne, and Mahin could not take her on this drive.

If you are blessed with your loved ones and can make a meaningful difference in their lives, whether by taking them on a nice holiday, having a deep and meaningful conversation with them, being there when they need you, comforting them when they are worried, making time and listening to understand them with empathy, that can be very satisfying not only for them but also for you.

Often, we tend to choose things that give us raw pleasure (having a dessert) or achievement (hitting a business goal), which are essential and tempting. As mentioned earlier, pleasure is the most common, easy, and fun element for most. Things like watching a movie and having a few drinks make you feel good in the moment, but they are short-lived. You already know that, according to studies, pleasure has almost zero contribution to your life satisfaction. And meaning is the strongest, while flow and love & connections are also very strong.

If you spend $120 for dinner today, it gives you a good feeling, but it is gone once you finish. But, hypothetically, if you invest $10 each month in stock for a year (same $120), it can give you a compounding return of $500 over time. Likewise, if you spend one hour watching Netflix, it will give you raw pleasure, but if you spend even five minutes with your son every day for twelve days (totaling the same one hour), that will strengthen your deep and meaningful loving connection with your son, and it will compound over time as you continue.

Remember, whether it is about money, happiness, or satisfaction,

the compounding effect happens from many small actions over time.

If you spend time on health, no one can take that away from you. If you spend quality time with your loved ones, the loving connections you build will be deep and meaningful. If you experience flow regularly, you will be happy and satisfied every day. If you work on your meaning, you will feel a sense of fulfilment inside you from the compounding effect. The happiness and satisfaction will stay with you much longer than momentary pleasures.

I personally choose the things which help my health, love, meaning, and flow over only achievements or pleasure. What works best is to have a good harmony of all the six elements in your life.

Every day, your ability to choose wisely will help you stay happier and more satisfied.

REFLECTION

Being happy by yourself, loving your own company, and intentionally getting into flow are the skills not everyone has. Once you internalize and skill up, your happiness does not need to depend on anyone or anything. This is one of the best things that you can do.

Remember, you have greatness in you, and by noticing and nurturing yourself, you can bring it out.

PART 7:
Stay Happy at Home

In this part, we will discuss the following:

- how you can be happy at home
- seeing through the lenses of your loved ones
- how you minimize conflicts with people at home
- who needs your love and care at home but is not saying it

STAY HAPPY WITH YOUR LOVED ONES AT HOME

"You cannot judge what should bring others joy,
and others cannot judge what should bring you joy."
—Alan Cohen

When you are at home, you are either by yourself or with someone who lives with you, such as family members or maybe your best friend or a roommate. But, generally, when we talk about people at home, they are the people we love and care for. There are numerous ways that you can create loving connections with them. I want to share with you three key things that I learned over many years. They are very simple and easy to do and will make your loving connections with your loved ones at home deep and meaningful.

SEEING THROUGH THEIR LENSES

I have a special drawer where I keep things like papers, a wallet, bank cards, and my keys. I like to keep them always in the same place so I can find them easily. I usually put these back after I use them in my drawer. Last week, I was running late for an in-person meeting, so I rushed to my study and opened my drawer for my car keys, but they weren't there. I was stressing out a little because I did not have time to look for the car keys. But I remembered that my wife drove the car last time, and I realized she may not have put the key back in the drawer.

If it had happened ten years ago, I would have been very upset about it. But over time, I realized that she also has places for her own things, and she has her unique way of finding things that I have no idea about. But this is how she operates, and me telling her a thousand times was not going to help and would upset her.

So I guessed and looked at her walk-in robe and found it. I went out and came back, said nothing about this to her. It was not because I was angry with her, but because over the years I have realized that one of the most important things about people is that the things that are important to us are not necessarily important to others. They have their unique perspectives, and they interpret the same objects (car keys, in this case) in their own ways.

When I was about six years old, I took my grandmother's high-powered glasses just to see how things looked through them. I was looking at an apple, and the apple looked three times as big. I was like, "Wow!" Then I looked at the apple again with clear eyes, but it looked normal. I used to switch back and forth many times. It was fun.

People have their unique lenses to see things. Keeping the car keys in the right place was very important for me. They were three times as big through my own lenses, but for my wife, they were not as big.

She has told me a million times to put the rubbish bin outside on Monday nights. For some reason, almost every Monday, I forget to do that. It is not that I do not want to, but I keep forgetting because, through my lenses, putting the rubbish bin out does not look important. Many years ago, she used to tackle me for that, but lately she has been understanding, and she puts on her calendar reminder and tells me it is time. She could have just said to me, "You always forget, no matter how many times I tell you," or I could have said the same about the car keys to her. The funny thing is that even if we tell people with very clear and simple instructions over and over again, they may still fail to follow with correct actions. This is not because they ignore us,

but because they operate differently to us (and that's expected).

We learned to respect the difference between our lenses and accept it. It is not about winning or being right but is about accepting each other as we individually are. Issues regarding car keys or bins are small things, but they pile up and become big over time.

At home, you deal with people. One of the key elements of being and staying happy at home is your loving connections with them. Whether it is your parents, partner, or children, respecting and accepting their views with empathy makes them feel that their opinions matter.

Everyone wants to feel important and be heard, including you and me. This is one of the core desires we all have as humans.

For many years, I had never seen through the lenses of my loved ones at home. I had developed the idea that they were my family and they would love me unconditionally no matter what. So I did not need to think about them as much as I used to for my close friends outside the home.

Twenty-five years later, I realized how wrong I was. We take people at home for granted. They love and support me when I need them, look after me when I'm sick, become happy when I'm happy, are sad when I'm sad, and are there when I feel down. Basically, their emotional well-being is highly influenced by mine, and vice versa.

I understand that the dynamics of individual families are different, and your experience and perception of people at home might not be the same. But remember, the longest study on happiness, which has lasted over seventy seven years, found that your happiness is the quality of your close relationships. That means the people at home (or in your circle zero) have a powerful influence on your happiness. It is critical that you create strong, meaningful, and loving connections with them that you can count on at all times.

One of the many ways to bond with them is to accept them not just as your family members but also as human beings with lenses that are different to yours (in a non-judging way—I know it is hard, but it is important). Have you ever seen a movie that you like but your partner hates? My wife and I differ about the movie The Avengers. The movie is the same, but we see and interpret it very differently. Whether eating on time, studying a subject, evaluating career choices, handling money, or even organizing rooms, whatever it is, some things may be very important to you. And you may want your loved ones to live in a certain way, even if you have a valid point and you are right, but those things may not necessarily be important to them (and may never be in the future). By insisting on or tackling them, you may upset your loved ones even more and will feel more disconnection with them over time.

But isn't happiness about creating loving connections with them? Think about it. How good would it be if I took the bin outside without my wife reminding me every Monday? Or if she put back the car keys in the right place? These are little things, but once we try and understand our loved ones on how they operate as human beings and respect their views of the world, life will be much easier and more peaceful for us and for them at home.

CLEANING UP CONFLICTS

It was about 4:00 p.m. We were at Herald Square in New York City, visiting for the first time. I booked a sightseeing cruise at 7:00 p.m., starting from Forty-Second Street, a few blocks from where we were. So we had some time, and my wife wanted to do some shopping at Macy's. So we went in. I was just wandering around as she was browsing through stores.

An hour later, I realized she hadn't picked anything and seemed confused. I asked her, "Are you looking for anything in particular?" She said, "I'm not sure. Give me some time." I said, "Okay, no problem. Call me if you need me. I will be in the men's section." Another half an hour passed, but she hadn't picked anything. It was almost 6:00 p.m., and I said, "Let's go. We must be at the pier by 6:45 p.m. to catch the cruise."

But she didn't like that and said, "Every time, during shopping, you always have something else planned out, and I cannot browse in peace." I said, "Every time? we need to go now, or we will miss the cruise." And we ended up in a little conflict and argued.

She said that she wanted to buy something for me as a surprise, and that something had to be from Macy's, and we couldn't come back to Macy's later, as we had a flight to catch to Toronto the next day. So she was stressing out, which I had no idea about. At that moment, I had two options: first, not to worry about what she thought and leave the mall, or resolve the conflict and continue shopping and risk the cruise at 7 p.m.

She had tears in her eyes (she doesn't cry very often), and I realized the depth of her wish, so it became important for me. Even though we had only thirty minutes, we stood in a corner. We had a chat with an open mind. She wanted to surprise me, but she couldn't find anything that she liked within the time she had already spent. I should have been happy that she wanted to surprise me, but I didn't want to miss the cruise either. But that was only my point of view. But for her, the cruise was not the priority; surprising me was. We have very different ways to show love to each other, which took me years to realize.

I said, "I'm surprised and humbled, but let me help you find something for me." We spent the next five minutes picking out something that we both liked (I'm usually very quick to pick something to buy). Then I felt bad that she had wanted to surprise me but I hadn't thought about buying anything for her. So I wanted to buy her something. She said, "We do not have time," but I insisted, and I bought her a pair of shoes that she chose, and we rushed out. I looked at my watch and saw it was already 6:30 p.m. We had about fifteen minutes to get to the pier on Forty-Second Street.

Google Maps said it was a twenty-minute walk, so we decided to walk to avoid New York traffic on a weekday. But it was not easy to just walk fast through the crowds. Anyway, after a few blocks of brisk walking and running, we reached the pier at 6:52 p.m. and were able to catch the cruise ship.

Misunderstandings and conflicts are meant to happen. My intent in including this story is to share at least one important aspect that we learned as a couple over more than sixteen years.

That is to not leave any conflict unresolved (no matter how small).

At the mall, we could have just left and resolved the issue later. But I knew that if we did that, both of us would hold a little grudge inside us, and this could pile up. We wouldn't have enjoyed the cruise either.

It was not a big conflict, but I took the risk of missing the cruise and prioritized resolving the conflict first. We were blessed that we could solve this in less than ten minutes on this occasion. I understand that not all conflicts can be resolved immediately. Sometimes it takes hours, if not days. But we make sure that we put in the time and effort to resolve any conflict as soon as we face it with an open mind and empathy.

How quickly you can resolve the conflict depends on how you practice it in your daily life. How do you treat your loved ones on an ordinary day? Is this person a priority for you? Do you feel what she feels?

Resolving conflict is also part of loving a person. If you do not initiate the uncomfortable conversation that is needed to resolve the issue, that means either your ego is stopping you or you do not really care. The ego in a relationship is evil, and if not managed, it can destroy a beautiful relationship. For the first few years, I would never initiate the conversation after an argument or conflict because it wasn't my fault (to my understanding). Also, most of the time, I thought I was right and felt that she needed to be the one who would need to initiate and apologize. But over the years, I understood and, most importantly, realized ego is part of human nature and will always be there for both of us. I had to be aware of it and decided that I would not let my ego win over my love.

One simple thing I always do when I face conflicts is ask myself, "Will this matter in a year?" If the answer is no, I just do not wait another three days or three months to act. Over time, I have trained my brain to bypass my ego and initiate the difficult conversation right now. And that's what I did on that day in New York. Also, I had to be kind, empathetic, and nice, because she is not just anyone. She is my better half.

It was not just me. She was also the same to me, because these values between two people come from awareness and practice over many years. They do not develop in a few weeks or months.

You might easily think that you are kind but your partner is not, or that you are nice but your partner is not. That's easy to think for yourself, but guess what? That's your thinking. And your partner thinks the same way, and like you, she is right in her own ways and holding on to her ego. As a result, the conflicts start to pile up, no matter how small they are.

You and I cannot get rid of ego; it is built into every one of us, but you must be aware of its impact on you and anyone you love and care for.

On that day, we resolved the conflict in ten minutes—not because it was easy, but because we live our daily lives like that. Some conflicts took us hours to resolve in the past, and we now think about them and laugh. But we make sure we put in the time and effort to resolve them. It is similar to cleaning your house. If you clean your house every day, there will not be much dust accumulation, and it will be easy to clean. But if you clean every three months, there will be a lot of dust to clean, and it will be harder and will take much longer to clean.

What I can say for sure is that in any relationship (not only a romantic one), when conflicts happen and you are having an argument with the other person, one thing leads to another. Most of the time, you start with one single issue, but a few hours later, you may end up talking about things which happened five years ago. If you have unresolved conflict today and keep that with you, be assured these conflicts will pile up and come back to hit your relationship later.

As I said, that day, walking and running down the crowded streets of New York, looking at the clock every minute to catch that cruise ship, was a great experience. I realize this may not make any sense to you. But we felt so free that we had resolved the issue. We laughed, ran, and were panting, and people were looking at us as we were running, but who cares? We reached the pier on time, felt more connected, enjoyed the cruise, and had a nice dinner later.

That day in New York was not special. It was just an ordinary day. What you do with your loved ones on your ordinary days determines the quality of your loving connections with them. Remember, ordinary days make up most of our lives, not our special days. It was a simple conflict for us, and I still talked about it because holding grudges regarding small conflicts leads to bigger issues later.

Resolving the conflicts with your loved ones as soon as possible is one of the best ways to keep your relationships clean. And that cleanliness creates room for more respect and love.

WHO NEEDS YOUR LOVE AND CARE BUT IS NOT SAYING IT?

When I was about nineteen years old, I was obsessed with computer racing games. I loved the game Screamer. In our group of friends, we used to challenge each other on race lap times, and we spent hours breaking each other's records. I also loved computer coding.

At the time, my dad was working on a large telecom project with a Canadian company. He knew that computer programs could help him plan his project better. He knew how to code, but he did not know the programming language required for his project. He wanted to get some help from me because I had some experience with it.

Just to set the context, my dad likes to do things himself if he can. He would not even ask for a glass of water if he could get it himself. Also, he is very kind and will never push anyone to do anything. So, he asked me nicely for help writing the computer program for his project. One day, we went through the plan together, and it didn't seem overly complicated, so I said, "Sure, I can help."

In the meantime, one of my friends broke my lap record in Screamer. Well, it was a big deal for me at that time. So, I dropped everything (including my dad's project) and put all my focus on breaking my friend's record. But despite all my efforts over almost two weeks, I wasn't able to break it. During this time, my dad nicely asked me a few times whether I'd had a chance to look at his program. I started to procrastinate, and I kept saying, "Give me two days. I shall get to it."

More than three weeks passed. My dad did not say anything else to me, but he started to write the program himself. He would spend hours on it every day. I pretended that I was busy studying and didn't look at him, but I was busy breaking the lap record challenge set by my friend. My other friends started laughing at me and said I could never break that record. I was so upset with myself, and I was surprised with my skills, which could not have been any better. The gap was only thirty milliseconds; how could I not break that?

One day, I came home and saw dad was working on the program himself. It was pretty late at night. I asked him how it was going. He said that he wrote a draft program, and it gave the results all right, but they were not always accurate. He was looking into the issue.

I felt so bad that he was not angry with me and didn't confront me. Instead, he was very kind as usual and asked me, "Do you think you have some time? Maybe you would understand the issue quicker than me." I had just come home, and I needed some rest, but then I caught myself doing the same pattern of procrastinating (and I was already feeling so bad). I said, "Sure, I shall look at it right now." I spent less than two hours and made some changes to simplify his program. I got my dad to do some testing, and it gave accurate results.

He was amazed. I still remember that his face was full of joy not only because his program worked but also because we had written it together as a team and as a family. I had spent countless hours playing Screamer in the last three weeks but was not getting any closer to breaking the record, and that made me very upset, but the two hours I spent with my dad made me so much happier and fulfilled that I almost forgot about the racing. It made me feel as if I did matter. I contributed to something that truly was meaningful to someone I love and care for.

What I had not been doing over the past three weeks was paying attention to my dad at all. Even if I listened to him, I did not take any action for him.

We take the love from our family and friends for granted. We think that when it comes to unconditional love, we can always count on them. But we forget that they are also human beings and they also crave love and care from us. Even if you do not love them back with your meaningful actions, they might still love you, but the purity of their love will fade away over time. Even if they hug you, there will be no affection to it.

Even if they say, "I love you," they may not mean it. They might just support your endeavors out of obligation instead of genuine love. They might not tell you this; you must pay attention to them to feel it.

I was receiving love from my dad but wasn't returning enough. I ignored him for a long time and took his love for granted. All that time, he was kind and nice, but he wasn't happy inside because I kept ignoring him. He didn't express his unhappiness, but I felt it. I realized on that day that I also needed to play my part to give love and care to the person I received unconditional love from, because one-way love does not persist and loses its purity and strength over time. Would you continue to genuinely love someone who ignores you day after day and does not love you back?

Just as my dad needed my attention, love, and care, which I didn't notice, does anyone need yours at home?

Whether it is our partners, parents, children, or whoever, most of the time, our loved ones do not ask for big things. It is the little things that make a lot of difference in their lives and ours. We need to pay attention to them through meaningful actions because they are our loved ones, not strangers.

Note: By the way, I finally broke that lap record after six weeks.

REFLECTION

Take a piece of paper and write down a secret you haven't shared with anyone yet. If you could, whom would you share this with? And why?

In our busy lives, in which we are distracted by many things, we often fail to pay attention and take meaningful actions for our loved ones. If you have someone you love at home and she loves you, how can you love her back? How can you pay attention to her? How can you understand her perceptions? It could be anyone you love and care for.

It is your little actions on your ordinary days that matter the most.

Remember, if your loved ones are happy with you, you will be happy with them.

PART 8:
Stay Happy at Work

In this part, we will discuss the following:

- why being happy at work matters
- what happiness at work means
- how you can be happy at work
- how you can handle stress at work
- if you hate your job
- how you can be happy with others at work
- how you deal with conflicts
- do you hate your boss
- why and how to create a happy workplace
- how to inspire employees with your company's purpose
- how to measure the engagement and happiness of your employees

WHY DOES HAPPINESS AT WORK MATTER?

A long time ago, I had a colleague who was a true gentleman in his late forties. One day, I saw him in the office kitchen, and he didn't seem very happy. I asked him, "Are you all right?" He said, "Sanju, I'm okay, just tired of working. I can't wait to retire, but I need to keep going for another ten years." I said, "Why do you feel the need to retire?" He said, "I do not really want to retire, but I feel that I've just been working like a machine over the last twenty years. Everything is the same old, and I have no excitement about this job. I feel like I have had enough and want to do something which makes sense to me. But I cannot leave this job because I need to pay my bills. I do not know how long I can survive like this."

He had lost his excitement at work. Most people spend at least eight to ten hours at work, which is almost one-third of one's adult life. Feeling good and fulfilled at work matters. Many people believe in working hard for the whole week like a machine and somehow getting to the end of the week and living for the weekend. Hypothetically, if your whole life is seven days, your weekend is only 28 per cent, and the weekdays make up the other 72 per cent of your life, which you are not really living. Many just cling to their jobs because they have to, not because they love to. A recent Gallup study found that more than 80 per cent of the global workforce are not engaged at work. They cannot leave their jobs because they have to pay their bills. More than 50 per cent of your waking hours are spent at work, including travelling to and from work. Regardless of the type of work you do, if you want a happy and satisfying life, you must stop and wonder, are you truly happy and fulfilled at your work? Because that accounts for more than 50 per cent of your happiness.

WHAT DOES IT MEAN TO BE HAPPY AT WORK?

According to leading happiness researchers, being happy at work is not about just having fun all the time but is also about having a meaningful workplace. Happiness researchers at the University of California–Berkeley define happiness at work with four key pillars: purpose, engagement, resilience, and kindness (PERK). Firstly, you should have a purpose attached to your work. You should not go to work just because you have to, but rather because you want to. You should feel that the work you do every day matters more than just having a paycheck. Do you believe in what your organization believes? For example, if you work for an organization that believes in and produces fresh food for people, do you also believe that everybody deserves to eat fresh food? By working with that company, are you helping people to have fresh food every day?

Secondly, how do you engage in your daily tasks? Are you excited about the things that you are going to do? Are you engaged? Do you feel total immersion? Do you feel a sense of independence and responsibility in what you do? For example, if you do sales presentations, as you present, do you feel that time stops for you? Do you experience flow?

Thirdly, how do you handle stress at work? Do you take regular time off from work? Are you present at the task at hand? Or do you wander around the future or past? For example, if you have to finish writing an email in the next half an hour, do you focus on writing the email or worry about a presentation you have tomorrow? How quickly and efficiently can you bounce back from setbacks at work?

And finally, do you care about the people you work with? Are you being kind to them? Do you feel empathy toward them? For example, if one of your colleagues needs some help with her speech and you are good at speechwriting, do you offer help without her asking for it? Or if somebody needs time off in your team but needs to offload some work before she goes, do you offer help to cover for her?

We need to have these 4 pillars (PERK) at work. This can be practiced on three different levels. Firstly, how can you use PERK as an individual every day? Secondly, how can you use PERK with people you work with? And finally, how can you, as a leader of an organization, implement the strategies of PERK, and make the whole workplace happier? We will discuss these items in the next few chapters.

HOW CAN YOU STAY HAPPY AT WORK

"Once you do something you love, you never have to work again."
—Willie Hill

WHY DO YOU WORK?

In 2017, Mark Zuckerberg, the CEO and founder of Facebook (Now Meta), in his Harvard commencement speech, said, "One of my favorite stories is when John F. Kennedy visited the NASA space center, he saw a janitor carrying a broom, and he walked over and asked what he was doing. The janitor responded, 'Mr. President, I'm helping put a man on the moon.' Purpose is that sense that we are a part of something bigger than ourselves, we are needed, that we have something better ahead to work for. Purpose is what creates true happiness."

No matter how small his contributions were, the janitor at the NASA space center was still part of something much bigger than himself or his family. He belonged to something that created a historic moment for humanity.

Mark Zuckerberg is the leader of Facebook, and he has a purpose attached to his role. His mission is to connect the world. Recently, I attended a seminar. One of the Facebook employees in Australia came over and talked about how business owners can use Facebook to attract more customers for their businesses. That man's purpose for his work could be "He personally believes small business owners can truly attract more customers using Facebook, and his presentations educate people to do that." He helps people grow their businesses using Facebook, but it is different to Mark's purpose to connect the whole world. But both of their roles uniquely contribute to the overall operation and success of Facebook, which is bigger than both of them individually.

And the impact? More than 2 billion people are connected to their friends and families worldwide as the end customers of Facebook.

In the 1960s, my dad was a talented young man and was doing research on long-distance telecommunication at the University of Tokyo. Dad's work was widely recognized and was selected to be a case study for undergraduate students. It was very rare for an international student in Tokyo at the time. Later, he started working for NEC Corporation, one of the world's leading companies. In 2020, they reported a revenue of 3.1 trillion JPY. His mentor, Professor Miyakawa, was so impressed with his research that he insisted on staying in Tokyo. So my dad had a great job at NEC with decent pay and more research opportunities with his mentor. But he always wanted to do something meaningful for his country, and he turned down his research and job opportunities in Japan and returned to Bangladesh (West Pakistan at that time).

He spent his life as a telecommunication engineer for the government of Bangladesh. He was the director of research and development. He led the very first project for replacing all analogue telephone systems with modern digital systems across the country. He worked days and nights for a few years and was travelling back and forth to Tokyo as they were installing Japanese digital exchanges and systems. He was away from his family for a long time as part of that project. He successfully completed the project and was recognized widely. During his career, he was recognized for various other projects numerous times and featured in local and international media and on national television.

I'm not telling this story to brag about my dad, but because he turned down opportunities in Japan, where they were very easy for him to take. He sacrificed his potentially lucrative career and returned to his own country, where the opportunities were very limited. The country was politically unstable, and the pay was nowhere near what he was earning in Japan. But he still took the risk and came back to Dhaka to serve his country. During his career, every success he had in Bangladesh was a recognition of the sacrifice he made for his country. Those successes fulfilled him, and during his career, he felt that he had played a small part in his country's development in telecommunication.

Did anybody tell my dad to give meaning to his work? Not really. He gave his own meaning to his work. Every day, he had a mission in front of him. He had a purpose, and he used to look forward to being part of something much bigger than himself. The impact of the work my dad did was not limited to himself or his family, but the people of Bangladesh, who now have a much better and smarter telephone system than before. But most of all, he went to work for his country, which made his days meaningful. He was fulfilled not just on the days he was rewarded but every single day for over thirty-three years.

Rakib is a specialist eye surgeon based in Dhaka. He has been helping people around the country recover and improve their eyesight for over twenty-five years. He is a professor of ophthalmology for the BIRDEM hospital, one of Dhaka's leading research and rehabilitation centers. Also, every Thursday of the week, he travels to a small city called Tangail to help underprivileged people who cannot afford to come to Dhaka for treatment for various reasons, including financial inability. This gives him an additional purpose. His commitments to his patients are unbelievable. He can make someone's eyesight better or even recover a patient's sight with his skills in surgery and treatment. He has already helped thousands of people to have better vision. He is still going, and that is the purpose for him.

According to Global Purpose Index 2016, People associate their work with either status, money, or purpose. Studies suggest in the report that purpose-oriented employees scored higher than non-purpose-oriented employees on every measure studied. They have 64 per cent higher job fulfilment, are 50 per cent more likely to be in leadership positions, and are 47 per cent more likely to be promoters of their employers. These results are across all races, ethnicities, and income levels. Obviously, money is one of the top reasons people work, because everybody has to pay their bills. Learning is another reason people work, because they want to develop their skills personally and professionally. Sometimes, people's work or titles are symbols of power or accomplishments. For example, if they are asked, "Where do you work?" They may say, "I am an astronaut at NASA," or "I am a professor at Oxford." The position can be a form of status and a symbol of achievement for them, and many have a sense of contribution beyond themselves. Whatever reason people may give to their work, they generally come down to those three factors: money, status, and purpose.

It does not matter how big or small your role is; if you are part of something big, you always have a role to play that contributes to the company's overall success. Every business in the world serves people. And you either directly or indirectly serve the end customer.

Randi Zuckerberg is the creator of Facebook Live and former director of marketing for Facebook. She once said that she used to get up in the morning and work for twenty hours a day to empower someone across the world to have a voice. That was the purpose she gave for her role on Facebook.

If you think about people like Mark Zuckerberg, his purpose is to connect the world, and he has connected more than 2 billion people through Facebook. Bill Gates's purpose is to eradicate diseases from the world, and he has played a vital role in eradicating polio from the world. My dad's purpose was to serve his country by building a modern and sustainable telecommunication system. Rakib's purpose is to help people improve their eyesight, and yes, there are countless examples.

How do you define your purpose? How does your work impact others? Think about it.

You do not have to have a purpose to change the world. You can always define your purpose based on what you truly care for. I wasn't born with a purpose either. After spending thirty-five years on this planet, I understood that purpose keeps me going, gives me a sense that my work matters, and keeps me truly alive. I believe most people do not realize their true brilliance in their lifetimes. I help people discover and nurture their natural talents and educate them with the science of happiness so they live more fulfilled lives, which is my purpose.

Last month, one of my private student groups just finished a six-month-long program with me. I asked them individually how the sessions reshaped their lives and work. They ended up crying out of gratitude to each other for more than an hour and shared how they were able to redesign their lives to live more on their terms. It was a very emotional experience. When I see people drive eight hours just to have a catch-up with me, when I get a phone call from an old client saying, "I fell in love with a girl and wanted to tell you first," or when I hear someone tell me, "Because of you, I didn't give up," those words give me true fulfilment for what I do.

You do not have to work for a big corporate or own a business or make sacrifices like my dad to have a purpose at work. One of many ways to give meaning and have purpose is to ask yourself, "Does my work matter? How does my role directly or indirectly impact people by doing what I do at work? Because of my work, do people live better lives?"

When we look at the seven billion people globally, I am just one of them and so are you. No matter how small we think we are, we all have roles to play, and that matters at work.

DO YOU FEEL ENGAGED?

I was working on a presentation for a group session on how to use your natural talents in your everyday role at work. I had a call with the group leader and discussed their expectations and priorities, the group dynamic, how they operate as a team, and the topics to focus on. After the discussion with the leader, at 10:30 a.m., I started working on planning the topics that I wanted to talk about in the session and things like designing the slides, doing the necessary research, incorporating scientific tools, modifying, adjusting, and many other things, and suddenly, my phone rang. I picked up the phone. It was one of those telemarketing calls asking whether I wanted to switch my energy provider. We have all been there. I felt interrupted and annoyed because I was in the middle of something.

Then I looked at the time. It was 4:30 p.m.

Notice that I started working on the slides at 10:30 a.m. But before I realized it, six hours had passed, and I was still going until my phone rang. I forgot to eat my lunch, had the doors of my study closed, wasn't doing anything else, was completely immersed in creating the slides, and lost track of time. You know what I'm talking about. I'm talking about flow. I was completely engaged in creating the slides for my session the following week. I couldn't feel anything. I had a sense of great control over everything

I was doing during that time. As I said above, my phone rang suddenly. It didn't feel like six hours. Time flew by for me. My phone rang, but I would have continued to work on my slides otherwise.

My session with the group was not until the following week, and I had more than seven days to prepare the slides. But I was continuing to work on the slides—not because I had limited time, but because I was enjoying the process of creating those slides so much that I lost myself in the process.

Everything I said that I felt and experienced during that six hours are the signs when you experience flow. For me, just creating PowerPoint slides is not very exciting itself, but the content I develop using PowerPoint is exciting and gets me into flow.

Remember that the two critical components must be met for flow to occur. One is your skill. You must have the necessary skills to do the task. And the second is a challenge. There should be some level of challenge, (though it should be comfortable for you). The challenge should not be so high as to make you anxious or worried and should not be so low as to make you feel bored. The challenge and the skill should meet in the sweet spot, where you don't feel anxious or bored but feel a great sense of control over the task with satisfaction as you do that.

One of my previous clients is an accountant, and she loves numbers. She works on her own business. When she goes through each transaction of the bank statements or works on an income statement or a balance sheet, she never gets tired, and time stops for her. She doesn't eat, doesn't talk to anyone, and feels "in the zone." She does not like any distractions during those times. Once she finishes, she feels satisfied and wants to do it again.

Her business partner hates looking at numbers. But she is the head of sales. She started on her own, and now she has a team of people working for her. She excels in sales, and she loves talking to people. She developed the skills to win her potential customers. She never gets tired, and she can do it all day without stopping. Again, time stops for her. She wouldn't stop doing it unless interrupted.

You see, two different people love very different things in the same business. One is an accountant and loves numbers but hates talking to people. The other is the opposite. She loves talking to people but hates numbers. Their combination couldn't be more perfect for this business. Their skills complement each other. It does not matter whether you are in sales, marketing, research, development, or any other area of a business; you can get flow from any task you love doing. Ideally, you should be in those roles where you can use your strengths and skills with a challenge to experience flow.

Is there a task or activity you do daily in your role that you get flow from? If the challenge and skill you have do not match your role, you will still perform your tasks, but it will be very hard to experience flow.

You can technically get flow from almost any activity, depending on your skills, the challenge level, and the things you love to do. One of the key things to be aware of is accidental mind wandering. You must avoid thinking about things other than the task at hand. Even if you know you can achieve flow in a certain task or activity, you still need to start doing it. The key here is to pay 100 per cent of your attention to the task for the whole duration.

If you are trying out a new role at work or a new task that you have been assigned, be aware of how that particular task makes you feel during and after you do it. If you experience flow, build up your skills by doing the task or activity more and more, but also increase the level of challenge gradually over time so you do not feel bored.

This feels awesome when you are in a role with a challenge you love and have the skills to do it. Nothing can stop you from excelling in that role at work. The more engagement or flow you have in any role, the more results you will get, and they will speak for you. When you finish work for the day, you will not be tired. Instead, you will feel satisfied and have a sense of achievement. Your peers and management will notice you for your great results and how you show up at work every day.

How good would that be?

ARE YOU STRESSED AT WORK?

Many years ago, I was nominated to lead a high-profile project at work. In the first meeting with the project team, I provided insights into how it could work with a draft plan. The project manager said to me, "This is a high-visibility project. What's the ETA on the delivery?"

I said, "Well, ideally this should take about ten to twelve weeks, but given the priorities, I think we should be able to deliver in ten weeks." The project manager said, "We do not have ten weeks. What is the best you can do?" I hesitated and reluctantly agreed to six weeks.

But the project delivery in six weeks was a real challenge for us. I tried to compact everything into the short amount of time with limited resources, which kept the project team working extra hours for a whole month. Being the lead, I had to make sure that everyone was delivering on time, and I was stressing out almost every day and blaming myself for agreeing to six weeks.

I'm telling you the story for two reasons. First, in the project meeting, I should not have agreed to six weeks. I did because I was new to leading a project and wanted to prove myself to the management, as it was a highly visible project. So I overestimated my and my team's ability to deliver the project in six weeks. That not only stressed me out but also caused my team members to suffer. I should have explained and been firm with a ten-week time frame. I was not being authentic to myself and my team.

Secondly, during the project's delivery phase, which was six weeks, almost every night after work, I came home and worked on the project, which took away from my time with my family. Whenever I talked to my family at dinner, I was again thinking about the project delivery and worrying about what could go wrong. Some of it did go wrong, but we managed to deliver on time. But I was not present in the moments most of the time during the delivery phase, whether at work or home.

According to studies, being authentic to yourself and being mindful are both critical when it comes to handling pressure and stress at work, which I had no idea about at that time. I could have saved myself and my team from all that pressure.

Dr. Emiliana Simon Thomas from the University of California Berkeley said, "We define mindfulness as maintaining a moment-by-moment awareness of our thoughts, feelings, bodily sensations, and surrounding environment through a gentle nurturing lens." Learning the skills of mindfulness can reduce stress and help you handle stress much better. Also, being authentic means expressing yourself with authenticity, which I couldn't do at the project meeting. I should have expressed what I was capable of and should not have overpromised, which kept me and my team stressed out for six weeks.

You may think your stress will go away after you finish your current project, but the truth is that you will be applauded and given an even bigger project, and you will then have more stress. Keep in mind that you will always be part of some project, and stress will always follow you unless you take care of yourself first.

It is not the project that gives you stress; it is you who gives yourself stress. We like to be recognized, applauded, and appreciated, and we want to feel that we matter. Delivering the projects on time gives us gratification and a sense of achievement. But the gratification and recognition I got from delivering my project lasted only a few days before I was assigned to another project and started to stress out about my new project.

See, three days of gratification does not (or should not) outweigh the six weeks of stress.

Delivering a project on time is essential. But having a good balance of the expectation from management and your team's ability to deliver should be aligned (or very close) so that you have some level of challenge to get out of your comfort zone, meet the business's needs, and manage stress comfortably. Pressure and stress at work are inevitable not only in project spaces but also in almost any industry.

Remember, things like purpose and flow will give you satisfaction. Even if you have a solid purpose for your role and love your job, which fulfils you every day, you still can get stressed, and you do not need me to talk about why chronic stress is bad for you.

But understand that stress is a form of fear we all have and is not going anywhere. It is part of who we are. The only way to deal with it is to manage it.

Practicing mindfulness and being true to yourself can save you. I understand that the moments I'm living right now are given to me and limited. Worrying about the uncertain future or regretting the past keeps me from enjoying and living the moments right now. The moment you are reading this sentence, for example, will never come back to you.

Another way to reduce stress is to take time off work. Research suggests that spending good quality time off work helps reduce daily stress and pressure. If you can have good sleep every night, that is also critical to handling everyday work worries. A good holiday can help us rebound from a setback at work.

Honestly, if you are in a job with no purpose or flow and it stresses you out every day, you are in the wrong job or with the wrong leader, which will destroy your happiness, and over time, that can lead to depression, chronic anxiety, or other mental issues. If this sounds like you, it is time to adjust how you think, feel, and behave at work. Seek professional help or make an immediate change in your role at work.

Most people at work think about things that haven't happened yet. They may or may not happen. Instead, learning to live in the moment helps you manage your worries. Yes, this is easier to say than it is to do. But this is a learnable skill you and I can learn.

For many years, I thought being mindful was useless and did not add any value to my life. So I never consciously practiced it. I ignored being in the present, but now when I look back fifteen years in my life and think about the moments when I was stressed out, I feel silly about it. Honestly, today I wonder why I was stressing out at that time. I feel that I should have been present at home with my family and friends instead of worrying about the project delivery.

If you are stressing out about something today, you may not even remember this moment in a year. Eventually, someday you will move on to other, more important things.

But why someday and not today?

ARE YOU TOO HARD ON YOURSELF?

Joshua was impatiently waiting for the traffic lights to go green. He was driving to a client site for an urgent call he had received stating that one of his client's email systems had broken down. He is a very experienced IT consultant with a good client base which he had built over the previous ten years. Joshua holds himself to a very high standard of service for his clients. They trust and count on him. So, as he was at the traffic light to attend to this client, he couldn't wait to get to the client's site as soon as possible. After all, it was a matter of his reputation, and he was stressing about the possibility of getting stuck in traffic.

Even though he was starving, he skipped lunch, as there was no time for it. He was running on the coffee that he had in the morning. Because of traffic, he arrived at the client site about thirty minutes late. He apologized to them for being late and started working on the issue right away. After a few hours of work, he was able to get them back online again. It was 7:00 p.m. when he finished. He had a very stressful day, but it felt good for him because he solved the client's problem and felt he had achieved something.

In the next couple of years, his demand and reputation in the market became much better, and his client base grew. But he was diagnosed with chronic anxiety, as he was constantly worrying about his clients and his reputation. It was also causing him sleeplessness at night.

One thing was obvious—that he put his clients first before himself. That is an attitude that many people have. They put their work before themselves. If your leader assigns you a task to complete in a short time, you may be tempted to reprioritize everything and do that right away because you may want to deliver or overdeliver and set a higher standard for yourself as a responsible team member with an outstanding work ethic.

But in that endeavor, many of us are guilty of putting ourselves at the bottom of our priorities. If you are a leader of a team or the owner of a business, this tendency can be worse. The higher your position in an organization, the more responsibilities you will have and the more stress you will likely experience.

Whenever you deliver something at work, you feel a sense of gratification, but you may worry about failing to deliver good-quality work on time. Yes, we all have a role to play to be outstanding. Yes, we need to be congruent with what we promise. Yes, we must hit our targets and make a profit. Yes, we must keep our customers happy. Yes, we must pay our employees on time, and yes, we must do many other things, so we deliver and we grow at work. But these things come at the expense of self-destruction in some way.

All our achievements fade away if we are not physically and mentally sound. In recent years, we have been hearing a lot about mental health at work. And this is not by chance. Big and innovative companies like Google, Facebook, and Apple have been focusing on the mental well-being of their employees, and other businesses are doing the same. They understood and realized that their employees would never be at their best if they were in a constant state of worry or stressing out. Salesforce and many other organizations have taken initiatives like practicing mindfulness, self-compassion, mental habits, and bringing your authentic self to work so you can perform at your best. These are remarkable and timely initiatives because businesses that are not seriously taking care of their employees will not last, regardless of their current standings.

The same idea applies to you as an individual, regardless of your role. If you are always in an anxious or worried state, needing to deliver more and more, you will not be able to sustain your achievements and reputation, which you worked so hard for.

If you are an employee and have a good boss, the boss you may love may not be there for the rest of your career. She may take another role, retire, or die. You might worry about that, but there is not much you can do about it. Then, with your new boss, you will have to start again from zero. Then the same pattern continues.

Generally, if you run your own business, your revenue comes from customers. You may have killed yourself to get them and to build a good reputation (as did Joshua, mentioned earlier), but your clients can surely change providers (which happens more often than you may wish to believe) or can go out of business. Then, with your new clients, you will have to start from zero again.

Regardless of how much power and status you have in your role at work, if you worry about your boss or clients, it's because, deep down, you are fearful of the power that is in their control. So you do everything in your power to keep them happy, and in that endeavor, you make yourself unhappy by constantly worrying about them.

What does that do to your happiness? Think about it.

Remember, change is inevitable for you, me, and everyone else. I have learned not to worry about things that I don't control. I have been on both sides as an employee and a business owner. I have realized that there is no reason to put yourself at the bottom of your priorities.

In fact, to thrive, you will need to do quite the opposite. Taking care of yourself comes above everything else. The project or task that you are worrying about will be completed whether it is completed by you or someone else. God forbid, if anything happens to you, your project will carry on, and your organization will find someone else. Or maybe your company will not be able to afford you anymore and will have to let you go. Or you will find another role in another organization, and the same story will repeat.

The bottom line is that you are replaceable as an employee or a business owner, but your body and mind are not.

Remember, your mind and body don't care about your projects, boss, or clients. You do. You may put your work first and your happiness last, and that's where all the worries start.

DO YOU HATE YOUR JOB?

If you hate your job, why are you still doing it? The truth is, we all have to pay our bills. The job you may hate is one way to pay your bills, but it is not the only way.

A Gallup study revealed that a surprising 85 per cent of the global workforce are not engaged at work. How can you be happy at work when you are not engaged?

The answer is that you cannot.

So what options do you have? To keep it simple, firstly, if you hate your boss, please read the next chapter. But if you feel that you are on the wrong team or do not get along with team members, that can impact how you feel every day at work. As human beings, we crave to be included and want to belong. If you feel that you do not belong to your team, the easier option would be to find a role on another team where you will be valued, appreciated, recognized for your work, and feel included. But you will never know it unless you change your team.

The alternative is harder. If you try to fit in on the team where you do not feel you belong, you will have to intentionally change how you think, feel, dress, talk, or even eat. In other words, you will have to change who you truly are, which will stress you even more and make you unhappy.

Secondly, Author Leigh Branham states in his book The 7 Hidden Reasons Employees Leave that only 12 per cent of employees leave an organization for more money. But if you feel that you are not paid fairly and you believe you deserve more money, there are two ways to make it happen. Either you have a conversation with your manager, which may or may not go your way, or you change to your next-level role, where generally your pay will be higher than in your existing role.

Finally, if you are bored with your current role or skill, you may want to try something new, whether a new skill, something that gives new meaning to your work, or even a career change. Many people change their careers at some point to reset their purpose and engagement. Many people start their own businesses and do something entrepreneurial to follow their passions or purposes or both.

Carefully evaluate your current role and consider whether it is time for a new chapter.

If you believe it is, you may decide to transition from your day job to something entrepreneurial. You may want to think about a plan for how you will continue to pay your bills during the transition. How are you going to develop those skills that are required to pursue your passion? Do you have a financial safety net? As it might take a long time to make money from your passion. What is the time frame for this transition?

How committed are you to meeting that time frame? Do you have a mentor who can help you during this process?

I know there are many things to consider if you are going down that path on your own. This will be much more challenging than finding another job. There will be ups and downs. There will be rejections, obstacles, failures, emotional trauma, and many other things. You constantly have to push your boundaries and get uncomfortable on a regular basis to get to where you may want to go. Honestly, you may feel alone for a long time until you are able to build your own team. But as you go through this process to pursue your true passion, that will be your new work.

There will be no boss. You will work on your own hours, with no annoying colleagues; you will work only with the people you decide to work with; you will handle your own pay; and you will have complete control over almost everything about your new work. And most importantly, you will work on something that you truly love. Most people are not engaged in their jobs is because, one way or the other, every day, they have to work with people or things against their will.

The challenges you will face as an entrepreneur are not as scary as if you are ninety years old and sitting in your rocking chair and regretfully thinking, "I wish I had taken the leap of faith and followed my passion." When you work on something that you truly love and care for, even when you face challenges, it will be very hard for you to be unfulfilled or bored, because almost everything you do at work will be done according to your will. And in your old age, you will have no excuse or regret for not trying.

REFLECTION

The four pillars—purpose, engagement, resilience, and kindness, are the fundamentals to be and stay happy at work. Think about how you can use PERK strategies.

Ponder upon what else you get beyond your paycheck from work?

Do people live better lives because of your role?

Are you engaged?

Are you mindful and kind to yourself?

How do you handle stress?

Remember, your happiness happens in your head. It does not matter whether you are by yourself, at home, or at work.

If you can be and stay happy at work, it will not even feel like work

HOW TO STAY HAPPY WITH OTHERS AT WORK

"The greatness of a man is measured by the way he treats the little man. Compassion for the weak is a sign of greatness."
—Myles Munroe

THE TWO-WAY ROAD

Sheryl is an interior designer and works for a medium-sized business. She has a two-year-old son. She and her husband are both full-time workers. She used to send her son to childcare when she was at work. But because of COVID-19 restrictions, they have been working from home and haven't been able to send her son to childcare. Being two years old, her son needs a lot of attention from both parents during work hours. So she has been putting in a lot of extra after-hours work over the last few months. She loves her work and has delivered numerous successful projects.

Her manager told her to keep a count of the extra hours so they can reimburse her with money or time off. In December, she emailed her manager the number of extra hours she put in. Her manager replied that she is entitled to take time off for half of the hours she put in. That is, for each ten hours extra she worked she would get only five hours off.

That was a surprise for her, as she assumed she would get time off equal to the extra hours, and her manager initially did not communicate clearly about it. She became very upset about it because she took full responsibility for delivering the projects on time, and she had done so. She worked hard in accordance with her passion, and the projects were close to her heart. Her deliveries allowed her company to sign new contracts and keep existing ones, and she made a measurable difference to the business.

She felt that her hard work had gone unnoticed. She said, "It was not the number of hours I was offered to take time off. It was much more about recognition in that email from my manager. He said that I could take fifty per cent of my extra hours of work as time off. It felt that I didn't work as much as I said I did. He didn't explain why

I would get 50 per cent of those hours and not 100 per cent. And that bothered me the most, as it means to me that my efforts have been only 50 per cent recognized."

It was not about whether her manager was right or wrong; some companies do have these policies, and they widely vary across various industries. Working extra hours when needed is nothing new. Some employees get paid hourly; some are salaried and expected to work "reasonable" extra hours as part of their package. Some businesses pay or give time off to even salaried employees for putting in extra hours. But in all those situations, a good manager communicates policies accordingly to their employees in advance so there are no surprises to the employees later.

During the COVID-19 pandemic, many businesses had to create such policies as working-from-home arrangements for employees, which they didn't need before. Honestly, during these uncertain times, businesses even didn't know what their policies should look like. And if Sheryl's company didn't already have such a policy for the new working arrangements for their employees, they should have had open and clear communication and set the expectations accordingly with their employees.

In Sheryl's case, the issue was not about fairness or unfairness but rather her manager's need to have an open and honest conversation with Sheryl to make sure that she felt recognized, important, and appreciated for her efforts. And from Sheryl's point of view, she also had to realize that her manager and her company's management are also human beings and also make mistakes, especially during these uncertain times. With so many businesses trying to figure out their course of action, it would have been challenging for her management as they navigated these times.

As human beings, we always crave recognition. As managers learn to communicate better with their teams, their team members will also need to understand and realize the manager's position.

What I'm talking about here is empathy with kindness. This empathy is not just one-sided from the manager to Sheryl but also from Sheryl to her manager. You may think you are not empathetic, but research suggests that empathy is not a personality trait but a skill you can learn over time by intentionally practicing on others.

If you are a leader, being empathetic to your employees and truly caring for them will make your team members listen to you even more. Your employees look up to you for guidance and inspiration. What you tell them matters. It impacts their mental well-being and emotions. No matter how "right" you are and how aligned your words are with the company policy, at the end of the day, the question is,

do your employees feel that they are included, recognized, and appreciated?

Studies suggest that 79 per cent of employees leave an organization because they lack recognition from their leader. No matter how small their efforts seem to be, if you, as their leader, can take a moment and genuinely appreciate them, you can make them feel appreciated, and they will feel that they are needed. This is one of the core human needs we all have, including you as a leader.

A simple thanks to your employees takes less than ten seconds, whether it is carried out face-to-face, by a quick call, or even via text or email. It is your awareness as the leader and your conscious effort to genuinely appreciate your employees that make the difference. It is silly for your people to leave you because you do not give them recognition or appreciation on a regular basis. Once in a while (e.g., yearly or half-yearly) is not enough. Your employees should not have to move mountains for your thanks.

No matter how small or regular your appreciation is, be genuine in your compliments because the recipients can sense your honesty.

But caring is not just a one-way road. Somehow, over time, we have developed the notion that all the caring must be from the employer to the employees. If you are an employee, it is also your job to understand and focus on the priorities of your leader and the organization. When your manager tells you something, it may or may not be a direct reflection on you. Maybe the manager is not skilled enough to communicate efficiently with empathy; maybe she was having a hard day at work herself. There could be hundreds of reasons why your manager treated you the way she did.

According to Forbes, research shows that about 58 per cent of managers said that they did not receive any management training. That is worrying. But one thing to remember is that your leaders are also human beings. They are also learning as leaders. Give them a chance and see whether they can do better in their roles as managers. If or when you become a leader, it is likely that you will also make mistakes, and your employees will do the same for you.

At work, you will always be working with people. Whatever the context is, whether you are an employee or a leader, treating people with empathy, kindness, and appreciation will help you stay in peace.

THE RIPPLE EFFECT

> Hi Ellen,
>
> I just wanted to say that the project we worked on together was an exceptional experience for me. I learned a number of strategies and skills from you, especially how to handle customer complaints. I appreciate the additional time and effort you spent to help me with the project.
>
> I sincerely thank you for that.
>
> Your work ethics and determination are very inspiring.

Truly.
Alicia

Ellen opened her email in the morning and saw this and was pleasantly surprised. Alicia used to be her colleague, but she moved to another team recently. They worked on a project two months ago. But she realized that Alicia still remembered and recognized her work as a colleague. Ellen couldn't believe that people could be so nice. There were other people on the same project that Ellen had helped, but none of them said thanks but Alicia. It was a nice gesture from her.

One of the best types of recognition you can possibly get is that which comes from colleagues on your own team. They know you more than other people in the organization. Alicia didn't just acknowledge Ellen's help but also took the time to send Ellen this quick note. It may have taken just a few minutes for her, but Ellen felt more connection toward Alicia because of that. Whom do you think Ellen will remember and feel connected to—Alicia or other team members she helped?

We do not say "thank you" to our colleagues enough. Their work may or may not directly impact us, but it is not always only the manager's or leader's job to recognize team members. If you are a team member and someone in your team has done amazing work, a simple note of recognition or appreciation from you to that colleague can make her day. She will then feel happy like Ellen did, and you will also become happier.

Even if you truly want to recognize your colleague, you may still forget to do so. The trick is not to procrastinate or add a task to your to-do list, so you do not forget.

Laura has been working for a leading pharmaceutical company for a few years. One day, she asked her manager whether she could take a few days off and go for surgery, as she had a minor heart condition. Most of her colleagues didn't know that. On the same day, one of their top-level executives, Jason, was meeting with the wider team, including Laura. In this meeting, employees can freely talk about their wins, struggles, processes, or generally anything, with a few senior leadership team executives participating informally.

In the meeting, some of Laura's colleagues talked about her going for the surgery soon. Jason did not really know Laura very well, but he attentively listened to what Laura shared about the surgery, and he said that if she needed any help, she could reach out to her manager or Jason directly. That was a nice gesture on Jason's part. Technically, Jason is a top executive who literally oversees a couple of hundred people in his wider team and is five levels higher than Laura.

Laura had the surgery in a few days and returned to work after two weeks. On her return, everybody supported her with best wishes, greeting cards, flowers, and such. But the next day, something happened that Laura did not expect. She received a call from their senior leader, Jason. He asked about the surgery and spoke to her for a few minutes to show his support to her. She was overwhelmed with gratitude and compassion from all over the floor and from Jason. Even though it was a minor surgery, she felt that people cared about her, she felt that she belonged to the wider team, and, of course, the direct support from Jason meant a lot to her.

Jason did say in the initial meeting that if Laura needed any help during the surgery from her organization, she could ask for it. But he did not stop there and went the extra mile to follow up on her status after her surgery. It was a quick phone call, but it greatly impacted his wider team, and he set an example of true compassion for the existing managers and other future leaders.

When we go through tough times, we all need support. If you know someone is going through hardship, reach out and have a quick chat and say that you are there for him or her. Offer the person support and do what you can. Even if he or she does not need any support, just your simple phone call can help him or her go through tough times emotionally.

Many years ago, I used to work for a large corporate. I was sitting at my desk. At the time, it was located near the exit door. Earlier in the morning, we'd had a meeting with one of our senior leaders, Roy. He had just been appointed in Sydney but was visiting his team in Melbourne for the day. In the afternoon, he was heading back to Sydney and walked past my desk to the exit door.

I said, "Bye, Roy, see you soon." By the time I finished saying that, he had already walked past my desk, but he stopped, turned around, and walked back to my desk. He was holding a bunch of files in his right hand. He stood by my desk, shifted those files to his left hand, and then offered me his right hand for a handshake, and then he smiled and said, "See you soon."

He could have just raised his hand on his way out and said, "See you," or he could have just pretended that he didn't hear my goodbye and kept walking, but he didn't do any of that. He seemed to be in a hurry, but he still stopped, walked back to my desk, freed his right hand, shook my hand, and properly said goodbye. Honestly, for many people, it may not be a big deal, but it was and still is to me, no matter how small or simple an act it may seem. I do not think he remembered who I was, but he knew that I was on his team. The time he took for this gesture was less than twenty seconds, but the impact he made on me lasted for years.

He positioned himself not just as a leader but as a person that I would naturally respect. I would listen to him more than others because he was kind and made me feel important, even if to him I wasn't at the time.

When it comes to company culture, kindness, compassion, and gratitude can put you and your team in a state of creativity, motivation, belonging, and many other positive vibrations. These acts will not only make you and your team happy at work but will also help your team thrive, perform better, and produce results for the organization.

If you become kind to someone, there is a good chance that she will be kind to you or someone else. If you show compassion to someone in need, someone else from your team will do so too, as Jason did for Laura. If you genuinely say "thank you" to someone from your team, she will likely learn from you and thank someone else, as Alicia did. These acts not only create meaningful and stronger connections among the team members but also create a ripple effect of positive emotions across the organization.

Sometimes, if you do not like someone or hold a grudge towards someone, it might be hard for you to be kind or compassionate or even thankful to the person. But remember that these acts also make you happy. They release tension between two people and help make a stronger connection. Kindness and compassion always have a high return on investment for you and others. If your work environment is toxic, by not practicing kindness and compassion, you are also helping the culture to remain toxic. Hatred only increases hatred. This is clichéd, but it is true. One way to tackle that is to practice the opposite—a culture of kindness, compassion, and gratitude. The toxic environment should not define you, whether as an employee or a leader. If you are a kind person or have compassion and gratitude toward others, do your part anyway. You owe it to yourself more than to them.

DEALING WITH CONFLICTS

Rachel is a single mother and a business analyst. She drops her son at the childcare facility and then starts work at 8:30 a.m. and leaves at 3:30 p.m. to pick up her son. She does not take a lunch break, and if needed, she works on the weekend. She has flexible working arrangements with her manager. She is a valuable team member and always delivers.

One day, she found that her manager had taken another role and would be leaving soon. She became a little worried about her flexible working arrangement. When the new manager joined, he seemed friendly to the team and started to understand how his team worked. But he noticed that Rachel was the only one with a flexible working arrangement in the team. No one else had one. The new manager didn't think that was fair to the other team members so, he caught up with Rachel and mentioned that she had to think of an alternative to stay till 5:00 p.m. like the others.

Rachel became very worried and upset, as she had been working the existing flexible working hours for a while. She had been outstanding and had no issues. So she stood up for herself and politely made her points. But the new manager was not easily convinced. He said, "I understand the context, but I believe everyone should be treated equally."

Without having any other options, Rachel involved human resources. They had a meeting and agreed that the existing arrangement for Rachel would continue for another eight weeks. The manager would see whether this worked for the team and the organization, and they would have another review after that.

In the next few weeks, Rachel did not do anything extra to impress her manager. She performed and collaborated with her colleagues face-to-face or on video conferencing, and business continued as usual.

The manager noticed and noted his remarks. Two months later, in the review with HR, the manager said, "Earlier, I mentioned fairness for everybody. I realized that sometimes one size does not fit all, we are all different, and I underestimated your abilities to perform in your flexible arrangement. I'm happy for you to continue with your existing hours." Even though it was a conflicting situation, Rachel's manager learned and decided what was best for Rachel, his team, and the organization.

It was a good outcome.

But what if the manager didn't learn and was holding on to his belief of fairness? The manager's ego would kick in, and he would try to defend his position about fairness. And Rachel's ego would tell her that the flexible working had worked for four years already and there was no reason not to continue. See, your ego will not allow you to be open to any change because you will be tempted to stick to what you said already. If you are reading this as a manager, you might think you should stick to your guns no matter what. But if you are reading as an employee, you might think you should fight for your entitlements.

That's where conflicts are born.

We are all part of someone's story, and that someone's beliefs are likely to be different to ours. Conflicts are meant to happen not only at work but also in life in general. It is essential to understand that we are all driven by our beliefs and values as human beings—you and I included. You just cannot expect others to always understand your beliefs, as they are driven by their own beliefs and not yours.

If you are in a conflict situation, the first thing to acknowledge is that the other person is driven by her own beliefs (e.g., fairness for all), and your own beliefs (e.g., one size does not fit all) can be very different. Your brain's job is to abide by your beliefs no matter what. Any potential change creates a threat to your brain, and you start to worry. Some people can adapt to changes better than others. You may decide to hold on to your existing beliefs, and that's the default behavior for most people. But that strategy will not work. Your ego will influence you. The ego is one of your brain's ways to stick to your beliefs. From that standpoint, it is almost impossible to resolve a conflict situation with another person, because her brain will also do the same.

It does not matter who is right or who is wrong. Being right or wrong is only a perspective from the person saying it and is entirely driven by her beliefs. For example, if you have only seen the clear sky without clouds, it will be blue for you, and you will believe the sky is blue. If someone else sees the sky with clouds, she will believe the sky is grey. Both of you are right. But this is a rare condition when no one wins.

Accept and respect that other person is (and will be) different to you. This acceptance is not about being defeated in the conflict. Instead, accepting and respecting the other person's position (e.g., the sky can also look grey) will help you become more open and understanding to the other person with empathy.

Regardless of what you believe about the conflict situation, chances are you may not know the other person's full story. Yes, maybe she has wronged you. Yes, maybe it is hard for you to be empathetic, but think about it; she did all of this because the sky looks grey to her.

You may think you must win the conflict with another person for whatever reason. But ask yourself who is stressing out every day. Who is constantly worrying about winning? There is a good chance that you are. If that is the case, you will need to set yourself free from that, rather focusing on what is best for both parties. How can you create a win-win situation?

Honestly, some conflicts do not add any value to you. Ask yourself whether it is worth the fight. How is it making you feel on a daily basis? Often, we forget our own mental well-being in the endeavor to win over another person. Sometimes, letting go of your ego and choosing an easier option is healthier and is needed for you and the other person to move on.

Even if you think you have won over the other person and you may feel good for some time, your hedonic adaptation will kick in, and eventually that good feeling will go away. Over time, you will notice that fight you were in to win did not even matter, and you will find that the many sleepless nights worrying about it, the calls to other people for support, and anything else that you might have done to win the conflict was in vain.

If you are in a conflict, complementing and flattering the other person often works very well (unsurprisingly, as almost everybody likes to receive compliments). One of the hardest yet most powerful things that you can do when it comes to conflict resolution is to take responsibility and apologize when appropriate (don't let you ego dictate but choose wisely). You may think you would never apologize to the other person, as you are right and she is wrong; however, either party who can take that initiative of apologizing can benefit both. Professor Dacher Keltner from UC Berkeley said, "Really interesting study showing just simply saying you are sorry in the heat of a moment where you may have sort of pushed too hard can lower stress."

And finally, if you have the courage to be the bigger person and forgive the other person for her wrongdoings, you save yourself from holding a grudge. Forgiving the other person is really for you and your happiness more than the other person.

In a conflict situation, there are many things to consider, but I have learned to understand and respect the other person's point of view. As human beings, people are not perfect and may lack skills—communication skills, emotional skills, or leadership skills. I'm just part of his story, and that is not permanent. I put my emotional well-being first. Often, it is just healthier to let go of my ego and choose the easier option.

It is not always worth stressing yourself out for other people. It is much easier and safer for you and your mental well-being to be open to understanding the other person's side of the story and his or her motivation, and to then ask yourself what you can do to create a win for yourself and the other person—not as a manager or employee, but as a human being.

IF YOU HATE YOUR BOSS

Steve is a business analyst, and he has been part of his team for a few years, but he thinks that his boss plays favorites with the team. Only two people get most of the credit and recognition. Others, including him, do not get enough recognition for their work and always feel like second-class citizens in the team. Over time, all those disappointments have piled up for Steve, and he is considering quitting because he hates his boss.

A Harvard business review survey revealed that 58 per cent of people say that they trust strangers over their bosses. Your boss could be one of the primary reasons why you may hate your job.

If you are like Steve, you are not alone. According to a study by Gallup that looked at 7,000 US adults, about 50 per cent of people leave an organization because they do not get along with their managers. If you are employed and part of a team, you will always have someone managing you, and she will also be managed by someone else.

That's just how it is.

An article published by CNBC mentioned that playing favorites by managers is at the top of the list of the behaviors that employees hate the most. Taking credit for employees' work and not recognizing them, making informal threats to fire them, making romantic advances towards employees, and mentioning poor performance to coworkers are some of the top ten sabotaging behaviors by managers.

In the conflict section, I mentioned that everyone in an organization, including you and your boss, is driven by his or her unique beliefs and core values. What you truly believe in your core and your boss's beliefs can be very different on the same subject (The sky is blue or grey). Another study mentioned that 58 per cent of managers say that they did not receive any management training. That makes a lot of sense and explains some of the negative behaviors by the managers.

Even managers who get management training hardly change their core values unless they adopt them and consciously implement their learnings. We have developed this belief that managers are supposed to be honest and open, treat everyone equally, communicate better, and have so many other desirable traits. But the truth is, the managers are just like other people who play the role of managing you. They are not perfect, and they have many shortcomings, like everybody else.

If you are the employee with the best skills and results from among your peers, you will have a better chance to be the leader of your team. If that happens, you might be happy and excited to get promoted to that role and have some level of authority over your peers for the first time. You may not receive any management training before transitioning to your new role, because of other organizational priorities. But you will be expected to perform your role as a leader, and you must deal with uncomfortable situations and make decisions involving your previous peers, which you never had to do before.

And guess what? As a new leader, you will likely make decisions that will upset some of your team members. You might become a pain in the neck to some of them over time, not because you are right or wrong, but because your beliefs and values will not align with those of some of your team.

Remember, being a people manager is a skill in itself and has very little to nothing to do with any other professional skill that you had before. If you keep learning the principles of a good leader and apply them to your employees consistently, over time, you will become a better leader. Your employees will value and admire you for that.

Now think about your boss you hate.

Ask yourself, "Is he a new manager? Has he got management training? How many years of experience he has as a manager?" He might be experienced, but was he a successful leader in the past, or is he an absolute idiot who just wants to use his power and get what he wants? Such people do not deserve to be leaders, but sadly many of them are.

You likely already know why you hate your manager, but if you ask these questions to yourself, you might get different perspectives. I personally came across a few managers who didn't perform well as leaders. One example is that of a manager who speaks for fifty minutes in a sixty-minute meeting, while the other eight team members get only ten minutes (often less) to discuss. You get the idea.

Was he a new leader? Yes. Did he improve over time? Not really. He lacked leadership, listening skills, and determination and did not learn as a leader. But some leaders do get better at leading their teams. When you become a new leader and genuinely want to serve your employees, would you not learn from your mistakes and deserve a second chance? I'm sure most people would.

But yes, your boss can make your life miserable if you are managed by an abusive person.

So what are your options?

After spending fifteen years in corporate business, I understood that there would be no perfect boss for me who would be there for me forever. Even if I had a boss earlier who was seemingly perfect, my current boss was not perfect. Well, I had my time with my perfect boss, and it was finished. My first option was to take another role and gamble for a new seemingly perfect boss in another team or organization. And I might get a better one. But this way, my happiness at work would be at the mercy of my fate of having a boss that I love.

What are the odds?

Remember, you are responsible for your own happiness. This is a change in perception. Your boss is not perfect, and it is not his job to make you happy (even though many think this way).

Please read that again.

It is your job.

The second, and most viable, option is understanding that we are highly driven by our beliefs, values and emotions. Loving or hating your boss are also your emotional responses. The quality of your relationship with your boss determines your emotional response towards your boss. And there is no guarantee that you will have a perfect boss at work.

Does that mean that you cannot be happy at work?

No. You totally can.

Sometimes, it is not the problem you need to solve but the perception you need to change.

The reason why your second option is most viable is that it is backed by thousands of data points from hundreds of studies. Focus on the four pillars of happiness (PERK) at work, and understand how empathy, kindness, gratitude, and compassion play in your daily interactions with your boss and peers. What can you do on your part consistently to make a difference in your relationship with your boss? Your boss is also a human being and craves to be treated with kindness, empathy, and compassion.

But yes, of course, after you have tried these things for a while and nothing has worked, and your boss has turned out to be a complete idiot, sure, get a new boss, by all means. If you think that your boss has done something abusive, unethical, or unfair, you may escalate the issue with human resources, and the issue can be taken care of by them.

However, if you always complain about every move that your boss makes, you might have to watch your own thought pattern. For some people, complaining about the boss is a habit, and they will always have issues with their bosses (no matter how many new bosses they get). If you find that to be the case for yourself, you should be your own boss.

Remember, your boss is not perfect and makes mistakes, but in a work context, bosses need to be trained and build up skills to manage employees in ways that facilitate good leadership.

If you can consciously try being empathetic, grateful, kind, and compassionate with people at work, including your boss, that is probably the best investment. It wouldn't hurt to try thinking about the good things that your boss has done for you, genuinely complimenting your boss, empathize with his position, or doing an act of kindness. You, as a human being, have these qualities in you. Even if your boss does not respond as you would like, you still are the bigger person.

Most people spend half of their waking hours at work, and the person in charge of you can influence a lot about how you feel every day.

But if you own your happiness and consciously use PERK strategies, you will own how you feel at work, and not your boss.

REFLECTION

As long as you work in an organization, you will always work with people. You will inevitably come across people you like, but there will be some you won't like. Honestly, there isn't much you can do about changing their behavior. But by using PERK strategies, you can learn to change your own behavior. If you can do that, it will help you stay happy and satisfied at work.

CREATING A HAPPY WORKPLACE

"Coming together is a beginning; keeping together is progress; working together is success."
—Edward Everett Hale

WHY CREATE A HAPPY WORKPLACE?

In 1880, John was the owner of a farm in Idaho. He had a few people working for him. As the busiest season of the year was approaching for harvesting crops, John urgently needed at least one more full-time farmer to get through the season. A few days later, two guys showed up for the job. John spoke to both of them separately. Both seemed to have enough skills and experience. John became a little confused, and he actually needed a tie-breaker to offer the job. He looked at their physical builds for strength because farming is hard work and requires a lot of energy. He decided to offer the job to the one who had the better physical build and was stronger.

In those old days, many roles required physical strength. Over a couple of hundred years, we have seen the emergence of various technologies, including artificial intelligence and robotics. In today's workforce, physical strength generally is not a tie-breaker anymore. Rather, creativity, problem-solving, having a proactive and can-do attitude, and other things like these are at the top of the list for hiring managers. These are purely human skills and are not specific to any industry or profession. These qualities apply to almost any team today.

Employers look for these prime human skills in their employees, depending on the role. Suppose you have advertised a role in which the candidate needs to be creative, and you have found that person. You would expect her to produce consistent creative results in some way that helps your business. But how can she produce consistent creative results in her role? Being creative is a human quality that no machine (including AI) can do as well as human beings. Your employee's creativity will surely wax and wane depending on how she feels in her environment. If she feels safe and comfortable at work, she will be more creative; if not, she will struggle.

Many studies suggest that the prime human qualities most employers look for in a candidate come down to one thing: how happy and safe your employees feel at work.

While quite a number of studies support this, I would like to highlight a few related to productivity, which is the most common trait that employers look for in any existing employee or a potential candidate. A research by Oxford University's said business school in collaboration with British multinational telecoms firm BT, has found a conclusive link between happiness and productivity. Other studies found that people are 31 per cent more productive when their brains are at positive states. When it comes to sales, they are 37 per cent better. When they are in positive states their dopamine levels rise which not only make them happy but also it turns on all of the learning centers on their brains which helps them learn quicker and perform better. One of the recent article in Forbes (which analyzed a number of other studies) concluded that employee happiness is a leading indicator of profitability and productivity. I can go on and on with more references but the point is, most companies want to thrive, make differences in people's lives, make a profit, and hit their business goals. But it was not until recent times that productivity, creativity, performance, and many other desired qualities were linked with employee well-being and happiness. That's why most businesses are not even aware of how important their employees' well-being and mental states are, and what roles those states play in their success.

You already know that your individual success depends on how happy you are. Likewise, the success of your business depends on how happy your people and customers are.

If you are the leader of a business, you know, in most cases, that your employees are the front door of your company. Ultimately, customers do not usually care who the owner of the business is as long as they are being served to their expected levels. At the end of the day, what matters for any business is happy, loyal, and returning customers.

One way to make your customers happy is through great customer service. The experience you give to your customers is given by your employees. Now, it is a no-brainer that a happy employee would provide a better experience to your customers than an unhappy employee. You do not need science to tell you this. But think about it—would you go back to a shop where you were not treated well or not given the attention and care you expected? Probably not.

If you are a business leader and you are not already doing so, it is never too late to invest in the happiness and well-being of your employees. Professor Jennifer Aaker and her team from Sanford Business School wrote in their business case for happiness, "We care, because investing in happiness, both for employees and customers, drives profit for firms. For example, employees are more likely to come up with a creative idea when they are in a better mode than normal, and customers will pay more for a great experience." If you are the leader of an organization and your people are not satisfied or motivated at work, they feel less purpose and more stressed. They also have less engagement and lack positive emotions. Also, they feel less resilient and have a lot of uncertainty.

Also, it is not only about new hires. It is even more important for the existing people in your organization so they can flourish in their own uniqueness and willingly contribute to your business. So their successes become yours. The only reasonable way to achieve that is by caring about their mental well-being and happiness. Employees are more creative, proactive, ambitious, responsible, and, of course, productive if they are happier. In today's world, to thrive, you will need people who are happier and not necessarily physically stronger.

You might think, "What about the skills?"

Happy people learn better than unhappy people. In one study by the Harvard Graduate School of Education, they wanted to find out how much happiness matters when it comes to learning. They wrote, "The answer is clear. It matters a lot."

Did you know that in recent years almost 50 per cent of every dollar spent in the United States eCommerce market went to Amazon? According to a CNBC report in 2018, this totals about $258 billion. The founder of Amazon, Jeff Bezos, said, "I work with people who are missionaries for what they do. The only way to do it is with happy people. You cannot do it with miserable people watching the clock all day." People like Jeff know the importance of happiness for their employees. They focus on and invest in their people's happiness, which is one of the reasons behind their success.

As a business leader, you know that your people run your business. If you help them become happier, they will help your business thrive.

HAPPINESS FIRST AND THEN SUCCESS FOLLOWS

Tim said, "Jack, you are fired. Even though you are the top performer, you are not a good fit for the rest of the team." Jack was saddened, as he brought in over 70 per cent of the sales for the company.

Tim is the new owner. He is a world-renowned venture capitalist in Australia. Earlier, before acquiring the company, Tim and his team went through the acquisition process and found that the products and services were great but the marketing and sales were not. The sales team was struggling to convert quality leads to sales. They wanted to find out where the gap was. After a detailed analysis of the sales reports and numbers, they found that Jack was bringing in more than 70 per cent of the sales for the company alone on a seven-member sales team, and the other six members were bringing the rest, which seemed to be very odd and lopsided.

Tim wanted to find out why.

Earlier, Tim met and spent some time with the previous management, and he wanted to discover their wins and challenges. After talking to teams and carefully reviewing other reports, he realized the potential of the business, and he decided to acquire it. After the formalities, the first thing Tim did was fire the top performer, Jack.

You might be thinking, "Seriously, why Jack?" Let's find out.

After talking to the sales team members individually, Tim found that Jack was performing the best, but he was undermining everyone else. He was generating toxicity within the team. The previous leadership was focusing only on the numbers generated by Jack and ignoring the rest of the team. As a result, the rest of the team members were not trusting each other. They were always let down by the previous leadership, were not given enough opportunities, and did not have appreciation either. In other words, the rest of the team was very demoralized, and they stopped trying to make sales. They believed that no matter how hard they tried, they would never be appreciated within the company.

After Jack was fired, Tim revamped the whole team, inspired the employees with the company's mission, and created a culture of trust and collaboration. They became more empathetic and kinder to each other and started to believe in themselves more than ever before.

Tim's whole company became happier.

The salespeople were able to push their boundaries, and in the next eight to ten months, the sales team was able to increase the company-wide sales by 33 per cent with everyone's contribution.

The happier your employees are, the more success they will bring to your business.

The widely used classic (but mistaken) formula for happiness and success is that if you work hard enough, you will achieve success, and then you will become happy. That is how most of us have been programmed and what we grew up believing. Every time you have a success, you have a little boost of happiness, like a spike, and then it fades away, and you set a higher target, and the same pattern repeats, so your lasting happiness is always on the other side of success.

Author Shawn Achor is one of the world's leading experts in relation to happiness and success. In his TEDx talk, he said, "The real problem is our brain works in the opposite order. If you can raise somebody's levels of positivity in the present, then their brain experiences what we now call a happiness advantage, which is your brain at positive performs significantly better than it does at negative, neutral, or stressed, your intelligence rises, your creativity rises, your energy level rises. Your brain is 31% more productive than your brain at negative, neutral, or stressed. You are 37% better at sales, doctors are 19% faster and more accurate at coming up with correct diagnosis."

Whether for individuals or businesses, success works the same way because every team in business is nothing but a collection of people.

Every business leader wants success for his or her company. I believe that if you are a leader, you do too. A positive environment and a positive culture for your employees are critical. World-leading companies like Google, Facebook, Zappos, and many others are constantly investing in their employee well-being programs. They ask how they can implement strategies so their employees feel at ease and have a better environment and culture to allow them to be and stay happy at work. That way, companies get the most and best out of their employees.

Basically, every business wants more performance and productivity from their employees. That means that more employee engagement will be required, which is unlikely to happen unless your employees are happy and cared for.

It is easy to think companies like Google, Facebook, Apple, and the like produce amazing products and services, but it is their employees who make all the difference. These brands would not be where they are today if their employees were not at their best, which requires them to be happy and fulfilled at work.

HOW TO MAKE YOUR ORGANIZATION HAPPIER

I hope that even if you are not totally convinced yet, you may have started to think about how you can create a more positive and happier culture in your organization.

When we talk about people's happiness in your organization, what does it really mean?

Happiness at work is still relatively new for many businesses and leaders. The link between employee happiness and business success is slowly becoming more visible and tangible.

As a business leader, you may be wondering, "Well, I get it, but where or how do I start this process in my organization?"

There are truly unlimited ways you can achieve this. But the best approach would be to develop a framework recommended by the world's leading happiness researchers and systematically implement those strategies in your organization to create that positive change.

Dr. Emiliana Simon Thomas is a leading expert on neuroscience and psychology of compassion, kindness, gratitude, and other pro-social skills from the University of California–Berkeley. She said, "And we look at the scientific evidence about the factors that most reliably support or contribute to happiness at work, we find four key pillars, purpose, engagement, resilience, and kindness." In short, P-E-R-K.

The PERK strategies we discussed in this book are inspired from the study of hundreds of successful organizations—how they operate, motivate, and inspire their people through the company's mission and purpose; sustain that motivation and engagement; and create cultures with empathy, kindness, and resiliency; as well as how those initiatives resulted in their business successes.

The vision or mission of your company can be accelerated by making your employees happier.

You already know that happiness is much more than just feeling good at work. For your employees, it is also about having a true purpose, having an overall sense of enjoyment, and being internally motivated (rather than just receiving a paycheck or bonus) to make progress towards their goals that align with your business. They feel that they truly matter with their individual contribution.

When it comes to implementing PERK, it must be understood and actioned across the whole organization. If you are a business leader and you have five thousand employees, it can be challenging to make your people understand and implement the concept of PERK. But it needs to start somewhere. You may remember that PERK spans across three levels. Firstly, what can you do as a leader on your own to implement PERK? Secondly, how can you use PERK with your direct reports and peers? And finally, how can PERK be implemented at every level of your organization in different teams?

One way to start implementing PERK is by first finding out your organization's current state. Then analyze and define strategies to implement the PERK model and implement it across the business. It can be started with one team being the pilot for a few months and measuring the team's happiness and performance over time. When you get positive results, educate the other teams and implement the model (or similar model) in them. Your teams will need multiple iterations to adjust and tweak to find out what works for them. Every team has its own dynamics and operates differently and so the strategies might not be exactly same.

You want to ensure your leadership team follows this model by walking the talk and implements PERK at every level across the organization. Once PERK is implemented, it is important to maintain the momentum, as this is an ongoing process. People within your organization will understand, appreciate, and become happier. And when that happens, the success of your business will only accelerate in a positive direction.

If the whole organization operates as one team and that one team is happy, that team can not only make your business thrive but can also change the world for the better.

HOW TO INSPIRE EMPLOYEES WITH THE COMPANY'S PURPOSE

KPMG is one of the world's leading professional services firms, originally founded in 1818. Over time, it has evolved and gone through mergers, but the KPMG we know today was founded in 1987 and has become one of the world's big four accounting organizations. In 2020, they had a revenue of $29.22 billion, and they have over two hundred twenty-seven thousand employees worldwide. According to Harvard Business Review, KPMG could "convince" their employees that they could change the world.

KPMG has always been a purpose-led organization. But just having a purpose for the organization is not enough to inspire people. KPMG shared, "Most importantly, we recognized that just telling people from the top down about their higher purpose would not succeed. We encouraged everyone—from our interns to our Chairman—to share their own stories about how their work is making a difference."

KPMG has its employees annual surveys to understand how they feel in general and how they relate to the organization. They also have a "purpose initiative." Six months later, 85 per cent of its employees said it was a great place to work. Communicating a higher purpose within the company at all levels raised engagement and morale. 76 per cent of the employees said their "job had special meaning (and was not just a job.).."

A few years ago, KPMG launched an initiative to strengthen their people's pride, engagement, and emotional connection to the company by encouraging them to recognize and celebrate the meaning of the positive impact of their work. They started asking questions like, "What do you do at KPMG?" and invited employees globally to share their own purpose-driven stories. The company wanted ten thousand stories, but they ended up with forty-two thousand. These stories were then featured in the campaign across a variety of channels, including print, digital, and various electronic live communications.

Daniel works for KPMG, and he said, "I help farms grow." When family farms and ranches need loans, KPMG works with the credit system to help secure them, furthering America's proud tradition of family farming. Notice that Daniel's statement reflects that the farms believe in Daniel. And he feels responsible for helping the farms grow. That's the meaning he gives to his role every day. Jo, Steph, Heidi, and Gary have similar roles. They said, "We restore neighborhoods." KPMG audits development programs that contribute to the revitalization of low-income communities in Boston, which opens new possibilities for every resident. Vinit is another employee at KPMG. He said, "I stop cyber-crime." During a widespread cyber-attack, KPMG collaborated with their client to develop innovative ways to protect critical systems, making the digital world safer. Notice Vinit, Daniel, and others are very clear on their roles at KPMG, and they feel how their work impacts their end customers. It's not a job for them, but rather a responsibility they feel as individuals.

These employees know and feel that they are at KPMG for a purpose.

Research within KPMG found that managers and leaders who talked about the purposeful work with employees were more inspired, motivated, and engaged than the other employees with managers who didn't.

According to Global Purpose Index 2016, 58 per cent of companies from 2013 to 2016 with a clearly communicated and understood purpose organization-wide experienced a growth of 10 per cent. The companies without a genuine purpose and lack of communication showed a drop in company revenue. Also, research from E. Y. Beacon Institute and Harvard Business School shows that companies with purpose are more likely to be profitable.

It is essential that as a leader you become a role model for your employees. For example, do you talk about the business's core values or advocate the purpose in conversations with your leaders and employees? Do they bring up these things in their meetings and negotiations? Is that what you and your leadership team reflect in your communications and attitude towards each other? In other words, as a leader, you are the one who can inspire and motivate your people. It always starts with the leader.

KPMG's story is one of the many ways organizations can inspire and engage their employees. Every employee has his or her own set of core values, and every organization also has its purpose and core values. But are your employees aware of and aligned with your company's mission and core values? As a leader, it is critical for the mental well-being and happiness of your employees to bring those into alignment. Making specific structural changes and implementing PERK strategies across the organization will eventually not only help you succeed in the business but also fulfil your company's purpose.

ARE YOUR EMPLOYEES ENGAGED?

Chris was working on a problem and was looking at his computer screen. One of his team members, John, called him. "Hey Chris," Chris didn't reply. He kept looking at his screen. A few seconds later, John called him again. "Can you hear me, Chris?" Again, there was no reply from Chris. Colin was sitting next to Chris, and he saw that John was calling Chris, but he didn't respond to John, so Colin leaned in and tapped on Chris's shoulder. "Hey, John is calling you," Chris seemed to have been electrified. He said, "Sorry, what?" Colin said, "John is calling you." Chris said, "Ah, okay, sorry, I didn't notice. I was just working on a problem." Chris works for a problem-management team in a large corporate. His job is to find solutions to long-term or reoccurring issues in the company's IT systems. He loves solving problems. When working on a problem, he gets total immersion, loses track of time, and forgets his surroundings. He experiences the state of flow.

In the PERK model, we are talking about the E for "engagement," which does not relate only to asking a bunch of survey questions to your employees on how engaged they are in a year; It is much deeper than that. Professor Dacher Keltner from the University of California–Berkeley said that engagement is really autonomy, curiosity, and flow. A leader of an organization would probably want to understand how the employees are being engaged and how he or she can facilitate those three elements in the employees so they feel engaged in their roles.

For your employees, you want to ask three questions, "Do they experience flow? Do they have autonomy? Are they curious?"

One of the most important elements of the facilitation of flow is minimal distraction. Distractions can include internal messaging services like Skype, Teams or Slack, constant checking of emails, interruptions by colleagues (as Chris was interrupted by Colin), received phone calls. Flow is not about encouraging work in a silo but is rather about immersion in what someone is doing with enjoyment, and respect of that immersion by others on the team.

When employees in an organization experience flow very frequently during the day, they are much more productive and have satisfaction with what they do. Their performance increases for particular tasks. Employees can experience flow from almost everything they love doing, including solving problems, creating new designs, having conversations, or presenting in meetings. Employees who love their roles are more likely to experience flow than those who do not.

Kirk is a project manager for a multinational company. His current project delivery time and funds are very tight, and he is responsible for ensuring that the project is finished properly on time and within the budget. He has three full-time employees in his project. But he realized that he initially underestimated the efforts, and halfway through, he needed at least one more person to complete this project on time. But there was no budget for hiring contractors. However, he originally put aside $20,000 for any additional equipment the project might need. He had two options: to either keep that $20,000 untouched and risk the project missing the deadline or to spend $10,000 of that to hire a contractor to finish the project. After talking to the project team, he realized that the need for additional equipment was not very high. So he decided to hire a contractor with that additional money and was able to finish the project two days before the deadline without asking the program manager for more money.

This is a classic example of autonomy. But it relates not only to spending money but also to how employees do things in terms of process, innovation, efficiency, and so forth. Google allows its employees to spend 20 per cent of their time exploring and enquiring about what their employees are interested in, which might benefit Google. Professor Keltner also talked about the opposite of autonomy, where people feel micromanaged or bored and constrained, either by managers or in any other way, which makes things hard for engagement. One of the qualities of the work is the sense of freedom that the employees have.

When it comes to autonomy, freedom must be associated with responsibilities. Remember, Kirk had the freedom to spend that $20,000, but he also was responsible for finishing the project properly and on time. There must be a balance when both freedom and responsibility complement each other. Over many years, Netflix has learned to create a culture in which freedom and responsibility are harmonious. It has built an innovative culture in which its employees know and understand how exactly they create value for their customers and Netflix. Patty McCord, former chief talent officer at Netflix, said, "We didn't mean to give freedom to people to do anything. We coupled freedom with responsibility. It also implies reliability and deliverables."

As Professor Keltner mentioned, another way to increase employee engagement is curiosity. A couple of years ago, Logi (formerly Logitech) made a deep investment in employee training specifically focused on strengthening the skills of PERK. They found more meaning and joy. Most importantly, they found more inspiration in their work. They focused on human-centered experiences. They made high-quality connections with their peers and wider team members, solved problems as a team, had meaningful conversations, and were curious about the other team members. Their employees did strength assessments to gain insight into their strengths and learned to use them at work.

Whether it is Netflix, Logi, Google, or any other company, they understand how critical their employees are for their business. If your employees are not engaged and inspired when they come to work, you are not getting enough value from them for the paycheck you give to them. Great organizations pay attention to this, and by investing in their employees, they are constantly improving their culture of innovation, autonomy, and engagement and still getting the job done.

Not all your employees look, talk, perform, contribute, and innovate the same way. They are all different, but they all bring their own strengths and diversity to your business's mission and success.

But they can do it best when they are truly engaged at work.

HOW DO YOUR EMPLOYEES HANDLE STRESS?

Rachel has moved to a new team. But working with her new boss has made her life very difficult. She said, "He never appreciates anything that I do correctly but picks up the smallest things and makes me feel guilty about them. I feel like he does not trust me enough to give me responsibilities. And it is almost impossible to make him happy. He has always got this tough look on his face. He does not make himself approachable. It is also impacting my personal and social life, as I'm working extra hours, but it feels like I'm not going anywhere in my life. I feel anxious most of the time at work."

Rachel contacted HR after a few weeks, and they suggested taking two weeks of stress-related leave. In the meantime, HR contacted Rachel's manager. He said, "If someone cannot take the pressure, she should consider another role. In fact, I was not aware of her stress. She never told me about it. I thought everything was normal and didn't think she needed any help. I'm not sure what else I could have done for her."

After Rachel's leave finished, she was not willing to go back to work. She said, "I doubt I can go back to work and deal with this person. Earlier, I constantly felt anxious about making mistakes and not being valued or appreciated around him. I have never felt so low."

HR arranged individual meetings with Rachel and with her manager. From the conversations, the HR manager understood and said, "I do not think our line manager had a good understanding of work-related stress, and we may not have trained our managers on that line enough. We have a plan for Rachel and her manager and spoke to them individually."

A few weeks later, Rachel received a call from her manager, and after the conversation, she felt much more comfortable and returned to work only two days a week. She said, "I had a conversation with my manager. He called me, and he mentioned that the hard work that I had put in, he noticed, but he didn't think that he needed to explicitly appreciate my work to me. He thought I was just doing my duties, and I did what I meant to do. The appreciation part he missed out, which he realized after HR pointed it out to him. He also said that he would be open to hear any issue that might come in the future from my side and will try to be supportive."

She also said, "I needed to change my perception as well. When I got back to work, I started to talk with my team members more than I did before. We started to have regular meetings, and now my manager also appreciates the little things. Most importantly, he made me feel that I'm part of the team and I matter."

Her manager conceded, "HR asked me when was the last time I appreciated Rachel for her good work, but I could not remember any. That was a big one for me, because

I never thought I needed to appreciate the people on my team for their regular duties. HR has now arranged for me some more leadership and employee well-being training. The new things that I picked up from the conversation with HR have enabled me to look after Rachel and other people on my team. They are now more collaborative and seem encouraged to do their work than before—and, most importantly, more open and engaged."

Over time, many experienced managers develop their own styles of managing people. But they are not always open to learning or improvement as managers. Rachel was stressed out, and she suffered alone and did not share her issue with anyone but HR; her manager had no idea.

If you are the leader of your organization, it is essential that your line managers in various teams understand the work-related stress for your employees and how they can support them to alleviate their suffering. Many studies show that to ensure mental well-being, satisfaction, and engagement for your employees to create a culture of resilience, your line managers need to be aware and take action on how their people handle stress. Do they have enough time off? Do they have flexible working arrangements? Do they have support when they need it? Are the employees being who they are, or are they trying to just fit in? Do they feel safe? How efficiently can your employees bounce back when they are stressed out or have a setback at work or in their families?

All of these questions promote resilience inside your organization.

One of the ways to calm your mind is by practicing mindfulness. Many organizations have started to provide sessions for their employees to practice mindfulness at work to calm themselves during the day. They encourage people to take proper lunch breaks or go for a walk, provide gym access, and offer various other benefits, including childcare facilities in some companies. They also run sessions for their employees to become more socially and emotionally intelligent, which helps them create better social connections and trust.

Salesforce CEO Marc Benioff is a promoter of mindfulness, meditation, and yoga. He said to CNBC, "We do have a yoga class at Salesforce.com for our employees twice a week." There is no one type of practice that suits every organization, but companies that care about the mental well-being of their employees make a difference with mindfulness. They promote various activities within the organization to help their people do their jobs efficiently and increase performance by making sure they are happy and satisfied at work.

Often, we see many organizations promote people to managerial positions because they were good at their previous non-managerial roles. Such a person may not have prior management experience, or companies may ignore the importance of skilling the person before promoting her to a new managerial role. As mentioned previously, according to studies, 58 per cent of managers did not receive any management training. As a result, once the person is an employee after the promotion, suddenly she has power that she never had before. Now she is a manager without leadership skills. So she starts to lead using what she thinks about leadership instead of learning fundamental leadership skills. The leader who got promoted may be excited, but the team members may be worried. As human beings, when we are given some level of power because of our titles or promotions, we behave differently.

Professor Dacher Keltner from UC Berkeley said, "When we feel powerful, we read people's emotions less effectively, we express gratitude less effectively, we are less able to take the other people's perspective." He talked about another study where he found that people show less kindness and compassion to somebody describing something serious as a form of suffering in their lives. Even with experienced managers, this is not very uncommon. Some managers like to micromanage because it gives them a chance to practice their power more often and feel more powerful each time they practice that behavior. Often, we see people interrupting and talking over others or using their mobile phones at meetings, listening not to understand but to reply. Many people tend to behave in these ways when they feel powerful; Scientists call this phenomenon a power paradox.

In the PERK model, R stands for the resilience of your employees and how they handle pressure and stress at work. If they are resilient enough, they and their work suffer less. Stress is universal, and you cannot get rid of this. It is part of who we are, but managing and handling stress is key to being and staying happy at work.

At the end of the day, as a leader, it is important that the people you manage are stressing less, are not suffering alone, are being who they truly are, and are getting the support they need from you and your leadership team so they feel appreciated, more engaged, inspired, and resilient, and so they trust you more as their leader.

THE BOSS OVERHEARD HER CONVERSATION AND …

Emily had just gotten off the phone with a customer. She took her headset off and stretched her shoulders. She looked very tired. She was working in a customer service center in a very big enterprise. One of the top executives, Tom, was walking past and heard part of her conversation with the customer and noticed that she was tired and did not look very excited at work.

He came to Emily's desk. He didn't know her name, but he noticed her badge. He said, "Hi Emily, I'm Tom. How are you going?" Emily said, "I'm good, how are you?" with a smile. Tom said, "I'm great. I just wanted to say hi, and I kind of overheard your conversation with the customer, and you have done a great job on that. I liked it." Emily said, "Thanks, Tom, for noticing." Tom continued, "I also wanted to check on you, as you look a bit tired and probably need some rest. Are you feeling okay? is there anything that we can do to help?" Emily was tired, but she smiled and said, "Nah, I'm fine. It's just that today is my birthday but I'm working today. But no big deal, I'm good." Tom said, "Ah, okay. Happy birthday, Emily. I shall tell your manager so you can knock off a little early today, and you have a wonderful day," Emily was pleasantly surprised, and her face lit up with a smile. "Really? Thank you very much, Tom. You made my day." Tom smiled and walked away.

A small act can go a long way. Emily felt that her company cared for her. This little thirty-second conversation with Tom made her day. She felt important. She felt that she belonged in a place where she felt safe. Great leaders take care of their employees by having little one-on-one conversations with employees with kindness and empathy. Emily's company employs more than forty thousand people worldwide, and they understand how employee satisfaction works.

A few weeks later, Emily and her team got an announcement from the senior leadership team that every employee would have a paid day off once a year on their birthdays.

One of the basic elements of human nature is feeling important. It does not matter who you are or where you work; this is true for you, me, and everybody else. One of the best ways to deal with others in almost any circumstance is to employ empathy and compassion, such as by asking a simple question like "How would I feel if I were in her position?" We may not be born with a lot of empathy skills, but we can all learn them. One extremely important thing I learned from the executive chairman and former CEO of LinkedIn, Jeff Weiner, is that empathy is feeling what someone is feeling, but compassion is feeling what another person is feeling and doing something about it. In short, compassion is empathy plus action. Jeff learned this many years ago from a book by the Dalai Lama in which he explains the difference between empathy and compassion this way.

Jeff Weiner, in a commencement speech, said, "The long-term value of a company is based on the speed and quality of its decision-making. It's hard to make better decisions faster when people on the team lack trust in one another and are constantly questioning each other's motivations. In an environment like that, you'll spend most of your time navigating corporate politics rather than focusing on the task at hand. I've been there, and it's no fun. The flip side is developing a culture with a compassionate ethos. That's what our leadership team has tried to do at LinkedIn—create a culture where people take the time to understand the other person's perspective and not assume nefarious intentions; build trust; and align around a shared mission. After nearly ten years, I still celebrate the fact we can make important decisions in minutes or hours that some companies debate for months. Create the right culture, and you create a competitive advantage."

After Facebook's former chief operating officer Sheryl Sandberg suddenly lost her husband in 2015, Mark Zuckerberg and his wife, Pricilla Chan, supported Sheryl and her family in many ways to help her navigate the difficult times. But Mark and his leadership team at Facebook didn't just stop there. They realized that people who work for Facebook are like everyone else. They are all human beings, have families and kids, have older parents, and have other responsibilities, but when a death happens in a close or wider family, it is always a shock to everyone in the family. Facebook decided to honor its employees, and they changed their bereavement leave policy in the wake of Sheryl's personal loss. Now their employees are entitled to twenty days of paid bereavement leave, which is double what they had before.

In the PERK model, compassion, kindness, empathy, and gratitude are keys to building a culture that creates and enhances trust, innovation, collaboration, and many other desirable qualities in your employees.

Suppose you have an employee who spends more than one-third of her day at your company. If she spends ten years in your company, that means (excluding four weeks of annual leave) she would have spent 19,200 hours (800 straight days) in the environment that you have given as her leader. Would it be fair for her to ask that you give her such an environment, where she feels good, comfortable, valued, and respected? Everyone deserves to be treated with kindness and compassion, including you and me.

Whether it is your customers, community, or employees businesses always revolve around people, not the other way around.

MEASURING EMPLOYEE HAPPINESS AND ENGAGEMENT

As a business leader you might wonder how to know whether the PERK strategies and policies are working and making employees more engaged and happier at all levels? One obvious way is to measure happiness and engagement for employees at regular intervals and link this back to business performance numbers. This is an iterative process.

If you can have regular deep and meaningful conversations with a person, you can generally tell whether she feels a sense of purpose, is inspired, is engaged, or is happy. Often, we hide our emotions from others, and some people are good at this. Happiness and true fulfilment are very internal emotions, and it is not enough to just ask employees general social questions (e.g., "How are you?" "How was your weekend?" "Are you okay?"). While these questions provide some context, they are not deep enough to accurately measure the happiness and engagement of your employees.

That's why happiness researchers have designed specific survey questions that help measure happiness and engagement for employees in an organization. As mentioned previously, the Oxford Happiness Scale (Part 2, Chapter: "Measure Your Happiness") is one of them, which has twenty-nine specific questions that can accurately measure the happiness of your employees on a scale of 1 to 6.

Then there are a number of employee engagement questions that you can send out to your employees to find out their engagement levels. Companies like Culture Amp, Gartner, and others are already helping organizations with engagement surveys. In addition, organizations can add to the surveys their own specific questions they are interested in. Also, things like age groups, ethnicities, hobbies, and such can help. For example, if you analyze data for hobbies of your employees and 30 per cent of them say they love football, you may later organize a football match as a bonding event in your organization. This is just one idea among many possibilities.

The data you extract from those happiness and engagement measurements with your employees' permission can be analyzed and compared with business performance metrics. Then you can identify the areas where you would need to make improvements.

Then to model a strategy to implement policies.

Finally, implement those strategies and review the progress of employee engagement and business performance numbers (iterative).

So how frequently should a business leader measure employee engagement? It depends on how committed you are to taking meaningful actions for employee well-being and happiness to enhance business success. For example, Warby Parker has half-yearly surveys sent out to their people, and some organizations check their employee happiness and engagement levels every quarter.

Some world-leading companies take their employees' well-being very seriously. For example, the tech giant Hitachi has published a report to measure their employee happiness using wearable technology. In short, in addition to self-report, they also track employee physical activity, and they have done extensive research on this. They found that by considering their employees' self-reports and physical activities, they can more accurately measure their happiness.

Hitachi has a dedicated happiness unit that gathers voluntary ongoing physiological and self-reported data about employee happiness. The company believes that if their employees are happier, that increases innovation, improves management quality, and increases productivity and revenue.

As mentioned previously, Harvard Professor Daniel Gilbert and other scientists have used various methods to measure human happiness, including fMRI, brain scans, measurement of dopamine levels, and many other techniques, but it turns out that self-report surveys are almost as good as using those technologies in a lab environment. In fact, scientists have been measuring happiness for people in their studies by asking survey questions for many years.

Depending on where your organization is on this journey, for starters, you can get your employee happiness and engagement levels measured, get a happiness consultant involved, and take the next steps from there. I'm sure once you get the ball rolling, you will see how implementing PERK strategies can change your organization for the better.

REFLECTION

Like you and me, your employees are also human beings. They have emotions. They have the same needs and feelings as you and me. If your business is not making money, you might be stressed out. Then you go out and tell them that they must hit their sales target within a short time.

Guess what?

They will also get stressed out. How can a business thrive when the leader and the employees are stressed out?

Feeling pressure and having stress are part of our human emotions. We cannot avoid them, but stress related to work can be reduced by practicing the PERK strategies at senior leadership, mid-management, and employee levels.

Unfortunately, many leaders are very good at making people anxious. Employees get things done for them in exchange for high stress, sleepless nights, health issues, and the like. Over time, they all add up, and employees experience chronic anxiety, high stress levels, and sometimes even depression. According to a Gallup survey, about 67 per cent of employees in the US are not engaged. That is alarming for businesses, as it costs (Gallup estimates) somewhere between $483 to $605 billion annually in lost productivity. Globally these numbers are even higher.

There is a saying that goes, "Do not push your loyal employees to the level that they do not care anymore." Many leaders and managers use the fear factor to get things done by their employees.

What they really need to do is care.

Your caring will give your employees a sense that they belong and matter, which is one of the basic human needs.

That is true for you and me.

Professor Cynthia D. Fisher from Bond University, Gold Coast, Australia, published an article on happiness at work, citing 180 research studies. She said,

"Happiness at work is likely to be the glue that retains and motivates the high-quality employees of the future."

Sir Richard Branson is the founder of Virgin Group. The group owns more than forty companies in thirty-five countries, employs seventy-one thousand employees worldwide, and has been in the industry for over forty years. Richard said, "Clients do not come first. Employees come first. If you take care of your employees, they will take care of the clients."

What simple initiatives can you take right away to start to take care of your employees more?

Take a piece of paper and come up with some ideas you like.

If you are not doing so already, I invite you to focus and invest in your employees' happiness at work and join the global movement of a better and happier world that your organization is also part of.

MY EMBARRASSING STORY AND CONCLUSION

It was a Saturday, and my wife and I invited some close friends to our place for lunch. We cooked for them, they came over, and we had some great times together. Then we got into chatting, refreshing memories from the past. And without even realizing it, the time went by so fast that it was soon almost dinner time. But we ran out of the food that we had cooked, so we decided to go out to a restaurant. Everybody left our house and got into their cars and were waiting for us to come out so we could go together.

But I couldn't find my car key. I looked in my desk drawer, where I usually keep it. It wasn't there. I looked around the house but couldn't find it. After ten minutes or so, one of my friends came inside and asked, "What happened? What's taking you so long?" I said, "I lost my car key and cannot find it anywhere." He said, "Let us help you find it." All of my friends started to look around our house. They were very close and were familiar with our place. They looked under the couch, under the dining table, and inside the indoor plants, and after spending another twenty minutes, none of us had found my car key. So I told them, "You guys go ahead and settle down at the restaurant. In the meantime, I shall find it, and I will join you guys there."

It was very frustrating and embarrassing that I lost my key and none of us could find it. Some of my friends were even making fun of me. I felt more annoyed that not only my car key but also a bunch of other keys were on the same key ring.

After a few minutes, I was standing outside the house, trying to think of when and where I last saw my key. As I was thinking, I unconsciously put my hand in my back pocket. Suddenly I felt something. I usually keep my wallet in there, but it felt like something different, and I took it out.

Surprise! There was my car key.

I had been so absent-minded that I hadn't looked in my own pocket. The whole time, the key was with me, and I felt more embarrassed for not looking in my pocket, where the key was most likely to be found. But after I found it, I felt good, even though my friends were looking at me in disbelief. I was smiling, and we went out for dinner. My friends talked about how absent-minded I was for a long time.

Many years later, as I'm writing the conclusion of my book, I'm still smiling, but when I think about my happiness, it feels like the car key incident. When I was in my twenties and thirties, I used to look for my happiness everywhere but within myself, striving for things like getting a dream job, being approved for a credit card, buying a new car, fitting in with a friend's group, and so on. The time, effort, and money I spent to chase happiness in things, places, and other people kept me in a loop of constant searching. I was expecting other people to make me happy, but over time I realized that it is not their job to make me happy. Their job is to make themselves happy.

I also realized I wanted my happiness on my terms. But I didn't know my own terms. How strange was that? Like many others, I was told who should be my friends, which career path I should I choose, criteria to fall in love with, and where and when I should I travel. And I had hundreds of opinions imposed on me.

As a result, I lost myself and had no idea what my own terms were.

Like my car key, my happiness key was with me the whole time. I had to just look inside me. I started asking better questions to myself and honestly answered them. "What business do I want to be in?" "Where do I want to travel?" "Whom do I love?" "What is my dream?" "What job do I genuinely love and care about?" "How much money do I want to make?" "What would I spend it on?" "How do I want to be seen?" "What is my legacy?"

The answers to these questions are some of my terms.

Your terms and happiness are always with you. When you look inside yourself and honestly embrace them, you will make different decisions and take meaningful actions to be happy on your terms.

I sincerely thank you for taking the time to read my book, but do you remember the two simple questions I asked in the preface?

No matter who you are, what you do, or what you have, you want to ask yourself,

Do you live a happy life?

And do you have a satisfying life?

I believe that reading my book has enabled you to look inside yourself in an inspiring way and you will confidently say yes to both.

NOTES

PART 1: CHAPTER: THE POWER OF HAPPINESS

1. Wikipedia, "Tal_Ben-Shahar," last edited on 31 January 2025, at 18:29 (UTC), https://en.wikipedia.org/wiki/Tal_Ben-Shahar
2. Seph Fontane Pennock, "Positive Psychology 1504: Harvard's Groundbreaking Course," positivepsychology.com, 16 Jun, 2015, https://positivepsychology.com/harvards-1504-positive-psychology-course/
3. TED, "Robert Waldinger: What makes a good life? Lessons from the longest study on happiness | TED," YouTube video, 0:35, 10th Apr, 2025, https://www.youtube.com/watch?v=8KkKuTCFvzI&t=1s
4. Audrey Hamilton, "Recent Generations Focus More on Fame, Money Than Giving Back," www.apa.org, https://www.apa.org/news/press/releases/2012/03/fame-giving
5. Wikipedia, "John Dewey," last edited on 9 April 2025, at 17:01 (UTC) https://en.wikipedia.org/wiki/John_Dewey
6. Goodreads, "John Dewey > Quotes," www.goodreads.com, 10th Apr, 2025, https://www.goodreads.com/author/quotes/42738.John_Dewey
7. TEDx Talks, "TEDxBloomington - Shawn Achor - "The Happiness Advantage: Linking Positive Brains to Performance," YouTube video, 10:29, 10th Apr, 2025, https://www.youtube.com/watch?v=GXy_kBVq1M
8. Sonja Lyubomirsky, The How of Happiness (Piatkus, 2010), 25.
9. Ephrat Livni, "A Nobel Prize-winning psychologist says most people don't really want to be happy," qz.com, 21 Dec, 2018, https://qz.com/1503207/a-nobel-prize-winning-psychologist-defines-happiness-versus-satisfaction
10. Big Think, "Can technology make us happy?," Video, 00:56, 10 Apr, 2025, https://bigthink.com/videos/can-technology-make-us-happy
11. Leslie Williamson, LinkedIn, 10th Apr, 2025 https://www.linkedin.com/in/leslie-williamson-a506662a
12. Susie Steiner, "Top five regrets of the dying," www.theguardian.com, 1 Feb 2012, https://www.theguardian.com/lifeandstyle/2012/feb/01/top-five-regrets-of-the-dying

PART 1: CHAPTER: THE DEFAULT LIFE

13. WORLD.MINDS, "Dan Gilbert: Happiness: What Your Mother Didn't Tell You (2018 WORLD.MINDS Annual Symposium)," YouTube video, 9:21, 10th Apr, 2025, https://www.youtube.com/watch?v=b1Y2Z1BGwno
14. TED, "The surprising science of happiness | Dan Gilbert," YouTube video, 1:05, 10th Apr, 2025, https://www.youtube.com/watch?v=4q1dgn_C0AU&t=399s
15. The Aspen Institute, "Stumbling on Happiness with Daniel Gilbert," YouTube video, 6:20, 10th Apr, 2025, https://www.youtube.com/watch?v=GXy_kBVq1M
16. World Happiness Report, WHR 2019, page 88, 10th Apr, 2024, https://s3.amazonaws.com/happiness-report/2019/WHR19.pdf
17. World Happiness Report, WHR 2025, page 17, page 20, 10th Apr, 2025, https://happiness-report.s3.us-east-1.amazonaws.com/2025/WHR+25.pdf
18. Wikipedia, "GDP ranking" last edited on 3 April 2025, at 19:36 (UTC), https://en.wikipedia.org/wiki/List_of_countries_by_GDP_(nominal)

19. World Health Organization, "Depressive disorder (depression)," 10th Apr, 2025, https://www.who.int/news-room/fact-sheets/detail/depression
20. Wikipedia, "Midlife crisis," last edited on 12 January 2025, at 05:16 (UTC), https://en.wikipedia.org/wiki/Midlife_crisis
21. ADAA, "What are anxiety and depression?," 10th Apr, 2025, https://adaa.org/understanding-anxiety/facts-statistics
22. Happify, "90 Percent Of People Say They Have A Major Regret. Here's How To Move Past It," Huffpost.com, 26 Jun, 2014, https://www.huffpost.com/entry/regret-infographic_n_5529641#:~:text=90%20Percent%20Of%20People%20Say,Move%20Past%20It%20%7C%20HuffPost%20Life
23. JEFF HADEN, "New Research Reveals What People Regret Most of All: 5 Ways to Make Sure You Never Do," www.inc-aus.com, 4 Jun, 2018, https://www.inc.com/jeff-haden/new-research-reveals-what-people-regret-most-of-all-5-ways-to-make-sure-you-never-do.html
24. JEFF HADEN, "Research Shows People Become Increasingly Unhappy Until Age 47.2. Here's How to Minimize the Negative Effect of the 'Happiness Curve'," www.inc-aus.com, 10th Apr, 2025, https://www.inc.com/jeff-haden/scientists-just-discovered-mid-life-crisis-peaks-at-age-47-heres-how-to-minimize-effect-of-happiness-curve.html
25. 99U, "Brené Brown: Why Your Critics Aren't The Ones Who Count," YouTube video, 21:58, 10th Apr, 2025, https://www.youtube.com/watch?v=8-JXOnFOXQk

PART 1: CHAPTER: MY QUEST FOR LIFE BY DESIGN

26. Team Tony, "FEEL GOOD NOW," www.tonyrobbins.com, 10th Apr, 2025, https://www.tonyrobbins.com/leadership-impact/feel-good-now/
27. Wikipedia, "Tao Porchon-Lynch," last edited on 20 October 2024, at 13:56 (UTC), https://en.wikipedia.org/wiki/Tao_Porchon-Lynch
28. BETSY FARBER, "How This 98-Year-Old Yoga Teacher and Ballroom Dancer Stays Young," www.dance-teacher.com, 24 Jul, 2017, https://dance-teacher.com/how-this-98-year-old-yoga-teacher-and-ballroom-dancer-stays-young/
29. Confucius Quotes, "Confucius Quotes," www.brainyquote.com, 10th Apr, 2025, https://www.brainyquote.com/quotes/confucius_136802
30. LOGAN CHIEROTTI, "Harvard Professor Says 95% of Purchasing Decisions Are Subconscious," www.inc-aus.com, 27 Mar, 2018, https://www.inc.com/logan-chierotti/harvard-professor-says-95-of-purchasing-decisions-are-subconscious.html
31. WebMD Editorial Contributors, "Anatomy and Circulation of the Heart," https://www.webmd.com, 24 April, 2023, https://www.webmd.com/heart-disease/guide/how-heart-works
32. Netflix documentary, Human, the world within, 2021, pulse
33. Ali M Alshami, National Library of Medicine, "Pain: Is It All in the Brain or the Heart?," pubmed.ncbi.nlm.nih.gov, 14 Nov, 2019, https://pubmed.ncbi.nlm.nih.gov/31728781/
34. Howard E. LeWine, MD, Chief Medical Editor, Harvard Health Publishing, "A Broken-heart syndrome (takotsubo cardiomyopathy)," www.health.harvard.edu, 13 Jun, 2023, https://www.health.harvard.edu/heart-health/takotsubo-cardiomyopathy-broken-heart-syndrome
35. Stanford, "Steve Jobs' 2005 Stanford Commencement Address," YouTube video, 9:47, 10th Apr, 2025, https://www.youtube.com/watch?v=UF8uR6Z6KLc&t=307s
36. Goodreads, "Jim Rohn > Quotes > Quotable Quote," www.goodreads.com, 10th Apr, 2025, https://www.goodreads.com/quotes/1798-you-are-the-average-of-the-five-people-you-spend
37. Quotefancy, "Oprah Winfrey Quotes," quotefancy.com, 10th Apr, 2025, https://quotefancy.com/quote/879847/Oprah-Winfrey-The-way-through-the-challenge-is-to-get-still-and-ask-yourself-What-is-the
38. Brainyquotes, "Henry Ford Quotes," www.brainyquote.com, 10th Apr, 2025, https://www.brainyquote.com/quotes/henry_ford_122817
39. Mikhaila Friel, "Prince Harry implied that it was his decision to leave the royal family, not Meghan Markle's," www.insider.com, 20 Jan, 2020, https://www.insider.com/prince-harry-his-decision-leave-royal-family-not-meghan-markle-2020-1

NOTES

PART 1: CHAPTER: THE SCIENCE OF HAPPINESS

40. Museum of Science, "Positive Psychology: The Science of Happiness | Tal Ben-Shahar," YouTube video, 4:40, 10th Apr, 2025, https://www.youtube.com/watch?v=wBWejfL0xOA
41. Courtney E. Ackerman, MA., "What Is Positive Psychology & Why Is It Important?," www.positivepsychology.com, 20 Apr, 2018, https://positivepsychology.com/what-is-positive-psychology-definition/
42. Copernicus, "Daniel Gilbert, Happiness: What Your Mother Didn't Tell You," YouTube video, 1:20:20, 10th Apr, 2025, https://www.youtube.com/watch?v=7VuKfSdZWlg
43. The Guardian, "Take the Oxford Happiness Questionnaire," www.theguardian.com, 03 Nov, 2014, https://www.theguardian.com/lifeandstyle/2014/nov/03/take-the-oxford-happiness-questionnaire
44. Sonja Lyubomirsky, The How of Happiness (Piatkus, 2010), 20, 21.
45. Seph Fontane Pennock, "Who Is Martin Seligman and What Does He Do?," www.positivepsychology.com, 20 Sep, 2016, https://positivepsychology.com/who-is-martin-seligman/
46. Maria Cramer, "Smile? The results from the 2020 World Happiness Report Are In," www.nytimes.com, 20 Mar, 2020, https://www.nytimes.com/2020/03/20/world/europe/world-happiness-report.html
47. Melissa Madeson, Ph.D., "Seligman's PERMA+ Model Explained: A Theory of Wellbeing," www.positivepsychology.com, 24 Feb, 2017, https://positivepsychology.com/perma-model/

PART 1: CHAPTER: YOUR HEART, TIME, AND DECISIONS

48. Stephanie Watson, "Amazing Facts About Heart Health and Heart Disease," www.webmd.com, 2 Jul, 2009, https://www.webmd.com/heart/features/amazing-facts-about-heart-health-and-heart-disease

PART 2: CHAPTER: MEASURE YOUR HAPPINESS

49. The Guardian, "Take the Oxford Happiness Questionnaire," www.theguardian.com, 03 Nov, 2014, https://www.theguardian.com/lifeandstyle/2014/nov/03/take-the-oxford-happiness-questionnaire
50. P. Hills and M. Argyle, "Personality and Individual Differences," in The Oxford Happiness Questionnaire: a compact scale for the measurement of psychological well-being, 2002, 1073–82.
51. Sonja Lyubomirsky, The How of Happiness (Piatkus, 2010), 86.

PART 2: CHAPTER: HOW TO RECOVER FROM A SETBACK

52. SAMANTHA SCHNURR, "8 Celebrities Who Struggled More Than The Average Twenty-Something," www.businessinsider.com, 19 Jan, 2014, https://www.businessinsider.com/celebrities-who-struggled-in-their-twenties-2014-1?IR=T#walt-disney-ate-dog-food-5
53. Olivia Singh, "35 celebrities who have opened up about their struggles with mental illness," www.businessinsider.com, 16 May, 2020, https://www.businessinsider.com/celebrities-depression-anxiety-mental-health-awareness-2017-11?amp&fbclid=IwAR2deL_5uwk7UMnr4q5fjvevJHWvrokY7ZJ8hU-iftn5yLGMNZucvJACAL0
54. Diana Pearl, "The Fight to Fame: 14 Stars Who Struggled Before They Made it Big," www.people.com, 8 Apr, 2016, https://people.com/celebrity/stars-who-struggled-before-they-were-famous/?amp=true&fbclid=IwAR2Ya7-YpHOek2WgM5Nt7z690hGfEoSHvbXHmOvHIM80XYAOC-5U1i-1npY
55. Sonja Lyubomirsky, The How of Happiness (Piatkus, 2010), 154, 164, 167.
56. Daily Motivation, "Life is happening for you and not to you - Tony Robbins," YouTube video, 0:48, 10th Apr, 2025, https://www.youtube.com/watch?v=CWWoRLuLsUQ

57. Goalcast, "Why Am I Even Alive? | Muniba Mazari Speech | Inspiring Women of Goalcast," YouTube video, 5:40, 10th Apr, 2025, https://www.youtube.com/watch?v=LIF5BnugxYM

58. Madeleine A. Fugère Ph.D., "Don't Underestimate Your Psychological Immune System," www.psychologytoday.com, 15 Apr, 2020, https://www.psychologytoday.com/au/blog/dating-and-mating/202004/don-t-underestimate-your-psychological-immune-system

59. SIRI CARPENTER, "We don't know our own strength," www.apa.org, Oct, 2001, https://www.apa.org/monitor/oct01/strength

60. Seph Fontane Pennock, "50+ Positive Psychology Quotes: Our Favorite Reflections," www.positivepsychology.com, 11 Oct, 2014, https://positivepsychology.com/positive-psychology-quotes/

61. Sonja Lyubomirsky, The How of Happiness (Piatkus, 2010), 21.

62. Courtney E. Ackerman, MA., "What Is Neuroplasticity? A Psychologist Explains [+14 Tools]," www.positivepsychology.com, 15 Jul, 2018, https://positivepsychology.com/neuroplasticity/

PART 2: CHAPTER: HOW MUCH MONEY DO YOU NEED

63. Belinda Luscombe, "Do We Need $75,000 a Year to Be Happy?," www.content.time.com, 6 Sep, 2010, http://content.time.com/time/magazine/article/0,9171,2019628,00.html

64. PresidentialConf, "Prof. Dan Gilbert -- The Science of Happiness: What Your Mother Didn't Tell You," YouTube video, 8:10, 11:05, 10th Apr, 2025, https://www.youtube.com/watch?v=BwQFSc9mHyA

65. Robert Kiyosaki, The Cashflow Quadrant (TechPress, Inc, 1998), Sonja Lyubomirsky, The How of Happiness (Piatkus, 2010), 185-196.

66. Wikipedia, "Yanni," last edited on 8 April 2025, at 21:37 (UTC), https://en.wikipedia.org/wiki/Yanni

67. Celebritynetworth, "Yanni Net Worth $50 Million," www.celebritynetworth.com, 1 Mar, 2024, https://www.celebritynetworth.com/richest-celebrities/singers/yanni-net-worth/

68. Brainyquote, "Yanni Quotes," www.brainyquote.com, 10th Apr, 2025, https://www.brainyquote.com/quotes/yanni_541593

69. Wikipedia, "List of best-selling books," last edited on 7 April 2025, at 22:35 (UTC), https://en.wikipedia.org/wiki/List_of_best-selling_books

70. Heather Taylor, "How Rich Are JK Rowling, James Patterson and the Other Top 10 Richest Authors?," www.nasdaq.com, 19 Oct, 2023, https://www.nasdaq.com/articles/how-rich-are-jk-rowling-james-patterson-and-the-other-top-10-richest-authors

71. Brainyquote, "J. K. Rowling Quotes," www.brainyquote.com, 10th Apr, 2025, https://www.brainyquote.com/quotes/j_k_rowling_454009

72. https://www.brainyquote.com/authors/j-k-rowling-quotes

73. ABOVE INSPIRATION, "Put God First - Denzel Washington Motivational & Inspiring Commencement Speech," YouTube video, 5:56, 10th Apr, 2025, https://www.youtube.com/watch?v=BxY_eJLBflk

74. PresidentialConf, "Prof. Dan Gilbert -- The Science of Happiness: What Your Mother Didn't Tell You," YouTube video, 11:30, 10th Apr, 2025, https://www.youtube.com/watch?v=BwQFSc9mHyA&t=773s

75. Matthew Brown, "Fact check: Bill Gates has given over $50 billion to charitable causes over career," www.usatoday.com, 11 Jun, 2020, https://www.usatoday.com/story/news/factcheck/2020/06/11/fact-check-bill-gates-has-given-over-50-billion-charitable-causes/3169864001/

76. Hayley C. Cuccinello, "Elon Musk Has Promised To Give At Least Half His Fortune To Charity. Here's How Much He's Donated So Far," www.forbes.com, 8 Sep, 2020, https://www.forbes.com/sites/hayleycuccinello/2020/09/08/elon-musk-has-promised-to-give-at-least-half-his-fortune-to-charity-heres-how-much-hes-donated-so-far/?sh=6940bbcf3c8c

PART 2: CHAPTER: HOW TO ALLOW YOURSELF TO BE HAPPY

77. Team Fearless, "After This You'll Change How You Do Everything! - Tony Robbins," YouTube video, 10:30, 10th Apr, 2025, https://www.youtube.com/watch?v=CVP1CwEBz_Y

78. Jessica Swainston, Ph.D., "What Is Cherophobia? How to Overcome a Fear of Happiness," www.positivepsychology.com, 3 Dec, 2020, https://positivepsychology.com/cherophobia/

79. Netflix documentary, The Call to Courage, 2019.

PART 3: CHAPTER: MEANING

80. Marc Randolph, Private group conversation, 2018 Aaron Sansoni event in Melbourne.
81. Wikipedia, "Netflix," last edited on 8 April 2025, at 13:37 (UTC), https://en.wikipedia.org/wiki/Netflix
82. STEVE MOLLMAN, "Blockbuster 'laughed us out of the room,' recalls Netflix cofounder on trying to sell company now worth over $150 billion for $50 million," www.fortune.com, 14 Apr, 2023, https://fortune.com/2023/04/14/netflix-cofounder-marc-randolph-recalls-blockbuster-rejecting-chance-to-buy-it/
83. RITOBAN CHAKRABARTI, "#9 Out of 10 Start-ups Fail. Here's Why!," www.entrepreneur.com, 14 Jun, 2017, https://www.entrepreneur.com/article/295798
84. TED, "The new era of positive psychology | Martin Seligman," YouTube video, 19:27, 10th Apr, 2025, https://www.youtube.com/watch?v=9FBxfd7DL3E&t=2s
85. Ashley Lazaro, personal email and personal interview with the Author, 2019.
86. Medhavi Arora, "From filthy to fabulous: Mumbai beach undergoes dramatic makeover," www.edition.cnn.com, 22 May, 2017, https://edition.cnn.com/2017/05/22/asia/mumbai-beach-dramatic-makeover/index.html
87. James M. Rochford, "New Age Spirituality," www.evidenceunseen.com, 1 Mar, 2024, https://www.evidenceunseen.com/world-religions/new-age-spirituality/
88. Wikipedia, "Ruth Bader Ginsburg," last edited on 1 April 2025, at 05:59 (UTC), https://en.wikipedia.org/wiki/Ruth_Bader_Ginsburg

PART 3: CHAPTER: FLOW

89. Jeremy Sutton, Ph.D, "Mihály Csíkszentmihályi: The Father of Flow" positivepsychology.com, 31 Mar, 2025, https://positivepsychology.com/mihaly-csikszentmihalyi-father-of-flow/
90. Wikipedia, "Mihaly Csikszentmihalyi," last edited on 16 March 2025, at 05:43 (UTC), https://en.wikipedia.org/wiki/Mihaly_Csikszentmihalyi
91. TED, "The new era of positive psychology | Martin Seligman," YouTube video, 19:33, 10th Apr, 2025, https://www.youtube.com/watch?v=9FBxfd7DL3E&t=199s
92. Sonja Lyubomirsky, The How of Happiness (Piatkus, 2010), 188.

PART 3: CHAPTER: LOVE & CONNECTIONS

93. TED, "Robert Waldinger: What makes a good life? Lessons from the longest study on happiness | TED," YouTube video, 1:59, 10th Apr, 2025, https://www.youtube.com/watch?v=8KkKuTCFvzI
94. Berit Brogaard D.M.Sci., Ph.D, "How does Love Affect Happiness?," www.psychologytoday.com, 9 Mar, 2015, https://www.psychologytoday.com/us/blog/the-mysteries-love/201503/how-does-love-affect-happiness
95. Melissa L Davey, "Loneliness study finds one in five Australians rarely or never have someone to talk to," www.theguardian.com, 9 Nov, 2018, https://www.theguardian.com/australia-news/2018/nov/09/loneliness-study-finds-one-in-five-australians-rarely-or-never-have-someone-to-talk-to
96. National Library of Medicine, "Loneliness at epidemic levels in America," www.ncbi.nlm.nih.gov, 28 Jun, 2020, https://www.ncbi.nlm.nih.gov/pmc/articles/PMC7321652/
97. BBC, "Dunbar's number: Why we can only maintain 150 relationships," www.bbc.com, 9 Oct, 2019, https://www.bbc.com/future/article/20191001-dunbars-number-why-we-can-only-maintain-150-relationships
98. TED, "The power of vulnerability | Brené Brown | TED," YouTube video, 7:10, 10th Apr, 2025, https://www.youtube.com/watch?v=iCvmsMzlF7o
99. JESSICA STILLMAN, "Use the Magic 5:1 Ratio to Improve All Your Relationships," www.inc-aus.com, 31 Jul, 2020, https://www.inc.com/jessica-stillman/use-magic-51-ratio-to-improve-all-your-relationships.html

100. Wikipedia, "John Gottman," last edited on 29 March 2025, at 07:49 (UTC), https://en.wikipedia.org/wiki/John_Gottman

PART 3: CHAPTER: PLEASURE

101. TED, "The new era of positive psychology | Martin Seligman," YouTube video, 17:10, 10th Apr, 2024, https://www.youtube.com/watch?v=9FBxfd7DL3E&t=199s
102. USC Schwarzenegger Institute, "Mission," schwarzenegger.usc.edu, 10th Apr, 2024, http://schwarzenegger.usc.edu/about-the-institute/mission

PART 3: CHAPTER: HEALTH

103. World Health Organization, "WHO remains firmly committed to the principles set out in the preamble to the Constitution," www.who.int, 10th Apr, 2024, https://www.who.int/about/governance/constitution
104. Stephanie Watson and Kristeen Cherney, "The Effects of Sleep Deprivation on Your Body," www.healthline.com, 10th Apr, 2025, https://www.healthline.com/health/sleep-deprivation/effects-on-body#Prevention
105. TEDx Talks, "Happy Brain: How to Overcome Our Neural Predispositions to Suffering | Amit Sood, MD | TEDxUNI," YouTube video, 3:07, 10th Apr, 2025, https://www.youtube.com/watch?v=KZIGekgoaz4&list=PLPvbbwL31HUTLk5nRhWJqciD2H68ER67C
106. Steve Bradt, "Wandering mind not a happy mind," news.harvard.edu, 11 Nov, 2010, https://news.harvard.edu/gazette/story/2010/11/wandering-mind-not-a-happy-mind/
107. National Library of Medicine, "Toward mapping the human body at a cellular resolution," www.ncbi.nlm.nih.gov, 1 Aug, 2018, https://www.ncbi.nlm.nih.gov/pmc/articles/PMC6085824/
108. Kelly Burch, "How many days a person can survive without food or water," www.businessinsider.com, 4 Sep, 2021, https://www.businessinsider.com/guides/health/diet-nutrition/how-long-can-you-go-without-food
109. SUCCESS, "TED Talks: 'The Surprising Science of Happiness'," www.success.com, 8 Feb, 2017, https://www.success.com/ted-talks-the-surprising-science-of-happiness/

PART 3: CHAPTER: ACHIEVEMENTS

110. Wy-Lene Yap, "Richard Tan: The Man Behind A $100 Million Business Providing Educational Content," www.hnworth.com, 13 Oct, 2017, https://www.hnworth.com/article/spotlight/influential-brands/richard-tan-the-man-behind-a-100-million-business-providing-educational-content/
111. Peter Ludwig, Adela Schicker, The End of Procrastination (Murdoch Books, 2018), 47-63.
112. Ana Gajić, "Facebook Live Statistics," 99firms.com, 02 Mar, 2024, https://99firms.com/blog/facebook-live-stats/#gref
113. Wikipedia, "Randi Zuckerberg," last edited on 22 November 2024, at 11:10 (UTC), https://en.wikipedia.org/wiki/Randi_Zuckerberg
114. CNN Business, "Randi Zuckerberg on growing up with Mark," YouTube video, 0:48, 10th Apr, 2025, https://www.youtube.com/watch?v=zvd_RfQxsc4
115. Randi Zuckerberg, personal interview with author in Hack Success event, Sydney 2018.
116. Jim Kwik, "HOW TO GET UNSTUCK & BECOME CREATIVE," www.jimkwik.com, 29 Jul, 2019, https://www.jimkwik.com/podcast/kwik-brain-139-how-to-get-unstuck-become-creative
117. Joe Robinson, "Does Pursuing Our Passions Really Make Us Happier?," www.huffpost.com, 25 Jan, 2011, https://www.huffpost.com/entry/pursuing-passions-happiness_b_812881#:~:text=Robert%20Vallerand%20from%20the%20University,barrage%20of%20pressures%20and%20strife
118. Wikipedia, "Broaden-and-build," last edited on 1 January 2025, at 11:40 (UTC), https://en.wikipedia.org/wiki/Broaden-and-build
119. Ron Dicker, "Joe Biden Is Playing Way Less Golf Than Donald Trump Did As President," www.huffpost.com, 17 Sep, 2021, https://www.huffpost.com/entry/joe-biden-golf-donald_trump_n_614457c0e4b0556e4dd76c24

NOTES

120. Daniel Dale and Holmes Lybrand, "Fact check: Trump has spent far more time at golf clubs than Obama had at same point," www. edition.cnn.com, 25 May, 2020, https://edition.cnn.com/2020/05/25/politics/fact-check-trump-obama-golf/index.html

121. Herald Sun, "Areeb Alam is the youngest Aussie to complete a half-marathon, and he's already got his sights set on a bigger goal.," www.heraldsun.com.au, 6 Aug, 2017, https://www.heraldsun.com.au/subscribe/news/1/?sourceCode=HSWEB_WRE170_a_FBK&dest=https%3A%2F%2Fwww.heraldsun.com.au%2Fnews%2Fvictoria%2Fareeb-alam-is-australias-youngest-person-to-complete-halfmarathon%2Fnews-story%2F8b7afb536e5f4b53412d11bf5dcebb2f&memtype=anonymous&mode=premium&v21=GROUPB-Segment-2-NOSCORE

PART 4: CHAPTER: YOUR HAPPINESS IS YOUR RESPONSIBILITY

122. Big Think, "Can technology make us happy?," Video, 00:56, 10th Apr, 2025, https://bigthink.com/videos/can-technology-make-us-happy

PART 4: CHAPTER: THREE LANES OF HAPPINESS

123. Wikipedia, "Medical students' disease," last edited on 2 July 2024, at 00:06 (UTC), https://en.wikipedia.org/wiki/Medical_students%27_disease

124. STACY LIBERATORE, "Average person has over 6,000 thoughts per day, according to study that isolated a 'thought worm' in the human brain showing when an idea begins and ends," www.dailymail.co.uk, 17 Jul, 2020, https://www.dailymail.co.uk/sciencetech/article-8531913/Average-person-6-000-thoughts-day-according-study-isolated-thought-worm.html

125. Twitter(X), "Tony Robbins," www. twitter.com, 7 Oct, 2016, https://twitter.com/tonyrobbins/status/784141351646404608?lang=en

PART 4: CHAPTER: HOW TO BE HAPPY

126. Facebook(Meta), "Paulo Coelho," www.facebook.com, 8 Jul, 2021, https://www.facebook.com/story.php?story_fbid=10159097836596211&id=11777366210&p=30&_rdr

127. Heather Rudow, "Indecisiveness can lead to unhappiness in everyday life," www.counseling.org, 16 Dec, 2011, https://ctarchive.counseling.org/2011/12/indecisiveness-can-lead-to-unhappiness-in-everyday-life/#:~:text=This%20can%20then%20translate%20into,or%20applying%20for%20a%20job.

PART 4: CHAPTER: HOW TO STAY HAPPY

128. Sonja Lyubomirsky, The How of Happiness (Piatkus, 2010), 270-294.

129. Tom Bilyeu, "Billionaires Do This Every Morning - End Laziness, Escape Mediocrity & Master Success | Mel Robbins," YouTube video, 19:40, 10th Apr, 2025, https://www.youtube.com/watch?v=LCHPSo79rB4

130. Speakers Spotlight, "Motivation does not cause action, action causes motivation | Neil Pasricha," YouTube video, 4:10, 10th Apr, 2025, https://www.youtube.com/watch?v=FtWkQ-GPaRI

131. Team Tony, "FEEL GOOD NOW," www.tonyrobbins.com, 10th Apr, 2025, https://www.tonyrobbins.com/leadership-impact/feel-good-now/

PART 4: CHAPTER: THE ELEVEN HAPPINESS HABITS

132. Mandy Ferreira, "6 Essential Nutrients and Why Your Body Needs Them," www.healthline.com, 10th Apr, 2025, https://www.healthline.com/health/food-nutrition/six-essential-nutrients
133. Melissa Madeson, Ph.D., "Seligman's PERMA+ Model Explained: A Theory of Wellbeing," www.positivepsychology.com, 24 Feb, 2017, https://positivepsychology.com/perma-model/
134. Sonja Lyubomirsky, The How of Happiness (Piatkus, 2010), 322.
135. The Good Therapy Team, "How Many Friends Does the Average Person Have?," www.goodtherapy.org, 8 Feb, 2019, https://www.goodtherapy.org/blog/psychology-facts/how-many-friends-does-average-person-have-0208197
136. BBC, "Dunbar's number: Why we can only maintain 150 relationships," www.bbc.com, 10th Apr, 2025, https://www.bbc.com/future/article/20191001-dunbars-number-why-we-can-only-maintain-150-relationships
137. Berit Brogaard D.M.Sci., Ph.D, "How does Love Affect Happiness?," www.psychologytoday.com, 9 Mar, 2015, https://www.psychologytoday.com/us/blog/the-mysteries-love/201503/how-does-love-affect-happiness
138. Oliver Tham, personal interview with the Author, 2019.
139. Wikipedia, "History of the telephone," last edited on 25 March 2025, at 19:08 (UTC), https://en.wikipedia.org/wiki/History_of_the_telephone
140. GAIL FINEBERG, "Bell Papers Document Experiments, Family Life," www.loc.gov, April, 2004, https://www.loc.gov/loc/lcib/0404/digitize.html
141. Wikipedia, "Alexander Graham Bell," last edited on 7 April 2025, at 00:00 (UTC), https://en.wikipedia.org/wiki/Alexander_Graham_Bell
142. Wikipedia, "Wright brothers," last edited on 4 April 2025, at 04:43 (UTC), https://en.wikipedia.org/wiki/Wright_brothers
143. Wikipedia, "Apple Inc.," last edited on 4 April 2025, at 17:48 (UTC), https://en.wikipedia.org/wiki/Apple_Inc
144. Wikipedia, "Ronald Wayne," last edited on 1 April 2025, at 11:30 (UTC), https://en.wikipedia.org/wiki/Ronald_Wayne
145. Tiff any, Vietnam orphanage story, personal interview with the Author, 2019
146. Sonja Lyubomirsky, The How of Happiness (Piatkus, 2010), 188.
147. National Library of Medicine, "HAPPY PEOPLE BECOME HAPPIER THROUGH KINDNESS: A COUNTING KINDNESSES INTERVENTION," www.ncbi.nlm.nih.gov, Sep, 2006, https://www.ncbi.nlm.nih.gov/pmc/articles/PMC1820947/
148. Sonja Lyubomirsky, The How of Happiness (Piatkus, 2010), 95.
149. Facebook(Meta), "BuzzFeed," www.facebook.com, 27 Sep, 2017, https://www.facebook.com/BuzzFeed/videos/10156791799070329/?v=10156791799070329
150. Buddha Quotes, "Buddha Quotes," www.brainyquote.com, Mar 2, 2024, https://www.brainyquote.com/quotes/buddha_104025
151. Greater Good Science Center, "Three Good Things," www.ggia.berkeley.edu, 10th Apr, 2025, https://ggia.berkeley.edu/practice/three-good-things

PART 4: CHAPTER: THE 7 EMOTIONAL HABITS

152. Judy Carter, "Can You Laugh Away Anger?," https://www.psychologytoday.com/, 29 Sep, 2014, https://www.psychologytoday.com/au/blog/stress-is-laughing-matter/201409/can-you-laugh-away-anger
153. Healthline, "How to Hack Your Hormones for a Better Mood," www.healthline.com, 2 Mar, 2024, https://www.healthline.com/health/happy-hormone
154. Mayo Clinic, "Stress relief from laughter? It's no joke," www.mayoclinic.org, 2 Mar, 2024, https://www.mayoclinic.org/healthy-lifestyle/stress-management/in-depth/stress-relief/art-20044456
155. Kim Elsesser, "Power Posing Is Back: Amy Cuddy Successfully Refutes Criticism," www.forbes.com, 3 Apr, 2018, https://www.forbes.com/sites/kimelsesser/2018/04/03/power-posing-is-back-amy-cuddy-successfully-refutes-criticism/?sh=35cd5eae3b8e

156. https://journals.sagepub.com/doi/full/10.1177/0956797610383437
157. Team Tony, "TRAIN YOUR BRAIN FOR HAPPINESS AND FULFILLMENT," www.tonyrobbins.com, 22nd Nov, 2019, https://www.tonyrobbins.com/podcasts/how-to-live-in-absolute-abundance/
158. TED, "Your body language may shape who you are | Amy Cuddy | TED," YouTube video, 2:10, 10th Apr, 2025, https://www.youtube.com/watch?v=Ks-_Mh1QhMc

PART 5: CHAPTER: THE SIX-WEEK INTERVENTION PROGRAM

159. Michael Argyle, Peter Hills and Stephen Wright, "Take the Oxford Happiness Questionnaire," www.theguardian.com, 3 Nov, 2014, https://www.theguardian.com/lifeandstyle/2014/nov/03/take-the-oxford-happiness-questionnaire
160. Sonja Lyubomirsky, The How of Happiness (Piatkus, 2010), 95, 107-108, 133-134, 188, 179-180.
161. TED, "The new era of positive psychology | Martin Seligman," YouTube video, 16:40, 10th Apr, 2025, https://www.youtube.com/watch?v=9FBxfd7DL3E
162. Greater Good Science Center, "Three Good Things," www.ggia.berkeley.edu, 10th Apr, 2025, https://ggia.berkeley.edu/practice/three-good-things

PART 6: CHAPTER: STAY HAPPY BY YOURSELF

163. Wikipedia, "How to Win Friends and Influence People," last edited on 6 March 2025, at 16:01 (UTC), https://en.wikipedia.org/wiki/How_to_Win_Friends_and_Influence_People
164. Wikipedia, "You Can Heal Your Life," last edited on 6 April 2024, at 17:43 (UTC), https://en.wikipedia.org/wiki/You_Can_Heal_Your_Life
165. Louise Hay, You can heal your life (Hay House, 1985), Page before introduction.
166. TED, "Robert Waldinger: What makes a good life? Lessons from the longest study on
167. happiness | TED," YouTube video, 0:35, 10th Apr, 2025, https://www.youtube.com/watch?v=8KkKuTCFvzI&t=1s
168. Healthy Psych, "The Study of Authenticity (Positive Psychology Series #3)," www.healthypsych.com, 2 Mar, 2024, https://healthypsych.com/the-study-of-authenticity/#:~:text=In%20one%20study%2C%20researchers%20found,others%20and%20more%20personal%20growth.
169. TED, "The new era of positive psychology | Martin Seligman," YouTube video, 11:12, 10th Apr, 2025, https://www.youtube.com/watch?v=9FBxfd7DL3E
170. Wikipedia, "Michael Schumacher," last edited on 8 April 2025, at 15:29 (UTC), https://en.wikipedia.org/wiki/Michael_Schumacher
171. Michael Schumacher, "Michael Schumacher," www.brainyquote.com, Mar 2, 2024, https://www.brainyquote.com/authors/michael_schumacher
172. Melissa Madeson, Ph.D., "Seligman's PERMA+ Model Explained: A Theory of Wellbeing," www.positivepsychology.com, 24 Feb, 2017, https://positivepsychology.com/perma-model/

PART 7: CHAPTER: STAY HAPPY AT HOME

173. TED, "Robert Waldinger: What makes a good life? Lessons from the longest study on
174. happiness | TED," YouTube video, 6:07, 10th Apr, 2025, https://www.youtube.com/watch?v=8KkKuTCFvzI&t=1s
175. Dale Carnegie, How to win friends and influence people (HarperCollins Publishers 2017), 47.

PART 8: CHAPTER: HOW CAN YOU STAY HAPPY AT WORK

176. JIM HARTER, "Dismal Employee Engagement Is a Sign of Global Mismanagement," www.gallup.com, 10th Apr, 2025, https://www.gallup.com/workplace/231668/dismal-employee-engagement-sign-global-mismanagement.aspx
177. EDX, "BerkeleyX: The Foundations of Happiness at Work," www.edx.org, 10th Apr, 2025, https://www.edx.org/learn/happiness/university-of-california-berkeley-the-foundations-of-happiness-at-work
178. Kris Snibbe, "Mark Zuckerberg's Commencement address at Harvard," www. news.harvard.edu, 25 May, 2017, https://news.harvard.edu/gazette/story/2017/05/mark-zuckerbergs-speech-as-written-for-harvards-class-of-2017/#:~:text=Campus%20%26%20Community-,Mark%20Zuckerberg's%20Commencement%20address%20at%20Harvard,366th%20Commencement%20on%20May%2025.
179. Statista Research DePart ment, "Revenue of NEC Corporation from fiscal year 2014 to 2023," www.statista.com, 14th Mar, 2025, https://www.statista.com/statistics/1222885/nec-corporation-revenue/
180. Wikipedia, "BIRDEM," last edited on 16 March 2025, at 06:51 (UTC), https://en.wikipedia.org/wiki/BIRDEM
181. John F. Helliwell, Richard Layard and Jeffrey D. Sachs, "World Happiness Report," https://worldhappiness.report, 10th Apr, 2024, https://s3.amazonaws.com/happiness-report/2019/WHR19.pdf
182. Imperative, LinkedIn, "2016 Workforce Purpose Index," www.cdn.imperative.com, 10th Apr, 2025, https://40823263.fs1.hubspotusercontent-na1.net/hubfs/40823263/Content%20Downloads/2016%20Workforce%20Purpose%20Index.pdf
183. CNN Business, "Randi Zuckerberg on growing up with Mark," YouTube video, 34:00, 10th Apr, 2025, https://www.youtube.com/watch?v=zvd_RfQxsc4
184. Mike Oppland, BA, MBA, "8 Traits of Flow According to Mihaly Csikszentmihalyi," www.positivepsychology.com, 2 Mar, 2024, https://positivepsychology.com/mihaly-csikszentmihalyi-father-of-flow/

PART 8: CHAPTER: HOW TO STAY HAPPY WITH OTHERS AT WORK

185. David Sturt and Todd Nordstrom, "10 Shocking Workplace Stats You Need To Know," www.forbes.com, 8 Mar, 2018, https://www.forbes.com/sites/davidsturt/2018/03/08/10-shocking-workplace-stats-you-need-to-know/?sh=5704c66f3afe
186. Kerri Anne Renzulli, "50% of people have quit because of a bad manager—here are the 10 boss behaviors workers hate most," www.cnbc.com, 7 Mar, 2019, https://www.cnbc.com/2019/03/07/the-10-bad-boss-behaviors-employees-hate-most.html
187. Peg Streep, "6 Things You Need to Know About Empathy," www.psychologytoday.com, 23 Jan, 2017, https://www.psychologytoday.com/au/blog/tech-support/201701/6-things-you-need-know-about-empathy
188. Camille Preston, PhD, PCC, "Promoting Employee Happiness Benefits Everyone," www.forbes.com, 13 Dec, 2017, https://www.forbes.com/sites/forbescoachescouncil/2017/12/13/promoting-employee-happiness-benefits-everyone/?sh=3c897dd3581a

PART 8: CHAPTER: HOW TO BUILD A HAPPY WORKPLACE

189. University of Oxford, "Happy workers are 13% more productive," www.ox.ac.uk, 24 Oct, 2019, https://www.ox.ac.uk/news/2019-10-24-happy-workers-are-13-more-productive
190. TEDx Talks, "TEDxBloomington - Shawn Achor - "The Happiness Advantage: Linking Positive Brains to Performance," YouTube video, 10:20, 10th Apr, 2025, https://www.youtube.com/watch?v=GXy_kBVq1M
191. Cindy Gordon, "Employee Happiness Is A Leading Indicator Of Profitability And Productivity," www.forbes.com, 30 Oct, 2022, https://www.forbes.com/sites/cindygordon/2022/10/30/employee-happiness-is-a-leading-indicator-of-profitability-and-productivity/?sh=10222b5d1f8f
192. Stanford Business School, "THE BUSINESS CASE FOR HAPPINESS," www.stanford.edu, 13 May, 2012, https://stanford.edu/class/gsbgen542/cgi-bin/files/M345_BusinessCaseHappiness.pdf
193. Ceri Parker, ""You can't do it with miserable people watching the clock all day": Jeff Bezos on work-life harmony," www.weforum.org, 2 Jun, 2016, https://www.weforum.org/agenda/2016/06/you-can-t-do-it-with-

miserable-people-watching-the-clock-all-day-jeff-bezos-on-work-life-harmony/?utm_campaign=buffer&utm_content=buffer16c3f&utm_medium=social&utm_source=facebook.com

194. Ceri Parker, "Watch out, retailers. This is just how big Amazon is becoming," www.cnbc.com, 13 Jul, 2018, https://www.cnbc.com/2018/07/12/amazon-to-take-almost-50-percent-of-us-e-commerce-market-by-years-end.html

195. Greater Good Magazine, "Emiliana R. Simon-Thomas," www.greatergood.berkeley.edu, 10th Apr, 2024, https://greatergood.berkeley.edu/profile/emiliana_simon_thomas

196. EDX, "BerkeleyX: The Foundations of Happiness at Work," www.edx.org, 2 Mar, 2024, https://www.edx.org/learn/happiness/university-of-california-berkeley-the-foundations-of-happiness-at-work

197. Wikipedia, "KPMG," last edited on 3 April 2025, at 07:33 (UTC), https://en.wikipedia.org/wiki/KPMG

198. Bruce N. Pfau, "How an Accounting Firm Convinced Its Employees They Could Change the World," www.hbr.org, 3 Mar, 2024, https://hbr.org/2015/10/how-an-accounting-firm-convinced-its-employees-they-could-change-the-world

199. Imperative, LinkedIn, "2016 Workforce Purpose Index," www.cdn.imperative.com, 2 Mar, 2024, https://40823263.fs1.hubspotusercontent-na1.net/hubfs/40823263/Content%20Downloads/2016%20Workforce%20Purpose%20Index.pdf

200. BILL MURPHY JR., "Google Says It Still Swears By the 20 Percent Rule to Find Big Ideas, and You Should Totally Copy It," www.inc.com, 1 Nov, 2020, https://www.inc.com/bill-murphy-jr/google-says-it-still-uses-20-percent-rule-you-should-totally-copy-it.html

201. Knowledge at Wharton Staff, "Learning from Netflix: How to Build a Culture of Freedom and Responsibility," www.knowledge.wharton.upenn.edu, 29 May, 2018, https://knowledge.wharton.upenn.edu/article/how-netflix-built-its-company-culture/

202. Jason Hiner, "Benioff: Salesforce was made possible by Steve Jobs, meditation, and perseverance," www.zdnet.com, 4 Oct, 2017, https://www.zdnet.com/article/benioff-salesforce-was-made-possible-by-steve-jobs-meditation-and-perseverance/

203. Courtney Connley, "Marc Benioff, Oprah and 3 other business leaders say this habit is key to their success," www.cnbc.com, 23 Jun, 2018, https://www.cnbc.com/2018/06/22/marc-benioff-oprah-and-others-say-this-is-key-to-their-success.html

204. Knowledge at Wharton Staff, "LinkedIn's Jeff Weiner: How Compassion Builds Better Companies," www.knowledge.wharton.upenn.edu, 17 May, 2018, https://knowledge.wharton.upenn.edu/article/linkedin-ceo-how-compassion-can-build-a-better-company/

205. VALENTINA ZARYA, "Sheryl Sandberg: Facebook Employees Now Get 20 Paid Days to Mourn a Family Death," www.fortune.com, 8 Feb, 2017, https://fortune.com/2017/02/07/facebook-sheryl-sandberg-bereavement-leave/

206. Gallup, "State of the American Workplace," www.gallup.com, 10th Apr, 2025, https://www.gallup.com/workplace/238085/state-american-workplace-report-2017.aspx

207. Cynthia D. Fisher, "Happiness at Work," www.researchgate.net, Dec, 2010, https://www.researchgate.net/publication/227533694_Happiness_at_Work

208. Virgin Group, "Richard Branson's story," www.virgin.com, 10th Apr, 2025, https://www.virgin.com/richard-branson/biography

209. Wikipedia, "Virgin Group," last edited on 21 March 2025, at 01:38 (UTC), https://en.wikipedia.org/wiki/Virgin_Group

210. Goodreads, "Richard Branson > Quotes > Quotable Quote," www.goodreads.com, 10th Apr, 2025, https://www.goodreads.com/quotes/7356284-clients-do-not-come-first-employees-come-first-if-you

211. JIM ASPLUND, "How Your Strengths Set You Apart ," www.gallup.com, 5 Nov, 2021, https://www.gallup.com/cliftonstrengths/en/356810/strengths-set-aPart.aspx

www.ingramcontent.com/pod-product-compliance
Lightning Source LLC
Chambersburg PA
CBHW071949070526
44583CB00015B/1119